MW01056251

STRANGERS
& NATIVES

STRANGERS & NATIVES

A Newspaper Narrative of Early Jewish America
1734–1869

RON RUBIN

Developed by Peri Devaney

Foreword by
Jonathan D. Sarna

URIM PUBLICATIONS

Strangers and Natives: A Newspaper Narrative of Early Jewish America, 1734–1869
by Ron Rubin
Developed by Peri Devaney
Foreword by Jonathan D. Sarna

Copyright © 2019 Ron Rubin

All rights reserved.
No part of this book may be used or reproduced in any manner whatsoever without
written permission from the copyright owner, except in the case of brief quotations
embodied in reviews and articles.

Cover photo: Page 1 of the *Gazette of the United States, December 18, 1790*,
featuring correspondence between the Hebrew Congregations of four major cities
and President George Washington (close-up and historic details on pages 192–193).

Typeset by Peri Devaney
Printed in USA. First Edition

ISBN 978-1-60280-328-2

Urim Publications
P.O. Box 52287, Jerusalem 9152102 Israel
www.UrimPublications.com

Library of Congress Cataloging-in-Publication Data

Names: Rubin, Ron, 1942- author. | Devaney, Peri, | Sarna, Jonathan D.,
    author of foreword
Title: Strangers & natives : a newspaper narrative of early Jewish America
    1734-1869 / Ron Rubin ; developed by Peri Devaney ; foreword by Jonathan
    D. Sarna.
Other titles: Stranger and natives
Description: First edition. | [New York] ; Jerusalem, Israel : Urim
    Publications, [2019] | Summary: "The cultural, political, and religious
    history of the Jews in America from the Colonial period through the
    Civil War, as told through original articles, advertisements, and
    notices appearing in U.S. periodicals of the day. This vivid newspaper
    narrative brings historic events to life, as the Jews, once strangers in
    America, began to emerge as natives in this young, uncharted country."--
    Provided by publisher.
Identifiers: LCCN 2019026440 | ISBN 9781602803282 (trade paperback)
Subjects: LCSH: Jews—United States—History—18th century—Sources. |
    Jews—United States—History—19th century—Sources.
Classification: LCC E184.352 .R83 2019 | DDC 973/.04924--dc23
LC record available at https://lccn.loc.gov/2019026440

In memory of Professors Abe and Debbie Karp
who sparked my love for Judaica Americana.

Before You Start Reading, Please Note:

The following information

will help you best understand the wealth of

original 18th and early 19th century material

reproduced throughout the book.

Until 1795, and sometimes as late as 1810, American printers used what is referred to as a **"long s"** – which looks more like an **"f"** – whenever the letter "s" appeared in the middle of a word or, occasionally, at the beginning. Until 1804, Acts of *Congreſs* were publiſhed using the "long s." For example:

"Jewiſh" is simply **"Jewish"** and

"Addreſs" is merely *"Address"*

Keeping this mind will help you more easily and **succeſsfully** understand what you read! (Note that when a word has a double "s" the "long s" is only used for the first of the two.)

Contents

Foreword
by Jonathan D. Sarna

When I was young, I enjoyed reading an imaginative history entitled *Chronicles: News of the Past,* edited by Israel Eldad and Moshe Aumann. The large-sized volume cleverly recounted biblical events as if they had appeared in contemporary newspapers. "WE QUIT EGYPT TODAY," one headline memorably screamed. Another read "JOSHUA CRUSHES FIVE KINGS." A third reported that "DEBORAH DECLARES WAR ON CANAANITES." Accompanying articles provided vivid details of these "breaking stories" as experienced journalists might have reported them. Instead of dry-as-dust textbook history, *Chronicles* offered the drama of a "this-just-in" newspaper account, complete with side-bar analyses, fascinating reports from the field, exciting features, mock editorials, even letters to the editor, photographs, and advertisements.

Chronicles: News of the Past sprang to mind when I read Ron Rubin's *Strangers and Natives: A Newspaper Narrative of Early Jewish America.* Here too readers will experience the past just as it appeared in contemporary newspapers. Here too one will find all varieties of articles, including advertisements. *Strangers and Natives,* however, differs from *Chronicles* in one absolutely crucial respect. It is based on *actual* stories that appeared in *real* newspapers. Ron Rubin has the originals to prove it.

The United States boasted over 200 different newspapers in 1800, and ten times that many in 1850. Freedom and democracy depended upon those newspapers. A free and robust press – the "fourth estate" – served as a check upon government and kept the populace informed. Newspapers covered every imaginable subject in early America; they reported, educated, and entertained. From time to time, therefore, they told readers about Jews.

Ron Rubin, in this marvelous book, reprints some 179 Jewish-related articles that appeared in American newspapers from 1734 to 1869. He had to select judiciously, for hundreds of other articles about Jews likewise appeared, more than any single book could contain. The urban character of early American Jewry, the exotic "otherness" of the Jew within an overwhelmingly Christian American society, and the fast-growing American Jewish population that mushroomed from less than a thousand in 1734 to more than 150,000 in 1869 all help to explain this journalistic fascination. News about Jews piqued the nation's curiosity.

Newspapers are said to be the "first drafts of history." So it is with Ron Rubin's "newspaper narrative." Replete with fascinating articles from American Jewry's early days, one hopes that it will stimulate readers to learn more about the American Jewish community's beginnings – based not upon faux sources, as in *Chronicles,* but on actual primary sources, early American newspapers.

Jonathan D. Sarna is a University Professor and Joseph H. & Belle R. Braun Professor of American Jewish History at Brandeis University and Chief Historian of the National Museum of American Jewish History. Recognized as a leading commentator on Jewish American History, he is also the award-winning author, editor or co-editor of more than thirty books, including American Judaism: A History; Lincoln and the Jews: A History; The American Jewish Experience; *and* When General Grant Expelled the Jews.

Preface

Newspapers are the first blush of history, providing in a sense a more authentic account than documents, diaries and memoirs. While there are numerous historical accounts of American Jewry, there are none based exclusively on newspaper sources. *Strangers and Natives: A Newspaper Narrative of Early Jewish America, 1734–1869* includes 179 scanned newspaper items – including reports, articles, advertisements, releases, announcements, obituaries and notices – each accompanied by descriptions and historical references. The descriptions, varying from a few sentences to a few pages, flesh out the people, events and scenes mentioned. The items, covering cultural, religious, commercial and political subjects, are organized chronologically within 12 topical chapters.

The theme of *Strangers and Natives* is based on the concept that both Jews and their fellow American gentiles saw this young, uncharted country from one or the other – or both – of these perspectives. The items included are curious, whimsical and often unknown to the public, such as an advertisement by the first Jewish bookseller in America, a description of a Chanukah Ball in New York City in the 1860s, the first benediction by a rabbi before a session of Congress, the give and take over the passage of the Maryland "Jew Bill," accounts about the Holy Land in missionary newspapers, advertisements by southern Jewish slave owners, rabbinic debate over slavery, Jewish synagogue memorial observances following Lincoln's assassination, ads by Jewish colonial brokers and merchants such as Haym Solomon, responses to General U. S. Grant's infamous Order No. 11 ordering the expulsion of Jews from Tennessee, the controversial and courageous career of Mordecai Manual Noah, a front page article in the Newport Mercury (1766) on the dedication of the London Great Synagogue, and much more.

The author is, himself, a collector and owns most of the newspaper issues from which the material was culled. We thank the New York Historical Society for their contributions of material from the March 13, 1784 issue of *The Independent Gazetteer/The Chronicle of Freedom* (see pages 132–133) and the August 13, 1800 issue of *Aurora General Advertiser* (see pages 140–143).

Acknowledgments

The role of newspapers in reporting the glorious, and sometimes tense, relations between Judaism and Americanism in the early years of United States history is the theme of this volume. My Jewish credentials came from the upbringing in the home of my parents, Robert and Blanche Rubin, inspirational rabbis and a yeshiva education. Growing up in the Bronx in the 1940s and 1950s, I benefited from nearly daily conversations with Aunt Rosie about current events, the source of my interest in what newspapers have to say about American society. Hopefully, my five daughters, their spouses and children will value these two main forces in my life, Judaism and Americanism.

I was helped in preparing this book by librarians of the New York Historical Society and the American Jewish Historical Society. My thanks to Professor Jonathan D. Sarna for his valuable input during the first drafts of the book and for his insightful *Foreword.* Tzvi Mauer and Michal Filiba Alatin of Urim Publications were always available and encouraging. My beloved wife Miriam played an instrumental, hands on role – scanning every newspaper issue in the book, making emergency runs to Staples, and discussing caption content – in addition to her vital supportive role. This work would not have come together in the absence of Peri Devaney's editorial and graphic genius. Peri, editor of one of my earlier works and developer of an anthology of my published commentary, believed fervently in the originality of this book's message. I also thank Peri's family for the patience and support they afforded her during the hundreds of hours she spent working on the book.

Most importantly, my humble gratitude to the Creator for giving me the strength to bring to light this story about how Jews changed their identities from *Strangers* to *Natives* in this new American Zion.

Introduction

Though Jews had been part of the American experience ever since 23 brave men, women and children fled to New Amsterdam in 1654 after the Dutch lost control of Recife, Brazil – and the American Jewish community had grown to more than 10,000 and had for the most part established itself legally and culturally by 1835 – the June 6, 1835 issue of New York's most conservative newspaper, *The New York Sun* (see page 155), included an article headlined "Jewing" that scoffed at Jews, referring to stereotypical traits. The article noted that:

> "a couple of Jews from New York with porcelain ware" appeared in Northampton aiming to deceitfully exchange their cheap merchandise for more expensive second-hand clothing. Making fun of the strange accents of these European-born Jews, the article claimed that they were more inclined to "jew" "de women" and not "de men."

Thirty years later, in the waning days of the Civil War, an abolitionist New York-based paper, *National Anti-Slavery Standard,* disparaged the Jews in its August 27, 1864 … not in terms of their character traits but by their physical features. Judah P. Benjamin (b. 1811; d. 1884), Secretary of State of the Confederacy, was described as "a short, plump, oily little man in black, with a keen black eye, a Jew face, curly black hair…"

Countering the impact of hostile articles like these, many other newspapers in the young republic carried much more welcoming and tolerant messages. The September 15, 1790 issue of *Gazette of the United States* (see pages 190–191), in what has become the most venerated item of Americana Judaica, reported the exchange of greetings between Rhode Island's Newport Hebrew Congregation and the recently inaugurated George Washington. In this encounter, considered one of the central expressions of religious liberty in American history, Washington noted:

> "… the Government of the United States, which gives to bigotry no sanction, to persecution no assistance, requires only that they who live under its protection should demean themselves as good citizens."

Washington concluded his message with the biblically toned wish:

> "May the children of the stock of Abraham who dwell in this land continue to merit and enjoy the goodwill of the other inhabitants—while every one shall sit in safety under his own vine and figtree, and there shall be none to make them afraid."

Washington was not alone among those of his contemporaries in advocating safe harbor in this New Jerusalem to Jews seeking religious and personal freedom. Five years after Washington's celebrated message to the Jews of Newport, the noted lexicographer Noah Webster (b. 1758; d. 1843) discussed the ills of usury in the February 4, 1795 issue of *The Herald, A Gazette for the Country* (see page 139). Webster raised the issue of the role of Jews in this practice. Webster sympathized with the plight of Jews which forced them to become money lenders. "Proscribed and insulted, the poor Jews were compelled to turn their hand against every man in their own defense…. Hence the general character of the Jews and the prejudice against them that survives in this enlightened period."

Having survived in the Diaspora for 1,700 years at the time, the Jews who came to America's shores to flee persecution and to find opportunity were prepared for both types of treatment described here—acceptance and rejection. In their own way, the chosen people in this chosen land were reenacting the experience of Abraham, history's first Jew, in seeking to persuade the children of Heth to sell him a burial site for Sarah, "I am a stranger and a resident with you" (Genesis 23, 4).

Though the early experiences of Jews in America have been retold many times in biographies, diaries, letters, and political histories, no account has appeared exclusively relying on newspaper narratives, the first blush of history. Similarly, newspapers alone have never been used as a source in tracing the political trajectory of the republic from its earliest days of colonization until the Civil War as an Old Testament based or "Redeemer" nation. The immediacy and unadulterated quality of newspaper accounts underscore their value as primary sources inherent to the historical process.

The first newspaper to appear on American shores was the *Public Journal* in Boston, 1704. By 1754, four other newspapers were produced in New England with press runs of no more than 600 each. In colonial times, newspapers were four-page weekly publications, appearing usually on Mondays, sold only to subscribers. Typically, these emerging newspapers had short life spans. A substantial amount of space was devoted to ads, ship arrival and departure schedules, foreign news which was a few weeks old, and columns reprinted from other newspapers. Most newspapers carried definite political identities and affiliations.

Between 1760 and the outbreak of the Revolutionary War the number of newspapers doubled. Newspapers became a forum for debating and contesting new British taxes and the authority of the London Parliament. By 1800, there were some 150 separate American newspapers. By 1810, according to Isaiah Thomas (b. 1749; d. 1831), the leading American publisher and printer of the day, as a result of the American proclivity for journalism, this nation produced more newspapers than the United Kingdom. By that date, 360 national newspapers, including twenty dailies, were published.

In his tribute to the role of newspapers, Thomas noted:

> They have become the vehicles of discussion, in which the principles of government, the interests of nations, the spirit and tendency of public measures, and the public and private character of individuals, are all arraigned, tried, and decided.[1]

In addition to their central political role, newspapers according to Thomas had also become key literary vehicles:

> There are few of them, within the last twenty years, which have not added to their political details, some curious and useful information, on the various subjects of literature, science and art. They have thus become the means of conveying, to every class in society, innumerable scraps of knowledge, which have at once increased the public intelligence, and extended the taste for perusing periodical publications. The advertisements, moreover, which they daily contain, respecting new books, projects, inventions, discoveries and improvements, are well calculated to enlarge and enlighten the public mind.[2]

While recognizing the salutary role of newspapers, Thomas warned about the character shortcomings of their publishers or editors. From the standpoint of this work's analysis of Judaic themes in newspapers, these "depravities" might be considered as factors to have spurred negative portrayals when they appeared. "Too many of our gazettes are in the hands of persons destitute at once of the urbanity of gentlemen, the information of scholars, and the principles of virtue."[3]

Despite the rhetoric and writings of many of this nation's founders conflating the republicanism of ancient Zion with the republicanism of the young United States, very few Jews actually lived in this new world entity. The absence of Jews among colonists and early settlers was notwithstanding definitions of Jews as a religion, ethnicity, culture or people. The metaphor comparing the young America with the Holy Land or Promised Land was mainly one of thought or philosophy. Most observers in early America failed to associate the glories of the Book with the descendants of the personalities of the Book who dwelled among them. In building the New Israel, Jews were no more chosen than any other ethnicity. According to Eran Shalev:

> The majority of the Americans who believed that they were God's New Israel probably never interacted with or even saw real-life Jews who were relatively few before the closing decades of the nineteenth century, and mostly clustered in commercial centers in an overwhelmingly agricultural country. Yet that the American Hebraic imagination developed in the absence of Jews was in so sense unique: for

millennia Christians have conjured "the Jew" as a figure of thought for their particular needs (typically to serve as an ultimate Other), often with little regard to actual Jews.[4]

When this nation's first synagogue, Shearith Israel (the Spanish and Portuguese Synagogue) laid its foundation stone in 1730, only a few score Jewish families lived in New York City. By the time of the Revolutionary War, the country's Jewish population stood at a maximum of 1,000, out of a national figure of some 3,000,000, and concentrated mainly in the cities of Philadelphia, Charleston, Savannah, New York and Newport. In 1790, the 1,350 Jews constituted 0.03% of the 4.000,000 Americans. In 1820, 2,700 Jews (still 0.03% of the total) lived among 10,000,000 Americans. In 1860, Jews numbered 150,000 (0.48%) among an American population of 33,000,000.

Regardless of these small numbers of Jews, Hebrew Scripture or Old Testament biblical themes were central to colonial and early American descriptions of national mission. The application of Hebrew Scriptural themes to this early American experience is known as Biblicism. Shalev shows how these settlers saw themselves as Israelites experiencing an Exodus fleeing an updated Egyptian captivity, crossed a sea to find freedom and to take possession of a promised land. Biblical references whether in oratorical flourishes, projected national seals or names of new towns underscore the efforts of this elect nation to build in this New World a Second Israel endowed with liberty. In a most basic sense, these political-theological tropes about an American Israel or a Redeemer Nation were designed to show that God still operates in history.

Thus, the Rev. William Gordon, chaplain to both houses of the Provincial Congress, entitled his sermon on July 4, 1777, the first anniversary of the Declaration of Independence, "The Separation of the Jewish Tribes, After the Death of Solomon, Accounted and Applied to the Present Day" (which extended to 31 published pages). Rev. Gordon in likening the cause of the Americans to the Hebrews of biblical times emphasized that "the king hearkens unto the people for the cause was from the Lord. And it is upon that principle alone that we can rationally accept the separation that hath taken place between the United States of America and Great Britain."

Though newspapers, the subject of this work, have not been systematically researched as a source of Biblicism, they provide rich examples of this sentiment in the nation's early political imagination. Significantly, in a prominent London newspaper, *The Gentleman's Magazine,* February 1789, Benjamin Franklin took to task Antifederalists who opposed ratification of the proposed American Constitution drawn up in Philadelphia in 1787 as upstarts replaying the revolt of Korach against Moses and Aaron as described in the Book of Numbers:

> Many still retained an affection for Egypt, the land of their nativity; and there whenever they felt any inconvenience or hardship, through the natural and unavoidable effect of their change of situation…were not only for returning into Egypt, but for stoning their deliverers…He accused Moses of having, by various artifices, fraudulently obtained the government and deprived the people of their liberties; and of conspiring with Aaron to perpetuate the tyranny of their family.

Franklin, in advocating the Constitution, could not conceive of such a profound political transformation lacking the hand of Providence:

> I can hardly conceive a transaction of such momentous importance to the welfare of millions now existing, and to exist in the posterity of a great nation, should be suffered to pass without being in some degree influenced, guided, and governed by that omnipotent, omniscient, and beneficent Ruler, in whom all inferior spirits live and move and have their being.

Franklin, in addition to regarding the American political experience as an updating of the biblical experience, also was responsible for introducing a decidedly philo-semitic sentiment in contemporary Philadelphia. Perhaps twenty-five Jewish families lived in that city when Franklin praised the Jewish contribution to civilization in the *Pennsylvania Packet,* September 15, 1737: "The Jews were acquainted with the several Arts and Sciences long e're the Romans became a People, or the Greeks were known among the nations."

(continued)

In this Judaic-focused early American newspaper narrative, one event stands out in embracing the three themes examined in the pages that follow—Hebrew scriptural discourse on liberty, the political rights of disenfranchised Jews and the mission of America. Maryland's first Constitution, written in 1776, required all public servants to take a Christian oath. In 1818, Judge Henry M. Brackenridge and several other members of the Maryland House of Delegates launched an eight-year battle to overturn this discriminatory standard. This legislation, "The Jew Bill," was originally defeated in 1819, but became law in 1826. Brackenridge's speech on "The Jew Bill," published in an article titled "Religious Liberty" in *Niles' Weekly Register* in Baltimore on May 29, 1819 (see pages 196–197), ranks as one of the most powerful statements of Jewish civil liberties, and political freedom in American history:

> But, sir, is there really this inferiority in the Jewish race or character? The sacred book on which we ground our faith, teaches that they are not an inferior people. Else, wherefore should they be the chosen people of God, the favored depositories of the sacred law and holy prophecies. Do we forget that to these we are not only indebted for these, but even the blessings of Christianity? Its author was a Jew, his apostles were Jews. On the contrary, there is every reason to believe, that as a race, they are the first among men…

> Is there anything in the Jewish religious doctrines which disqualify the Jew from discharging the duties and fulfilling all the obligations of a citizen of Maryland? Sir, I boldly assert that there is not, and I defy any one to point it out…

> If we may venture to assign a cause why the discovery of America was permitted, I know of none more rational, than that it was the will of heaven to open an asylum for the persecuted of every nation. In my mind it excites the most pleasing reflections to behold even the Jew, to whom the world is dark and cheerless, exulting in finding a home in this land—in discovering here one sunny spot at last!

Two simultaneous cultural upheavals serve as a backdrop for the following newspaper narrative. For one, the colonies and later the new republic, and later the Union in fighting for its survival, were steadily and argumentatively working out definitions of freedom, equality and republicanism. Meanwhile, Jews who had never themselves experienced a secure civic culture in the western world were also trying to figure out their rights and responsibilities during the 130-year period explored here. In both trajectories, the national American and the specifically Jewish, democratically based solutions were easier to reach because this new world experiment did not inherit an embedded monarchical heritage or clerical class.

But the Jewish transition was much tougher. Jews, in addition to adjusting to changing definitions of civic humanism, as did all other of their fellow countrymen, faced the extra pressure of maintaining their minority religion within the dominant Christian culture. True, as William Pencak argues in *Jews and Gentiles in Early America 1654–1800,*[5] whatever anti-Semitism existed here was far less hostile and rooted than the European variety. But Jewish vulnerabilities often surfaced. Newspapers reported on vandalized Jewish graves, attacks on Jewish business practices, the schemes of missionaries to convert Jews, and outright attempts at ethnic cleansing such as the infamous Order Number 11 issued by General U.S.Grant that forced Jews to vacate – immediately – their homes in certain states during the Civil War.

During the period of this newspaper narrative, Jews, as peddlers or dry goods merchants, moved out of the security of their city neighborhoods to isolated, western pioneering towns. In the process, many faltered in their faith, succumbing to assimilation as a survival tool on the beckoning frontier. Responding to this precarious possibility, Rev. Isaac Leeser (b. 1806; d. 1868) of Philadelphia's Mikveh Israel synagogue, translator of many scriptural works, launched *The Occident and American Jewish Advocate* in 1843 and edited it until his death. Discussing religious doctrine as well as providing communal updates, *The Occident* reached subscribers increasingly scattered across prairie towns. For many subscribers, this publication represented their only ongoing contact with their faith. Ironically, Leeser's impact was limited, however, because *The Occident* was written in English at a time when more literate Jews read German than English.

What is the image that emerges of Jews and Judaism through the medium of newspapers? To begin quantitatively, Jews drew many more references in the press than their small size would indicate. For example, other religions or ethnicities containing small populations, such as Quakers or Moslems, received much scantier treatment than Jews. Early on in the Jewish American experience, an advertisement in *The New-York Weekly Journal,* May 20, 1734 (see page 49), illustrated an identifiable Jewish presence in New York City's lower Manhattan. The ad described a "dwelling" for sale on Duke Street fronting the alley leading to the Coentjes Market. Included in the property was a "good storehouse fronting the back street near the Synagogue." This historic issue published what was probably the first newspaper reference to a Jewish house of worship in North America. The nondescript brick home of Congregation Shearith Israel, America's first synagogue, measuring 35 square feet and 22 feet tall, purposely avoided outside Jewish symbols such as the Star of David in order not to attract attention. Yet this physically inconspicuous structure was well known enough to serve as a geographic marker in a general newspaper! At the time, there were no more than fifty Jewish families in town.

Newspapers reveal that Jews, despite their small numbers and non-Christian heritage, did not feel alienated, actually contributing significantly in the development of the federal republic. This conclusion particularly emerges based on ads, which in most newspapers comprised at least half of the edition's space. These ads testify to the activity of Jews in many diverse fields in advancing the nation's welfare such as commerce, finance, crafts, shipping, book sales and journalism. Jewish family connections abroad, making it easier, for instance, to secure loans or letters of credit or introductions, many times factored into their business success. Based on press accounts, we learn that Jews traded on the frontier, worked as administrators in schools for the deaf, announced marriages (sometimes with non-Jews), paid for ads about returning lost wallets to their owners, sold their used furniture and, to be sure, also owned slaves. Newspapers also reported on foreign developments, ranging from Napoleon's establishing a Jewish Sanhedrin Court, to the investments of the Rothschilds, to the bouts of the Jewish bare-knuckled British boxing champ, Daniel Mendoza (b. 1764; d. 1836).

Politically, newspapers show that Jews were very devoted to the American enterprise. Jewish names were included in published protests against British taxation. In a celebration in Philadelphia, on Independence Day, 1788 marking the ratification of the Constitution, the *Pennsylvania Packet,* July 9, 1788, noted that in the parade were "the Clergy of the different Christian denominations, with the rabbi of the Jews walking arm in arm" (see pages 18–19). In response to President George Washington's request, Rev. Gershom Mendes Seixas (b. 1745; d. 1816), of New York City's Congregation Shearith Israel, delivered a lengthy Thanksgiving Day Discourse on November 26, 1789. An advertisement in *The New York Daily Gazette,* December 23, 1789, selling copies of the sermon, noted that it was "the first of its kind ever preached in English in this State, is highly deserving the attention of every pious reader, whether Jew or Christian, as it breathes nothing but pure morality and devotion."

In the eighteenth and nineteenth centuries, newspapers reported on rabbinic sermons in connection with nationally declared Days of Fasting and Humiliation. The first rabbinic prayer opening a session of Congress was recorded. Press reports described Jewish military enlistment drives for both the Blue and Gray in the Civil War, debates from the pulpit about biblical support for slavery, and funeral ceremonies for Jewish troops. Synagogue services marking the assassination and funeral of Abraham Lincoln were front-paged in black bordered New York City dailies.

Despite strong Jewish political identity with this new nation, certain newspapers carried insults and smears. Some of these attacks were based on alleged character shortcomings such as greed, dishonesty and uncouthness. Another line of attack was to identify someone as "a Jew," indicating an inherently inferior status. John Fenno, publisher of the *Gazette of the United States,* unhappy with the Jewish presence here, urged that "they live in the wilderness like their biblical ancestors." Someone could become a victim of anti-Semitism without even being a Jew! Thus, the anti-Jeffersonian *Tree of Liberty,* September 13, 1800, seeking to undermine John Israel's support for Jefferson's presidential campaign, referred to his office as "a synagogue." Israel's father was a baptized Christian, showing that in this anti-Semitic aspersion, the term Jew meant more ethnicity than religion. The most powerful Jewish response to editorial anti-Semitism was the claim that the perpetrator was not only bigoted, but also guilty of undermining the American belief in equality. Though French born, Benjamin Nones

(b. 1757; d. 1826) had fought heroically in the battle of Savannah during the American Revolution; he was attacked as a Jew in the *Gazette of the United States,* August 5, 1800. Nones's proud, patriotic reply in the Philadelphia *Aurora,* August 13, 1800 (see pages 140–143), stated:

> I am a Jew, and if for no other reason, for that reason am I a republican... Among the nations of Europe we are inhabitants everywhere but citizens, nowhere unless in republics. In republics we have rights, in monarchies we live but to experience wrongs.

Newspapers of all political persuasions featured material on diverse aspects of Judaism, including Jewish rituals, holidays, festive Purim Balls, Hebrew calligraphy, levirate marriage, the principles of Moses Maimonides, biblical legends, the Talmud, wedding practices and kosher diets. By the midpoint of the nineteenth century, articles appeared on synagogue dedications, efforts to form national Jewish umbrella groups, fundraising events, and Hebrew school graduations. As Jews grew in prominence on the national scene, newspapers published lengthy obituaries. The death of Mordecai M. Noah (b. 1785; d. 1851), a politician, newspaper publisher, New York City sheriff, synagogue president, and more—the most famous American Jew in the first half of the nineteenth century—was front-paged. A more secure American Jewry staged public demonstrations in 1840, protesting what came to be known as the Damascus Affair, where Jews were falsely charged with killing Christian children (see page 201). Missionary conversion tactics both here and abroad were debated. A new interest in the Holy Land was reflected in articles that described scenes, pilgrimages and geography.

Given the small Jewish population numbers in the period examined in this work, the prospect of increasing circulation figures among potential Jewish readers cannot be cited as a motive for the substantial journalistic attention to things Jewish. Yet, indirectly, such steady references to Jewish "news" must have enhanced Jewish pride, security, and self-awareness. Two examples relating to the Newport, Rhode Island Jewish community are cited later in this collection. *The Newport Mercury,* in its December 29, 1766 to January 5, 1767 issue, carried a front-page report on the festive dedication of the London Great Synagogue (see page 51). Similarly, twenty-two years later, the *Newport Herald,* February 26, 1789, eulogized Jacob Rodrigues Rivera (b. 1717; d. 1789) as "an Israelite indeed" (see page 95). Rivera, reported the newspaper, was "exemplary in his observance of the Jewish Ritual, intelligent and upright in commerce, and an ornament to all the social virtues." Newport's Jewish population in both journalistic examples likely did not exceed three hundred members.

Newspapers played a transformative role in building a new America, or, in political-theological terms, an American Zion. This narrative argues that Jews who reached these shores not only found a haven, but robustly contributed to making this new country a flourishing home for all. This process meant maintaining a delicate balance between their ancient Jewish culture while adapting to the yet uncharted American dream. Hopefully, this newspaper account, in showing how Jews were seen by a wider America and by themselves, will add to the understanding of the forces that made this young country thrive.

FOOTNOTES

1. **Isaiah Thomas, *The History of Printing in America*,** Barre, Mass. 1970 (reprint of 1810 edition), Weathervane Books, New York, P.18
2. **Ibid.**
3. **Ibid.** P. 20
4. **Eran Shalev, *American Zion: The Old Testament as a Political Text from the Revolution to the Civil War,*** New Haven, Conn., Yale University Press, 2013, P.189
5. **William Pencak, *Jews and Gentiles in Early America 1654–1800,*** Ann Arbor, Michigan, The University of Michigan Press, 2005.

Religious Equality
in
A New Nation

The Pennsylvania Packet, and Daily Advertiser.

[Price Four-Pence.]   W E D N E S D A Y, July 9, 1788.   [No. 2943.]

Bank of North-America. | Coke on Littleton. | GRAND Federal Proceſſion. Philadelphia, July 9.

PHILADELPHIA – 1788
THE CLERGY...
WITH THE RABBI
The Pennsylvania Packet and Daily Advertiser,
p. 1 (col 4) – p. 3 (col 4)
July 9, 1788

Philadelphia's Grand Federal Procession was not only the largest civic event thus far in American history, but it marked the first national celebration where Jewish clergy was treated on an equal level with Christian counterparts. Organized by Federalist politicians to link Independence Day with Pennsylvania's ratification of the Constitution, this July 4, 1788 event drew some 5,000 marchers grouped in 88 trades, military and political categories. The pageant, covering one and one-half miles was seen by 17,000 onlookers. The hope was that this great outpouring of nationalism would influence the three states which had not yet ratified the Constitution to follow suit.

Francis Hopkinson, a signer of the Declaration of Independence, described the festivities in a July 4th edition of this newspaper. But in that issue's account, Hopkinson omitted the crucial one sentence description of the interfaith amity in connection with the celebration of the Constitution's ratification victory. It remained for *The Pennsylvania Packet*'s July 9th edition to detail the good spirits between Jew and Christian:

The clergy of the different Christian denominations,
with the rabbi of the Jews, walking arm in arm.

Historians consider this "arm in arm" reference as a landmark evidence of Jewish recognition and equality in the early republic. The rabbi* cited among the marchers was Jacob Raphael Cohen (b. 1738, d. 1811).

(continued)

* Actually, at that point in history there were no ordained rabbis in the nation; Cohen served as Hazzan (i.e., cantor) in Philadelphia's only synagogue, Congregation Mikveh Israel

LXXXIV.
The gentlemen of the Bar, headed by the Honorable Edward Shippen, Esquire, President of the Common Pleas, and William Bradford, Esquire, Attorney General, followed by the Students of Law.
LXXXV.
The Clergy of the different Christian denominations, with the rabbi of the Jews, walking arm in arm.
LXXXVI.
The College of Physicians, headed by their President, Dr. John Redman, and followed by the students in physic.

Watching the scene, Dr. Benjamin Rush (b. 1746, d. 1813), a signer of the Declaration of Independence and a delegate to the Pennsylvania ratification convention, wrote:

The clergy formed a very agreeable part of the procession. They manifested the connection between religion and good government. Pains were taken to connect ministers of the most dissimilar religious principles together, thereby to show the influence of a free government in promoting charity. The Rabbi of the Jews, Jacob Raphael Cohen of Congregation Mikveh Israel, Philadelphia's only synagogue, locked in arms of two ministers of the gospel was a most delightful sight. There could not have been a more happy emblem contrived of that section of the new Constitution, Article VI, prohibiting religious qualifications for holding office, which opens all its power and offices alike not only to every sect of Christians but to worthy men of every religion.

Furthermore, contemporary accounts of this Procession note that tables serving kosher food at the parade's conclusion were available for Jewish celebrants, "with a full supply of soused salmon, bread and crackers, almonds and raisins."[1]

[1] www.israpundit.org/an-eye-opening-introduction-to-the-jewish-influence-on-americas-founding/

Above drawing: "Philadelphia's Grand Federal Procession" by Caroline Logan, originally published in the Tredyffrin-Easttown History Club Quarterly, *July 1938. Courtesy of the Tredyffrin Easttown Historical Society, http://www.tehistory.org/hqda/html/v01/v01n4p002.html*

Chapter #1

Daily Life &
Customs of the
Jewish Community

ADVERTISEMENTS.

Mr. *Zenger*;

If you insert the following in your next, you'll oblige a Friend of one of your Subscribers.

Greenfield in *Conecticut,*
March 20

Lately ftray'd away a large Catamount about 5 Foot 2 Inches high, of a dark Colour; he is extreemly fiery in his Afpect, he fhew's his Teeth on all Occafions, he has a large Hump upon his Shoulders, his Mouth is generally filled with all Manner of Naftinefs, when he went away he had a long Tail, but we hear he has fince loft it; on any furprife he is apt to catch fomething into his Paws, and endeavours to imitate a Man, he is very fond of the Female *Indians*, we hear that he is lately mated with another mifchievous Animal that's come from the South ward, and that they both burrow in one Hole tho' not at one and the fame Time.

Whoever fhall take up the faid Catamount, and bring him to his Mafter *Richard Crane*, fhall have two Pair of Gold Buttons and two Gold Rings, as a Reward.

To be fold, at publick Vendue the 25th Day of this inftant Month of *March*, at Ten o' Clock in the Morning, the Dwelling Houfe and Bolting Houfe, of *Fredrick Willemz.*, fcituate near the Fort, there's belonging to them, a large Oven for Baking, a good Well, a Ciftern and fundry other good Conveniencies, for a Bolter and Baker; likewife to be Sold the 26th Inftant, at Three of the Clock in the Afternoon, two Lott of Ground, lying Contiguous to the Ground of *John Ellifon*, deceas'd, near the *North River*, and on the 27th, Inftant, at Three a Clock in the Afternoon, two Lots of Ground lying a little beyond *Abraham Palding*, each Lot containing 25 Foot in Breadth, and one Hundred and Ten Foot in Length. If any Perfon inclines to Purchafe any of the Particulars above-mentioned, before the feveral Days above limited for the Sale at Vendue may apply to Mefs. *Herman Winckler*, *John Sprat*, and *Simon Johnfon*, and agree on very reafonable Terms.

Jeremiah Lattouch, and *Friend Lucas*, having broke up Partnerfhip, give this publick Notice to all Perfons that have any Demands on them, to bring in their Accompts in Order to be fatisfied; and thofe that are indebted to them, are defired to Ballance their Accompts, to prevent further Trouble. They have alfo fundry Sorts of Goods to difpofe of, either for ready Money or Credit at reafonable Terms.

Very good Chefhire Cheefe to be Sold, by Nathaniel Hazard, near the Old Slip Market, in New-York.

This is to give Notice to all Gentlemen Ladies and others, that at the Houfe of Charles Sleigh, in Duke Street is to be feen the famous German Artift, is to perform the Wonders of the World by Dexterity of Hand: The Things he performs are too many to be enumerated here. He here with invites all to be Spectators of his Ingenuity: the Prices for Admittance are, beft Seats one Shilling, farther off Nine-Pence, and fartheft off Six-pence. He begins at Seven o'Clock in the Evening. To be continued every Night in the Week. To be performed by.

Jofeph Broome

To be Sold, a Lot of Land at the Head of Cow Bay, on Long-Ifland, containing about 40 Acres, there is on it now a very good Houfe and Barn, there is a good Stream of Water fit for either Fulling or Grift Mill, there is very good Water. The whole lies very Convenient for a Trader or Tradefman. Whoever inclines to purchafe may enquire of John Byvanck or David Provooft, both of the City of New-York.

All Perfons that have any Demands on the Eftate of *Benjamin Elias*, are defired to bring in their Accounts, to *Abraham Ifaac's* in Order to be fatisfied. And thofe that are indebted to the faid Eftate, are defired to fend in their Accounts, to prevent further Trouble.

Jofeph Scot of *NewYork* Merchant, intending for London in the Spring, gives this timely Notice, to all the Perfons indebted to him, to Pay the Ballance of their Accounts. Alfo, any Perfon that has any Demands on the faid *Scot* by Application may receive Satisfaction.

Dr. John Van Solingen, *intending to Remove out of this City, he gives this publick Notice, to all Perfons that have any Demands on him, to bring in their Accounts, in order to be fatisfied. And thofe that are indebted to him are defired to Ballance their Account, to prevent further Trouble. He has fundry forts of Shop Goods to fell, either at Wholefale or Retail at very reafonable Rates of him, at his Houfe in Hanover-Square.*

N. B. He intends to remove to Long-Ifland.

TO BE SOLD,

Sundry Lots of two Hundred and three Hundred Acres in a Lot, of very good arable Land, in Middlefex County, in the Eaftern Divifion of the Province of New-Jerfey, about 3 Miles from New-Brunfwick, the Road call'd the George's Road, runs through the whole Tract; it lies upon Lawrences Brook, which is a good ftream convenient for either Grift or Saw Mills, it is ftored with abundance of very good Timber, and rich low Meadow, Grounds. Whoever inclines to Purchafe any Part of the faid Lands, may enquire of Mr. James Nealfon, in New-Brunfwick, where he will find further Direction for taking a View of this Land, and alfo hear of the Proprietor thereof.

There are Printed and Sold, by the Publifher hereof fome Obfervations on the Charge given by the Honorable *James De Lancey*, Efqr; Chief Juftice of the Province of *New-York*, to the grand Jury, on the 15th Day of *January* 1733. Price, 1 s.

The Printer hereof intends to remove to Broad-Street near the upper End of the Long Bridge.

N E W-Y O R K: Printed and Sold by *John Peter Zenger*: By whom Subfcriptions for this Paper are taken at three Shillings *per* Quarter; and Advertifements at three Shllings the firft Week, and one Shilling every Week after.

Dedicated in 1730, the Mill Street Synagogue of Elias's congregation, Shearith Israel, was the first synagogue in America. Illustration "from an old etching" courtesy of Congregation Shearith Israel, New York.

ALL Perfons that have any Demands on the Eftate of *Benjamin Elias*, are defired to bring in their Accounts, to *Abraham Ifaac's* in Order to be fatisfied. And thofe that are indebted to the faid Eftate, are defired to fend in their Accounts, to prevent further Trouble.

NEW YORK CITY - 1734
ESTATE ANNOUNCEMENT
The New York Weekly Journal, p. 4 (col 2)
March 25, 1734

One of the earliest newspaper references to Jews in American history was this classified announcement in *The New York Weekly Journal*: "All Persons that have any Demands on the Estate of Benjamin Elias are desired to bring their Accounts to Abraham Isaacs in Order to be satisfied. And those that are indebted to the said Estate are desired to send in their Accounts to prevent further Trouble."

Elias had been a merchant as well as a Hebrew teacher and shochet (ritual slaughterer) at Congregation Shearith Israel—the Spanish and Portuguese Synagogue. Shearith Israel was the first Jewish congregation in North America.

Isaacs, a merchant, was naturalized as a citizen of New York on July 6, 1723, the same date as John Peter Zenger, publisher of the newspaper.

PHILADELPHIA – 1750
STOLEN ITEMS
The Pennsylvania Gazette, p. 3 (col 2)
March 13, 1750

Michael Israel was among the first Jewish settlers of Philadelphia, though there are no accurate records as to his dates of birth and death. It is known that he married Mary J. Paxton, an Episcopalian. Together they parented Israel Israel (b. 1743; d. 1821), the American Revolutionary War patriot.

The younger Israel was a farmer near Wilmington, Delaware, in 1777 when he was captured by the British on the way to bringing relief to his family in Philadelphia. The thrilling account of Israel Israel's capture and escape is a matter of historical record. Later in life he became the high sheriff of Philadelphia (1801–1803).

This request, placed by Michael Israel in Benjamin Franklin's newspaper, describes the types of garments worn by Philadelphia colonists, and the value placed upon them.

ON Wednesday at night, the 21st of February last, was stolen out of the house of Michael Israel, on Society-Hill, at the sign of the Blue-Lion, a short scarlet cloak, a woman's holland cap, with a cambrick border, a new check apron, a white homespun shirt, a superfine blue broad-cloth coat, lined with blue taffety, a scarlet double-breasted cloth jacket, with brass buttons, lined with double alopeen, the body with fustian, a black taffety jacket, double-breasted, lined with crimson colour'd taffety, without pockets, a man's English velvet jockey cap, a fine holland shirt ruffled, two linnen petticoats with calicoe borders, a pair of check trowsers, an old long lawn handkerchief, sundry baby-cloaths, and sundry things unknown. Any person that any of the said things are offer'd to sale, are desired to stop the thief, so as he may be brought to justice, and the subscriber will pay the person for so doing THREE POUNDS.   MICHAEL ISRAEL.

N. B. The said Israel lost a sorrel horse last September, about 14 hands high, a white mane and tail, branded on the near shoulder M, and on the near buttock S, lame behind, several saddle spots, and shod all round, with a bald face. Whoever secures said horse, so that the owner may have him again, shall be paid by said Michael Israel TEN SHILLINGS.

THE
NEW-YORK MERCURY.
Containing the freshest Advices Foreign and Domestick.

MONDAY, DECEMBER 6, 1756.

NUMB. 226

NEW YORK – 1756
FOUND – PARCEL OF PAPER MONEY
The New-York Mercury, p. 3 (col 2)
December 6, 1756

WHEREAS a parcel of PAPER MONEY was found within these few days, near the Meal-market; if the person who lost it, will describe the number of bills, to the amount of the sum found, they may, on paying the charge of advertising, have it again, by applying at the house of Mr. JACOB FRANKS.

Though the British colony of New-York numbered only some 100 Jews at the period two decades before the American Revolution, Jews showed a strong sense of civic mindedness and political identity with the province's other 15,000 inhabitants. Illustrating this attitude was an advertisement placed by merchant Jacob Franks (b. Germany, 1688; d. New York City, 1769) seeking to return a lost sum of money to its rightful owner.

Franks, the wealthiest Jewish merchant in the colony, was learned in Jewish law and was often called rabbi. He was instrumental in building Congregation Shearith Israel's Mill Street Synagogue, the first synagogue in the thirteen colonies. As a businessman, he was the King's Agent in New York. The letters his wife Bilhah Abigail (b. London, 1696; d. New York City, 1756) wrote to her son Naphtali (b. 1715; d. 1796) are among the few extant – and possibly the earliest – letters written by an eighteenth-century woman of New York.

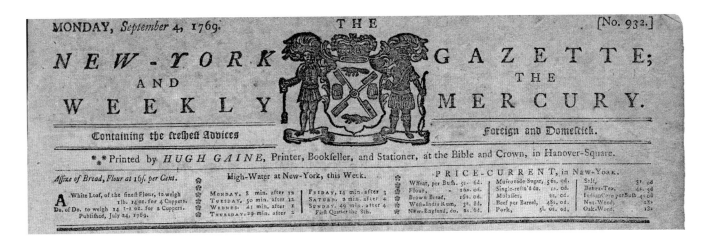

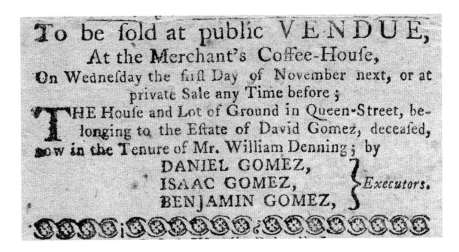

NEW YORK – 1769
ESTATE SALE
The New-York Gazette and the Weekly Mercury, p. 1 (col 1)
September 4, 1769

The Gomez family, a Marrano family hailing from Madrid, Spain, established itself in the United States in the early eighteenth century. Lewis Moses Gomez (b. Madrid, Spain, 1654; d. New York City, 1740) established the American branch of the family. He became a merchant in New York, exporting wheat to Portugal. He also was involved in congregational affairs. As *Parnas* (president) of Congregation Shearith Israel, he presided at the consecration ceremony at its Mill Street location.

In this front-page announcement, the public is notified of the sale of the "The House and Lot of Ground … belonging to the Estate of David Gomez, deceased…." David was one of Lewis Moses Gomez' six sons. The notice is signed by three brothers of the deceased, Isaac, Daniel and Benjamin. The son of Daniel married the daughter of Isaac, and the son of Isaac married the daughter of Benjamin. Benjamin (b. 1759; d. 1826) was the first Jewish bookseller in New York.

LONDON – 1781
JUDAH LEVY'S DAUGHTER
WEDS IN LONDON

The London Chronicle, p. 2 (col 3)
April 3–April 5, 1781

Almost half a column was devoted to a report of the April 4, 1781 marriage of Minka Levy, daughter of American Jewish merchant Judah Levy, to Henry Noah of London's Crosby Square, at London's Great Synagogue in Duke's-Place.

The report describes the processional "three times round [Duke's-Place] according to their custom," with the "High Priest" of the synagogue leading. The list of participants, ending with "above three hundred Jew Gentleman and Ladies," is followed by information about the ceremony, dinner and dancing and a final note that at midnight the bride and groom retired and "the company sat down to a cold supper."

Last Wednesday was married, at the great synagogue in Duke's-Place, by the Rev. Mr. Tavely, the High Priest of that synagogue, Mr. Henry Noah, of Crosby-square, to Miss Minka Levy, daughter of Mr. Judah Levy, an eminent American merchant, in Heydon-square, in the Minories. At 12 o'clock the bride and bridegroom, and all that were invited to the ceremony, assembled in Duke's-Place, and walked in procession three times round it, according to their custom, in the following order:—First, the High Priest, followed by the two readers of the synagogue, each holding in their hands the laws of Moses, written on parchment; then went the bride and bridegroom; after them the fathers, mothers, and other relations of both; then Mr. Jacob Salomons and Mr. Barnet Monk, the two Elders of the synagogue; after them Mr. Nepthtali Myers, the treasurer to the subscriptions for the poor Jews; then followed, two and two, above three hundred Jew Gentlemen and Ladies. After their having walked the third time round Duke's-Place, they entered the synagogue, and were married according to the Jewish rites and ceremonies. Immediately after the ceremony, the whole company retired to the great hall adjoining the synagogue, where an elegant dinner was provided, consisting of four courses, and a dessert, which was provided by Mr. Hoffman. After dinner the company entered the ball room; and minuets were danced till seven o'clock, when country dances began, and continued till twelve; at which time the bride and bridegroom retired, and the company sat down to a cold supper.

Minka Levy Noah, who was later known as Amelia Noel after "Noah" was Anglicized to Noel, became an artist and art advisor to England's Princess Charlotte. Two of her nephews were among the most prominent American Jews of the nineteenth century – Mordecai M. Noah, the son of her husband's brother Manuel, was a statesman, newspaper editor and Tammany Hall politician, and Uriah P. Levy, son of her brother Michael, was the naval officer responsible for the abolition of corporal punishment in the Navy, and the purchaser of Monticello, following the death of Thomas Jefferson.

> Laft Wednefday night, departed this life, Mr. HAYMEN LEVY, Merchant, of New-York, and one of the Hebrew religion; a gentleman much refpected by all denominations who had the pleafure of his acquaintance. This gentleman lived in this city during the late war; his character as a merchant was without a blemifh; he was a true patriot and friend to the United States, an affectionate hufband, a tender father, and a fincere friend. The widow, the orphan and poor, will lament the lofs; he was benevolent and charitable to a great degree—his houfe was open to all ftrangers of good character to partake of his liberality.
> HAYMEN is gone where there is no labor or toil; In him died an Ifraelite, in whom there was no guile.

PHILADELPHIA – 1789
OBITUARY OF "HAYMEN" LEVY
Independent Gazetteer, or the Chronicle of Freedom, p. 3 (col 2)
August 25, 1789

The *Gazetteer* posted this most complimentary obituary of "Mr. Haymen [sic] Levy, Merchant, of New-York, and one of the Hebrew religion; a gentlemen much respected by all denominations who had the pleasure of his acquaintance."

"… his character as a merchant," the blurb continues, "was without a blemish; he was a true patriot and friend of the United States … his house was open to all strangers of good character to partake of his liberality."

"Haymen [sic] is gone where there is no labor or toil. In him died an Israelite, in whom there was no guile."

According to the *Universal Jewish Encyclopedia,* vol. 7, p. 10, Hayman Levy (b. Germany, 1721; d. New York, 1789), "was one of the leading merchants in New York and the largest fur traders among the colonists.... There are entries in his books to show that he employed John Jacob Astor to beat furs at $1.00 a day. Levy was one of the signers in 1770 of a resolution to make more stringent the Non-Importation Act of 1765." (See page 85.)

Levy escaped from New York and went to Philadephia during the Revolutionary War. He was one of the founders of Philadelphia's Congregation Mikveh Israel and served on its first board of trustees. In 1784, he returned to New York where he helped reorganize Congregation Shearith Israel.

The engraving on the "first recorded Jewish medal"[1] – one of the first of the more than 100 attributed to the Slovakian-Jewish engraver Moritz Fürst during his years in America – reads "GERSHOM M. SEIXAS CONGREGATIONIS HEBRÆÆ SACERDOS NOVI EBORACI." The photo at left is of a modern strike from the die in the collection of the American Jewish Historical Society; at right (courtesy of University Archives, Rare Book and Manuscript Library, Columbia University Libraries) is a silver casting that was donated to Columbia University in 1933.

[1] Daniel Friedenberg, *Jewish Minters and Medalists* (Philadelphia,1976), p. 67.

NEW YORK CITY – 1816
"DIED" – REV. GERSHOM SEIXAS
New York Evening Post, p. 2 (col 4)
July 2, 1816

In this death notice, Rev. Gershom Mendes Seixas (b. New York City, 1745; d. 1816) was referred to as "the venerable Pastor of

DIED,
Departed this life, at 9 o'clock this morning, the Rev. Mr. GERSHAM SEIXAS, the venerable Pastor of the Hebrew congregation, in the 71st year of his age.
The funeral of the deceased will take place tomorrow morning at 8 o'clock from his late residence in Mill-street.

the Hebrew congregation." He died "in the 71st year of his age," continues the notice, and the funeral will take place "tomorrow morning at 8 o'clock from his late residence on Mill street."

Rev. Seixas, the most prominent American rabbinic figure from colonial times through the early years of the republic, was known as the Jewish minister of the American Revolution and "the patriot rabbi." He was the minister of Congregation Shearith Israel beginning in 1766, and at the outbreak of the Revolution he espoused the patriot cause. Rather than having his congregation function during the British occupation of New York, he fled to Philadelphia where he invoked the blessings of the Almighty on Congress and General Washington during the dedication ceremony of Congregation Mikveh Israel. He was one of thirteen clergymen who officiated at Washington's inauguration.

Seixas was an incorporator and trustee of Columbia College, and a bronze medal in his memory (pictured above) was struck by the college following his death.

BOSTON – 1816
"OBITUARY NOTICE" –
REV. GERSHOM SEIXAS
Columbian Centinel, p. 2 (col 3)
August 17, 1816

The *Columbian Centinel* published this tribute to Columbia trustee, Rev. Gershom Mendes Seixas (see above). The notice praises Seixas highly, indicating that "the demise of this Israelite indeed, has made a great breech in the primitive church… his life was consecrated to learning,

OBITUARY NOTICE.
A few days since we announced the decease, in New York, of the Rev. GERSHOM MANDES SEIXAS, late Minister of the Hebrew Congregation in that city, in the 71st year of his age, and 50th of his ministry. The demise of this Israelite indeed, has made a great breech in the primitive church. From its earliest date, his life was consecrated to learning, piety and benevolence ; and in the ancient scriptures he was an oracle of consultation to all sects and denominations. No Minister ever lived more respected, nor died more universally lamented. For the last years of his life he experienced the excruciating pains of a chronic disease ; but supported his sufferings with true resignation, and closed a long life in full confidence of the abounding mercy of the God of Abraham, Isaac and Jacob.

piety and benevolence … he was an oracle of consultation to all sects and denominations. No Minister ever lived more respected, nor died more universally lamented."

Poulson's American Daily Advertiser.

VOLUME XLIX.]   WEDNESDAY MORNING, NOVEMBER 8, 1820.   [NUMBER 13,711.

PHILADELPHIA—Printed by ZACHARIAH POULSON, No. 106, Chesnut street—where SUBSCRIPTIONS and ADVERTISEMENTS will be gratefully received.

OBITUARY.

DIED, yesterday morning, at 6 o'clock, Miss RACHEL, daughter of Benjamin Nones, Esq. of this city, after a painful illness, sustained, in every part of its progress, with the meekness and resignation which innocence and virtue inspire.

Possessing all the advantages of education, amiable in her manners, with every accomplishment that enhances the charms of female character, she was esteemed wherever known: yet all these exterior accomplishments, the graces of person and manner, that rendered her valuable and acceptable to society, derived a higher lustre from the inestimable qualities of her mind;—The sweetness of her disposition, the benevolence of her heart, and the genuine worth that shone in every part of her conduct, endeared her to her family and friends. Her early fall is a severe visitation to her fond and disconsolate parents, and to those friends and relations who knew and admired her virtues.   J.

PHILADELPHIA – 1820
"OBITUARY" – RACHEL NONES
Poulson's American Daily Advertiser, p. 3 (col 3)
November 8, 1820

The passing of Rachel Nones was reported in a most flattering obituary. Rachel was the daughter of Benjamin Nones (b., Bordeaux, France, 1757; d. Philadelphia, 1826), who shortly after immigrating to Philadelphia had enlisted as a private in the new American army. After establishing a record for gallantry in the war, he returned to Philadelphia, set up a brokerage office, and became an ardent supporter of Thomas Jefferson.

Together with his wife Miriam, Nones fathered fourteen children. As reported here, one of his daughters, Rachel, died at a young age. According to the obituary, though she suffered a painful illness, she endured it "with the meekness and resignation which innocence and virtue inspire.... The sweetness of her disposition, the benevolence of her heart, and the genuine worth that shone in every part of her conduct, endeared her to her family and friends."

Another of Nones's daughters, Miriam, married the grandson of Haym Salomon, the financier of the Revolutionary War (see page 94).

Interesting Obituary Notice.—Died, on Friday last, Abraham Touro, Esq. merchant, of this city, aged 48 ; a gentleman whose urbanity of manners, and hospitable disposition had secured him the esteem and respect of all who were personally acquainted with him. His death was occasioned by an accident. While viewing the militaay parade on the 3d inst. in a chaise, his horse was frightened, by the firing of the artillery, and became unmanageable, and in leaping from the carriage, fractured his leg so severely, that, notwithstanding the best surgical aid, a mortification ensued, which terminated his existence in this world. Besides several gifts and remembrances to private individuals, amounting, it is said, to upwards of $10,000, he has bequeathed $50,000 to the following institutions :

Massachusetts General Hospital,	$10,000
Synagogue, New-York,	10,000
Synagogue, Newport,	15,000
Boston Female Asylum,	5,000
Asylum for Indigent Boys,	5,000
Humane Society,	5,000

The remains of Mr. Touro are to be deposited in the Synagogue at Newport.—*Boston Gazette.*

Black and white copy of Gilbert Stuart's oil portrait of Abraham Touro, procured by Massachusetts General Hospital in 1825 to commemorate Touro's generous bequest. Photo courtesy of Massachusetts General Hospital Archives and Special Collections.

NEW YORK – 1822
"INTERESTING OBITUARY NOTICE"
New-York American, p. 1 (col 2)
October 26, 1822

Abraham Touro (b. 1777; d. 1822), among the most prominent Jews of his day, was the brother of the philanthropist Judah Touro (b. 1775; d. 1854) and son of Rev. Isaac Touro (b. 1727; d. 1784), founding minister of the historic Touro Synagogue in Newport, R.I. Abraham was trained in commerce by his uncle, Moses Michael Hays, and spent most of his life in Boston.

This front-page death notice, originally published in the *Boston Gazette,* describes the strange circumstances of Touro's death. His horse had become unmanageable after being frightened by the firing of artillery at a ceremony. As a result of the horse's leaping, Touro fell off "and a mortification ensued which terminated his existence."

In addition to noting that Touro's remains "were deposited in the synagogue at Newport," the notice mentions his substantial bequest of $50,000. Six beneficiaries are listed, including the "Synagogue, Newport, $15,000," and the "Synagogue, New-York, $10,000."

THE NATIONAL ADVOCATE.

VOL. XII.   NEW-YORK, FRIDAY MORNING, JUNE 11, 1824.   NO. 3270.

> MARRIED,
> Last evening, by the Rev. Mr. Piexotto, Mr.
> Morland Micholl, to Miss Hetty Isaacs, daugh-
> ter of Mr. Abraham Isaacs, deceased.

NEW YORK CITY – 1824
MARRIAGE ANNOUNCEMENT
The National Advocate, p2 (col 4)
June 11, 1824

Among the marriage announcements in this issue of the *Advocate* was the one performed "last evening, by the Rev. Mr. Piexotto [sic]" of Miss Hetty Isaacs, daughter of the deceased Abraham Isaacs, to Mr. Morland Micholl. In later years, Micholl, a garment manufacturer, would become the second president of New York's Hebrew Benevolent Society and an officer of Congregation B'nai Jeshurun.

Nothing in the listing indicated the Jewish nature of the marriage – unless one was aware that "Rev." Mr. Peixotto was the *hazzan* (cantor) and minister of Congregation Shearith Israel. Moses Levi Maduro Peixotto (b. Curacao, 1767; d. New York, 1828) arrived in New York in 1807, having lived the first forty years of his life in Curacao and Amsterdam. He became a merchant, a freemason, a synagogue trustee and occasional *hazzan*. He took over as *hazzan* and minister of Shearith Israel after the passing of Rev. Gershom Mendes Seixas in 1816.

Though his spoken English was not good in his early years in New York, eventually it improved to the point where Rev. Peixotto delivered discourses on Thanksgiving Day and other special occasions. When certain synagogue members criticized his unmusical reading of the Torah, Rev. Peixotto replied, "Please remember that it says in the Torah that the Lord said to Moses, or He spoke to Moses, never that He sang to him."

NEW YORK HERALD.

NEW YORK, FRIDAY MORNING, OCTOBER 28, 1842.

Price Two Cents

NEW YORK – 1842 ROSSINI'S "ISRAELITES IN EGYPT"

New York Herald, p.1 (col 5) October 28, 1842

The front page of this issue of *The New York Herald* included several stanzas of Rossini's opera, "Israelites in Egypt," scheduled to debut that evening.

The second page of the issue contained an article in which James Gordon Bennett, founder and editor of *The Herald*, attacked Mordecai M. Noah (see Chapter 8).

The Principal Passages

From the Sacred Musical Drama of the Israelites in Egypt, music by Rossini, to be performed at the Park Theatre, for the first time, on Monday, the 31st instant.

SONG OF MOSES AND THE ISRAELITES.

CHORUS OF ISRAELITES.

God of Israel! oh, deign to hear
Thy children's moan, their suppliant pray'r!
Grant, O Lord! that thy chosen band
May once more see their native land!
In bondage vile we toil and groan,
'Neath an impious tyrant's reign,
Who bows to gods of senseless stone,
And treats our law with foul disdain!

CHORUS OF ISRAELITISH WOMEN.

A prey every day to new tears,
How, alas! can we cease our tears!
Almighty God! Wilt thou ne'er more
Our husbands, our fathers, our children restore?

Enter Moses from the tent.

Moses (rebuking them) Your impious complainings end,
God and Moses still are high!
Midianites! these murmurs high
You jealous God o'ermuch offend!

CHORUS OF ISRAELITES.

Forgive to wretched grief
These tears, our sole relief;
Think what ills our hearts have borne!

MOSES.

Filled with love towards God, e'er just,
Still let your hearts his mercy trust;
He will make the impious mourn;
The Lord of Grace, from heaven's high sphere,
The contrite heart will ever hear;
Led by his hand, his chosen band
Will see, ere long, their native land!

CHORUS.

God of love! shall we then behold
Our fathers, our husbands? Our children again unfold?

MOSES.

The Lord of Grace, from heaven's high sphere,
The contrite heart will ever hear;
Led by his hand, his chosen band
Will see, ere long, their native land!

ISRAELITES.

God of Israel, oh! deign to hear;
Thy children's moan, their suppliant pray'r!
Grant, O Lord! that thy chosen band
May once more see their native land!

SONG OF LOVE AND ADORATION.

DUETT.

Amenoph. (*Detaining her.*)—
Ah! if thou whom I adore
Must forever leave me,
Peace, alas! will never more
In this bosom smile again!

Anai. Do not seek my heart to move;
Duty's sacred voice commands me!
I may ne'er accept thy love,—
Heav'n itself doth so ordain!

Amenoph. One kind smile to calm this anguish,
Anai, oh, why deny me?
Depriv'd of thee, to joy farewell!

Anai. Cease, oh, cease! In vain's thy anguish!
Hapless youth, oh, seek to fly me;
I thy love must still repel!

Amenoph. Those in hopeless love who languish,
Can alone my torments tell!

Anai. We must part; thy passion vanquish;
Absence soon will break Love's spell.
(*A trumpet is heard without.*)

Anai. Hark! yonder sound calls Israel's children,
And I must stay no longer near thee.

Amenoph. (*seizing her*)—
Who shall dare from me to tear thee?
By this hand he surely dies!

Anai. Ah! yet tremble——

Amenoph. To fear a stranger——

Anai. Oh! for mercy!

Amenoph. Ev'ry danger
I'll confront, howe'er impending,
Ev'ry terror brave, unbending!

Anai. Dread the Pow'r thou'rt now offending!

Amenoph. Ev'ry fear my soul defies!
Amenoph. One kind smile to calm my anguish,
Anai, oh, why deny me?
Depriv'd of thee, to joy farewell!
Those in hopeless love who languish,
Can alone my torments tell!

Anai. Cease, oh, cease! In vain's thy anguish!
Hapless youth, ah, seek to fly me!
I thy love must still repel!
We must part; thy passion vanquish;
Absence soon will break Love's spell!
(*The trumpet sounds again.*)

Anai. Hear'st thou?

Amenoph. Distraction!

Anai. Farewell!

SONG OF FEAR AND JOY.

CHORUS.

Egyptians. Oh, awful darkness! Oh, fear!
Ah! when will disappear
This veil that hides the day?

Amenoph. Oh, punishment severe!
My heart is all dismay!

Phar. Will ne'er again appear
Sinaide. The Sun's all-cheering ray?

Egyptians. Oh, God of Israel, hear!
Let thine anger burst
Upon the head accurst
That made great Egypt's Lord
Forswear his plighted word!

Phar. These harsh and sore reprovings,
Rending my breast, give over!
Too late I now discover
The error we all deplore!

Amenoph. Ah! what conflicting passions
(*aside.*) Now are my bosom tearing!

Sinaide. Of future joy despairing,
Will Egypt smile no more!

Egyptians. (*kneeling to Pharaoh*)—
Thus, prostrate, King, we pray thee
In error's path persist not!
The wonders dire resist not
Which Heav'n doth on us pour!

Pharaoh (*commandingly.*)
Be Moses called!
(*Attendants go to summon Moses.*)

Amenoph. (*aside.*) Confusion!
Sanaide (*aside.*) Oh, joy!

Egyptian (*anxiously.*) Moses, haste thee!

Sinaide (*to Pharaoh.*)
At last art thou decided?

Phar. By reason I am guided.

Amenoph. (*aside.*)
I love thee, Anai!

Sinaide (*aside.*) Oh, delight!

Egyptians. Hope from despair awakes,
And on our hearts beams bright!

Amenoph. (*aside*)
All hope my heart forsakes!
My soul feels double night!

Egyptians. Oh, God of Israel, hear!
That hence thy Chosen may go,
Thy mercy, Pow'r of Fear,
Now deign to show!

SINNERS GROANING.

DUETT.

Amenoph. In vain I try,—oh, torture!
(*aside.*) To hide these pains that overbear me;
And yet the pangs that tear me
Must in my breast remain!

Phar. Once more joy smiles o'er all the land,
So late my fears tormented,
And soon thy heart, by love contented,
Will banish ev'ry pain!

Amenoph. No! Joy for ever flies me!

Phar. What mean'st thou? Thy words surprise me!

Amenoph. Father! Thou suspect'st not——

Phar. What say'st thou?

Amenoph. No more! Oh, never may'st thou
Learn what doth cause my pain!

Phar. Wherefore such grief betray'st thou?
Thy strange discourse explain!

Amenoph. (*aside.*)
Of ev'ry joy despairing,
This heart must hopeless sigh!
The fiercest dangers daring,
To death from woe I'll fly!

WASHINGTON. D.C. – 1844
"RELIGIOUS REVIVAL AMONGST THE JEWS"

National Intelligencer, p. 1 (col 4)
September 26, 1844

This front-page news item expresses admiration for the "outburst of religious enthusiasm" from worshippers at New York City's Crosby Street Synagogue in the "season of penance" preceding the "day of atonement" [sic].

"Few of our Christian sects excel in a devotion which arouses one from the balmiest moments of morning sleep to mingle in spiritual exercises."

REVIVAL OF RELIGION AMONGST THE JEWS.—The Crosby street Synagogue has been the scene of an unexampled outburst of religious enthusiasm on the part of some of its members during the last fortnight. This is the season for penance, and, until the day of atonement, which ensues on Monday, the 23d instant, this period is peculiarly marked by the offering of prayers, supplicating pardon for the numerous transgressions by which they have offended against the law during the preceding year. One of the peculiarities of the service is the necessity of its repetition before the dawn of morning, to accomplish which the faithful congregate at four o'clock, and present a most interesting and unique appearance. Assembled in half dress, like travellers hastily aroused, by the glare of the lamps dimly lighting the extensive building, it seems some hurried assemblage appealing to ward off a suddenly expected calamity ; and when the clear tones of the reader is heard rehearsing in musical chantings the aspirations for pardon, our thoughts are carried back to the better days of Judaism, when the children of Israel "abided under the shadow of the Almighty." Few of our Christian sects excel in a devotion which arouses one from the balmiest moments of morning sleep to mingle in spiritual exercises, disturbing the rest and sacrificing the sweetest comfort of nature.—*N. Y. Express*

JEWISH FESTIVALS. Thursday was the commencement of the New Year, and the Synagogues throughout New York were crowded with the people of the ancient faith, who now number some fifteen thousand. Ten days hence in the solemn fast, the great day of atonement.

BOSTON – 1848
"JEWISH FESTIVALS"

Daily Evening Transcript, p.2 (col 2)
September 30, 1848

As the size of New York City's Jewish population increased – to "some fifteen thousand" by 1848 – "the Synagogues throughout New York were crowded" in celebration of the New Year.

In 1848, Ahawath Chesed (known today as Central Synagogue) was a two-year old congregation on the Lower East Side. In 1872 it built what is now a New York City Landmark and National Historic Landmark as the oldest synagogue in continuous use in the city. Photo courtesy of Central Synagogue Archives, C.K. Bill, 1872.

NEW ORLEANS – 1852
"MATZOT"

The Daily Delta, p. 2 (col 5) – February 10, 1852

By 1852, New Orleans had emerged as the nation's wealthiest and third most populous city, numbering several hundred Jewish families. What made this advertisement unusual was the use of an actual Hebrew type face to spell out the heading, *"Matzot,"* the principal Passover food.

Addressed "To the Israelites of New Orleans and other Cities," the ad notes that L. Regensburger, "having been appointed" to supply the Passover bread and meat, is soliciting orders. Judging from the advertiser's name, there is a good chance he arrived in the United States after 1840, together with other German refugees. It might be argued that the public printing of such an ad in a secular in a secular newspaper showed a high Jewish confidence level with life in New Orleans.

NEW YORK – 1853
"JEWISH FEASTS"

New York Tribune, p. 4 (col 3)
October 25, 1853

The article "Jewish Feasts" discusses the Feast of Tabernacles associated with Jews erecting outdoor huts in remembrance of the dwelling arrangement in the wilderness on the way to the Holy Land, the use of ceremonial palm branches, and animal sacrifices in the Temple in Jerusalem.

NEW YORK – 1859
"THE HEBREWS IN NEW YORK"
The New York Herald, p. 2 (col 1–2)
December 27, 1859

Two full columns in this issue of the *Herald*, excerpted here, focused on what was going on religiously and sociologically with "The Hebrews in New York" at the time. Included in the section were four sub-articles: Two covered appeals, one at Temple Emanuel and another at the Wooster Street Synagogue, for assistance for the thousands of Jews who had to flee to Gibraltar as a result of the French-Spanish invasion of Morocco; one described ceremonies relating to the Chanukah holiday they referred to as the "Feast of Dedication;" and the last discussed "An Interesting Jewish Ceremony," that being the conversion of a young Christian woman to the Reform branch of Judaism, at a public ceremony at Temple Emanuel.

THE HEBREWS IN NEW YORK.

THE SUFFERING JEWS OF MOROCCO.
APPEAL FROM THE TEMPLE EMANUEL.

At half-past ten o'clock on Saturday morning the Temple Emanuel, a Jewish place of worship in East Twelfth street, was crowded with a highly respectable congregation of Israelites. It being the Jewish Sabbath, the usual solemn and imposing ceremonies incident to that day were performed, and a very eloquent discourse on charity was delivered by the Rabbi, Rev. Dr. S. Adler. In the course of his remarks, Dr. Adler alluded to the hapless condition of the Israelites of Morocco, who, in consequence of the French-Spanish invasion, were obliged to flee from their homes in that country, and seek shelter in the more hospitable region of Gibraltar. The heart of all Israel, he said, bled for the sufferings of their unfortunate brethren, and he appealed to the congregation of Temple Emanuel to come forward with every assistance in their power. This appeal, couched in the most pathetic language, made a powerful effect upon his hearers.

The text of an appeal circular followed, ending with:

Any donation you may be pleased to bestow may be handed to Mr. Mayer, the bearer of this circular, or to either of the undersigned committee, who will promptly forward the same to its destination. We have the honor to sign, most respectfully,
A. MICHELBACHER, 39 John street.
S. J. SPIEGELBERG, 32 Vesey, corner Church st.
ISAAC BERNHEIMER, 199 Broadway.

THE ANNUAL JEWISH FEAST OF DEDICATION.

The annual Jewish festival in commemoration of the Purification of the Second Temple, a feast among the Israelites corresponding to our holiday week between Christmas and New Year, commenced evening of the 19th inst., and will be continued eight days. With the Jews it is a time for social enjoyment; for balls, parties, tableaux, the frequenting of theatres—to be sure not so

The principal peculiarity in the observance of this feast is the burning of lamps in the synagogues, and also in all the private residences of the Jews, the lamps being fed by pure olive oil. On the first night of the festival one lamp is lit; on the second, two; on the third, three; and so on ... This feast commemorates the Purification of the Second Temple by the sons of the Grand Priest, John, the son of Mattathias, and sometimes called Hashmonaee, or Maccabee. ...

SERVICE IN THE WOOSTER STREET SYNAGOGUE.

Saturday being the Jewish Sabbath, and the 4th day of the Jewish Feast of Dedication, which the Jews will continue to celebrate four days longer, an extra service was performed on that morning in all the synagogues, and in the Wooster street synagogue a sermon was delivered in English by the Rev. S. M. Isaacs, embracing a stirring appeal in behalf of the suffering Jews at Gibraltar. The Rev. Mr. Isaacs took his text from Zachariah. ...

After quoting Rev. Isaac's discourse, the article speaks of his smooth segue into *his* appeal before the last article…

INTERESTING JEWISH CEREMONY.
RECEPTION OF A FEMALE CHRISTIAN PROSELYTE.

A very large congregation assembled at the Jewish Synagogue, No. 84 East Twelfth street, on the 17th inst., for the purpose of Divine worship, and to witness the rare and interesting ceremony of the reception of a Christian proselyte. The services of the day were conducted in the ordinary form of Hebrew worship, and the chanting of some of the Psalms of "the Sweet Singer of Israel." ...

The article devotes almost half a column describing the morning service, including the reading of Torah ("the law") and the discourse that followed, before it discusses the actual "Interesting Jewish Ceremony."

At the conclusion of morning service the Rev. Dr. Adler ascended the rostrum, and a very fine looking young woman, of middle stature, and apparently not more than twenty-three years of age, plainly and respectably attired, boldly advanced from among the congregation ... The utmost stillness prevailed throughout the synagogue as Dr. Adler proceeded to address the proselyte. Addressing her by her name, he said:—

"Mrs. ——, I have to inquire of you whether you have duly prepared yourself for the solemn step you are now about to take ...

The lady then made the following confession of the faith of an Israelite in full and distinct tones, and with a very perfect English pronunciation:—

"I acknowledge and confess that God, the creator, supporter and ruler of the whole universe, is an only God... and I promise solemnly to live henceforth with all my heart, with all my soul, and with all my might, according to this holy belief, and to deviate neither toward the right nor toward the left from the obligations arising from the same. Living and dying I will confess by word and deed the truth.

"Shemang Yisrael, Adonai Elohim elohino achod."
Hear, O Israel—the Lord our God, the Lord is one.

The long conversion ceremony, explained in detail, ended with the priestly benediction which concluded:

"God lift up his countenance upon thee and give thee peace—peace now, peace forever and ever."
The congregation answered, "Amen."

> PASSOVER.—The Passover, or Hebrew feast,
> in commemoration of the sparing of the Israel-
> ites, when the first-born of the Egyptians per-
> ished, and of their escape out of Egypt, com-
> menced last night. The Hebrew congregation
> in Madison numbers seventy-five or eighty
> souls. During the eight days of the feast, they
> eat unleavened bread only, because their hasty
> departure from Egypt obliged their ancestors
> to take their dough with them before it was
> leavened. To the festival of the Passover, so
> long as the Israelites remained in possession of
> Palestine, they assembled originally at the Tab-
> ernacle, and from Solomon's time at the Tem-
> ble. Since their dispersion, wherever two or
> three of them are together, it is celebrated by
> eating unleavened bread and by public prayers.

MADISON, INDIANA – 1860
"PASSOVER"
The Daily Evening Courier, p. 3 (col 1)
April 7, 1860

In the "Local Matters" column of this issue, a paragraph on Passover talks about the holiday, indicating that the "seventy five or eighty souls" belonging to the Hebrew congregation in Madison will observe the holiday by eating unleavened bread for eight days. The paragraph ends with the notation that "since their dispersion [from what the paper refers to as Palestine], wherever two or three of them are together, [the holiday] is celebrated by eating unleavened bread and by public prayers."

What the Jews Have Done the Last Year.
[From the New York Evening Post.]
The *Jewish Messenger* of this week sums up what the professors of the Hebrew faith have accomplished, as an Ecclesiasticism, during the past year, 5620 of the Jewish calendar.
The editor deplores the "lethargic indifference" which has characterized the Hebrew community of this country, but observes that this indifference is compensated, in some degree, by

ST. LOUIS, MISSOURI – 1860
"WHAT THE JEWS HAVE DONE THE LAST YEAR."
The Weekly Missouri Democrat, p. 2 (col 8)
October 9, 1860

This assessment of how Jews have fared around the world in the Hebrew year 5620, taken from the *New York Evening Post*, is based on information published in "The *Jewish Messenger* of this week." The article reports that while deploring the spiritual "lethargic indifference" of American Jewry, the *Messenger's* editor found several developments to praise. The founding of the Board of Delegates of American Israelites, and the efforts to organize a similar body in Italy, constituted "a great advance towards the [much hoped for] union of Israelites throughout the world."

The article includes an extensive quote from the *Messenger's* report on the "progress of liberal ideas and tolerance" in Europe, giving country-by-country updates.

The *Messenger's* information led the *Post* to conclude in the article that Jewish literature apparently flourishes better in Europe than here, "but two books have been printed in Hebrew on this side of the Atlantic." Three Jewish papers have been added overseas while the number has decreased here, and only "one or two have any influence." A Jewish professor is reported as now being attached to the University of Gottingen and another has been "elevated to an important professorship in the Warsaw University."

The article next reports on the five new congregations organized during the year and lists several "places of worship [that] have been dedicated" in such far apart locations as Fort Wayne, Indiana; Long Island, New York; and Macon, Georgia.

The Jews, according to the *Post's* deductions, were not particularly affected by the disturbances in Syria and Morocco, nor in Palestine by the contending factions of Moslems and Christians.

The article closes by quoting the *Messenger's* summary which notes that "our [Jewish] community, as a whole, has [not] progressed as it should," referring to the lack of "improvement in the religious spirit." Politically, however, the Jews' status "is probably better" and "their social position about the same."

the establishment of the "Board of Delegates of American Israelites," and adds:

"The consummation of this measure, with the recent efforts—promising a successful issue—to organize a similar central body among our *Italian* co-religionists, and to carry out the design for some time agitated of a 'Universal Israelitish Alliance,' we consider a significant realization of the hope we expressed a twelvemonth ago, and—as constituting a great advance towards the union of Israelites throughout the world—we deem these matters of greater importance than a casual observer might be disposed to concede."

A similar hope, we may remark, has been expressed for centuries; the dream of "United Israel" is the one sweet dream of every Israelitish breast; but it seems as far from fulfillment now as in the day when Solyman I. held mosque services in the holy city of Palestine.

The *Messenger* adverts with a spirit of gladness to the progress of liberal ideas and the tolerance extended toward the Jews of Europe during the year past. We may quote:

"In Great Britain, France and Holland our co-religionists retain the same high standing, which, in a free country, they are certain to secure. Distinguished honors have been paid to several Israelitish citizens of these sovereignties. From Russia we have intelligence of continued progress in liberal enactments, and the condition of our community is one of prosperity and advancement. In Poland, likewise, old prejudices are wearing off. Dr. Hirshfield, for instance, has been elevated to an important professorship in the Warsaw University. In Galicia, illiberal measures are yet being enforced. Austria has witnessed some little improvement in the position of her Jewish population during the past year, though whether it is likely to last we have our fears. In Prussia, and the minor German States, nothing worthy of particular mention has transpired, although, on the whole, the condition of things is favorable. The Grand Duchy of Hesse boasts of a Jewish mayor. Our Italian brethren are doing well. * * * In Spain and Portugal Judaism is once more openly practised, where, since the close of the fifteenth century, it has been interdicted."

In what other age of the Christian world could this have been asserted?

Jewish literature seems not to flourish here, but two books have been printed in Hebrew on this side of the Atlantic during the year past, though in Europe the labors of Auerbach, Philipsohn, Stauben, &c., are eminently appreciated. A Jewish professor, Stern, is now attached to the University of Gottingen. Three Jewish papers have been started during the year, viz: at Tunis, Mayence and Odessa. The number of papers has decreased in this country, and the *Messenger* deplores the fact that "but one or two have any influence."

Five new congregations have been organized during the year, viz: "One at Portland, Oregon; one at New Brunswick, New Jersey; one at St. Joseph, Mo., and two in this city. The number of consecrations of new synagogues rather exceeds the average. Places of worship have been dedicated at Fort Wayne, Indiana; Milwaukee, Wisconsin; Macon, Georgia; Plaquemine, Louisiana; Montreal, Canada East; Philadelphia, Pennsylvania; two at Cincinnati, Ohio; Brooklyn, Long Island, and three in this city."

The Hebrew Benevolent society has established an Orphan Asylum in this city. One also has been established in Charleston, South Carolina. No mention is made by the *Messenger* of any other bevolent institutions under Hebrew auspices.

The recent disturbances in Morocco and Syria did not affect the Jews particularly. In Morocco they receive a ready protection from Moorish vengeance, and are now peacefully enjoying their usual immunities. In Palestine the Hebrews were not disturbed at all by the contending factions of Moslems and Christians.

The *Messenger* says, in closing its summary:

"We cannot claim that our community, as a whole, has progressed as it should. There has been, we are obliged, to our regret, to confess, no improvement in the religious spirit of our co-religionists; and on this point we forbear to speak more at length. Their political status is probably better than when we entered on the year which has just come to a close; their social position about the same."

National Anti-Slavery Standard.

VOL. XXIII. NO. 32.   NEW YORK, SATURDAY, DECEMBER 20, 1862.   WHOLE NO. 1,176

NEW YORK –
1862
"MANNERS AND
CUSTOMS OF THE
MODERN JEWS"
*National Anti-Slavery
Standard,
p. 4 (col 3–4)
December 20, 1862*

An article about Jewish customs, featured in the *National Anti-Slavery Standard,* an abolitionist newspaper, touched on topics such as the circumcision of a male infant, the Bar-Mitzvah of a 13 year old boy (referred to as a "ceremony akin to that of confirmation"), the wedding day customs and ceremony, affixing a *Mezuzah* – a container with verses from *Deuteronomy*, as pictured above – on the doorpost, burial rites and the mourning period, and a distinction between the sexes.

MANNERS AND CUSTOMS OF THE MODERN JEWS.

[The magazine, *Once a Week,* contains in one of its late numbers an interesting sketch of the peculiar customs of the modern Israelites. We extract a few of its passages for the benefit of readers to whom those customs are unfamiliar :]

THE STAGES OF LIFE.

ON the eighth day after the birth of the young Jew, he is taken to the synagogue by his father, accompanied by a godfather for circumcision. If the infant happens to be a first-born son, he is, according to Jewish jurisprudence, the property of the Cohen (who is supposed to be a descendant of the house of Aaron, but has no longer any priestly functions to perform), and must be redeemed on the thirtieth day after his birth; therefore, certain ceremonies take place, during which the father tenders the figurative sum of five shekels to the Cohen, who accepts them as a ransom.

Until he attains his thirteenth year, the young Jew is entirely under the control of his father and mother, who are supposed to be accountable for all the sins he may commit up to that period; but their responsibility ceases on the Sabbath day succeeding his thirteenth birthday, when a ceremony akin to that of confirmation takes place. The boy is called up to the reading-desk in the synagogue, and is required to read a portion of the law. If he cannot read, the chazan, or minister, does it for him, after which the father places his hands on his son's head, and solemnly renounces his accountability for his future actions.

The next important step in his career is his betrothal, which usually takes place at an early age, in accordance with the recommendation of the Jewish law. A number of friends being present, the *Kenas,* or bond inflicting a penalty on either party who shall be guilty of a breach of the agreement, is read, after which a cup is broken, as a ratification of its provisions, by the parties concerned. The marriage follows the betrothal, it may be six or twelve months afterwards, or more.

Due notice having been given at the synagogue, the minister, on the Saturday eve preceding the day fixed for the marriage, chants some sentences referring to the approaching event, and the next day the intended bridegroom has to appear in the synagogue and have certain portions of the law read over to him, and pay any arrears he may owe to the congregation.

The way in which the parties spend the morning in their respective dwellings on the wedding-day resembles, I suppose, the manner in which it is employed by Gentiles on similar occasions; those who rightly realize the awful nature of the ceremony they are about to perform, spend the hours in fasting and reading the service prepared for the day of atonement. As soon as the clock strikes the appointed hour, two men present themselves before the bridegroom, and carry him off to the synagogue, where he meets the bride, whom two female friends have brought there with her head enveloped in a veil. The same persons place the two principal performers facing each other under a silk or velvet canopy supported by four long poles; the shamas, a kind of curate and clerk combined, brings a glass of wine, which he hands to the Rabbi, who thereupon offers up a short blessing, and then gives the glass of wine to the bridegroom, who tastes it and passes it to the bride, who does likewise.

The bridegroom then takes the ring from his pocket and places it on the finger of the bride, saying after the Rabbi (in Hebrew) as he does so: "Behold! thou art betrothed unto me with this ring, according to the rites of Moses and Israel." The Rabbi then reads the marriage contract, which is written in Chaldee, and is not understood by the parties concerned, who therefore take it on trust; after this the Chazan takes a glass of wine, and pronounces a form of words longer but similar to that pronounced by the Rabbi; the wine is given to the bridegroom and bride, and an empty glass having been placed at the feet of the former, he stamps upon it and breaks it, whereupon all present wish him *mazel tov* (good speed), and the ceremony is at an end.

If the newly married Jew has a proper sense of his religious duties, one of his first proceedings, on taking possession of his domicile, is to prepare a mezuzah. This is a tube nailed to the door-post, and contains a strip of parchment, on one side of which is inscribed one of the names applied to the Supreme Being, and on the other from the 4th to 9th verses of the 6th chapter of Deuteronomy, and from the 13th to the 21st verses of the 11th chapter of the same book. A similar tube is fastened to the jambs of the other doors in the house; and the Jew who is a strict observer of the old customs of his forefathers never leaves his house for the first time, daily, without touching the mezuzah with his lips, or bending his head to it as he passes from room to room.

DEATH AND BURIAL.

The Jew has no reason to complain of lack of seasons for rejoicings, but days of mourning and sorrow visit him as well as his Gentile brethren. But the manner in which he mourns for the dead is different as regards certain forms from that of the latter, who simply buries his grief in his own heart, and suffers it to exibit itself as little as possible. The coffin is of the simplest construction, and before the lid is placed upon it, a little earth, brought from Jerusalem, is put in. The nearest relatives of the deceased approach in succession, and request pardon of the deceased for any offence they may have given him in his lifetime, and a favorable recollection of them in the world to which he has departed. The Rabbi then makes a slight cut in the upper part of the garments of each mourner, and tears it slightly, and this rent must not be sewn up till after a certain number of days.

No woman is allowed to accompany the corpse to its last resting-place, so that the wailing of women which has chilled the heart of every traveller in the East, and which may be heard even in those islands at the antipodes where scarcely a European has set his foot, is never heard here now.

A singular custom is sometimes observed on occasions when there have been several deaths in the family within a short period. A padlock is locked and placed in the grave and the key thrown away, the object being to delay the entrance of death into the house for a longer period.

The seven days which succeed the funeral of a Jew are given up entirely to mourning. Unwashed and with naked feet the mourner sits upon the bare ground in a room open to all comers; not even a change of dress is permitted; and the only consolation which the afflicted can have during this period is derived from the perusal of religious books which cheer them with the hope of meeting the deceased hereafter. When they visit the synagogue, during the continuance of these days of mourning, a touching reception is given them by the congregation, who all rise as they enter, and make a movement towards them, the Rabbi uttering a short prayer that they may be comforted. Business may be attended to after the lapse of the seven days, but no amusement may be indulged in for thirty days thereafter; and if the mourning be for a father or mother, this rule is to be observed for a year.

DISTINCTION BETWEEN THE SEXES.

In every day life the sexes are as much on an equality as among other civilized people, but in religious matters the case is slightly different. It is in acknowledgment of this difference that the Jew is taught to offer up the following short thanksgiving along with his daily prayers: "Blessed art Thou, O Lord our God, king of the universe, who hast not made me a woman." The female infant is named in the synagogue, and that is the only ceremony to which she is subjected.

NEW YORK CITY – 1863
THANKSGIVING AND "THE ISRAELITES"

The New York Times, p 8 (col 4)
August 7, 1863

Three front page columns focused on the National Thanksgiving which took place the day before. Reporting continues with another four additional columns, on the back page, devoted to this event. Coverage consists of highlights of sermons delivered at respective synagogues and churches.

The interfaith coverage opens with descriptions of the Jewish synagogue observance of this National Thanksgiving. The article's complimentary introductory paragraph to the Jewish prayer service, headed "The Israelites," acclaims:

The precepts of the Old Testament enjoin upon the Children of Israel the strict and close observance of all the public festivals proclaimed by the nations among whom they sojourn, and this highly intelligent class of our fellow citizens were among the foremost yesterday in doing honor to the National Thanksgiving, which they made a high and universal holiday to all their people.

The article continues, summarizing sermons delivered at three synagogues – Shaarai Tephila, Bn'ai Jeshurun and Shearith Israel.

The National Thanksgiving was observed throughout the City yesterday by an almost entire abstaining from secular pursuits. The stores throughout were closed, and there appeared to be a very general desire to unite in the purposes of the day—Thanksgiving and Praise. Very many of the churches were open, where proper observances were had, and each was crowded to overflowing. A large number, however, and many of them among the most prominent, were closed, this being "vacation season" with the pastors. It was a matter of disappointment and remark that on such an occasion the pulpits of all the churches in the City were not filled, either by the regular officiates, or from the many who would have volunteered. In a number of the churches no discourses were delivered, the services consisting of special prayers and hymns.

In the different institutions, public and private, due notice of the day was taken and proper solemnities observed.

In short, it can be said that on no previous occasions of a similar character, have the People of this City evinced so thorough an appreciation of its solemnity, or entered into an observance of it with more full and devout hearts.

The Israelites.

The precepts of the Old Testament enjoin upon the children of Israel the strict and close observance of all the public festivals proclaimed by the nations among whom they sojourn, and this highly intelligent and patriotic class of our fellow-citizens were among the foremost yesterday in doing honor to the National Thanksgiving, which they made a high and universal holiday to all their people.

THE SHAARAI TEPHILA,

Or Synagogue in Wooster-street, was opened for service at 7 A. M., and after the usual exercises of the Jewish rite pertaining to the solemn offering of thanks, Rev. S. M. ISAACS discoursed from the following text from the 105th Psalm:

"Give thanks unto the Lord, Call upon His name, make known His deeds among the nations."

The Rev. gentleman opened with an impressive recognition of the Divine mercy extended to the American people in the signal successes which had recently blessed their arms and had uplifted them from the depths of foreboding and humiliation to the summit of hope and rejoicing. The gloom and sorrow that had fallen upon us might be regarded among the dispensations of Providence as a chastisement for our sins. The long trials through which we were passing had, he fervently trusted, inclined our hearts more and more to the acknowledgment of the Supreme Will, and curbed the haughty spirit engendered by unexampled prosperity. He then referred feelingly to the unswerving loyalty manifested by the Jewish people in America, and expressed the hope that all our citizens would ere long be living together in the bonds of brotherhood. Not forgetting our own deficiencies, we must hereafter cultivate a loftier purity of principle, and rise superior to those mercenary aspirations which had been so frequently charged against Americans. Dr. ISAACS concluded with an earnest prayer for the complete restoration of peace and unity, for the safety and wise direction of the Government, and for consolation from the Great Disposer of events to those who had suffered from the dread calamities of war.

A large and attentive congregation followed the exercises and the sermon with the most marked interest.

THE BNAI JESHURUN,

or Jewish Synagogue, in Greene-street, was opened at 10½ A. M., in expectation that the Rabbi, M. J. RAPHALL, would deliver the day's discourse. It was learned, however, that the reverend gentleman was suffering from an attack of apoplexy, superinduced by the sudden return of his son from the seat of war, mutilated by the loss of an arm—a circumstance delicately alluded to in prayer by Rev. Mr. ISAACS, at the Wooster-street Synagogue. The building was then closed until 5 P. M., when Rev. J. S. KRAMER read the exercises appropriate to the day, offered up the prayer for Government, and concluded with a few brief remarks enjoining harmony among brethren. A full choir sang the Thanksgiving Hymn, assisted by a considerable and devout congregation.

THE SHEARITH ISRAEL,

On West Nineteenth-street, near Fifth-avenue, was thrown open at an early hour in the morning, and being regarded as a representative church by the Jewish community, second only to the Rabbis, was well attended. Rev. J. J. LYONS, pastor, read the services and pronounced the prayer for our National Government. There was no set lecture, but the brief pastoral invocation of the preacher was addressed to the speedy restoration of the Union and national peace and prosperity.

THE NEW YORK HERALD.

WHOLE NO. 9821.   NEW YORK, FRIDAY, AUGUST 7, 1863.   PRICE THREE CENTS.

NATIONAL THANKSGIVING.

Sermons by Bishop Upfold, of Indiana, the Rev. Dr. Cox, Dr. Tyng, Dr. Osgood, Dr. Osbon and the Rev. Mr. Cox.

THE SERVICES IN THE SYNAGOGUES,
&c., &c., &c.

TRINITY CHURCH.

ST. GEORGE'S CHURCH.

CALVARY CHURCH.

MADISON SQUARE PRESBYTERIAN CHURCH.

REV. DR. OSGOOD'S (UNITARIAN) CHURCH.

PRESBYTERIAN CHURCH, YORKVILLE.

THANKSGIVING AMONG THE JEWS.

NEWS FROM THE SOUTHWEST.

Everything Quiet on the Mississippi River.

Location and Condition of Johnston's Rebel Army.

Organization of Secret Union Societies in Mississippi.

The Rebels Strengthening the Defences of Mobile,
&c., &c., &c.

THANKSGIVING DAY IN THE PARK.

THANKSGIVING IN BROOKLYN.

SERIOUS ACCIDENT AT A PICNIC.

ANNUAL CROWDER OF THE BROOKLYN YACHT CLUB.

MANHATTAN ASSOCIATION.

THE DAY ELSEWHERE.

NEWS FROM THE SOUTH.

Charge of the police at the Tribune office during the New York Draft Riots of 1863. Possible wood engraving from Harper's Pictorial History of the Civil War, *v. 2, p. 653, ca. 1894. <www.loc.gov/item/2006688448/>*

NEW YORK CITY - 1863
"THANKSGIVING AMONG THE JEWS"

The New York Herald, p. 1 (col 4–5)
August 7, 1863

In 1863, there were protests against the draft throughout the North, but the greatest trouble occurred in July in New York City. These riots, the worst thus far in American history, consisted of a wave of working-class looting, fighting and lynchings claiming the lives of 105 people. The riots were quelled only when units of the United States Army were rushed to New York City from the battlefield at Gettysburg.

Yet one month later, New Yorkers responded wholeheartedly to President Lincoln's call for a National Thanksgiving to be held on August 6th. Nearly the entire front page is taken up with a description of religious events and programs in response to the President's request.

One such description, under the subhead "Thanksgiving Among the Jews," reports how the city's some 50,000 Jews marked the occasion. The names, addresses and spiritual leaders of New York City's twenty two synagogues are listed. "The services in the different synagogues consisted of the singing of several hymns selected by the priests officiating." At the end of each service, a seventeen-line prayer for the government, whose text is printed in full in the article, was recited.

THANKSGIVING AMONG THE JEWS.

Together with the many of her sects which offered up services yesterday in accordance with the proclamation of President Lincoln were many members of the Jewish persuasion. In this country, probably more than in any other, the Jews are guaranteed the right to their peculiar form of worship. They are protected in business as well as in religion; and the equality which has hitherto existed relative to every person in this quarter of the globe has attracted hither not alone believers in the Jewish doctrine, but of every doctrine which has originated since the advent of Christianity among us.

In accordance with the President's call for a general thanksgiving on the part of the nation yesterday, several of the synagogues were open in the afternoon and evening. Services were held and discourses given—some in English and some in German—relative to the events of the day. The following are the synagogues of the city, in nearly all of which services were held yesterday:—

Shearith Israel, West Nineteenth street, near Fifth avenue. Minister, J. J. Lyons.

Shaaer Hashamoin, 122 Attorney street. Minister, R. Lasker.

Temple, 84 East Twelfth street. Rabbi, Samuel Adler.

Adnareth El, 106 East Twenty-third street.

Ahawath Chesed, 127 Columbia street. President, Ignatz Stein.

Anshi Bikur Cholim, 150 Attorney street. President, M. Westheimer.

Anshi Chesed, 146 Norfolk street. President, M. Schwab.

Beth Israel Bikur Cholim, 56 Chrystie street. President, L. Levy.

Rodeph Shalom, No. 8 Clinton street. President, M. Schutz.

Beth Hamidrash, Mott street, corner of Chatham. President, Isidor Raphall.

Poel Tsedek, West Twenty-ninth street, corner of Eighth avenue. President, D. Kempner.

Shaarai Tephila, 112 Wooster street. Minister, S. M. Isaacs.

Bnai Israel, 41 Stanton street. President, M. S. Cohen.

Beth Joseph, 41 East Broadway. President, W. Alexander.

Bass Naamen, 136 Delancey street. President, N. Anstein.

Beth Hamidrash, 78 Allen street. President, A. Bohm.

Bnai Jeshurun, 164 Greene street. Rabbi, M. J. Raphall.

Bikur Cholim, U-Kadischa, 63 Chrystie street. President, E. Elbthal.

Shaarai Rach Mim, 156 Attorney street. President, N. Sonneberg.

Bnai Sholom, Third street, corner avenue C. President, J. Altmeyer.

Shaarai Berocho, 275 Ninth street. President, J. Abrahams.

Shaarai Zedeck, 38 Henry street. President, S. D. Moss.

The services in the different synagogues consisted of the singing of several hymns selected by the priests officiating, at the end of which the following prayer for the government was offered up:—

May He by whose dispensation assistance is granted unto kings and dominion unto princes—whose kingdom is an everlasting kingdom—who delivered his servant David from the destructive sword—who maketh a way in the sea and a path through the mighty waters—bless, preserve, guard, assist the constituted officers of the government, the President and Vice President of the United States. May the Supreme King of Kings, through His infinite mercy, preserve them, grant them life and deliver them from all manner of troubles and danger. May the Supreme King of Kings, through His infinite mercy, incline their hearts and the hearts of their counsellors and officers with benevolence towards us and all Israel. In other days and in ours may Judah be saved and Israel dwell in safety, and may the Redeemer come unto Zion, and may this be the will of God, and let us say Amen.

In the synagogue at No. 164 Greene street the Rev. S. T. Kramer officiated. The services consisted of singing the sixty-seventh, seventy-fifth, one hundredth and one hundred and fifth Psalms, after which the prayer for the government, as above, was read.

The Alexandria Gazette

MONDAY EVENING, SEPT'R. 14.

THE HEBREW HOLIDAYS.—Yesterday at sundown, the Jews inaugurated the series of Fall holidays by the celebration of the feast of Rosh-Hashana, or the New Year. The year thus entered upon, according to the Jewish Era, is 5,624 since the creation of the world. The holiday is considered by every Jew as one of the most holy in the year, second only to the day of Attonement. On Wednesday the 23d inst. the solemn fast of Your Kipur, or day of atonement, will be celebrated On this day every Israelite of the age of thirteen years and upwards keeps a rigid fast "from even to even." Every strict Jew is expected to be reconciled to such of his coreligionists as he may be at variance with, and the reconciliations thus effected are usually sincere and permanent. This fast is enjoined in the twenty-third chapter of Leviticus.

ALEXANDRIA, VIRGINIA – 1863
"THE HEBREW HOLIDAYS"
The Alexandria Gazette, p. 2 (col 1)
September 11, 1863

This Confederate newspaper informs its readers that the "Hebrew Holidays" have begun and gives a brief explanation of what they are, citing the biblical basis. The information they gave is accurate except for the names they gave Yom Kippur. In the first instance, it is referred to as the "day of Attonement," but since atonement is spelled correctly later on, this was most likely simply a typographic error. The second reference speaks of the "solemn fast of Your Kipur." It is possible that the typesetter, not familiar with the holiday, read the reporter's "Yom" as "Your."

NEW YORK – 1863
"THE 'CHANUKA' BALL"
The New-York Times, p. 2 (col 1–2)
December 12, 1863

Despite the stress of the Civil War, New York City's Jewish community sponsored a Chanukah masquerade ball which drew the admiration of *The Times* in an article covering more than one column.

After noting that, unlike Paris, New York City does not yet "observe the delightful institution" of the masquerade, the article praises "a portion of our community that does not always receive due credit for the good that it accomplishes…".

Stating that it is not speaking here of the Jewish community's judicious charity and commercial excellence, but to the fact that "Probably no class in our community are more choice and generous in their social enjoyments." It mentioned the grand Purim masquerade they held the previous two years which "emboldened" them to hold one on the holiday of Chanukah. The *Times* proceeded to explain the history of this holiday.

The event was by invitation only, in truth "a gathering of prominent Hebrew families." Irving Hall, where the ball was held, was decorated with red, white and blue patriotic bunting. Dancing commenced at 9:30 in the evening and lasted until four o'clock the following morning. Masqueraders – listed individually as, for example, "Miss K--- M---ers," were dressed in such costumes as Sultans and beggars, Greek girls and Irishmen, Italian bandits and Mexican cavaliers, the Goddess of liberty and Highland lassies. Notwithstanding the international backdrop of this merriment, "the viands were prepared in strictly Jewish style."

THE "CHANUKA" BALL.

Grand Masquerade at Irving Hall by the Hebrew Residents of New-York.

A successful masquerade is an incident in the records of a metropolis, upon which chroniclers may well dilate with pride and satisfaction. The difficulties naturally attending an entertainment of this character have probably deterred the usually enterprising Gothamites from naturalizing the *bal masque* here, as has been the case with pleasure-loving Paris. They say New-York resembles Paris, yet where, among the many particulars in which a metropolis should excel provincial cities, and in which we claim especial credit for *our* rising town, do we observe this delightful institution?

There is a portion of our community that does not always receive due credit for the good that it accomplishes. The Jewish population, though confessedly less numerous than the members of other denominations, is by no means inconsiderable in New-York. It is not to their monuments of judicious charity, any more than to their excellent position in the commercial world, that we propose referring. It is of another phase in their local history that we shall now speak, and a pleasant phase too. Probably no class in our community are more choice and generous in their social enjoyments. A most delightful illustration of this position was afforded by the " Chanuka" Fancy Dress Ball and Masquerade, given at Irving Hall, on Tuesday evening, under the auspices of the Orpheus Club, to which yesterday we had space only to make brief reference.

The Jewish festivals are not all of the same character as regards solemnity. The peculiar ceremonials attendant on most of these festivals, partake mainly of a religious nature. There are several exceptions, however. " Purim," or the Feast of Esther, celebrated in the month of March, is one of these. It is a season annually given over to jollity and humor, mirth and gladness. For the past two years it has been well commemorated in this City by grand masquerades, the last given at the Academy of Music during March, 1863, being the most brilliant social gathering witnessed here for many years.

Emboldened by the absolute success of these entertainments, they determined that the festival of Chanuka should receive the like attention. This festival is celebrated in memorial of the deliverance of Israel from Antiochus Epiphanes, King of Syria, about two thousand years ago, when, in consequence of the valorous deeds of the Asmonean family, Judas, son of Mattathias the Maccabee, and his valiant brothers, the barbarian hosts that had exercised an oppressive dominion over the Jewish people, were driven from their soil and the Hebrew commonwealth restored. As a memorial of the miraculous preservation of the holy oil in the sanctuary, where-

continued...

"THE 'CHANUKA' BALL," *continued...*

by there sufficed for lighting the holy lamps eight days, it is customary for each Jewish household to burn a so-called "Chanuka" lamp, consisting of eight branches, one for each day of the festival. In the synagogues there is also a candlestick, like that used in the ancient temple, wherein tapers are lighted—one the first night, two the second, and so on.

So much for the occasion.

The "Chanuka Ball" was given under the auspices of the "Orpheus Club," an Association of Jewish young men who evidently understand how to invest an affair of this character with the elements of success. It is surprising how they manage to exclude all that savors of impropriety. The company was unexceptionable, thus triumphantly answering one serious objection urged against masquerades. A genial air of sociability was diffused, contributing most essentially to the enjoyment of the guests. It was, in truth, a gathering of prominent Hebrew families, and the concomitants were as might have been foreseen, the same precautions exercised as in a similar affair at a private residence.

Admission was only by card of "Invitation," bearing the name of the guest and the member of the Committee by whom issued. Accompanying the tastefully engraved card was an invitation in manner following:

NEW-YORK, Nov. 17, 1863.

DEAR SIR: The Orpheus Club request the pleasure of your company at their first Invitation Fancy Dress Masquerade Ball, to be held on Chanuka night, Tuesday, Dec. 8, at Irving Hall. Inclosed is a ticket of admission for yourself and ladies.   Yours respectfully,

LIONEL DAVIES, President.
ARNOLD TANZER, Vice-President.
JACOB S. ISAACS, Treasurer.
BERNARD LEMANN,
MANUEL A. KURSHEEDT,   } Directors.
LOUIS M. PHILLIPS,
SOLOMON MOSES,

GEORGE LEVY, Secretary.

Upon the fly leaf of the invitation were printed the

REGULATIONS.

1. Admittance to the ball will be restricted to those having *cards of invitation*, bearing their name and that of the member of the Club by whom introduced.

2. Cards of invitation are *not transferable* under any circumstances.

3. All persons must unmask to a member of the Committee on entering.

4. Persons representing drunken, offensive, or other improper characters, will not be admitted.

5. Until 12 o'clock, no person will be *allowed* on the floor unless in costume.

During the evening, choice refreshments were furnished, under the direction of Mr. HARRISON, the gentlemanly proprietor of Irving Hall, the viands being prepared in strictly Jewish style.

In fine, taking the Ball in its entirety and in detail, it was a splendid success throughout, and we congratulate our Hebrew fellow-citizens on the high tone their social gatherings assume—on this "Masquerade" in especial. It might be as well to add

that another Fancy Dress Ball, on a still grander scale, will be given at the Academy of Music in the latter part of March, in commemoration of the well-known festival of "Purim."

THE COSTUMES.

This account would not be complete were we to omit all special reference to the costumes. The following were among the most noticeable:

Miss K—— M——rs, as a Spanish dancer, plying her castanets in approved style, and very becomingly attired; as was also her sister, Miss S—— M——rs, in the character of the Dumb Girl of Portici. Miss L——a J——n was another bewitching Spanish girl, her costume being especially becoming. Mrs. J——a was handsomely attired as a Marchioness. Miss F——s H——s made a pretty Russian peasant, with pink waist and black gown. Miss H—— K——n was a charming Chinese lady of very high rank; while her sister, Miss A—— K——n, as an applewoman, made a collection among the guests for a charitable object, and did excellently. Mrs. L. W. M——s was a capital Irishwoman, with her sweet little infant, a regular doll. Mrs. J—— A——t, a Turkish Princess, in robe of white satin, richly embroidered. Miss R—— L——i made a splendid Italian bandit's wife, in a handsome dress of black, with scarlet trimmings. Miss G——e R——l was neatly and becomingly dressed as Lady Gay Spanker, her sister, Miss M——n, being a charming peasant girl of French extraction. Miss M—— W——f was clad in the characteristic garb of Helen McGregor. Mrs. A—— C——n, and Mrs. A—— S—s, were neatly made up as peasant girls. Miss E——r C——n wore one of the most becoming costumes in the room—that of a Spanish lady, with fan and jaunty little cap—all forming a bewitching picture. Miss C——n was a capital fortune teller; being generally acquainted, her revelations as to the future naturally created considerable merriment. Miss F—— L——y and her sister, Mrs. A. H——g, wore elegant dominoes—the first of yellow satin, with black trimmings; the latter of pink satin. Mrs. H. L. S——r was a lively Tamborine Girl. Mr. M——e M——r wore the most elegant costume among the gentlemen, that of his Satanic Majesty, the king of the devils. Mr. J—— C. L——i was a positive Proteus. He made a comical Irishwoman, with superabundance of cap; then was transformed into a Yankee, and finally a gallant Zouave. Mr. L—— J. P——s was a first-rate Irishman, with a rich brogue and not ashamed to acknowledge it. Mr. H—— K——n was a regular curbstone broker, with his book and pencil ready for a spec. He reported the gold market as rather dull. Mr. L—— F——r wore a rich blue tunic and leggings of a dashing Mexican cavalier. Mr. L. W. M——s was a jolly little fellow in jacket and pants, pursuing his infantile gambols with apparent zest. Mr. I—— C——n looked well as Don Cæsar de Bazan, Mr. L—— L——n as his double.

The New-York Times.

VOL. XIII—NO. 3899.   NEW-YORK, WEDNESDAY, MARCH 23, 1864.   PRICE THREE CENTS.

NEW YORK – 1864 "PURIM"

The New-York Times, p. 1 (col 6) March 23, 1864

The Times devoted almost a full column on the front page describing the frolicking and excitement of the Purim Grand Fancy Dress Ball put on by New York's City's three-year-old Purim Association.

After not-quite accurately summarizing the Biblical story of Purim in two lengthy paragraphs, *The Times* reported how "Our Jewish Citizens in Their Glory" celebrated the costumed event held at the Academy of Music. Long lines of flowers festooned the hall; guests were dressed as Joan of Arc, Lucretia Borgia, the Duke of Ellington, and "several Jewish maidens."

"Wives, well disguised, teased their liege lords almost to distraction; sweethearts by sly winks and actions, drove their devoted lovers almost frantic; husbands thinking they were not known or noticed, paid sweet compliments to fair maidens only to be rapped over the knuckles for not reserving them for their wives, and staid old bachelors and maidens entered into the spirit of the fun in a manner which fairly astonished themselves."

While the watchword of the Ball was fun, it was staged in the name of charity, and monies raised were presented to the Orphan Asylum and other charitable institutions. It was only because of their dedication to their tradition and to helping the needy that the Jewish community was able to celebrate the joys of Purim despite the wartime atmosphere.

PURIM.

GRAND FANCY DRESS BALL.

BRILLIANCY AT THE ACADEMY OF MUSIC.

Our Jewish Citizens in Their Glory.

Last evening the Purim Association gave their third Grand Fancy Dress Ball, at the Academy of Music. The Association was formed in 1862 by nine young men of the Jewish faith, its first ball was given at Irving Hall in 1862, its second at the Academy of Music in 1863, and its third at the same hall last evening.

The festival of Purim is one of the oldest and most important festivals recognized by the Jews, commemorating, as it does, one of the most important events in their history as a nation. It was instituted by Queen Esther and by Mordecai about the year 510 B. C., and commemorates the remarkable deliverance of the children of Israel from the tyranny and machinations of Haman, who was Prime Minister to King Ahasuerus, who reigned from India unto Ethiopia, over a hundred and twenty-seven provinces. Mordecai had been carried captive from Jerusalem, and with him the fair and beautiful maiden Hadassah or Esther, whom Mordecai, when her father and mother were dead, took for his own daughter. Esther being exceedingly beautiful and pleasing found favor in the eyes of King Ahasuerus, who married her and made her his Queen. About this time Haman was appointed to the high position of Prime Minister to the King, and he demanded and received homage from all except the Jew Mordecai, who not only refused to pay homage, but also refused to give any reason why he would not. Haman, highly incensed at the conduct of Mordecai, ordered made a gallows of extraordinary height, on which to hang him for the insult he had offered to one in high office and favored by the King. Queen Esther, hearing of this, informed the King of the relation which existed between her and Mordecai, and also of the great benefit Mordecai had done the King some time previous in informing of two men in his confidence, Bigthana and Teresh, who sought to lay violent hands upon the King and kill him. The King remembering all these things and the iniquity of Haman, ordered him hanged upon the gallows erected for Mordecai, placed Mordecai in the position held by Haman, made him chief over the house of Haman, and released the children of Israel from bondage. This was celebrated by great rejoicing all over th[e] [l]and and, in every way the joy and happiness of the people was exhibited. From that to the present the festival of this deliverance of the Jews has been celebrated by the most extravagant expressions of happiness, calling upon each other at their houses, in every dress and guise which could possibly add merriment or joy to the occasion, and using every means they could devise for the utmost enjoyment and celebration of this great and happy event. Of late years their number has so increased that time would not allow them to visit all the friends they wished, nor would their houses hold all the friends they wished to entertain.

To obviate this difficulty, nine young gentlemen of the Jewish faith, in the year 1862, organized the "Purim Association," the object of which was to collect all the parties together for the general enjoyment of the festival, and that all friends might meet. Thus far they have been particularly fortunate, nothing has occurred to mar their pleasure, and they have also by this means been enabled to do a great deal of good. Last year they presented to the Orphan Asylum and other charitable institutions a handsome sum and this year they intend, first, to present to the officers of the association, who have been and are working hard and steadily for the promotion of this society and its good influence, and to whom, in a great measure, the success of the ball is due, are as follows: M. H. MOSES, President; Jos. A. LEVY, Vice-President; A. H. Schutz, Treasurer; A. L. Sanger, Secretary; B. Lemann H. H. Stettheimer, S. Weill, L. G. Schiffer, T. Hellman, Directors.

The Academy was beautifully dressed; long lines of flowers were festooned along each tier, between the lights, and about the boxes vases and baskets of flowers in great abundance; over the third tier a beautiful drapery of orange and blue, ornamented with stars; at the back of the stage a large gas-light on which, in a scroll, were the words "Merry Purim ;" below it the monogram of the Society, and below the entire fixture, on the floor, a beautiful fountain, sending forth showers of cologne water, the exquisite perfume of which pervaded the entire hall, almost intoxicating the senses, and adding greatly to the luxury of the occasion.

The parquet was floored even with the stage, affording, with that, the most ample room for enjoyment of the dance.

The hall was crowded with a most brilliant assemblage, who entered into the enjoyments of the occasion with a zest seldom equaled ; the costumes were very rich and beautiful ; the diamonds worn by the ladies magnificent, and in brilliancy almost rivaled the bright eyes of their fair owners. Among the best of the characters represented were those of Mrs. Partington, Lucretia Borgia, Penobscot Squaw, Chippewa Chief, Joan of Arc, several beauties of the Court of Charles II., the Duke of Buckingham, Faust, a Priest, and several Jewish maidens. Merriment reigned supreme within the hall. Wives, well disguised, teased their liege lords almost to distraction ; sweethearts by sly winks and actions, drove their devoted lovers almost frantic ; husbands thinking they were not known or noticed, paid sweet compliments to fair maidens only to be rapped over the knuckles for not reserving them for their wives, and staid old bachelors and maidens entered into the spirit of the fun in a manner which fairly astonished themselves. HELMSMULLER'S and GRAFULLA'S Bands gave constant music, to which the feet of the merry dancers kept time. At twelve o'clock they unmasked and then what surprise was created. Husbands found they had been flirting all the evening with their own wives ; lovers had been confidentially extolling the beauties of their sweethearts to their sweethearts themselves ; old maids had been telling old bachelors how disagreeable they thought that class of men to be, and old bachelors had been sympathizing, perhaps, with the old maids themselves, upon the unhappy condition of these unfortunate ladies. The mistakes, however, were speedily and amicably settled, and after the excellent supper prepared by the caterer, M. S. COHEN, had been fully enjoyed, were entirely forgotten.

Mayor GUNTHER, Maj. JOLINE and numerous other distinguished gentlemen were present, and by their presence added greatly to the brilliancy and dignity of the festival.

FAST DAY.

HUMILIATION AND PRAYER.

NEW YORK – 1865 "FAST DAY... BNAI ISRAEL"

The New York Herald,
p. 1 (col 1–3)
June 2, 1865

Though Lee surrendered to Grant at Appomattox on April 9, 1865, skirmishes continued through the next month. President Andrew Johnson designated June 1st as a "fast day" of humiliation and prayer as a step towards national reconciliation.

The front page of the next day's *New York Herald* was taken up with

The silence usually noticed in the city upon a sunny Sabbath day was observable during all of yesterday. The hum of busy industry was almost entirely suspended, and the street cars and omnibuses were running as on other days; but there was in the various branches of trade, commerce and shipping, and in the public offices, the courts, the mart of the money changers and the chambers of the merchants, the silence that accompanies the absence of the industrious throng known to these localities during the six days of the week generally given up to the accumulation of money. The day was, in accordance with the proclamation of President Johnson, followed by that of the Governor of the State and the Mayor of the city of New York, given over almost literally to humiliation, fasting and prayer. Little else of importance was done within the city limits.

There was not the same sadness to be seen upon the face of the multitude that rested there so conspicuously when the news of the death of President Lincoln was fresh upon the printed page, and the breath but lately passed from that great and good man's body. But there was none the less mourning. The funeral records that clung about the marble pillars of the mansions and the public places, when the sacred remains were here to be viewed by the weeping multitude, had all been removed, but the grief that hung upon the public heart had not been taken away with them. That remained and gave character to all the ceremonies and religious observances of the day. It filled the churches with a people who came to weep anew. It gave tone to the words upon the pages of the minister's manuscript, and found a ready response in the tear-dimmed eyes of those who listened. Whether in Jewish synagogue, or meeting house of other denomination, the same scene, the same feelings were uppermost.

The addresses at the different houses of worship are given below.

Bnai Israel.
ADDRESS OF REV. M. R. DESAUN.

There was a fine attendance at the Jewish synagogue, Bnai Israel, corner of Stanton and Forsyth streets, and the ceremonies performed were more than usually solemn. Rev. M. R. Desaun was the officiating minister, and spoke from the following text:—

"Through we do kings reign and chieftains give decrees in righteousness."—Proverb, viii., 15.

By these words it is clear that obedience to those in authority is a holy duty; this injunction is essential to the existence of government. Had the reverence due it

been paid no such thing as rebellion would have found the means to exist, and we would have been spared on this day the solemn task of blending a day of joy with one of humiliation. But emanating as it does from the Chief Magistrate of the nation, we Israelites, as an obedient people, are prepared to observe it. Wanting the proclamation of the President, we have the observance of this particular day enjoined on us by the King of Kings in commemoration of the giving of the law upon Sinai as a day of rejoicing. It is also customary on this day to offer prayers for the repose of the souls of departed relatives, friends and prominent men of Israel. Had the President done so wittingly he could not well have chosen a day more fitting the object of his proclamation. In the words of the prophet:— "Weep not for the dead, and do not bemoan him."— Jer. xxii., 10.

The external signs of mourning have disappeared, the earth has closed upon the remains of Abraham Lincoln, and the loud wailing and cry of anguish consequent on the first intimation of the horrid deed have subsided, as it is natural in man that they should. But even if these have disappeared to our hearts the details are yet fresh, as they will ever be, and upon its tablets are deeply and ineffaceably graven a pure and solemn memory; his kind nature cannot so easily be rejected from our disturbed minds, and assuredly by those who loved the man for his principle. It must be clear to all that it was the Divine will to remove Abraham Lincoln from our midst. To his relentless foes his magnanimity was incomprehensible; and, despising it by their crowning wickedness, they have drawn upon themselves the just deserts of their iniquity. A punishment such as no human mind would have devised was meted to the assassin. For three long hours, in the full possession of his clear mind, and yet physically unable to execute its vindictive dictates, beyond all human aid he lay slowly dying, his pangs increased by the sting of his black conscience until he was dead. If we reflect on this the majesty of avenging justice is belittled by the command so literally carried out— "Vengeance and recompense is mine saith the Lord." And we know, Oh Lord, thy judgment is righteous. We have humbled ourselves beneath the stroke of the hand of God, and we prayed to Him, in the midst of our distress, to direct the angel of destruction to stay his hand, and the Lord has heard our supplications. "Broken has the Lord the staff of the wicked."—Isaiah xiv., 5. "I will thank thee, Oh Lord, that thou was angry with me. Thy anger now is turned away and thou comfortest me."—Isaiah, xii., 1.

Therefore, war no longer rages in the land. Under the inspiration of our dead President the strife has ceased, and the glory of victory sits proudly on our banners, while balmy peace fills the land. His own life sealed the flow of blood, as it likewise marked the epoch that the task that he assumed at the commencement of his first term had been grandly and successfully accomplished. The successor of our late President has thus far, under Heavenly guidance, fully succeeded. We beseech thee, Oh Lord, not to withhold thy inspiration from him, to enable him to be a successful ruler. And now, my friends, we will pray for the repose of the soul of the illustrious dead.

news of the Fast Day and the mood of the defeated and ruined South. In an article, *Results, the South after War*, the correspondent in a tone of understatement notes, "War is a pastime that it is safe to presume the South will not be very soon inclined to renew."

"Fast Day," a three-column front page article, focused mainly on observances in churches. Significantly, the second paragraph mentions the Jewish association with the special day – "Whether in Jewish synagogues, or meeting houses of other denominations, the same scene, the same feelings were uppermost" – and Bnai Israel synagogue, located at Stanton and Forsythe Streets, is the first house of worship noted in the newspaper's roundup of church and other institutional observances.

In his sermon, the Rev. M. R. Desaun, clearly having in mind the assassinated Abraham Lincoln, pointed out that the national Fast Day coincided with the observance of the Jewish holiday of *Shavuot* (Pentecost), and the memorial prayers customarily accompanying the holiday's observance.*

* According to historians Jonathan Sarna and Benjamin Shapell, in their book <u>Lincoln and the Jews</u>, many Jews were angry that Johnson called the fast day to coincide with Shavuot.

Chapter #2

Communal Affairs: Congregations & Organizations

Numb. XXXV

THE New-York Weekly JOURNAL

Containing the freshest Advices, Foreign, and Domestick.

MUNDAY May 20th, 1734.

...de went a ... Signs of the Men ... ir Departure for *New-York*. ... *Boston*, that a large Ship was run a ... d on Cape Cod, but there is no certainty as yet who she is ; some say she belongs to *Leverpool*.

ADVERTISEMENTS.

* *Peter Delage*, of the City of *New-York* Merchant, intending to depart this Province in short Time, gives this timely Notice to all Persons that have any Demands on him to bring in their Accounts in order to be satisfied ; and those that are indebted to him are desired to ballance their Accounts and, prevent further Trouble.

‖ To be sold, at public *Vendue* on *Fryday* the 17th of this Instant May, a Lot of Land at the Head of Cow-Bay, on *Long-Island*, containing about 40 Acres ; there is on it now a very good House and Barn, a very good Stream fit for a Fulling-Mill, and very good Water. The whole lies very convenient for Land or Water Transportation.   Enquire of *John Eyvanck* or *David Provoost*, both of the City of *New-York*.

‡ All Persons that are indebted to the Estate of *Lena Cooper* are desired to ballance their Accounts with *John Lemontes,* and *Mary Campbell, the* Executors of the said Estate, and thereby prevent farther Trouble.

ALL Persons that have any Demands on the Estate of *Peter Brolicade, late of the City of New-York, Black-smith, deceased,* are desired to bring in their Accounts to *Charles Sleigh, of the same City, Baker,* in order to be satisfied. And those that are indebted to the said Estate are desired to ballance their Accounts, and prevent farther Trouble.

TO BE SOLD.

A dwelling House in *Duke Street fronting the Alle that leads to Coentjes Market, now in the Tenure of Lawrence Wessel,* it has a large Oven and other Coveniencies for Baking and Bolting : There is also belonging to the said House a good Store House fronting the back Street near the Synagogue. Inquire of *Hermanus Rutgers* or *John Garreau* in *New-York, or the Widow of* James Poillon *on Staten Island.*
N. B. *The Store House is to be let till the whole is sold.*

† To be sold, 18 Lotts of Ground fronting the King's high Road or the Street that leads from Smith's Fly to the Fresh Water : They begin from the House of *John Elsworth, and front the Road :* They are bounded by the Lots of *Patrick Macknight, and the rear Lots are bounded by the Swamp or Tan-Yards, by a Street called Skinners Street. Enquire of Cornelius Clopper, who will give a good Title.*

§ To be sold, a House and Lott of Ground in Elizabeth-Town *containing about 3 Acres, belonging to the Estate of the late Mr. James Banks, deceased. Enquire of the Executors* Hans Hansen *and* Rutger Bleecker *at Albany,* David Abeel *at New-York, or* Dirk Schuyler *at New-Brunswyk.*

...E SOLD, ... of two Hundred and three Hundred Lot, of very good arable Land, ... ounty, in the Eastern Divisi... of New-Jersey, about 2 Miles ... the Road call'd the George's ... gh the whole Tract ; it lies upon ...es Brook, which is a good stream convenient for either Grist or Saw Mills, it is stored with abundance of very good Timber, and rich low Meadow. Grounds. Whoever inclines to Purchase any Part of the said Lands, may enquire of Mr. *James Nealson,* in *New Brunswick,* where he will find further Direction for taking a View of this Land, and also hear of the Proprietor thereof.

JAmes Wallace, *who sells the Beatman Drops, removes from where he now lives, to a House belonging to Mr.* James Levingston, *in the Broadway, a little below* Alderman Van Gelder *his House on the other Side of the Street, where every one that wants those Drops may be supplied, and also at the Shop of Mr.* Proctor *Watch-maker, living in the Square, next Door to Mr.* John Waters Merchant. *and also at the Shop of Mr.* Thomas Hall Shoemaker *at the Corner House near the Old Slip Market, they having a Power from the said Wallace to dispose of those Drops.*

† *To be sold,* 22 *Lots of Ground fronting the King's high Road, or the Street that leads from Smith's Fly to the Fresh Water : They are bounded by the Lotts of* Alderman Rosevelt *and* Cornelius Clopper ju.r. *the rear Lotts are bounded by the Swamp or Tan Yards, by a Street called* Skinner Street. *Enquire of* Anna Macknight, *or* Alderman Rosevelt, *concerning the Title and Conditions of Sale.*

† *Very good Cheshire Cheese to be sold, by* Mary Campbell *in the Broad-Street, opposite to the Jew's Synagogue Alley, at* 9 d. 8 d. & 7 d. per Pound.

† *Very good Mackrel to be sold, by* Fredrick Becker, *living in Beekmans Street, opposite to Capt.* Ware, *in* New-York.

THere is to be sold a Tract of Land near the South Branch of Raraton River, *in the Province of* East New-Jersey, *and in the County of* Somerset, *containing about* 550 *Acres, now in Possession of* Aart Aarsen, *whereof there is about* 80 *Acres clear Land, with about* 8 *or* 10 *Acres of low Land which bears good* English *Grass ; there is upon it a good Grist Mill, a large new Barn, and a good dwelling House ; it lies about* 18 *Miles above* New-Brunswick.

As also another Tract of Land adjoyning to it, containing about 2500 *Acres, upon which are* 5 German *Families settled and have cleared good Part of it.*

There is also a fine Farm near Mill-stone River *now in Possession of* Hendrick Weaver, *about* 13 *Miles from* New-Brunswick *containing about* 550 *Acres, whereof a good Quantity is cleared, there is upon it a fine large dwelling House and Barn, with a large Orchard bearing several Sorts of Fruit : All the above Lands belong to the Estate of* Isaac Governeur, *deceased. Whoever has a mind to purchase any Part of the above-mentioned Lands, may apply to* Lewis Morris junr. *or* Nicolas Governeur *in* New-York, *or* Cornelius Low *on* Raraton Landing.

The Printer hereof is removed to Broad-Street near the upper End of the Long Bridge.

NEW-YORK : Printed and Sold by *John Peter Zenger* : By whom Subscriptions for this Paper are taken at three Shillings *per* Quarter ; and Advertisements at three Shillings the first Week, and one Shilling every Week after.

TO BE SOLD.

A dwelling Houſe in Duke Street fronting the Alle that leads to Coentjes Market, now in the Tenure yf Lawrence Weſſel, it has a large Oven and other Conveniencies for Bakeing and Bolting : There is alſo belonging to the ſaid Houſe a good Store Houſe fronting the back Street near the Synagogue. Inquire of Hermanus Rutgers or John Garreau in New-York, or the Widow of James Poillon on Statten Iſland.

N. B. The Store Houſe is to be let till the whole is ſold.

NEW YORK CITY – 1734
"TO BE SOLD. A DWELLING HOUSE IN DUKE STREET…"
The New-York Weekly Journal, p. 4 (col 2)
May 20, 1734

This advertisement describes a "dwelling House in Duke Street fronting the Alle[y] that leads to Coentjes Market … [with a] good Store House fronting the back street near the Synagogue."

This historic ad contains what is likely the first newspaper reference to a synagogue in North America, referring to the synagogue structure of Congregation Shearith Israel, the first synagogue erected on the continent.

In September, 1654, twenty-three Jewish refugees from the West Indies arrived at the harbor of New Amsterdam, a colony established by the Dutch West India Company.
Following a contest with Peter Stuyvesant, the colony's leader, and with the help of fellow Jews in Amsterdam, these Jewish settlers in 1656 were given the right "to exercise in all quietness their religion *within their houses*." Thus, public worship was denied to this new Congregation Shearith Israel, similar to the treatment accorded all groups other than the established Dutch Reformed Church.

In 1664, Dutch New Amsterdam became British New York. The Jewish population consisted of some fifty souls. Towards the end of the decade, this congregation seemed to have rented a home on Mill Street (known as South William Street today) in order to hold services. In 1728, congregations in New York City were started by Baptist and Lutheran churches. According to Abraham J. Karp in *Haven and Home: A History of the Jews in America* (New York, 1985), "In December of that year, for seven hundred pounds, a loaf of sugar and a pound of Bohea tea," the Jews purchased an adjoining lot to build a house of worship.

On the seventh day of Passover, April 9, 1730, the Mill Street synagogue, the first in North America, was dedicated. New York's Jewish population totaled less than one hundred. The congregation had received contributions from fellow Jews in London, Curacao, Jamaica, Barbados, Dutch Guiana and Boston. Structurally, this brick building was 35 feet square and 22 feet high. In order not to call attention to its purpose, the synagogue contained no obvious Jewish symbols on the outside, such as the traditional Star of David. Six months later, the congregation's *cabana (sukkah),* was built in the yard behind the synagogue. Early on, a *Mikveh* (ritual bath), drew power from the spring that powered the mill for which the street was named.

559

[NUMB. 435]

THE NEWPORT MERCURY.

From MONDAY, *December* 29, 1766,——to MONDAY, *January* 5, 1767.

The Rigour of the Season, which has prevented the Eastern and Western Posts from performing their Stages, will, it is hoped, be sufficient to excuse the Smallness of our Paper this Day.

CONSTANTINOPLE, August 16.

ON the 5th instant, at half an hour past 12 o'clock, we had a most violent shock of an earthquake, which lasted near a minute, and has done great damage at Constantinople, having thrown down or damaged greatly almost all the stone edifices that were shook by the first, and was of greater extent than that of the 22d of May, as it has ruined almost all the villages on the road to Adrianople, and thrown down four mosques and many houses there, Rodosto on the white sea, Gallipoli, many villages on the canal of the Dardanells and the island of Tonedos, have suffered greatly. We had two slight shocks the same evening; and on Thursday night a fire broke out at Fondukli, which has destroyed eight or nine houses.

BERLIN, Sept. 23. Sir Andrew Mitchell, minister plenipotentiary from Great-Britain, has had some private audiences of his majesty within these few days, since which he has dispatched a courier to his court. It is not doubted, that some important negociation is upon the carpet between the two courts.

HANOVER, Sept. 23. A regulation has been made, by virtue of which, the troops of this electorate will consist for the future of 25,000 men.

STOCKHOLM, Sept. 12. The harvest all over this kingdom has answered the wishes of the inhabitants, and according to our advices from the diocese of Wybourg, it has proved so very plentiful there, that they have not barns sufficient to hold all their corn.

PARIS, Sept. 26. It is reported that there is a plan formed for uniting the sovereign court of Lorrain with the parliament of Metz, but that the former makes great opposition to it, and has remonstrated to the King against it.

The house of M——t G———t and Co. has just failed for about 5,000,000 livres; by which some of the principal merchants of Lyons will be very considerable sufferers.

Sept. 27. Since the unfortunate expedition of Larache, an exchange of the prisoners which fell into the hands of the King of Morocco has been negociating, and we were in hopes was almost brought to a happy conclusion; but we have lately received advice that the Barbarian king will not listen to any reasonable proposition, that he expects to have all our prisonere redeemed at once, and demands a ransom of 18,000 livres for each of them.

The great bankruptcy which lately happened here, has thrown a damp for the present on publick credit; nevertheless, such steps are said to be taken as will set all their affairs to rights in about a year's time.

An agent of the late Mr. de la Bourdonnaye, is taken up for counterfeiting a draught for the sum of 180,000 livres in the name of Mr. Mory, cashier of the East India company. He had received the money for the true draught, and negotiated the counterfeit one; Mr. Mory, when the counterfeit was presented to him for payment luckily recollected his having paid such a sum, and upon referring to his books, detected the roguery; but it is said that his signature was so well imitated, that he did not perceive the forgery.

MADRID, Sept. 16. The Sieur de Bouganville is arrived at St. Ildephonso, from Paris, with the ratification of the cession of the Malonines islands, which France has made to this court; and he will soon embark at Ferrol for those islands, in order to deliver the same to the commissaries appointed to receive it.

ALTORF, in the Canton of Ury, in Switzerland, Sept. 15. A fire broke out a few days ago in a village of Andermalt, the most considerable in the valley of Urser, which burnt down 600 houses. The miserable state to which the inhabitants are reduced is deplorable, there being no timber in the valley to rebuild their houses; so that the buildings cannot be gone about till next summer, and in the mean time the distressed inhabitants are obliged to implore an asylum among their neighbours.

PARIS, Oct. 3. Maria-Victoria Sophia de Noailles, relict of Louis Alexander de Bourboun, Count de Toulouse, legitimated Prince of France, died the 30th of last month, aged 78. The court will go into mourning for her the 5th instant for three weeks.

Sept, 29. Last Thursday when the king was a hunting the wild boar at Compeigne, one of those animals seized the horse his majesty rode upon and wounded him; but happily the horse kept upon his legs, and the king received no hurt.

COPENHAGEN, Sept. 19. The King has admitted Prince Charles of Hesse-Cassel to be one of his five privy counsellors.

LONDON,

October 20. It is talked, that part of our most southerly possessions, in the continent of North-America, will be ceded to the King of Denmark for a valuable consideration.

From several parts of Norfolk we are told, that large numbers of the militia, have actually joined the rioters, and that there will be a necessity for a body of regular troops to quell the insurgents.

NEWPORT, January 5, 1767.

The Order for the Ceremony and Procession on the Dedication of the great Synagogue in Duke's-Place, London, on Friday, 29th August, 1766.

Service for the Dedication.

THE Persons appointed by the Presidents, to bring the several Books of Moses in Procession, are to repair into the Vestry Room, and return in the Order they are named in the List, each bringing a Pentateuch in the Ark of the Synagogue, preceeded by the Head Rabbi of the Congregation, with the white mantled Law, &c. supported by the Head Rabbies of the Portuguese and Mr. Isaac's Congregation, under a Canopy bore by four Persons, nominated by the Presidents.—The Overture of Samson to be immediately performed, by the Orchestra, in the Music Gallery, upon the Entrance of the Procession in the Synagogue, and the Doors of the Ark to be opened at the same Time.—The Laws being deposited in the Ark, the Rabbi, supported as before, to go to the Reader's Desk, from whence he is to pronounce the Prayer of Consecration; after which the Hymns on this Occasion to be sung by the Reader, and his Assistants; this being finished, the chief Rabbi is to read the Prayer for the King and Royal Family in English, which is to be immediately followed by Handel's Coronation Anthem, performed by the Orchestra.

The Order for the Ceremony and Procession of the Seven Circuits in the Synagogue.

1st CIRCUIT. The Coronation Anthem being finished, 7 Persons, viz. the Ruling Elders and Treasurer of the Synagogue to take each a Book of the Law out of the Ark, preceeded by the Head Rabbi as before, under a Canopy, make one Circuit in the Synagogue, and then deposit the Laws in the Ark.—Psalm the 91st to be chanted by the Reader at the Desk during this Procession, which, when finished, to be followed by a Piece of Musick by the Orchestra, viz. March in Oratorio of Judah Maccabeus, by Handel.

2d CIRCUIT. Seven other Persons, viz. the Ruling Elders and Treasurer of the Portuguese Congregation, preceeded by their Head Rabbi under a Canopy, make another Circuit as the foregoing. Psalm the 30th chanted by the Reader. Musick following, March in Derdamia, by Handel.

3d CIRCUIT. Seven other Persons, viz. the Ruling Elders and Treasurer of Mr, Isaac's Congregation, preceeded by their Head Rabbi as the foregoing. Psalm the 24th chanted by the Reader. Musick following, viz. Chorus in the Oratoria of Deborah, by Handel.

4th, 5th, 6th, 7th CIRCUITS, By seven different Persons, nominated by the Presidents for each Circuit, but without the Canopy, perform the same as before. 4th Circuit, Psalm the 84th to be chanted by the Reader, Musick following, viz. CHORUS, *Let the celestial Concerts all unite.* In Oratoria Samson.

5th CIRCUIT. Psalm the 122d chanted, Musick following, viz. Overture by Dr. Arne.

6th CIRCUIT. Psalm the 132d chanted, Musick following, viz. CHORUS, *My Heart is inditing.* Handel in Oratoria of Hesther.

7th and last CIRCUIT. Psalm the 100th chanted, Musick following, viz. A solemn Piece of Musick for Clarinets, Hautboys, and French Horns.

The Order for the Service for the Repose of the Benefactors to the Synagogue, deceased.

The Seven Circuits being finished, and the Laws deposited in the Ark, solemn Musick is to be performed preparatory to this Service, and followed by the dead March in Oratoria of Saul, during which the Presidents are to go with the Reader to the Ark, and take out the three white mantled Laws, whilst the three Head Rabbies of each Synagogue are to go up to the Reader's Desk, and there receive the said three Laws, when the Head Rabbi of the Congregation (supported by the other two) is to read the Prayer for the Repose of the Souls of the Benefactors to the Synagogue, assisted by the Reader; which being finished the three Rabbies, attended by the Presidents, are to deposit the Laws in the Ark; during which, a solemn Piece of Musick to be performed, viz. Musette for Clarinets and Horns; the Canopy not to be used in the Service; after which, a Hymn to be sung by the Reader, and afterwards the Prayer for the Congregation, and to conclude with a full Piece of Musick by Stamitz.

The Musick being finished, the common Service for the Eve of the Sabbath to be read as usual.

(The Hymn, used at the Opening of the Synagogue, will be inserted in our next.)

A Gentleman in London writes, That the Synagogue was esteemed, by foreign Jews, and travelling Christians, to be the finest in Europe: That there was an Audience of about 1500 at the Dedication, which, for the Regularity and Grandeur, was the finest ever attempted; the Band of Musick consisted of 27, the greatest Masters to be had in London, which was Mr N. Franks's Department, who chose the Pieces so well adapted to the Solemnity, that he acquired great Honour in the Choice.

BILL of Mortality for the Town of Newport.

A. D.		Whites.	Blacks.	1766.	W.	B.
1760	died	175	40	January	9	2
1761		123	35	February	10	4
1762		203	34	March	17	6
1763		158	50	April	12	3
1764		164	40	May	14	4
1765		225	49	June	7	0
1766		145	33	July	14	2
				August	5	0
		1193	281	September	11	3
		281		October	12	0
				November	18	3
Total,		1474 in 7 Years.		December	16	6
					145	33

This septennary Account shews, that, in this Town of about Seven Thousand Souls, there die yearly, at a Medium, 170 Whites, and 40 Blacks.

The largest Quantity of Snow fell last Monday Night, and the Day succeeding, that has been seen here for a great Number of Years. The Severity of the Weather last Week may be accurately known by the following

OBSERVATIONS abroad, in a North Shade, with Fahrenheit's Thermometer, whose freezing Point is 32 above the Cypher.

In Charlestown, S. Carolina. By Dr. Lining.	*Highest.*	*Lowest.*		*In Newport, Rh. Island.* By Dr. Stiles. *Highest.*	*Lowest.*
$174\frac{0}{1}$	63	31	January, 1766	$45\frac{1}{2}$	$1\frac{1}{2}$ above o
	68	30	February	56	16
1740	80	34	March	53	10
	83	51	April	$63\frac{1}{2}$	33
	87	56	May	$82\frac{1}{2}$	41
	90	66	June	84	51
	91	70	July	91	61
	90	67	August	$91\frac{1}{3}$	61
	84	56	September	77	57
	73	35	October	70	33
	67	32	November	58	27
	69	21	December	$49\frac{1}{2}$	20 by Xmas.

Dec. 31, o 3, i. e. 3 below o.

Last Tuesday Noon, Dec. 30, the Mercury stood at 28 Lines; by ten o'Clock at Night it had descended to 8: and by eight o'Clock, Wednesday Morning, it had fallen to 3 below o, or 35 Degrees below the freezing Point. It ascended to o at XIh. and at $I\frac{1}{4}$h. A. it rose to 2 above o, being the highest Altitude of the Day. By Vh. it fell again to o, and at Xh. at Night it was at 3 below o: So five Degrees only were the Limits of that Day's Variation. At VIIIh. on New-Year's Day Morning, it ascended two Degrees, and was found at 1 below o, and by Ih. A. it reached 7 above o, being the highest Altitude of the Day; and by XI at Night it fell to 5: So the Limits of this Day's Variation was eight Degrees,——On Friday Morning, the 2d Instant, at VIIIh. it had fallen to 2 below o; but by IIh. A. it arose to 10 above o, where it became stationary about two Hours; then it descended, and at VIIIh. in the Evening it was at 3 above o; and here the Intenseness of the Cold began to abate, for by IXh. it arose to $6\frac{1}{2}$, by XIh. at Night to 8—and on Saturday Morning, the 3d Inst. it was found at 12, and by Noon it was at 20, to which it had not been since Tuesday preceeding. For three entire Days the Cold was so uniformly and steadily intense as to be below 10, and for three Quarters of the Time below 5 Degrees on the Scale; and to be contained within the utmost Limits of thirteen Degrees, from 10 above, to 3 below o. In another Part of the Town the Cold was rather more intense, where the greatest Descent was $3\frac{1}{2}$ below o, and 1 above o was the highest Altitude on Wednesday.—January 27, 1765, the Mercury was at 5 below o before Sunrise, but then it arose above o before Xh. in the Forenoon, and descended no more below it; but on that Day arose to $11\frac{3}{4}$ above o, and the next Day to 18 above o. Whence the Severity of that Season came far short of the Intenseness of the present. In the hard

NEWPORT, January 5, 1767.

The Order for the Ceremony and Procession on the Dedication of the great Synagogue in Duke's-Place, London, on Friday, 29th August, 1766.

Service for the Dedication.

THE Persons appointed by the Presidents, to bring the several Books of Moses in Procession, are to repair into the Vestry Room, and return in the Order they are named in the List, each bringing a Pentateuch in the Ark of the Synagogue, preceeded by the Head Rabbi of the Congregation, with the white mantled Law, &c. supported by the Head Rabbies of the Portuguese and Mr. Isaac's Congregation, under a Canopy bore by four Persons, nominated by the Presidents.— The Overture of Samson to be immediately performed, by the Orchestra, in the Music Gallery, upon the Entrance of the Procession in the Synagogue, and the Doors of the Ark to be opened at the same Time.— The Laws being deposited in the Ark, the Rabbi, supported as before, to go to the Reader's Desk, from whence he is to pronounce the Prayer of Consecration; after which the Hymns on this Occasion to be sung by the Reader, and his Assistants; this being finished, the chief Rabbi is to read the Prayer for the King and Royal Family in English, which is to be immediately followed by Handel's Coronation Anthem, performed by the Orchestra.

NEWPORT – 1766-1767
DEDICATION OF SYNAGOGUE
The Newport Mercury, p. 1 (col 2)
From December 29, 1766 to January 5, 1767

In this two page issue of the *Mercury*, the entire center column and top of third column contain a January 5, 1767 report describing in great detail the dedication of the London Great Synagogue in Duke's Place that took place August 29, 1766. Quoting "A Gentleman in London," the report indicates that "the Synagogue was esteemed, by foreign Jews, and traveling Christians," there was an audience of 1,500, and the band "consisted of 27, the greatest Masters to be had in London." The bulk of the report focused on the pomp which included seven Circuits around the synagogue, as illustrated by its description of the first Circuit:

The Coronation Anthem being finished, 7 Persons, viz. the Ruling Elders and Treasurer of the synagogue to take each a Book of the Law out of the Ark, preceded by the Head Rabbi, as before, under a Canopy make one Circuit and then deposit the laws in the Ark.—Psalm the 91st to be chanted by the Reader at the Desk during the Procession, which, when finished, to be followed by a Piece of Music by the Orchestra, viz. March in Oratorio of Judah Maccabeus, by Handel.

The Order for the Ceremony and Procession of the Seven Circuits in the Synagogue.

1st CIRCUIT. The Coronation Anthem being finished, 7 Persons, viz. the Ruling Elders and Treasurer of the Synagogue to take each a Book of the Law out of the Ark, preceeded by the Head Rabbias before, under a Canopy, make one Circuit in the Synagogue, and then deposit the Laws in the Ark.—Psalm the 91st to be chanted by the Reader at the Desk during this Procession, which, when finished, to be followed by a Piece of Musick by the Orchestra, viz. March in Oratorio of Judah Maccabeus, by Handel.

2d CIRCUIT. Seven other Persons, viz. the Ruling Elders and Treasurer of the Portuguese Congregation, preceeded by their Head Rabbi under a Canopy, make another Circuit as the foregoing. Psalm the 30th chanted by the Reader. Musick following, March in Derdamia, by Handel.

3d CIRCUIT. Seven other Persons, viz. the Ruling Elders and Treasurer of Mr. Isaac's Congregation, preceeded by their Head Rabbi as the foregoing. Psalm the 24th chanted by the Reader. Musick following, viz. Chorus in the Oratoria of Deborah, by Handel.

4th, 5th, 6th, 7th CIRCUITS. By seven different Persons, nominated by the Presidents for each Circuit, but without the Canopy, perform the same as before. 4th Circuit, Psalm the 84th to be chanted by the Reader, Musick following, viz. CHORUS, *Let the celestial Concerts all unite.* In Oratoria Samson.

5th CIRCUIT. Psalm the 122d chanted, Musick following, viz. Overture by Dr. Arne.

6th CIRCUIT. Psalm the 132d chanted, Musick following, viz. CHORUS, *My Heart is inditing.* Handel in Oratoria of Hesther.

7th and last CIRCUIT. Psalm the 100th chanted, Musick following, viz. A solemn Piece of Musick for Clarinets, Hautboys, and French Horns.

The Order for the Service for the Repose of the Benefactors to the Synagogue, deceased.

The Seven Circuits being finished, and the Laws deposited in the Ark, solemn Musick is to be performed preparatory to this Service, and followed by the dead March in Oratoria of Saul, during which the Presidents are to go with the Reader to the Ark, and take out the three white mantled Laws, whilst the three Head Rabbies of each Synagogue are to go up to the Reader's Desk, and there receive the said three Laws, when the Head Rabbi of the Congregation (supported by the other two) is to read the Prayer for the Repose of the Souls of the Benefactors to the Synagogue, assisted by the Reader; which being finished the three Rabbies, attended by the Presidents, are to deposit the Laws in the Ark; during which, a solemn Piece of Musick to be performed, viz. Musette for Clarinets and Horns; the Canopy not to be used in the Service; after which, a Hymn to be sung by the Reader, and afterwards the Prayer for the Congregation, and to conclude with a full Piece of Musick by Stamitz.

The Musick being finished, the common Service for the Eve of the Sabbath to be read as usual.

(The Hymn, used at the Opening of the Synagogue, will be inserted in our next.)

A Gentleman in London writes, That the Synagogue was esteemed, by foreign Jews, and travelling Christians, to be the finest in Europe: That there was an Audience of about 1500 at the Dedication, which, for the Regularity and Grandeur, was the finest ever attempted; the Band of Musick consisted of 27, the greatest Masters to be had in London, which was Mr N. Franks's Department, who chose the Pieces so well adapted to the Solemnity, that he acquired great Honour in the Choice.

[*From the Savannah Republican, July 25.*]

CONSECRATION.

On Friday last, the new Hebrew synagogue, lately erected in this city, was consecrated in a solemn and impressive manner. At 4 o'clock in the afternoon, the congregation approached their temple, in procession, carrying the five books of Moses under a canopy. On the procession arriving at the door, it was thrown open, when they entered chaunting appropriate prayers and hymns, accompanied with an organ, that contributed to give great effect and solemnity to the occasion. The whole of the ceremony was performed agreeably to the ritual and canons of Judaism; and a suitable and eloquent discourse was pronounced by Dr. Jacob De La Motta.

WORCESTER, MA / SAVANNAH, GA – 1820
"CONSECRATION"
Massachusetts Spy or Worcester Gazette, p. 2 (col 2)
August 16, 1820

News about the July 21, 1820 consecration of a "new Hebrew synagogue" in Savannah, taken from a Savannah paper, was reported in this Massachusetts paper a month later. According to the report, the ceremony began with a procession to the newly erected synagogue with congregants carrying scrolls containing "the five books of Moses" under a canopy. Once inside the synagogue, organ music accompanying the "chaunting" of prayers and hymns enhanced the consecration's solemnity. A "suitable and eloquent discourse was pronounced" by Dr. Jacob De la Motta, M.D.

De la Motta (b. Savannah, 1789; d. 1845) was one of the most prominent Jewish figures of the day, and among those who had fought against the British in the siege of Savannah. He was one of two leading Jews in America with whom Madison and Jefferson corresponded on the topic of religious freedom. In his address at the "Hebrew synagogue" – which was actually Congregation Mikve Israel – De la Motta argued that the synagogue should not only serve Jewish religious interests, but also as an expression of patriotic obligation.

CONSECRATION OF THE JEWS' SYNAGOGUE. On the 29th of August, an interesting scene took place in the Great Synagogue, Jews' place, London. The building having been thoroughly overhauled and repaired, and fitted up in great splendour, the ceremony of consecration commenced.

"The gallery was crowded with females, many of whom were very beautiful, and all attired in that fashionable splendour which forms a principal characteristic of the nation. Soon after 5 o'clock, the hour appointed for the ceremony, the Chief Rabbi, attended by the Wardens, Elders, and other officers of the Synagogue, bearing the rolls of the Laws, appeared at the door of the Synagogue; the Chief Rabbi was in his full costume under a canopy of state, supported by six persons; the Chief Rabbi then exclaimed, " open unto us the gates of righteousness; we will enter them and praise the Lord;" they then all entered in procession, preceded by six little boys tastefully attired, each carrying a huge silver basket filled with different flowers, which they strewed along the path over which the procession passed. In this manner they circumambulated the Synagogue seven times, during which time seven appropriate psalms were chanted by the Reader and Choir, the music of which was exceedingly grand.

" Upon the procession approaching the Ark for the seventh time, the rolls of laws, which were all secured in peculiar cases, most splendidly ornamented, were severally placed within the Ark. The Chief Rabbi then delivered a prayer on behalf of the whole congregation, in which he particularly noticed the providential discovery of the state of the building. Three of the rolls were then taken from the Ark and conveyed in procession to an elevated spot in the centre of the Synagogue, when the Reader, surrounded by all the officers, delivered in a very solemn manner, in the Hebrew language, the following prayer for the King and the Royal Family :—

" He who disposeth Salvation unto kings and dominion unto princes, whose kingdom is an everlasting kingdom, who delivered his servant David from the destructive sword, who maketh a way in the sea, and a path through the mighty wilderness, may He bless, preserve, guard, assist, exalt and greatly aggrandize, our Sovereign Lord King George the Fourth, and all the Royal Family. May the Supreme King of kings through his infinite mercy, grant them life, preserve and deliver them from all manner of trouble, sorrow and danger. Subdue the nations under the soles of the king's feet, cause his enemies to fall before him, and grant him to reign prosperously.

" May the Supreme King of kings through his infinite mercy, inspire him and his Counsellors and Nobles with benevolence towards us and all Israel. In his days and in ours may Judah be saved, and Israel dwell in safety, and may the Redeemer come unto Zion, which God, in his infinite mercy, grant, and we will say—Amen."

" The rolls of laws being replaced in the Ark, and some other peculiar forms of service having been gone through, a subscription was opened towards defraying the expenses of the building, and in a very short time near £1000 was collected. The mode of conducting the subscription was a most curious one; for the Sabbath having just commenced as the subscription was opened, no money or cheques passed, and every moment one might see the officers who were collecting the names of the subscribers hold up their fingers to any friends whom they saw at a distance, which was to ask him how much he meant to subscribe. As many fingers as the individual held up in return he was immediately put down for so many guineas. The subscriptions were afterwards announced in Hebrew; after these were over the ordinary forms of the Sabbath eve commenced."

BOSTON – 1823
"CONSECRATION OF THE JEWS' SYNAGOGUE"
New-England Galaxy, p. 3 (col 1) – October 24, 1823

"Consecration of the Jews' Synagogue" describes in detail the consecration ceremony held in honor of the rebuilding of London's Great Synagogue following a devastating fire. It begins with a note that the gallery was crowded with well-attired females. This would be the case since most of the men would have been participating in the procession that had not yet reached the synagogue.

"Soon after 5 o'clock … the Chief Rabbi attended by the … officers of the Synagogue, bearing the rolls of the Laws, appeared at the door," the article reported. At the Chief Rabbi's exclamation of, "open unto us the gates of righteousness …" the procession entered and circled the Synagogue the traditional seven times before the rolls of laws, "all secured in peculiar cases, most splendidly ornamented" were placed in the Ark. After the Chief Rabbi "delivered a prayer on behalf of the whole congregation," three of the scrolls were taken to the reading table in the center of the Synagogue.

Two full paragraphs are devoted to the English translation of the Hebrew prayer for the King and the Royal Family that was delivered by the Reader "in a very solemn manner." The last paragraph speaks of a "subscription" held to defray the expenses of the building, noting that "in a very short time near £1000 was collected." The article reports that "the mode of conducting the subscription was a most curious one; for the Sabbath having just commenced …, no money or cheques passed…." After the individual donations were announced "in Hebrew," the regular Sabbath evening service commenced.

In New-York, on Thursday last, Mrs. Rebecca Lopez, wife of Mr. Joshua Lopez, and sister of the late Abraham Touro, of Boston, aged 54.

The Steamboat from New-York, which arrived here on Sunday, last, brought the body of Mrs. Lopez to be interred in the Jewish cemetery in this town. The corpse was placed in the Synagogue until Monday morning, at ten o'clock—when the service was performed, according to the Jewish ceremony, by the Rev. Isaac B. Seixas, in the presence of a large number of citizens—thence the body was conveyed to the cemetery and interred with additional ceremony at the grave.

This is the first time, for the last 40 years that the ceremony of the Jews has been performed in the synagogue.

NEWPORT – 1833
FROM NY TO NEWPORT TO BE INTERRED
Rhode-Island Republican, p. 3 (col 4)
December 23, 1833

This issue reported the death and funeral of Mrs. Rebecca Lopez, aged 54, wife of Joshua Lopez and sister of Judah and Abraham Touro. A steamboat from New York City arrived with her body, "to be interred in the Jewish cemetery in this town." Rabbi Isaac B. Seixas conducted the services in the Congregation Jeshuat Israel synagogue, which the Rhode Island legislature had already referred to as Touro Synagogue.

The synagogue's name change had come about when the state accepted bequests from Abraham Touro's will for the restoration and upkeep of the unused synagogue and for maintenance of the street between the cemetery and synagogue, which became known as Touro Street. In 1824, upon noting that nothing had been done with the monies her brother bequeathed, Rebecca petitioned the legislature to begin restoration and preservation. Her request led to one of the first American efforts to maintain a vacant historical site and to the beginning of Newport's efforts to maintain its architectural legacy.* The cemetery is the subject of a poem by Henry Wadsworth Longfellow (see sidebar).

The death notice showed how badly the Newport Jewish community had declined from the glorious days it had known in the decades preceding and shortly after the Revolutionary War. "This is the first time, for the last 40 years that the ceremony of the Jews has been performed in the synagogue." At the time there were no Jews living in the city, but a strong sense of responsibility for the community they had built led many who had been its members chose, like Rebecca, to be interred there.

* http://jwa.org/encyclopedia/article/lopez-rebecca-touro

The Jewish Cemetery at Newport
by Henry Wadsworth Longfellow

How strange it seems! These Hebrews in their graves,
Close by the street of this fair seaport town, Silent beside the never-silent waves,
At rest in all this moving up and down!

The trees are white with dust, that o'er their sleep
Wave their broad curtains in the south-wind's breath,
While underneath such leafy tents they keep
The long, mysterious Exodus of Death.

And these sepulchral stones, so old and brown,
That pave with level flags their burial-place,
Seem like the tablets of the Law, thrown down
And broken by Moses at the mountain's base.

The very names recorded here are strange,
Of foreign accent, and of different climes;
Alvares and Rivera interchange
With Abraham and Jacob of old times.

"Blessed be God! for he created Death!"
The mourners said, "and Death is rest and peace";
Then added, in the certainty of faith,
"And giveth Life that never more shall cease."

Closed are the portals of their Synagogue,
No Psalms of David now the silence break,
No Rabbi reads the ancient Decalogue
In the grand dialect the Prophets spake.

Gone are the living, but the dead remain,
And not neglected; for a hand unseen,
Scattering its bounty, like a summer rain,
Still keeps their graves and their remembrance green.

How came they here? What burst of Christian hate,
What persecution, merciless and blind,
Drove o'er the sea--that desert desolate--
These Ishmaels and Hagars of mankind?

They lived in narrow streets and lanes obscure,
Ghetto and Judenstrass, in mirk and mire;
Taught in the school of patience to endure
The life of anguish and the death of fire.

All their lives long, with the unleavened bread
And bitter herbs of exile and its fears,
The wasting famine of the heart they fed,
And slaked its thirst with marah of their tears.

Anathema maranatha! was the cry
That rang from town to town, from street to street;
At every gate the accursed Mordecai
Was mocked and jeered, and spurned by Christian feet.

Pride and humiliation hand in hand
Walked with them through the world where'er they went;
Trampled and beaten were they as the sand,
And yet unshaken as the continent.

For in the background figures vague and vast
Of patriarchs and of prophets rose sublime,
And all the great traditions of the Past
They saw reflected in the coming time.

And thus forever with reverted look
The mystic volume of the world they read, Spelling it backward, like a Hebrew book,
Till life became a Legend of the Dead.

But ah! what once has been shall be no more!
The groaning earth in travail and in pain
Brings forth its races, but does not restore
And the dead nations never rise again

PHILADELPHIA – 1834
"JEWISH SYNAGOGUE"
Atkinson's Saturday Evening Post,
p. 2 (col 3)
June 21, 1834

This news item covers the dedication ceremonies of the new building housing New York City's Congregation Shearith Israel on Crosby Street. Editor and diplomat Mordecai M. Noah, Esq. (b. Philadelphia, 1785; d. New York City, 1851), was the main speaker at the event. The *Post* described the new structure as "a very costly and beautiful one, fifty six feet in front by seventy five in depth."

Illustration of the Crosby Street Synagogue courtesy of Congregation Shearith Israel, New York (/shearithisrael.org/content/crosby-street-synagogue).

JEWISH SYNAGOGUE.—The Synagogue belonging to the congregation of Sherath Israel, just finished in Crosby street, New York, was on Thursday afternoon. consecrated, with the most imposing and interesting ceremonies, which were closed by an oration by M. M. Noah, Esq. The building is a very costly and beautiful one, fifty six feet in front by seventy five in depth. It was on this occasion filled in every part, and most of the clergy and magistrates were present.

NEW ORLEANS – 1841
NEW SYNAGOGUE MARKS
FIFTH IN NEW YORK CITY
The New Orleans Weekly Picayune,
p. 2 (col 3)
October 4, 1841

A report headlined "To Your Tents, O Israel" notes the dedication of a synagogue in New York City. This synagogue constitutes the fifth "in that city," serving a Jewish population numbering between eight and ten thousand. "This new congregation is wholly of Germans," the article notes, "many of whom have been driven to this country by the illiberal and oppressive laws of the Kingdom of Bavaria…. Among the oppressive laws were those forbidding certain occupations, and, in some instances, prohibiting the Jews to marry."

The New Orleans Weekly Picayune.

"TO YOUR TENTS, O ISRAEL!"—*A Jewish Synagogue* was consecrated in New York on the 15th instant, making the fifth in that city, comprising an aggregage number of that people of from eight to ten thousand. The new congregation is wholly of Germans, many of whom have been driven to this country by the illiberal and oppressive laws of the kingdom of Bavaria. Some are from the Duchy of Baden, Posen, &c. Among the oppressive laws were those forbidding certain occupations, and, in some instances, prohibiting the Jews to marry.

NEW YORK HERALD.
FIRST EDITION.
New York, Friday, August 27, 1841.

Important Religious Movement among the Jews.

We have received from Philadelphia several documents and circulars issued by the pious Jews of that city, developing one of the most important movements among the "ancient people of God" which has been attempted in many centuries.

It is no less than a novel and curious plan "for establishing a religious Union among the Israelites of America." In 1825, Mordecai Manuel Noah attempted to form a union at Grand Island, but his project fell to the ground, on account of want of talent and genius in the projector. That proposed by Noah was a sort of agricultural union on Grand Island, contingencies which were very convenient for smuggling purposes from Canada. Noah mixed with his project some religious features, and assumed the character and power of a prophet, priest and judge, but he did not command many converts.

The present project is altogether different in character. The following is the first document—the plan shall be given hereafter:—

CIRCULAR.
PHILADELPHIA, Ab, 5601, July, 1801.

To the President and Members of the Congregations throughout the United States, the Israelites of Philadelphia, send greeting:—

BRETHREN:—

May long life and spiritual and temporal prosperity be your portion from our father in heaven, and may He, the Most High, move your hearts to piety to himself, and good will towards all Israel your brethren. Amen.

In the full confidence that you will favorably entertain our plan for a general union, we on the part of the Israelites of this vicinity, affectionately invite you to deliberate well on the proposition and regulations which accompany this, and to elect without delay suitable persons for delegates, to meet us in general convention, on the first Sunday in November, being the 7th of that month, corresponding with the 23d day of Marcheshvan, 5602, at Philadelphia.

We deem it scarcely requisite to admonish you to select men who have the fear of God before their eyes, whose interest in the welfare of the House of Jacob is of an abiding nature, whose moral character is unblemished, and who are of sufficient intelligence to judge with impartiality and reasonable conviction, and of such men there are doubtless many among your number; and have the goodness to instruct them, without exacting pledges, with regard to the measures you wish proposed, and what persons elected for the high stations embraced in our plan, that they who are chosen may step abroad with the seal of public approbation stamped upon them and their characters.

Although we can scarcely believe that any congregation, who are duly impressed with the paramount obligation to uphold our blessed faith, can refuse uniting with us in a measure which evidently promises so much general good: we would, nevertheless, thank you to let us hear from you with the least possible delay, if you decline the union we herewith offer to you.

In the full confidence of a favorable issue, and a fervent hope that you will be found united with us in a common effort to spread the kingdom of Heaven, we remain, Beloved brethren,

Your friends and servants in the Lord.

J. L. HACKENBURG,
LEWIS ALLEN,
ISAAC LEESER,
SIMON ELFELT,   } Committee.
MAYER ARNOLD,
HENRY COHEN,
JACOB ULMAN,

We at once perceive that the object of this circular is union. The fact is, that there is not only no unity at present among the Dutch, Spanish, Portuguese, Polish, and German Jews, but there is actual jealousy, and even antipathy, between them. They all agree, however, in the articles of the Jewish faith, and therefore feel greatly alarmed at the conversions to Christianity which have taken place during the last and several preceeding years. There have been in the different parts of Europe from 3000 to 4000 who have gone over to Christianity. The Jews in America, as a body, are very ignorant of the Scriptures, and of course, of their own religion. That a powerful effort will now be made to regain the heretics, and so keep those who are still with them in the fold, there can be no doubt. The general wish among the Jews in this city, and also in Philadelphia, is, that Mr. Noah be not appointed to any office in this business. This, no doubt, arises partly from his Grand Island exhibitions and abortions. But we doubt the fairness of this policy. We know in this city nearly 12,000 Jews, and if they would return Noah as one of the principal delegates, we believe he would retrieve his character, and regain his position as a prophet—a successor of Moses, David, or Solomon. It certainly would be fair to give him a chance, and we advise the Hebrews to try him. There is salvation for the worst of sinners.

This religious movement is deeply interesting. No doubt this projected union has for its basis an expectation of the coming of the Messiah. The Hebrews have always believed that he will come—sooner or later—and we do not see why he should not come on this continent instead of the old. We say to all "watch and pray."

NEW YORK – 1841
IMPORTANT RELIGIOUS MOVEMENT AMONG THE JEWS
The New York Herald, p. 2 (cols 3–4) – August 27, 1841

This article discusses the beginnings of a campaign for a national union or federation among the nation's growing Jewish community. Seven signatories to a letter sent in July to the "Presidents and members of the Congregations throughout the United States," invite God-fearing delegates to a meeting the following November in Philadelphia to deal with this pressing issue. Among the signatories is Rev. Isaac Leeser of Philadelphia's Congregation Mikveh Israel, probably the most noted Jewish scholarly author of the day.

The anonymous author of the paragraph following this invitation endorses the letter's call. "The fact is, that there is not only no unity among the Dutch, Spanish, Portuguese, Polish and German Jews, but there is actual jealousy, and even antipathy between them." Yet these various ethnicities all agree on the main articles of the Jewish faith. In addition, threats of conversion face American Jews based on the success that missionaries have accomplished in Europe. The "ignorance" of many American Jews about their faith, argues the article, makes them prime targets for missionaries.

Finally, the article touches on the possible role for Mordecai M. Noah, the famed Jewish public figure (see Chapter 8). "The general wish" from all Jewish sources, is that Noah not be appointed to any position "in this business" especially as a result of his exhibitionism in trying to establish a Jewish colony he called "Ararat" near Buffalo, New York. But the article advises the Hebrews to "give him a chance... There is salvation for the worst of sinners."

JEWISH.

CONSECRATION OF A JEWISH SYNAGOGUE.—Friday afternoon the Synagogue of Congregation Rodolph Shalom, was consecrated with great solemnity to the worship of God. The galleries were occupied by the women only, and the body of the edifice by the men. About 1,500 persons were present.

The exercises were opened with a grand symphony by Hirschman's Band. Rev. Drs. Lillienthal and Raphall, followed by the President and Trustees of the Congregation brought the Scrolls of the Law to the closed doors of the Synagogue, where, standing under a canopy and knocking three times loudly at the door, they exclaimed :

"Open unto us the gates of righteousness, we will enter them and praise the Lord."

The doors were then opened, and the Preachers, President, and Trustees entered in procession with the scrolls, the Rev. N. Davidsohn, accompanied by the choir and band singing,

"Blessed be he who cometh in the name of the Lord ; we bless ye from the house of the Lord."

The procession, headed by the preachers, next advanced slowly up the isles, until arrived at the ark, the Rev. N. Davidsohn meantime singing the following :

"How Goodly are thy tents, O Jacob! thy tabernacles, O Israel! And in the greatness of thy benevolence will I enter thine house ; in reverence of thee will I bow down toward the temple of thine holiness. O Lord! I have loved the habitation of thine house, and the dwelling place of thy glory. I therefore will worship, bow down, and bend the knee before the Lord my Maker. And I will offer my prayer unto thee, O Lord! in an acceptable time ; in thine abundant mercy, O God! answer me in the truth of thy salvation."

The nine scrolls containing the five books of Moses, written in the Hebrew language on parchment, were given into the hands of different members of the congregation, and seven circuits performed under the canopy and in front of the ark. During the first circuit, Rev. Mr. Lyon chanted a Song of Degrees of David, commencing,

"I rejoiced when they said unto me, let us go into the house of the Lord. Our feet stood within thy gates, O, Jerusalem."

Rev. N. Davidsohn chanted an Ode at the dedication of the House of David, during the second circuit.

During the third circuit a Psalm of David was chanted by Rev. Dr. Haelmer.

Rev. Mr. Sternberg chanted a Psalm to the Chief Musician upon the Getteth by the sons of Korah, during the fourth circuit, as follows :

"How delightful are thy tabernacles, O Lord of Hosts! My soul longeth, aye yearneth, for the courts of the Lord : my mind and my body triumph in the God of life. As the sparrow found her house, the swallow a nest for herself, where she may foster her young, so I thy altars, O Lord of Hosts! my King and God. Happy are they who dwell, in thy house, unceasing they praise Thee. Selah! Happy is the man whose might is in Thee. Its paths are in their hearts, when passing through the arid vale of Bacha, a fountain they deem it, even their autumnal rain teemeth with blessings. Thus they march on from strength to strength, till they appear before God in Zion. O Lord God of Hosts! hear my prayer; give ear, O God of Jacob! Selah! Behold, O God! our shield; look upon thine anointed. For one day in thy courts is better than thousands. Rather would I stand at the threshhold of God's house, than dwell in the tents of wickedness. For the Eternal God is sun and shield; grace and glory God giveth; he withholdeth no happiness from those who walk uprightly. O Lord of Hosts! happy is the man who trusteth in Thee."

During the fifth circuit a psalm was chanted by Rev. N. Davidsohn, commencing,

"The voice of song and salvation is in the tabernacles of the righteous; the right hand of the Lord hath done valiantly."

Rev. Mr. Lyon chanted a psalm during the sixth circuit, and the Rev. Mr. Rubin a song of degrees during the seventh circuit.

The procession after the seventh circuit approached the Ark, accompanied by Rev. Mr. Haelmer, and with their faces to the Ark sung a Psalm of David, commencing,

"Ascribe unto the Lord, O ye sons of the mighty; ascribe glory and might unto the Lord."

At the conclusion of the psalm, the members of the procession, one by one, placed his scroll in the Ark, after which the doors were closed, and the following benediction pronounced by the Rev. Mr. Lillienthal :

"Blessed art thou, O Lord our God! King of the Universe, who preserved us alive, and brought us to this season."

The same clergyman then delivered an eloquent discourse in Hebrew, at the conclusion of which a prayer was delivered by Rev. N. Davidsohn.

A collection amounting to $1,025, was then taken up.

An eloquent address in English was then delivered by Rev. Dr. Raphall, after which a hymn was sung by Rev. N. Davidsohn, and the congregation dismissed.—*Tribune.*

NEW YORK –
1853
"CONSECRATION OF JEWISH SYNAGOGUE"
New York Observer, p. 3 (col 4–5) – April 21, 1853

The pageantry of the consecration of Congregation Rodolph Shalom is described in a nearly column length report. Some 1,500 people were present at the ceremony. The exercises were opened with a grand symphony by Hirschman's Band. Rabbis and officers of the congregation carrying Torah Scrolls knocked on the closed synagogue doors three times from the street. A procession which circled the Ark seven times followed. Psalms were sung and chanted. Sermons were delivered in both Hebrew and English. A collection amounting to $1,025 was taken.

316   ILLUSTRATED NEWS.   [MAY 14, 1853.

THE NEW SYNAGOGUE.

WE gave in our last number an exterior view of the new Clinton street Synagogue. Our present number contains a sketch of the interior In this synagogue, the reading desk, which is usually in the centre, is placed at the end. The seats also usually run parallel to the gall-ries—here they are transversely arranged. This is the thirteenth synagogue established in our city, the oldest being that in Crosby-street, which was originally founded in the early part of the seventeenth century. The largest synagogue, which is also one of the largest places of worship in the city, is in Norfolk-street. The German Israelites of New York have two rabbis (same as bishops). There are among the Hebrews no ministers, but the *leaders* and expounders. The principal portion of their service is chanted—one of the essential qualifications of a leader being a thorough knowledge of music, which art is probably more cultivated among the Jews than among any other race in the world.

INTERIOR VIEW OF THE JEWISH SYNAGOGUE, CLINTON-ST.

NEW YORK – 1853
"THE NEW SYNAGOGUE"
Illustrated News, p. 316 (col 3)
May 14, 1853

By 1853, New York City's Jewish population consisted of some 20,000 in a city of a half million inhabitants. Most Jews lived on the Lower East Side. This illustration shows the interior of the new synagogue on Clinton Street, the thirteenth synagogue in the city. The description notes that the reader's desk *(bimah)* is located at the front, unlike in older structures where it is found at the center, and the seats (where the men sit) are arranged transversely to the galleries (where the women sit) instead of parallel as in the past.

This article notes that the city's synagogues include two of the "German Israelites" which have rabbis ("same as bishops"), whereas the "Hebrews" have only "*leaders* and expounders." Because the main prayers of "their" (i.e., "Hebrews") synagogue service are chanted, therefore requiring knowledge of music "which art is more cultivated among the Jews than among any other race in the world."

NEW YORK – 1855
FIRST JEWISH TEMPLE
IN MISSISSIPPI VALLEY
The New York Herald, p. 2 (col 3)
September 15, 1855

Judah Touro

With the growing settlement of the West, Jewish migration was marked by the construction of new houses of worship. This article reports the dedication of Temple Baal El [sic – actual name is Temple B'nai El] in St. Louis, the first Jewish house of worship constructed in the Mississippi Valley. Mirroring the rise of the Reform Jewish movement in Europe, this Temple featured an organ. Above the Ark stood a plaque honoring Judah Touro (b. 1775; d. 1854), the philanthropist whose donation helped to construct the new Temple. Significantly, the main dedicatory address was delivered in German. Mr. Isadore Bush, who spoke in English, apologized for his "want of knowledge" in that language.

Dedication of the Temple of Baal El in St. Louis.

[From the St. Louis Intelligencer, Sept. 11.]

The first Hebrew temple erected in the Mississippi Valley was consecrated in this city, last Friday afternoon, in presence of a large concourse of both sexes, composed of members of the ancient Israelitist family, and others of our citizens.

The incident gives rise to so many reflections that we deem it proper to chronicle the event somewhat in detail.

The building is erected on the east side of Sixth street, just south of Cerro, and is octagonal in form, with a dome some fifty feet high, all substantially and neatly built and finished, and capable of seating some eight hundred persons. The whole presents a most unique appearance. The circular centre is some twelve inches or more below the floor of the main entrance; through this, from door to altar place, runs one main aisle, with seats on either side; surrounding this is a gallery, on the level of the main entrance, with an aisle next the wall, all round, and seats extending towards the centre. Above is another gallery, extending nearly all around the building, in the west end of which, over the main entrance, are the organ and choir, the balance occupied with seats. The eastern part of the building, in front of the main entrance, is occupied by the altar, which includes a reading desk; and raised some three steps above the floor of the lower

gallery is what may be termed a pulpit, behind which, in a recess in the wall, is built 'The Ark.'

The front or door of the Ark is covered with rich purple velvet, beautifully embossed in silver and gold, containing, beside some significant Hebrew characters and emblems, a crown, very handsomely wrought upon the velvet. All this has been wrought by some ladies of the congregation—sisters, we learn, of L. Block and Brothers, and exhibits a great degree of skill and taste, as well as persevering industry. Above the Ark is a tablet to the memory of Judah Truro, the patron friend whose liberal bequest has chiefly effected the erection of the building. Still above this is a likeness of the great Jewish Lawgiver, Moses, with the two tables of the law, handsomely wrought in worsted by two other ladies of the congregation. Over the altar hangs the sacred lamp, which is to burn continually, while on either side are the golden candlestick, (in this instance beautifully gilt,) each with its seven lights, three on each prong with one in each centre. On either side of the Ark is a raised wooden column, finely carved, surmounted each by a bouquet of various flowers, while on each side of the columns are the almond and myrtle trees, as seen in the ancient temple.

We do not intend to specify all of the ceremonies of the occasion, as many of them were not understood by us. Suffice it to say, that the door was opened by the President, and the ministers and elders brought in the law, and deposited the same in the Ark.

There were four copies, each of parchment, on which was written in Hebrew the whole of the Old Testament, beginning with Genesis and terminating with Malachi, the last of the "minor prophets." These parchments are done up in ancient form, upon rolls; to each there is a handsome metalic finger, so that the line and word may be pointed out to the reader, who goes from right to left, in the ancient form. These books are very carefully preserved, and greatly reverenced by all Israelites; and each new copy taken is carefully collated as written, so that no change takes place, even in the form of a letter, and thus change the sense.

Each was enclosed in a purple bag, with Hebrew characters, wrought in gold, after the book had been carefully bound with a white linen bandage.

After the books were deposited the officiating minister took one of them, when the elders removed the velvet covering, and then the linen bandage, and laid it on the desk, where the President unrolled it to the place in the Scriptures suitable to the occasion. He then took the metalic finger and pointed out the portions to be read, while sundry persons came forward from the congregation singly, to the number of twenty, and saw the Scriptures read. Each of these, on coming to the desk, had placed across his shoulders a vestment or scarf; he touched or kissed the book, made some remark, and then made an offering to the temple of whatever he chose—this done, he was divested of the scarf, which was then placed upon another.

After these offerings, the ministers and elders took the sacred books, and seven times made solemn circuit of the house, through its various aisles below.

This done, the Rev. Dr. Illowsy delivered a dedicatory address and prayer in German, which was attentively listened to by the large audience, and by those who understood it, was pronounced very eloquent, appropriate and affecting.

Next was an address in English by Mr. Isadore Bush, one of the most efficient members in getting this Temple built. He apologised for a want of knowledge of the tongue in which he spoke, suitably to express his emotions on this occasion, fraught with so much interest—described their difficulties—returned thanks to those friends of religious toleration who had aided them in their effort—spoke feelingly of the happiness of their condition in this great republic, where they had found a home, free from their persecutors—honored the memory of Judah Trouro, who had given their various congregations such efficient aid—thanked the ladies for the aid they had given in adorning the Temple with their handiwork, the labor of their needles—spoke of their efforts to restore to their worship its ancient musical interest, when David with harp and timbrel and song, praised God, and varied instruments were introduced in worship, and hoped although this practice had fallen into disuse, that it might now be restored to Israel; and in this connection he paid a well deserved compliment to the amateur musicians and vocalists, who had voluntarily come to their aid, and had so heightened the interests of this festive occasion by their admirable performances.

Mr. Bush spoke freely and with much feeling, and his eulogium on the choir was happy and well deserved, for they performed their interesting parts much to the satisfaction of the audience, closing with a beautiful anthem the services, which had begun with another from Israel's Royal Psalmist.

CHARLESTON – 1859
"THE JEWISH NATIONAL BOARD OF REPRESENTATIVES"

The Charleston Mercury, p. 1 (col 2)
November 10, 1859

"The leading Jews have come to the conclusion that their church affairs would be much benefited by the organization of a National Board of Representatives to attend to the general interests of the Israelites in the United States," notes this front page report. The article describes proposals for choosing delegates and drafting a constitution. Both the Hebrew and English dates – "Sunday, the first day of Kislay [sic], 5,620, corresponding with the 27th day of November, 1859" – are listed for the first meeting slated to be held in New York City. The Board was later named the Board of Delegates of American Israelites.

THE JEWISH NATIONAL BOARD OF REPRESENTATIVES.—The leading Jews have come to the conclusion that their church affairs would be much benefitted by the organization of a National Board of Representatives to attend to the general interests of the Israelites in the United States. They have formed a Committee in New York and drawn up the following plan, which they recommend to the attention of the Jewish congregations throughout the country:

" Two delegates to be elected from each congregation, to be divided into two classes, to serve one and two years respectively. The first delegates to be elected at a special general meeting of each congregation, and subsequently at such time and in such manner as the congregation may direct. The Board, when organized, to form its own Constitution and By-Laws, and select its name and title. The expenses to be defrayed by contributions from the congregations represented in such ratio as the Board may determine. The Board to take cognizance of temporal affairs only, and in no case to interfere with the internal administration of the Synagogues. The Board to lay an annual report of its proceedings before its constituents. The first meeting of the Board to be held at Cooper's Institute, in the city of New York, on Sunday, the first day of Kislay, 5,620, corresponding with the 27th day of November, 1859, at three o'clock in the afternoon. All congregations electing representatives, are requested to address a notification of the same to Asher Kursheedt, Chairman, 40 West Washington Place, or to Geo. Godfrey, Secretary, 74 Pine street.

SACRAMENTO DAILY UNION.

WHOLE NO. 2911. SACRAMENTO, THURSDAY MORNING, JULY 26, 1860. PRICE

SACRAMENTO – 1860
"THE JEWS IN CALIFORNIA HISTORY"

Sacramento Daily Union, p. 2 (col 6)
July 26, 1860

Jews played a major role in the history of California from the time it was annexed to the United States. On February 26, 1849, Jews were among those who arrived in San Francisco on the first Pacific Mail steamer. Later that year, a group of Jews met in a tent in San Francisco to hold Yom Kippur services. The following year, two congregations were organized in that city. This issue reports on a new Jewish burial ground that was dedicated at the Mission on July 25, 1860 "with appropriate ceremonies."

BY TELEGRAPH TO THE UNION.

BY THE STATE TELEGRAPH LINE.

Jewish Burial Ground — Republican Clubs.

SAN FRANCISCO, July 25, 1860.

The new Jewish burial ground at the Mission was dedicated to-day with appropriate ceremonies.

Two new Republican Clubs were organized last night—one composed entirely of German citizens.

Chapter #3

Education & Literature

CONNECTICUT MAGAZINE. IN B. 183

The NEW-HAVEN GAZETTE.
AND THE
CONNECTICUT MAGAZINE.

MANY SHALL RUN TO AND FRO, AND KNOWLEDGE SHALL BE INCREASED. Dan. Chap. XII. v. 4.

(VOL. II.)   Thursday, July 26, M.DCC.LXXXVII.   (No. 23.)

as ——— lambs. Let
the ———, ſhear their lambs, and
the ——— will furniſh hatters with excellent
materials for a part of their manufacture,
for which they will pay the caſh, and all
greatly advantage the animal. This mode
has been adopted in many places of late, and
they have found it extremely beneficial.
The lamb, before the heat of ſummer is
over, is clothed with ſuch a quantity of
wool that he often becomes poor, wherefore
let him be ſhear'd and the effect will be the
ſame as on ſheep. This method ought certainly
to claim the particular attention of
the farmers, and I venture to affirm that this
mode if adopted will annually produce a
conſiderable revenue as well as greatly advantage
our flocks of ſheep.
AGRICOLA.

Died, laſt Tueſday morning,
in the 70th year of his age,
the Rev. CHAUNCEY WHIT-
TLEſEY, of this City.
The harveſt in Pennſylvania has been uncommonly
plentiful. Double the quantity
of grain has been raiſed this year that there
was the laſt. The wheat is large and heavy,
nor is there any complaint of a deficiency of
ſtraw.
Laſt Sunday arrived in this city, from
Philadelphia, the Honourable ROGER
SHERMAN, Eſq. one of the delegates of
this ſtate to the Federal Convention.——
No particular intelligence, reſpecting the
proceedings of that illuſtrious aſſembly, is
communicated. We only learn, in general,
that a happy and auſpicious unanimity prevails
in their councils, and that they will
probably, finiſh the important buſineſs entruſted
to them, by the beginning of September.

We muſt beg our readers to excuſe us
for publiſhing a ſmaller ſheet than uſual, as
it was impoſſible for us to procure any other.

——, do.
——nce, White, Bath.

CLEARED.
Sloop Defiance, Venables, New Providence
Brig. Sally, Peck. Demarara.
Sloop Delight, Hſe, New York
Sloop Friendſhip, Bradley. Do.
Schr. Jolly Farmer, Allen, M. Vinyard.
Schr. Peggy, Goodſill, Fiſhing.
Sloop Delight, Hulls, New York.

Yale-College, July 20, 1787.
The Candidates for the
degree of Maſter of Arts, which is to be
conferred at the Public Commencement, on
the 12th of September next, are hereby notified
to ſend in their Requeſt to the Preſident,
and their QUAESTIONES MAGISTRALES
to Mr. Tutor Deniſon, and
give their Attendance at the Commencement.
The Catalogue of the Univerſity is to be
printed this Year.
EZRA STILES, Preſident.
[23 tw.]

For SALE, a Quantity of
SALT SHAD,
By the Barrel or Retail.
Enquire of Biſhop and Hotchkiſs.
New-Haven, July 24, 1787.   (2)

BY Direction of the
hon Court of Probate for the
Diſtrict of Danbury, we give Notice to all
Perſons who have any Demands upon the
Eſtate of DANIEL BALDWIN, late of
Newtown, in ſaid Diſtrict, deceaſed, to
bring in their Accounts for Settlement, within
Six Months from the Date hereof, and
if they neglect, they will be forever debarred.
CLARK BALDWIN,   Executors.
DANIEL BALDWIN,
ABIGAIL BALDWIN,
Newtown, Ju—— ——   (23 3)

——— GIVEN FOR
—— and Silver,
—— Ghittenden,
——RSMITH,
—— next to this OFFICE.
For Gold of the firſt
Quality Five Pounds per Oz.
will be given; and for Silver
of the firſt Quality, Six Shillings
and Eight Pence, per Oz.
and proportionably leſs for inferior
Qualities of either.
July 24.   (23)

HEBREW BOOKS.
To be ſold at this Office,
LEUSDEN's Hebrew Bible,
Buxtorf's Lexicon,
Schickard's Grammar, and
Bythner's Lyra Prophetica, or critical Analyſis
of the Book of Pſalms.
(23)

Elijah Auſtin, & Co.
HAVE juſt received from DUBLIN, a Quantity
of
IRISH LINNENS,
Printed do. &
Chintzes.
——— They have alſo for SALE, ———
A Variety of Piece Goods,
Gauzes,—Cutlery,—Hard-
Ware, &c.
ALL which they will ſell exceedingly cheap for
CASH.
Hollow-Ware by the Ton,
St. Croix Rum, by the hhd.
or bb.—A few Barrels of
exceeding GOOD SUGAR,
Seaſoned Pine Plank, Pine
Shingles, &c.
New-Haven June 4th, 1787.   [16]

JUST PUBLISHED,
Belknap's Hiſtory of New-
HAMPSHIRE. Sold by ISAAC BEERS.

> Yal.-College, July 20, 1787.
>
> The Candidates for the degree of Master of Arts, which is to be conferred at the Public Commencement, on the 12th of September next, are hereby notified to send in their Request to the President, and their *QUÆSTIONES MAGISTRALES* to Mr. Tutor Denison, and give their Attendance at the Commencement.
>
> The Catalogue of the University is to be printed this Year.
>
> EZRA STILES, *President.*
>
> [23 *tw.*]

> # HEBREW BOOKS.
>
> To be fold at this Office,
>
> L'EUSDEN's *Hebrew Bible*, Buxtorf's *Lexicon*, Schickard's *Grammar*, and Bythner's *Lyra Prophetica, or critical Analyfis of the Book of Pfalms.*
>
> (23)

NEW-HAVEN, CONNECTICUT
HEBREW IN U.S. COLLEGES
The New-Haven Gazette and the Connecticut Magazine, p. 3 (cols 2, 3)
July 20, 1787

Hebrew language studies were required in the nation's first universities where the main educational purpose was training future ministers. This advertisement – headlined "Hebrew Books" and listing works by Buxtorf, L'eusden, and *Lyra Prophetica, or c*ritical Analysis of the Book of Psalms – may well be the first advertisement in American newspaper history selling exclusively Hebrew books. Gentiles, rather than Jews, were clearly the intended audience for this ad since there were at most a handful of Jews in New Haven at this time.

The newspaper's adjoining column contained a notice from Yale College stating that "Candidates for the degree of Master of Arts … are hereby notified to send in their Requests … and *Questiones Magistrales.*" The notice was signed by Ezra Stiles (b. New Haven, 1727; d. 1795), who served as president of the College from 1778 until his death and as Yale's first Professor of Semitic Languages. Prior to being appointed to Yale, Stiles had been minister of the Second Congregational Church in Newport, R.I. (1755–1777). During that period he showed a strong interest in Hebraic and Judaic matters, attending many services at the Newport Hebrew Congregation where, in 1773, he met Rabbi Haim Carigal. According to a *diary* Stiles kept, he and Rabbi Carigal met at least twenty eight times during the rabbi's six month visit from the Holy Land. They discussed such topics as Kabala and the politics of the Holy Land, and Carigal tutored him extensively in Hebrew. Eventually, the two corresponded in Hebrew.

Ezra Stiles

As Yale's President and Professor of Semitic Languages, Stiles instituted a policy that all freshmen would be required to study Hebrew. In 1781, he delivered his first commencement address, notably in Hebrew. By 1790 he was forced to admit that requiring all students to study Hebrew was a mistake and the requirement was dropped, yet in both 1785 and 1792, Hebrew was the language in which the valedictorians delivered their speeches.

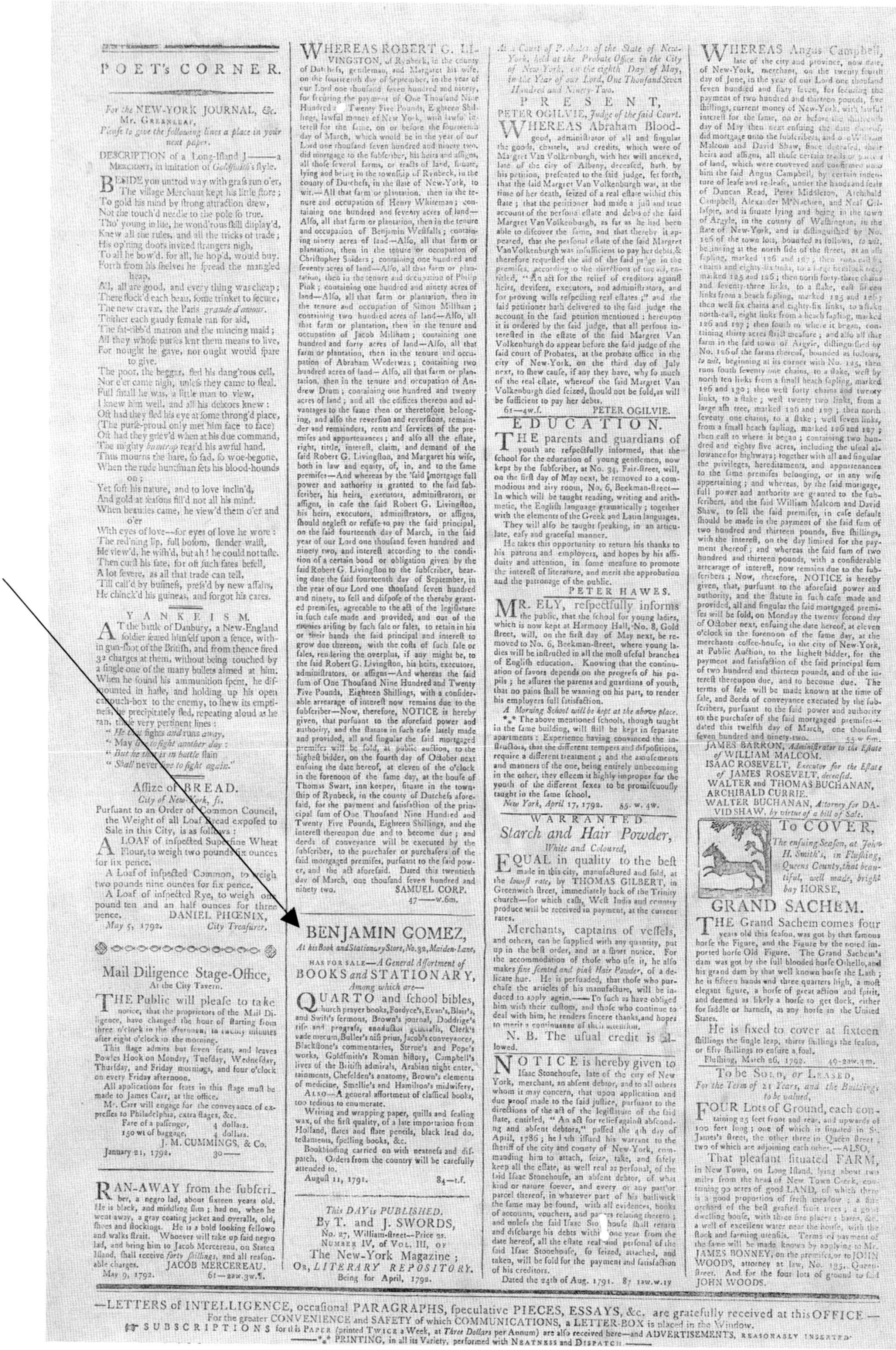

POET's CORNER.

For the NEW-YORK JOURNAL, &c.
Mr. GREENLEAF,
Pleaſe to give the following lines a place in your next paper.

DESCRIPTION of a Long-Iſland J——a MERCHANT, in imitation of *Goldſmith's* ſtyle.

BESIDE yon untrod way with graſs run o'er,
The village Merchant kept his little ſtore;
To gold his mind by ſtrong attraction drew,
Not the touch'd needle to the pole ſo true.
Tho' young in life, he wond'rous ſkill diſplay'd,
Knew all the rules, and all the tricks of trade;
His op'ning doors invited ſtrangers nigh,
To all he bow'd. for all, he hop'd, would buy.
Forth from his ſhelves he ſpread the mangled heap,
All, all are good, and every thing was cheap;
There flock'd each beau, ſome trinket to ſecure,
The new cravat, the Paris *grande d'amour.*
Thither each gaudy female ran for aid,
The fat-ribb'd matron and the mincing maid;
All they whoſe purſes lent them means to live,
For nought he gave, nor ought would ſpare to give.
The poor, the beggar, fled his dang'rous cell,
Nor e'er came nigh, unleſs they came to ſteal.
Full ſmall he was, a little man to view,
I knew him well, and all his debtors knew:
Oft had they fled his eye at ſome throng'd place,
(The purſe-proud only met him face to face)
Oft had they griev'd when at his due command,
The mighty *bumtrap* rear'd his awful hand.
Thus mourns the hare, ſo ſad, ſo woe-begone,
When the rude huntſman ſets his blood-hounds on;
Yet ſoft his nature, and to love inclin'd,
And gold at ſeaſons fill'd not all his mind.
When beauties came, he view'd them o'er and o'er
With eyes of love—for eyes of love he wore:
The red'ning lip, full boſom, ſlender waiſt,
He view'd, he wiſh'd, but ah! he could not taſte.
Then curſt his fate, for oft ſuch fates befell,
A lot ſevere, as all that trade can tell,
Till call'd by buſineſs, preſs'd by new affairs,
He chinck'd his guineas, and forgot his cares.

Y A N K E I S M.

AT the battle of Danbury, a New-England ſoldier ſeated himſelf upon a fence, within gun-ſhot of the Britiſh, and from thence fired 32 charges at them, without being touched by a ſingle one of the many bullets aimed at him. When he found his ammunition ſpent, he diſmounted in haſte, and holding up his open cartouch-box to the enemy, to ſhew its emptineſs, he precipitately fled, repeating aloud as he ran, theſe very pertinent lines:
" *He that* fights *and* runs *away,*
" May *live to fight another day:*
" *But he that is in battle* ſlain
" *Shall* never *live to fight again.*"

Aſſize of BREAD.
City of New-York, ſs.

Purſuant to an Order of Common Council, the Weight of all Loaf Bread expoſed to Sale in this City, is as follows:

A LOAF of inſpected Superfine Wheat Flour, to weigh two pounds ſix ounces for ſix pence.

A Loaf of inſpected Common, to weigh two pounds nine ounces for ſix pence.

A Loaf of inſpected Rye, to weigh one pound ten and an half ounces for three pence. DANIEL PHŒNIX,
May 5, 1792. *City Treaſurer.*

Mail Diligence Stage-Office,
At the City Tavern.

THE Public will pleaſe to take notice, that the proprietors of the Mail Diligence, have changed the hour of ſtarting from three o'clock in the afternoon, to twenty minutes after eight o'clock in the morning.

This ſtage admits but ſeven ſeats, and leaves Powles Hook on Monday, Tueſday, Wedneſday, Thurſday, and Friday mornings, and four o'clock on every Friday afternoon.

All applications for ſeats in this ſtage muſt be made to James Carr, at the office.

Mr. Carr will engage for the conveyance of expreſſes to Philadelphia, extra ſtages, &c.

Fare of a paſſenger, 4 dollars.
150 wt of baggage, 4 dollars.

J. M. CUMMINGS, & Co.
January 21, 1792. 30——

RAN-AWAY from the ſubſcriber, a negro lad, about ſixteen years old. He is black, and middling ſlim; had on, when he went away, a gray coating jacket and overalls, old, ſhoes and ſtockings. He is a bold looking fellowo and walks ſtrait. Whoever will take up ſaid negro lad, and bring him to Jacob Mercereau, on Staten Iſland, ſhall receive *forty ſhillings*, and all reaſonable charges. JACOB MERCEREAU.
May 9, 1792. 61—2aw.3w.¶.

WHEREAS ROBERT G. LIVINGSTON, of Rynbeck, in the county of Dutcheſs, gentleman, and Margaret his wife, on the fourteenth day of September, in the year of our Lord one thouſand ſeven hundred and ninety, for ſecuring the payment of One Thouſand Nine Hundred and Twenty Five Pounds, Eighteen Shillings, lawful money of New York, with lawful intereſt for the ſame, on or before the fourteenth day of March, which would be in the year of our Lord one thouſand ſeven hundred and ninety two, did mortgage to the ſubſcriber, his heirs and aſſigns, all thoſe ſeveral farms, or tracts of land, ſituate, lying and being in the townſhip of Rynbeck, in the county of Dutcheſs, in the ſtate of New-York, to wit.—All that farm or plantation, then in the tenure and occupation of Henry Whiteman; containing one hundred and ſeventy acres of land—Alſo, all that farm or plantation, then in the tenure and occupation of Benjamin Weſtfalls; containing ninety acres of land—Alſo, all that farm or plantation, then in the tenure or occupation of Chriſtopher Sniders; containing one hundred and ſeventy acres of land—Alſo, all that farm or plantation, then in the tenure and occupation of Philip Pink; containing one hundred and ninety acres of land—Alſo, all that farm or plantation, then in the tenure and occupation of Simon Millham; containing two hundred acres of land—Alſo, all that farm or plantation, then in the tenure and occupation of Jacob Millham; containing one hundred and forty acres of land—Alſo, all that farm or plantation, then in the tenure and occupation of Abraham Wedetwax; containing two hundred acres of land—Alſo, all that farm or plantation, then in the tenure and occupation of Andrew Drum; containing one hundred and twenty acres of land; and all the edifices thereon and advantages to the ſame then or theretofore belonging, and alſo the reverſion and reverſions, remainder and remainders, rents and ſervices of the premiſes and appurtenances; and alſo all the eſtate, right, title, intereſt, claim, and demand of the ſaid Robert G. Livingſton, and Margaret his wife, both in law and equity, of, in, and to the ſame premiſes—And whereas by the ſaid mortgage full power and authority is granted to the ſaid ſubſcriber, his heirs, executors, adminiſtrators, or aſſigns, in caſe the ſaid Robert G. Livingſton, his heirs, executors, adminiſtrators, or aſſigns, ſhould neglect or refuſe to pay the ſaid principal, on the ſaid fourteenth day of March, in the ſaid year of our Lord one thouſand ſeven hundred and ninety two, and intereſt according to the condition of a certain bond or obligation given by the ſaid Robert G. Livingſton to the ſubſcriber, bearing date the ſaid fourteenth day of September, in the year of our Lord one thouſand ſeven hundred and ninety, to ſell and diſpoſe of the thereby granted premiſes, agreeable to the act of the legiſlature in ſuch caſe made and provided, and out of the monies ariſing by ſuch ſale or ſales, to retain in his or their hands the ſaid principal and intereſt to grow due thereon, with the coſts of ſuch ſale or ſales, rendering the overplus, if any might be, to the ſaid Robert G. Livingſton, his heirs, executors, adminiſtrators, or aſſigns—And whereas the ſaid ſum of One Thouſand Nine Hundred and Twenty Five Pounds, Eighteen Shillings, with a conſiderable arrearage of intereſt now remains due to the ſubſcriber—Now, therefore, NOTICE is hereby given, that purſuant to the aforeſaid power and authority, and the ſtatute in ſuch caſe lately made and provided, all and ſingular the ſaid mortgaged premiſes will be ſold, at public auction, to the higheſt bidder, on the fourth day of October next enſuing the date hereof, at eleven of the o'clock in the forenoon of the ſame day, at the houſe of Thomas Swart, inn keeper, ſituate in the townſhip of Rynbeck, in the county of Dutcheſs aforeſaid, for the payment and ſatisfaction of the principal ſum of One Thouſand Nine Hundred and Twenty Five Pounds, Eighteen Shillings, and the intereſt thereupon due and to become due; and deeds of conveyance will be executed by the ſubſcriber, to the purchaſer or purchaſers of the ſaid mortgaged premiſes, purſuant to the ſaid power, and the act aforeſaid. Dated this twentieth day of March, one thouſand ſeven hundred and ninety two. SAMUEL CORP.
47——w.6m.

BENJAMIN GOMEZ,
At his Book and Stationary Store, No. 32, Maiden-Lane,
HAS FOR SALE—*A General Aſſortment of*
BOOKS *and* STATIONARY,
Among which are—

QUARTO and ſchool bibles, church prayer books, Fordyce's, Evan's, Blair's, and Swift's ſermons, Brown's journal, Doddrige's riſe and progreſs, conductor generalis, Clerk's vade mecum, Buller's niſi prius, Jacob's conveyancer, Blackſtone's commentaries, Sterne's and Pope's works, Goldſmith's Roman hiſtory, Campbell's lives of the Britiſh admirals, Arabian night entertainments, Cheſelden's anatomy, Brown's elements of medicine, Smellie's and Hamilton's midwifery,

ALSO—A general aſſortment of claſſical books, too tedious to enumerate.

Writing and wrapping paper, quills and ſealing wax, of the firſt quality, of a late importation from Holland, ſlates and ſlate pencils, black lead do. teſtaments, ſpelling books, &c.

Bookbinding carried on with neatneſs and diſpatch. Orders from the country will be carefully attended to.

Auguſt 11, 1791. 84—t.f.

This DAY is PUBLISHED.
By T. and J. SWORDS,
No. 27, William-ſtreet—Price 2s.
NUMBER IV, of VOL. III, OF
The New-York Magazine;
OR, *LITERARY REPOSITORY.*
Being for April, 1792.

At a Court of Probates of the State of New-York, held at the Probate Office in the City of New-York, on the eighth Day of May, in the Year of our Lord, One Thouſand Seven Hundred and Ninety-Two.

P R E S E N T,
PETER OGILVIE, *Judge of the ſaid Court.*

WHEREAS Abraham Bloodgood, adminiſtrator of all and ſingular the goods, chattels, and credits, which were of Margret Van Volkenburgh, with her will annexed, late of the city of Albany, deceaſed, hath, by his petition, preſented to the ſaid judge, ſet forth, that the ſaid Margret Van Volkenburgh was, at the time of her death, ſeized of a real eſtate within this ſtate; that the petitioner had made a juſt and true account of the perſonal eſtate and debts of the ſaid Margret Van Volkenburgh, as far as he had been able to diſcover the ſame, and that thereby it appeared, that the perſonal eſtate of the ſaid Margret Van Volkenburgh was inſufficient to pay her debts, & therefore requeſted the aid of the ſaid judge in the premiſes, according to the directions of the act, entitled, "An act for the relief of creditors againſt heirs, deviſees, executors, and adminiſtrators, and for proving wills reſpecting real eſtates;" and the ſaid petitioner hath delivered to the ſaid judge the account in the ſaid petition mentioned: hereupon it is ordered by the ſaid judge, that all perſons intereſted in the eſtate of the ſaid Margret Van Volkenburgh do appear before the ſaid judge of the ſaid court of Probates, at the probate office in the city of New-York, on the third day of July next, to ſhew cauſe, if any they have, why ſo much of the real eſtate, whereof the ſaid Margret Van Volkenburgh died ſeized, ſhould not be ſold, as will be ſufficient to pay her debts.
61—4w.ſ. PETER OGILVIE.

E D U C A T I O N.

THE parents and guardians of youth are reſpectfully informed, that the ſchool for the education of young gentlemen, now kept by the ſubſcriber, at No. 34, Fair-ſtreet, will, on the firſt day of May next, be removed to a commodious and airy room, No. 6, Beekman-ſtreet—In which will be taught reading, writing and arithmetic, the Engliſh language gramatically; together with the elements of the Greek and Latin languages.

They will alſo be taught ſpeaking, in an articulate, eaſy and graceful manner.

He takes this opportunity to return his thanks to his patrons and employers, and hopes by his aſſiduity and attention, in ſome meaſure to promote the intereſt of literature, and merit the approbation and the patronage of the public.

PETER HAWES.

MR. ELY, reſpectfully informs the public, that the ſchool for young ladies, which is now kept at Harmony Hall, No. 8, Gold ſtreet, will, on the firſt day of May next, be removed to No. 6, Beekman-ſtreet, where young ladies will be inſtructed in all the moſt uſeful branches of Engliſh education. Knowing that the continuation of favors depends on the progreſs of his pupils; he aſſures the parents and guardians of youth, that no pains ſhall be wanting on his part, to render his employers full ſatisfaction.

A Morning School will be kept at the above place.

*** The above mentioned ſchools, though taught in the ſame building, will ſtill be kept in ſeparate apartments: Experience having convinced the inſtructors, that the different tempers and diſpoſitions, require a different treatment; and the amuſements and manners of the one, being entirely unbecoming in the other, they eſteem it highly improper for the youth of the different ſexes to be promiſcuouſly taught in the ſame ſchool.

New York, April 17, 1792. 55. w. 4w.

W A R R A N T E D
Starch and Hair Powder,
White and Coloured,

EQUAL in quality to the beſt made in this city, manufactured and ſold, at the *loweſt rate*, by THOMAS GILBERT, in Greenwich ſtreet, immediately back of the Trinity church—for which caſh, Weſt India and country produce will be received in payment, at the current rates.

Merchants, captains of veſſels, and others, can be ſupplied with any quantity, put up in the beſt order, and at a ſhort notice. For the accommodation of thoſe who uſe it, he alſo makes *fine ſcented and pink Hair Powder*, of a delicate hue. He is perſuaded, that thoſe who purchaſe the articles of his manufacture, will be induced to apply again.——To ſuch as have obliged him with their cuſtom, and thoſe who continue to deal with him, he renders ſincere thanks, and hopes to merit a continuance of their attention.

N. B. The uſual credit is allowed.

NOTICE is hereby given to Iſaac Stonehouſe, late of the city of New York, merchant, an abſent debtor, and to all others whom it may concern, that upon application and due proof made to the ſaid juſtice, purſuant to the directions of the act of the legiſlature of the ſaid ſtate, entitled, "An act for relief againſt abſconding and abſent debtors," paſſed the 4th day of April, 1786; he hath iſſued his warrant to the ſheriff of the city and county of New-York, commanding him to attach, ſeize, take, and ſafely keep all the eſtate, as well real as perſonal, of the ſaid Iſaac Stonehouſe, an abſent debtor, of what kind or nature ſoever, and every or any part or parcel thereof, in whatever part of his bailiwick the ſame may be found, with all evidences, books of accounts, vouchers, and papers relating thereto; and unleſs the ſaid Iſaac Stonehouſe ſhall return and diſcharge his debts within one year from the date hereof, all the eſtate real and perſonal of the ſaid Iſaac Stonehouſe, ſo ſeized, attached, and taken, will be ſold for the payment and ſatisfaction of his creditors.

Dated the 24th of Aug. 1791. 87 1aw.w.1y

WHEREAS Angus Campbell, late of the city and province, now ſtate, of New-York, merchant, on the twenty fourth day of June, in the year of our Lord one thouſand ſeven hundred and ſixty ſeven, for ſecuring the payment of two hundred and thirteen pounds, five ſhillings, current money of New-York, with lawful intereſt for the ſame, on or before the thirteenth day of May then next enſuing the date thereof, did mortgage unto the ſubſcribers, and unto William Malcom and David Shaw, ſince deceaſed, their heirs and aſſigns, all thoſe certain tracts or parcels of land, which were conveyed and confirmed unto him the ſaid Angus Campbell, by certain indenture of leaſe and re-leaſe, under the hands and ſeals of Duncan Read, Peter Middleton, Archibald Campbell, Alexander M'Nachten, and Neal Gilleſpie, and is ſituate lying and being in the town of Argyle, in the county of Waſhington, in the ſtate of New-York, and is diſtinguiſhed by No. 126 of the town lots, bounded as follows, *to wit*, beginning at the north ſide of the ſtreet, at an aſh ſapling, marked 126 and 127; then runs eaſt ſix chains and eighty-ſix links, to a large hemlock tree, marked 125 and 126; then north forty-three chains and ſeventy-three links, to a ſtake, eaſt fifteen links from a beach ſapling, marked 125 and 126; then weſt ſix chains and eighty-ſix links, to a ſtake north-eaſt, eight links from a beach ſapling, marked 126 and 127; then ſouth to where it began, containing thirty acres ſtrict meaſure; and alſo all that farm in the ſaid town of Argyle, diſtinguiſhed by No. 126 of the farms thereof, bounded as follows, *to wit*, beginning at its corner with No. 125, then runs ſouth ſeventy one chains, to a ſtake, weſt by north ten links from a ſmall beach ſapling, marked 126 and 130; then weſt forty chains and twenty links, to a ſtake; weſt twenty two links, from a large aſh tree, marked 126 and 129; then north ſeventy one chains, to a ſtake; weſt ſeven links, from a ſmall beach ſapling, marked 126 and 127; then eaſt to where it began; containing two hundred and eighty five acres, including the uſual allowance for highways; together with all and ſingular the privileges, hereditaments, and appurtenances to the ſame premiſes belonging, or in any wiſe appertaining; and whereas, by the ſaid mortgage, full power and authority are granted to the ſubſcribers, and the ſaid William Malcom and David Shaw, to ſell the ſaid premiſes, in caſe default ſhould be made in the payment of the ſaid ſum of two hundred and thirteen pounds, five ſhillings, with the intereſt, on the day limited for the payment thereof; and whereas the ſaid ſum of two hundred and thirteen pounds, with a conſiderable arrearage of intereſt, now remains due to the ſubſcribers; Now, therefore, NOTICE is hereby given, that, purſuant to the aforeſaid power and authority, and the ſtatute in ſuch caſe made and provided, all and ſingular the ſaid mortgaged premiſes will be ſold, on Monday the twenty ſecond day of October next, enſuing the date hereof, at eleven o'clock in the forenoon of the ſame day, at the merchants coffee-houſe, in the city of New-York, at Public Auction, to the higheſt bidder, for the payment and ſatisfaction of the ſaid principal ſum of two hundred and thirteen pounds, and of the intereſt thereupon due, and to become due. The terms of ſale will be made known at the time of ſale, and deeds of conveyance executed by the ſubſcribers, purſuant to the ſaid power and authority to the purchaſer of the ſaid mortgaged premiſes—dated this twelfth day of March, one thouſand ſeven hundred and ninety-two. 55 w.6m.

JAMES BARRON, *Adminiſtrator to the Eſtate of* WILLIAM MALCOM.
ISAAC ROSEVELT, *Executor for the Eſtate of* JAMES ROSEVELT, *deceaſed.*
WALTER and THOMAS BUCHANAN,
ARCHIBALD CURRIE.
WALTER BUCHANAN, *Attorney for* DAVID SHAW, *by virtue of a bill of Sale.*

To COVER,
The enſuing Seaſon, at John H. Smith's, in Fluſhing, Queens County, that beautiful, well made, bright bay HORSE,

GRAND SACHEM.

THE Grand Sachem comes four years old this ſeaſon, was got by that famous horſe the Figure, and the Figure by the noted imported horſe Old Figure. The Grand Sachem's dam was got by the full blooded horſe Othello, and his grand dam by that well known horſe the Lath; he is fifteen hands and three quarters high, a moſt elegant figure, a horſe of great action and ſpirit, and deemed as likely a horſe to get ſtock, either for ſaddle or harneſs, as any horſe in the United States.

He is fixed to cover at ſixteen ſhillings the ſingle leap, thirty ſhillings the ſeaſon, or fifty ſhillings to enſure a foal.

Fluſhing, March 26, 1792. 49-2aw.3m.

To be SOLD, *or* LEASED,
For the Term of 21 *Years, and the Buildings to be valued,*

FOUR Lots of Ground, each containing 25 feet front and rear, and upwards of 100 feet long; one of which is ſituated in St. James's ſtreet, the other three in Queen ſtreet, two of which are adjoining each other.—ALSO,

That pleaſant ſituated FARM, in New Town, on Long Iſland, lying about two miles from the head of New Town Creek, containing 90 acres of good LAND, of which there is a good proportion of freſh meadow; a fine orchard of the beſt grafted fruit trees; a good dwelling houſe, with three fire places; barns, &c. a well of excellent water near the houſe, with the ſtock and farming utenſils. Terms of payment of the ſame will be made known by applying to Mr. JAMES BONNEY, on the premiſes, or to JOHN WOODS, attorney at law, No. 185, Queen-ſtreet. And for the four lots of ground to ſaid JOHN WOODS.

—LETTERS of INTELLIGENCE, occaſional PARAGRAPHS, ſpeculative PIECES, ESSAYS, &c. are gratefully received at this OFFICE—For the greater CONVENIENCE and SAFETY of which COMMUNICATIONS, a LETTER-BOX is placed in the Window.
☞ SUBSCRIPTIONS for this PAPER (printed TWICE a Week, at *Three Dollars* per Annum) are alſo received here—and ADVERTISEMENTS, REASONABLY INSERTED.
——*** PRINTING, in all its Variety, performed with NEATNESS and DISPATCH.——

NEW YORK CITY - 1792
PROMINENT JEWISH BOOKSELLER
The New York Journal & Patriot Register,
p. 4 (col 3)
May 15, 1792

Benjamin Gomez (b. 1769; d. 1828) was the great-grandson of Lewis Moses Gomez (see page 25).

While historians identify Benjamin Gomez as New York City's first *Jewish* bookseller, Gomez showed no hesitation in being ecumenical in his products. The first items announced in his advertisement are "[Christian] school bibles and Church prayer books," including Philip Doddridge, DD's spiritual guide, *The Rise and Progress of Religion in the Soul.* In addition to titles such as these, Gomez's store on Maiden Lane carried "a general assortment of classical books too tedious to enumerate" as well as sundry stationary products.

BENJAMIN GOMEZ,

At his Book and Stationary Store, No. 32, Maiden-Lane,

HAS FOR SALE—*A General Affortment of*

BOOKS *and* STATIONARY,

Among which are—

QUARTO and fchool bibles, church prayer books, Fordyce's, Evan's, Blair's, and Swift's fermons, Brown's journal, Doddrige's rife and progrefs, conductor generalis, Clerk's vade mecum, Buller's nifi prius, Jacob's conveyancer, Blackftone's commentaries, Sterne's and Pope's works, Goldfmith's Roman hiftory, Campbell's lives of the Britifh admirals, Arabian night enter. tainments, Chefelden's anatomy, Brown's elements of medicine, Smellie's and Hamilton's midwifery,

ALSO—A general affortment of claffical books, too tedious to enumerate.

Writing and wrapping paper, quills and fealing wax, of the firft quality, of a late importation from Holland, flates and flate pencils, black lead do. teftaments, fpelling books, &c.

Bookbinding carried on with neatnefs and difpatch. Orders from the country will be carefully attended to.

Auguft 11, 1791.   84—t.f.

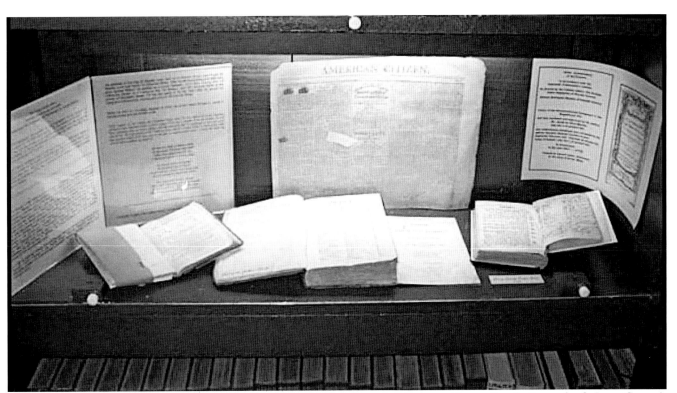

The Gomez Collection: From Right to Left open on the shelf in the Nan Boas Library — Gomez Family Prayer book, Isaac Gomez's "Selection of a Father," and David Levi's "Answer to Dr. Joseph Priestley's Letter to The Jews..." (published by Benjamin Gomez). In the background is a history of Benjamin and a newspaper front page with a copy of his store advertisement on Maiden Lane in NYC. Courtesy of the Gomez Foundation for Mill House.

PHILADELPHIA – 1802
HEBREW MANUSCRIPT
Gazette of the United States,
p. 2 (cols 2–3)
July 7, 1802

Solomon Simson (b. New York City, 1738; d. New York City, 1801) was the second son of Joseph Simson (b. London, 1686; d. New York City, 1787). The senior Simson, a freeman of New York, was actively involved with Congregation Shearith Israel, whose presidency he held for several terms. He also was learned in Hebrew and carried on a correspondence with a Dr. B. Kennicott of Oxford and Dr. Myles Cooper, president of Kings (later known as Columbia) College.

In this article, Solomon Simson describes the odyssey of a work, "A Hebrew Manuscript of the Jewish Scriptures," which was referred to as volume 144 in the 700-volume library collection of Columbia College. Originally, this volume was brought from Turkey to England where it was acquired by Joseph Simson. The son, Solomon Simson, describes the layout and typography of the text. For example, "The songs of Moses, Deborah, and David are poetical, written with the greatest uniformity and neatness, with black shining ink...The 119th Psalm is written in two columns of four lines each, each eight verses beginning with the *aleph,* the next eight with the *beth,* and proceeding through the alphabet in that order."

Following Simson's description of the work are letters between Simson and Drs. Kennicott and Cooper, dated 1770 to 1772, regarding Dr. Kennicott's request for, receipt, acknowledgement and return of the book which Simson lent to Oxford for a year. Dr. Cooper served as the intermediary for its transfer to England.

AN ACCOUNT OF A
HEBREW MANUSCIPT COPY,
OF THE
JEWISH SCRIPTURES,
NOW IN NEW-YORK:

In a Letter from Mr. Solomon Simson, the Proprietor, to Dr. Mitchell, dated March 26, 1802.

SIR,

"The old Manuscript Bible in my possession, of which you have desired some information, was brought from Turkey to England by a gentleman who left his library to a relation of his in this country, and from the latter my aged father purchased it with some other books. It is written in a character something resembling Rosha, or rather, it is to be presumed that Rosha borrowed or copied his from it. It is very different from the square character we have in use, and is about the size of a large octavo written in two columns, on parchment, or vellum, as fine as silk. The songs of Moses, Deborah, and David, are poetical, written with the greatest uniformity and neatness, with black shining ink. It is also accompanied with marginal notes, written, so fine and small that it requires good eyes, or glasses, to distinguish them. The Psalms appear to be a most masterly performance, and the diversity of the measure seems pleasingly to strike the eye, even of those who are unacquainted with the language, and is supposed to be the original poetry in which they were written by David, &c. There appears a great play of words and letters, ... beginning with the alphabet; and in order going through the same, with many variations. The 119th Psalm is written in two columns, of four lines each, each eight verses begining with the *aleph,* the next eight with the *beth,* and proceeding through the alphabet in that order, which is probably the reason of its being marked, in our English Bible with *aleph, beth,* &c.

"The two first chapters, and part of the last, in the book of Job, are written in prose in two columns. The other part of the book is in short Hemistich verse, beautifully written, and the whole handsomely pointed. The accents appear to be the same as in our printed books, except the ten commandments, which are only with single accents.

"In Joshua, chap. xxi. between the verses 35 and 36, two verses are inserted, with the names of four cities of refuge, of the tribe of Reuben, &c. which are not in our Hebrew or English Bibles: and Everardo Van der Hooght, in his edition, printed in Amsterdam, in 1705, mentions, in his preface, that these two verses are only to be found in three old, corrected manuscript books, but which he supposes to be an error. The order of the books in the manuscript is as follows:

"The Law, in five books.
"Joshua, Judges, and Samuel, each in one.
"Kings in one, without any division.
"Isaiah, Jeremiah, Ezekiel, Hosea, Joel, Amos, Obadiah, Jonah, Micah, Nahum, Habakkuk, Zephaniah, Haggai, Zechariah, Malachi, Ruth, Psalms, Job, Proverbs, Ecclesiastes, Song of Songs, Lamentations, Daniel, Ezra, Nehemiah, Esther, and Chronicles, each in one.

"The late Myles Cooper, L. L. D. President of King's College, delivered my father, Joseph Simpson, the following letter, with the book therein mentioned.

"Sir,

"I have been informed by Dr. Cooper, that you benevolently intend to lend me your curious Hebrew M. S. and when you have so done,

I shall celebrate, in the most grateful manner, your public spirit and generosity. I will take the utmost care of it, and it shall be returned in twelve months, to the person in London you appoint to receive it; and for this I will give a note of hand, or (if you require it) a bond of obligation. You will receive of Dr. Cooper the present of a book of mine, in which I have published your kind intention; and I hope you will accept that book as a mark of the gratitude of, Sir,

'Your highly obliged, and
'Very obedient servant.
B. KENNICOTT.
'Oxford, March 4, 1770.'

"In May following my father received the following note:

"Mr. Cooper's compliments to Mr. Simson, returns him Dr. Kennicott's letter, which he did not send for yesterday, but only for his own, and hopes that Mr. Simpson's determination on the point in question, viz. the transmission of the M. S. to England, is favourable to the grand scheme of collation, which the learned gentleman has now in hand.

"King's College, May 8, 1770."

"The June following the manuscript was delivered to Dr. Cooper, with the following letter:

'Sir,

'In obedience to my father's commands which gives me particular pleasure, I now answer your esteemed letter, by the hands of Mr. President Cooper; and though the M. S. is highly valued, it is cheerfully lent to promote the great work you have undertaken. The President has engaged to return it safe in one year. Permit me to mention, that in the book you have favoured my father with, instead of his name (Joseph), mine has been inserted, which, no doubt, will be rectified. My good father commands his respects and best wishes with mine, that you may be blest with health to go through the arduous work you have in hand—that it may be completed with the strictest regard to truth, to your honour, and the good of mankind.

'I am, with respect, Reverend Sir,

'Your most obedient humble servant.
'SAMPSON SIMPSON

'Rev. B. Kennicott.'

"In 1772 Dr. Cooper returned the M. S. with the following letter:

'Sir,

'I beg you to accept of my best thanks for the use of your valuable Hebrew M. S. which I am very glad of returning to you so safely as by the hands of Dr. Cooper. I shall take care publicly to express my gratitude* for this act of your kindness.

'And am, sir, your highly obliged & ob't svt.
'B. KENNICOTT.
'Oxford, May 11, 1772.'

"There does not appear any certainty when this Hebrew M. S. was written. Gentlemen learned in the Hebrew language have differed greatly in there opinion—from 700 to 1700 years ago. Some have gone so far as to suppose it to have been written by Ezra the scribe; but all agree that it is ...

I am, sir, with due respect,
your most humble servant,
"SOLOMON SIMSON."

*"Mr. Simson's manuscript is mentioned in the second volume of Kennicott's Bible in folio, of which there is a copy in the library of Columbia College. In the catalogue of the seven hundred which he consulted, this is the 144th, and is distinguished by the words, "Americ. Neo-Ebor." It is conjectured by him, to have been written between the years 1300 and 1400 of the christian æra."

THE SALEM GAZETTE.

Published on TUESDAYS and FRIDAYS, by THOMAS C. CUSHING, Essex-Street, SALEM.

VOL. XVIII—1350.]   FRIDAY, AUGUST 3, 1804.   [Price THREE per DOLLARS Annum.

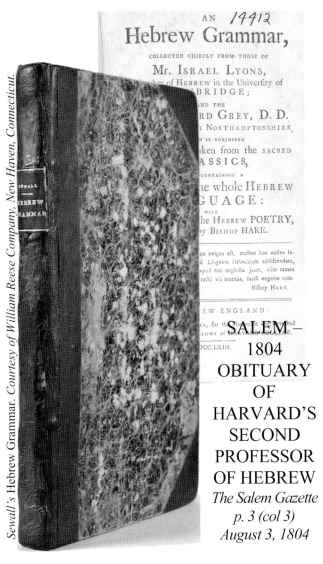

Sewall's Hebrew Grammar. Courtesy of William Reese Company, New Haven, Connecticut.

AN *14912*

Hebrew Grammar,

COLLECTED CHIEFLY FROM THOSE OF

Mr. ISRAEL LYONS,
...er of HEBREW in the Univerfity of
...BRIDGE;

...AND THE

...RD GREY, D. D.
...: NORTHAMPTONSHIRE,

... IS SUBJOINED

...ken from the SACRED
...ASSICS,

...CONTAINING A

...he whole HEBREW
...GUAGE:

...WITH

...he HEBREW POETRY,
...y BISHOP HARE.

...on exigua eft, multos hoc noftro la-
...d Linguam Hebraïcam addifcendam,
...apud nos neglecta jacet, cùm tamen
...recta via incedas, facili negotio com-
Bifhop HARE.

...EW·ENGLAND:

...r, for the ...
...LLOWS of ...

...DCC.LXIII.

SALEM–1804 OBITUARY OF HARVARD'S SECOND PROFESSOR OF HEBREW

*The Salem Gazette
p. 3 (col 3)
August 3, 1804*

.........DEATHS.........

At Cambridge, on Monday the 23d ult. after a very long and gradual decay, Stephen Sewall, Efq. formerly Hancock Profeffor of Hebrew, and other Oriental Languages. He was born at York, in the Diftrict of Maine, in April 1734—his circumftances being narrow, he was firft taught the trade of a joiner, by which he acquired the means to purfue his claffical inquiries. At the age of 24 he was admitted a ftudent in the Univerfity of Cambridge, and purfued his literary courfe with unabating ardor.— After graduating in 1761, he remained a refident graduate, and fupported himfelf by teaching the grammar fchool in Cambridge. The place of Hebrew Inftructor became vacant about that time by the refignation of Mr. Munis. An American who had acquired a fufficient knowledge of Hebrew to be qualified for an Inftructor, was a phenomenon at that time feldom feen. Mr. Munis was a Jew of Algiers. To the difadvantage common to all foreigners, there was added a peculiar unhappinefs in teaching. This had funk the reputation of Hebrew into a ftate of contempt. Mr. Sewall undertook the tafk of recovering it. His reputation rofe with that of his department, and when the late Mr. Hancock founded a profefforfhip for the Hebrew and other oriental languages, Mr. Sewall was the unrivalled candidate. He continued in this office above twenty years. His lectures were models of Englifh compofition, and the fuavity of his difpofition infured him the efteem of his pupils. Once only was he married. His wife was daughter of the firft Dr. Wiggelfworth, and died a year or two before he loft his profefforfhip. After that event, he led a very retired life. He was early in the revolution, and continued a warm friend to it. In 1777, before republicanifm had gone out of fafhion among the learned he was honoured with a feat in the Houfe of Reprefentatives, by the election of the town of Cambridge. To an elegant tafte in compofition, of which fpecimens in feveral languages have been publifhed, he added a modefty not only unaffuming but perhaps in fome cafes exceffive. He died in his 71ft year. His only child died in infancy.   *Reg*

In this town, widow Sarah Aborn

This issue reports the death of Stephen Sewall (b. 1734; d. 1804), an American-born Christian who became the second Professor of Hebrew at the "University of Cambridge" (Harvard), following the resignation of "Mr. Munis" (i.e., Judah Monis, see page 148). Sewall's obituary was especially impressed with the erudition in Hebrew of the Cambridge educated, Sewall: "An American who had acquired a sufficient knowledge of Hebrew to be qualified for an Instructor was a phenomenon at that time seldom seen." Sewall, who wrote a Hebrew Grammar, had a more extensive and impressive knowledge of Hebrew than did Monis considering Monis was born a Jew.

The obituary also notes that the reputation of Hebrew had sunk "into a state of contempt" and that Sewall "undertook the task of recovering it."

TO THE PATRONIZERS OF MY EDITION
OF
VANDER HOOGHT'S HEBREW BIBLE.
BE IT KNOWN, that an edition of the same work, advertised in the New-York Commercial Advertiser, by Messrs. Whiting & Watson, has no connection with the edition I am now about publishing. I therefore beg my indulgent patrons not to confound them. And humbly supplicate the further patronage of all those that are interested in the undertaking ; as it has been a considerable expence to me in travelling through New-England, with a view of obtaining subscribers ;— and where I may say, with pleasure, I have received the patronage of both Harvard College and Andover Theological Institution, who each subscribed for 40 copies. At the same time, I will be obliged to all those who hold subscription papers, to send them in as soon as possible, as the work is going on.

J. HORWITZ.

Jan. 16   3t

נביאים וכתובים

BIBLIA HEB[RAICA]

SECUNDUM ULTIMAM EDIT[IONEM]
IOS. ATHIAE,
A
JOHANNE LEUS[DEN]
DENUO RECOGNITAM,
RECENSITA VARIISQUE NOTIS LAT[INIS]
AB
EVERARDO VAN DER [HOOGHT]
V. D. M.

EDITIO PRIMA AMERICANA, SINE PUNCTIS MASORETHICIS.

TOM. II.

PHILADELPHIÆ:
CURA ET IMPENSIS THOMÆ DOBSON EDITA EX ÆDIBUS LAPIDEIS.
TYPIS GULIELMI FRY.
MDCCCXIV.

NEW YORK – 1813
FIRST HEBREW BIBLE IN U.S.
New York Evening Post, p. 3 (col 1)
January 18. 1813

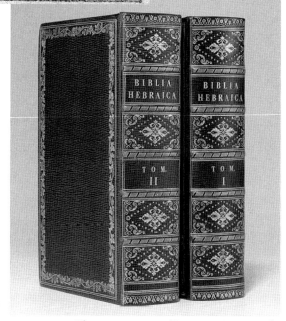

Photos courtesy of Bauman Rare Books

The first Hebrew Bible published in the United States (1814) was a reprinting of the second edition of the Joseph Athias *Biblia Hebraica,* with introduction and Latin notes by Evarado Van der Hooght, that was published in Amsterdam in 1667. In this advertisement, Jonathan Horwitz, who had proposed this as yet unpublished edition after arriving in from Amsterdam with a font of Hebrew type, notified the public that a rival edition to be published by Messrs. Whiting and Watson had no connection with his edition. Horwitz "humbly supplicates" the public not to purchase the competing edition. Furthermore, he proudly noted that both Harvard College and the Andover Theological Institution had each placed orders for 40 copies of his future edition.

Not long after posting this notice, Horwitz succumbed to the competition from Whiting & Watson and others. He sold the publishing rights and list of subscribers to Thomas Dobson and his Hebrew type to William Fry. Horwitz soon afterwards went to medical school and became an M.D., and Dobson's edition of the Bible, printed by Fry, was published in 1814. The title page and bound volume are pictured above.

PENNSYLVANIA INSTITUTION
FOR THE DEAF AND DUMB.

THE undersigned having been appointed the Committee of Admission for this Institution, inform the Public, that the Directors have fitted up and furnished a large and commodious building, situate on the south side of High street, between Schuylkill Sixth and Seventh streets, for the present residence of Pupils entrusted to their care; the house is capable of accommodating sixty Pupils.

A Matron has been selected to superintend the domestic duties of the establishment, in whose tenderness and ability the Board have great confidence.

A committee of twelve highly respectable Ladies, is associated with the Directors, to aid in the domestic arrangements of the Institution, whose zeal and assiduity will be directed to contribute to the comfort and regularity of the family, and by whom the utmost attention will be exercised to inculcate decorous and exemplary habits.

Two regular Physicians are appointed to afford medical services to the family.

The instruction of the pupils is confided to Mr. David G. Seixas, a gentleman whose talents and acquirements for this province are well ascertained by the board, and are evinced by the rapid improvement of the Scholars.

The family consists of eighteen pupils, fourteen of whom are gratuitously maintained and educated by the Institution—the Directors lament that the state of their finances, does not at present warrant the admission of a greater number of this description; they however confidently trust, the liberality of the public will soon enable them to afford the benefit of education to all their unfortunate fellow beings, whose desolate condition is aggravated by being the victims of Poverty. Surely none who have the means of contributing to ameliorate the moral condition of the Deaf and Dumb, will withhold aid to this infant Institution.

Applications for the admission of a sufficient number of Pupils to form a new class, the instruction of which, will commence on the 1st April, 1821, will be received by the committee, who will reply to such communications. It is desirable the applications should be made early, in order to afford sufficient time for the necessary arrangements; they should state the name, age, and sex of the proposed pupil.

The terms for the Instruction, Boarding, Lodging and Washing of each Pupil, are one hundred and sixty dollars per annum, one half of which is payable in advance.

The committee also solicit communications, stating the name, age, sex and residence, of Deaf and Dumb persons in indigent circumstances, as it is the wish of the Directors to admit an additional number of such pupils, as soon as an increase of funds will justify them so to do.

Subscriptions and donations will be received by JOHN BACON, City Treasurer, at the corner of Chesnut and Fifth streets.

(Signed,)

Jacob Gratz,
No. 2 South Seventh street.
William Price,
No. 225 Market street.
Samuel Canby,
No. 56 South Wharves.
Franklin Bache,
No. 163 Spruce street.
Samuel R. Wood,
No. 73 south Fifth street.

Editors of newspapers in this and the adjacent states, are solicited to give the above notice a few insertions.   dec 22   oc

PHILADELPHIA – 1820
INSTITUTE FOR THE DEAF AND DUMB
Poulson's American Daily Advertiser, p. 4 (col 3)
December 30, 1820

The Pennsylvania Institution for the Deaf and Dumb, in a back-page announcement that covers most of the fourth column, informs the public of its opening and invites applications for its eighteen available places. Twelve "highly respectable ladies" will serve in the "commodious" facility, and two physicians will be on call. David G. Seixas (b. 1788; d. 1864) will direct instruction for the "scholars." Seixas was the eldest of the twelve children of Rev. Gershom Mendes Seixas, minister of Congregation Shearith Israel in New York, whose loyalty to the young republic earned him the title "the patriot rabbi" (see page 28).

Jacob Gratz (b. 1788; d. 1836), of the prominent Philadelphia Jewish family, is the first name listed in the list of the institution's five directors.

8　　　　　　　　NEW YORK HERALD, FRIDAY, JUNE 16, 1865.

Dedication of a Hebrew Free School.

The first Hebrew free school ever established in this city was dedicated yesterday afternoon, with imposing ceremonies, at the new edifice which has been selected by the committee, No. 36 avenue C, near Fourth street. Mr. M. S. Cohen, the President of the association, under whose auspices the school has been established, presided, and a large number of prominent Israelites, patrons of the new institution, were present, among whom we noticed the following:—Dr. Raphall, S. M. Isaacs, J. Kramer, Mr. Sternberger, J. J. Lyons, Rev. Wm. Hoffman, and the presidents and trustees of several Hebrew congregations.

The exercises consisted of the performance of the Mincha service, by Rev. Dr. Hoffman; singing of a German hymn by the choir, after which prayer was offered by Rev. Dr. Raphall.

The chairman of the Building Committee then delivered up the keys of the school house to the President, after which that officer delivered a lengthy address, explaining the object of establishing such schools—the benefit of the children of Jewish parents in this country. He said that several educational institutions had at various times been started by individual congregations for their own members, or those who could afford to pay for tuition, and some few who were unable to pay were admitted gratis; but each of them had failed to receive that support which institutions of this kind require. Either from hostility to the institution or some misunderstanding among the teachers, or other causes, they had to be abandoned. But since then sufficient circumstances have transpired to convince the community that institutions of this particular kind are wanting for the proper training of the rising generation of Israelites, whose education has been neglected in many respects; some by inability to pay and others by an oversight that such institutions were not known among the Hebrews of this part of the world. A short time ago they were awakened from their lethargy, on finding that their children were receiving instruction in their own beautiful and native language from apostates from their own faith, and unbelievers in their doctrines, under the plea of ameliorating their condition, and trying under the garb of charity to poison the young minds of their children, in order to seduce them from their true God. This it was which aroused several of the presidents of the various congregations and called for their action in this matter. After mature deliberation they formed this association for the establishment of Hebrew free schools, as well as for the various branches of English, and other useful studies, as taught in the common free schools of this city, in order that those who come here from those schools to acquire their Hebrew studies may not lose what they have learned, but, on the contrary, advance; and those who commence here, when they leave, can continue their studies in the common schools, so that a uniform course of tuition is pursued; for in that no improvement can be made, as its system is perfect, and has been tried and even copied in foreign countries. To show the necessity of establishing schools on this principle he cited the fact that in this city alone there are more than fifty thousand Israelites, who have built within a few years twenty magnificent synagogues, hospitals and orphan asylums. He said, in conclusion, I would ask the assistance and co-operation of all the congregations and societies in this city to assist in keeping up and supporting this and similar schools, by using their influence in obtaining subscribers and donations, in order, as soon as possible, to enlarge the sphere of usefulness of this association, by the establishment of more schools, or by adding more talent to enlarge the facilities of studying the modern languages, literature, fine arts or music—in short, anything that may tend to enlighten, polish or adorn the minds of the young, teach them to become good, moral and useful citizens, bright ornaments of society, an honor to our people, and credit to the Hebrew free schools.

The President, after concluding his address, read letters from Comptroller Brennan, City Inspector Boole and Mayor Gunther, expressing their regret at not being able to be present at the dedication, but offering their hearty co-operation in the enterprise. Dr. Bergeman, on behalf of the Mayor, addressed the audience in German, which our reporter, not being versed in that language, was unable to report.

Rev. S. M. Isaacs and Rev. L. Sternberger also delivered addresses, and the exercises were concluded by the choir singing a hymn.

The school will go into operation at once, and the enterprise promises to be a very successful one.

NEW YORK CITY – 1865 "DEDICATION OF HEBREW FREE SCHOOL"
The New York Herald, p. 8 (col 1)
June 16, 1865

A milestone in the growth of New York City's Jewish community was the dedication of its first Hebrew Free School. At the time, the city's Jewish population consisted of some 50,000 members served by twenty congregations and various orphanages and hospitals. The new edifice was located at "No. 36 avenue C, near Fourth street."

The article reported that a "large number of prominent Israelites" were present at the dedication ceremony which began with the afternoon Mincha prayer service, and later featured songs from a choir. In recognition of the presence of significant number of Jews born in Germany, some remarks were delivered in that language. Speakers noted that individual congregations were unable to sustain a school of this advanced caliber. The vulnerability of the Jewish population to Christian missionaries was cited among the factors justifying a more intense Jewish education: "A short time ago they were awakened from their lethargy, on finding that their children were receiving instruction in their own beautiful and native language from apostates from their own faith, and unbelievers in their doctrines, under the plea of ameliorating their condition, and trying under the garb of charity to poison the young minds of their children, in order to seduce them from their true God."

Chapter #4

Jews in Journalism

NEW YORK – 1823
The Jew;
Being a Defence of Judaism Against All
Adversaries, and Particularly Against
the Insidious Attacks of
'ISRAEL'S ADVOCATE'
March, 5583 (1823)

The first Jewish periodical printed in the United States was aimed at discrediting the missionary efforts of the American Society for Meliorating the Condition of the Jews (ASMR). Solomon Henry Jackson (b. England; d. 1847), the first Jewish printer in New York City (see page 105), used both English and Hebrew fonts in *The Jew* in attacking the ASMR and its periodical deceptively known as *Israel's Advocate.*

According to Jackson, "Not to defend our character as a people would be a dereliction of duty." Jackson argued that the reason the ASMR had such poor results in their goal of converting Jews was because their arguments were so weak. In response to these missionary projects, Jackson attacked the theological underpinnings of Christianity challenging the divinity of Jesus and the Christian interpretation of the Hebrew Bible. He drew strength in asserting his beliefs based on the political equality that he claimed he deserved as an American.

Jackson published this periodical on a monthly basis between 1823 and 1825. During that time he also translated the Sephardi version of the daily prayer book into English, and in 1837 he published the first American translation of the Passover Haggadah into English.

THE JEW;

BEING A DEFENCE OF JUDAISM AGAINST ALL ADVERSA-
RIES, AND PARTICULARLY AGAINST THE
INSIDIOUS ATTACKS OF

ISRAEL'S ADVOCATE.

Psalm cix. 127. : עת לעשות לה' הפרו תורתך
ואענה חרפי דבר כי בטהתי בדנרך :

" 'Tis time to work for the Lord; they make void thy Law.
"And I will answer the blasphemers of the word, for I depend on thy words."
Psalm cix.

Vol. I.	*March,* 5583.	*No.* 1.

THE Advocate being three numbers before me, and be-ing confired to one sheet to answer them, I must, without prefatory remarks, proceed to their examination.

In the consideration of " The importance of converting the Jews," the writer* reminds his readers† of the claims they (the Jews) have on their benevolent exertions. He then enumerates: 1st, " The obligations we are under to them;" 2nd, the injuries we have formerly done them; 3d, the very awful apprehensions we are compelled to en-tertain concerning them, while they remain unconverted: 4th, the visible and glorious display of divine power and mercy, in their conversion; 5th, the aspect this great event will have on the salvation of the world at large. The two last, I cannot at present notice at all: and the first three but lightly; weightier matter precluding them from the consideration they perhaps merit.

In regard to the 1st, on the obligations they are under to the Jews, he says, that all their blessings came to them through the instrumentality of Jews. " The first propa-

* A. S. M. C. J., as a body, are considered the writer.   † No. ii.

1

Published (*Daily*) at No. 48 Wall-street,
fifth door below the City Bank,
BY N. PHILLIPS.
The NATIONAL ADVOCATE, (*for the country*)
is published every TUESDAY and
FRIDAY, at $4 per annum,
payable in advance.

NEW YORK – 1824
MASTHEAD
The National Advocate, p. 4 (col 7)
January 7, 1824

Jews were drawn to journalism in the early decades of the nineteenth century. Among the more prominent journalists were three Jews who were also significantly active in Jewish community affairs.

Isaac Harby (b. Charleston, S.C., 1788; d. New York City, 1820), editor of Charleston's *Southern Patriot* and *The Investigator*, was active in Charleston's Congregation Beth Elohim where he advocated increasing the amount of English in the congregation's services.

Naphtali Phillips

Naphtali Phillips (b. New York City, 1773; d. New York City, 1870) was, as shown in the above masthead, publisher (as well as proprietor and editor) of *The National Advocate,* the favorite paper of New York City's anti-Federalists and the political mouthpiece of the "Society of Tammany," the regional political machine of the Democratic-Republicans. He was the first Jew in America to publish a general interest newspaper. He was also the author of a history of New York's Congregation Shearith Israel. Phillips was the son of Jonas Phillips (b. Germany, 1736; d. Philadelphia, 1803), the celebrated American patriot who in 1770 signed the Non-Importation Agreement protesting British taxation and who served as president of Philadelphia's Congregation Mikveh Israel during its consecration year, 1782.

The third Jewish journalist was Phillips' nephew, Mordecai M. Noah, the editor of many newspapers and the most well-known and controversial Jew of his time (see Chapter 8).

NEW YORK – 1828
ENDORSING JACKSON / DENOUNCING ADAMS
New-York Enquirer, p. 1 (col 1) – April 1, 1828

By the time Mordecai Manuel Noah (see Chapter 8) launched *The New-York Enquirer* in July 1826, his grandiose personality had manifested itself in both New York political and Jewish circles. The symbolism of the ark (i.e., Noah's Ark) as an instrument of refuge appeared prominently on the *Enquirer's* masthead. In 1819, Noah published his memoir on his diplomatic assignment as the United States Consul in Tripoli, *Travels in England, France, Spain, and the Barbary States.* He had received an appointment in 1821 as Sheriff of New York City. As a Tammany Hall partisan, he was a declared "Bucktail" enemy of Governor DeWitt Clinton, the head of the other faction of the state's Democratic Party. Journalistically, Noah expressed his clearly partisan views as editor of *The National Advocate,* the newspaper owned by his uncle, Naphtali Phillips.

By early 1829, Noah had drifted into the camp of his previous rivals, the Clintonians, and merged his newspaper, *The New-York Enquirer* with *The New York Morning Courier.* While on good terms at first with James Watson Webb, who managed the newspaper, Noah's friendly feelings eventually abated over his disagreement with the Jacksonians about renewing the charter of the Bank of the United States. But before Noah's falling out with the Jacksonians, his newspaper vigorously campaigned for Old Hickory's election to the presidency in 1828.

In this front-page editorial endorsement of Jackson, Noah attacks the White House incumbent, John Quincy Adams:

We have been sold and betrayed. There is no other language strong enough to describe the political fraud which has brought the aristocracy and tory party into power, or to mark that disgraceful and confirmed bargain which has introduced Adams into the Presidency...

THE NEW-YORK ENQUIRER is published at No. 3 William-street.

TERMS—Daily Paper $10 per ann.; Country Paper Tuesdays and Fridays) $4, payable in advance.

FRIDAY MORNING, MARCH 28.

REPUBLICAN TICKET.

FOR PRESIDENT,
ANDREW JACKSON.

FOR VICE-PRESIDENT,
JOHN C. CALHOUN.

" Hang out your Banners on the Outward Walls."
SHAKSPEARE.

It will be seen, that according to custom, we have placed at the head of our paper, the names of the Democratic candidates for President and Vice-President of the United States. In less than six months this great contest will be ended—that is, it will be placed beyond any cavil or doubt, who is to be the successful man. The time has therefore arrived, to nail the flag to the mast, and, confiding in the justice of our cause, to adopt such measures as will lead to victory and success in the state of New-York ; for, we repeat it, in this state, the battle will rage the fiercest ; the enemy has abandoned Pennsylvania and Virginia, and concentrates his force in New-York.

We have been sold and betrayed. There is no other language strong enough to describe the political fraud which has brought the aristocracy and tory party into power, or to mark that disgraceful and confirmed bargain which has introduced Adams into the Presidency, and Clay into the State Department.

It were a waste of time to go over the particulars of this foul transaction—the people know them ; they feel their effect, and will resent this traffic of their rights at the next election.

Mr. Adams was educated and schooled in the belief of ultra federal doctrines. A strong national and consolidated government. A President and Senate for life, and hereditary succession—doctrines which have been confirmed during his long residence in foreign Courts. The attempt is now making to revive that very aristocracy and hereditary succession which the people triumphantly prostrated in 1800. A few misguided republicans have joined the Adams flag, who are as yet ignorant of the ultimate views of that confederacy. The time has arrived for the Republicans of 98 to unite and rally—to lay aside all local views and conflicting opinions, and save the country. The nation is at present in one feverish state of excitement. We are neither respected abroad, nor are we tranquil and prosperous at home. Every measure that can sustain a desperate and tottering administration, is resorted to without reference to consequences. The patronage belonging to the people, is use to aid the Cabinet, and the subsidized presses are filled with slanderous attacks on the best men of the nation.

The people, in the majesty of their strength, have nominated as *their* candidate, a man of tried patriotism, stern integrity, sound sense, and impayable public services. A man of honesty and firmness, who, in the darkest hour, led our armies to victory, and has, in every respect, "filled the measure of his country's glory." Associated with general Andrew Jackson, is the actual Vice President of the United States, Mr. Calhoun, in whose talents and public experience and patriotic attachment to the true interest of the country, we have the surest guarantee. With such men the republic will be safe, the rights of the States supported, the cardinal interests of the nation protected, the old republican party revived, and the power of the people perpetuated.

Sanguine as we are of the Jackson ticket in this State, we must not sleep on our arms, while a desperate faction is abroad. We must be up and doing—organize our town and country committees, keep up an active correspondence, prepare for the convention and fall election, act with energy, prudence and industry, and we shall be ready to take the field like men who know how to conquer.

John Quincy Adams

Andrew Jackson

.... Sanguine as we are of the Jackson ticket in this State, we must not sleep on our arms, while a desperate faction is abroad. We must be up and doing – organize our town and country committees, keep up an active correspondence, prepare for the convention and fall election, act with energy, prudence and industry, and we shall be ready to take the field like men who know how to conquer.

Having backed the winning candidate, Noah was appointed Surveyor and Inspector of the Port of New York. In 1832, Jackson was re-elected with New York's Martin Van Buren as his vice president. By this time, however, Noah had switched his allegiance to the Whig Party, choosing in 1840 to back William Henry Harrison rather than Van Buren, who in many ways had been his political mentor in New York.

The Beginnings of American Jewish Journalism

PHILADELPHIA – 1843
The Occident, and American Jewish Advocate.

When Isaac Leeser (b. Germany, 1806; d. 1868), a pioneering Philadelphia rabbi, launched *The Occident, and American Jewish Advocate: A Monthly Periodical* in April 1843, not only did he start this nation's first successful Jewish periodical, he also brought a sense of belonging and community to an emerging American Jewry. An earlier publication, *The Jew*, published from 1823 to 1825, was mainly a polemical response to a missionary publication and therefore not considered a true periodical.

During *The Occident's* quarter century life span, from 1843 to 1868, America's Jewish population grew almost nine-fold – from 20,000 to 175,000 – while the national population doubled from 17,000,000 to 35,000,000.

Leeser received his Jewish education in Germany. He arrived in the United States at age eighteen. After assisting Rabbi Isaac B. Seixas in Richmond, Virginia, he moved to Philadelphia's Congregation Mikveh Israel where he served for some forty years. About 1,500 Jews lived in Philadelphia at that time. Leeser was considered America's most important Jewish spiritual voice in the mid nineteenth century. According to Abraham J. Karp, *(From the Ends of the Earth: Jewish Treasure in the Library of Congress, 1991)*, "[Leeser] was the most prolific American Jewish writer and the most creative Jewish communal architect."

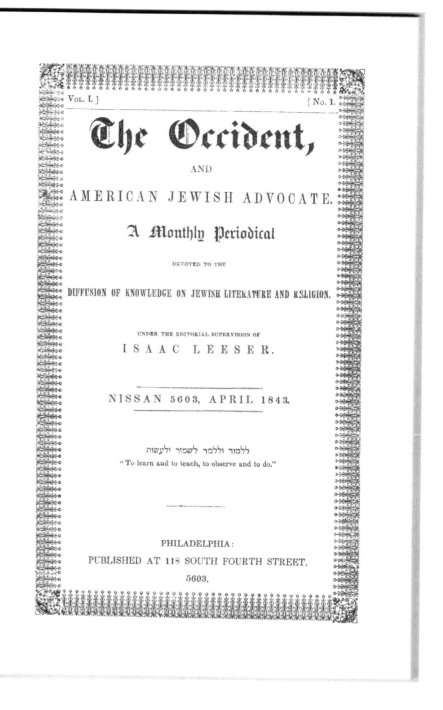

VOL. I.] [No. 1.

The Occident,

AND

AMERICAN JEWISH ADVOCATE.

A Monthly Periodical

DEVOTED TO THE

DIFFUSION OF KNOWLEDGE ON JEWISH LITERATURE AND RELIGION.

UNDER THE EDITORIAL SUPERVISION OF

ISAAC LEESER.

NISSAN 5603, APRIL 1843.

ללמור וללמר לשמור ולעשות

"To learn and to teach, to observe and to do."

PHILADELPHIA:
PUBLISHED AT 118 SOUTH FOURTH STREET.
5603.

In addition to his congregational responsibilities, Leeser wrote philosophical studies, translated the Bible and the prayer services, and edited (occasionally doing the typesetting himself) some 300 issues of *The Occident*. He was instrumental in founding the Hebrew Education Society in 1848 and Maimonides College, America's first, but short lived, Jewish theological seminary, in 1867, and he laid the groundwork for this nation's first representative body of American Jewry, the Board of Delegates of American Israelites.

(continued)

Among the main editorial themes advanced by Leeser was the moral rectitude of Judaism, the strength of Jewish family life, defenses of traditional or Orthodox Judaism as opposed to the incipient movement of Reform Judaism, and a policy of respectful noninterference with Christianity. Leeser strongly advocated the retention of Hebrew in synagogue worship. *The Occident* regularly reprinted sermons (many of them Leeser's), educational articles about the Sabbath and Jewish holidays, news about the burgeoning American Jewish community, reports from benevolent societies and Sunday schools, obituaries, and news about Jewish events from abroad, especially about Palestine.

Representative of this treasure trove of American Jewish theology, history and identity are items from four of *The Occident's* twenty five years:

In 1849 – Leeser focused on identity conflicts facing American Jews. On the one hand, he wrote, Jews are delighted at the prospects of religious freedom in the young republic: "For centuries maltreated and spit upon, they are overjoyed now at seeing a possible end to their spiritual warfare, they were delighted as one who finds an unexpected treasure at the opening prospect of civil equality" (p. 3). Yet, in an essay titled "The United States Not a Christian State," Leeser warned that on the other hand, "The proposition we always thought was so evident, that we could not help wondering, and our astonishment is not lessened at this day, that people should even dare to call this a Christian country, and speak of the population as a Christian people" (p. 563).

Mrs. N. Hyneman penned poetic tributes to four Jewish heroines – Jochebed, Deborah, Huldah and Hannah. Literary pieces explored Jewish poetry and reviewed newly authored works. News articles reported on congregational activities, the work of Hebrew benevolent societies, and relief efforts for Palestinian Jews. In addition to sermons from various American rabbis, the periodical published the sermon delivered by Rabbi Abraham De Sola at London's Spanish and Portuguese Synagogue giving thanks on the ending of the "grievous disease" that had afflicted so many English inhabitants.

In 1853 – Several articles, including "On the Value of the Study of Talmud," argued for the validity of Orthodox Judaism. "Palestine and its Prospects" promoted the settlement of Palestine, comparing the Jewish claim to the Holy Land with the allegedly weaker Christian case. Other articles warned about the lurking danger of Christian missionaries; indeed, a speech by the twelve-year-old Leon Cohen is noted on the need to protect Jews in China from Christian conversion schemes (p. 81). A lengthy obituary of Judah Touro (b. 1775; d. 1854), among the nation's most philanthropic Jews of the early eighteenth century, was published. This 600-page annual volume also carried about 100 news items describing Jewish communities both in the United States and abroad.

In 1856 – Reflecting on the steady growth of American Judaism, *The Occident* proudly listed various communities coast to coast, and counted a total of 118 synagogues nationally. Yet, noted Leeser, painful spiritual questions remained, "Why do the Jews suffer so much, and are so poor and despised, if it is not God's just punishment upon them?" (p. 122). The periodical continued confronting the young Reform movement in articles such as, "Life and Orthodoxy," "The Nature of Hebrew Theocracy," and "The Sabbath." Feature pieces included "Sunday School in Savannah," "The Jews' Hospital in New York," "England and its Jews," and "Conference of French Rabbis."

In 1862 – This twentieth anniversary volume carried an opening editorial by Leeser describing the havoc brought by the Civil War on *The Occident:* "The experience of the last year has already proved to us what a serious drawback the present deplorable war is to our circulation and the prospect for a return to peace and good-will is too gloomy at the time of writing this to expect any marked improvement shortly" (p. 1). The publication's twelve monthly issues reprinted sermons, reported congregational and communal news including obituaries from both the United States and abroad, described programs of Hebrew benevolent societies and Sunday schools, reported news about the "sufferings" of Palestinian Jewry, and introduced fiction pieces. The publication also reported on the activities of the newly organized national Board of Deputies of American Israelites, the first national representative body of American Jews, among whose aims were to foster religious education, collect statistical data, and arbitrate disputes within the Jewish community.

The Occident strongly attacked General Order No. 11, issued by General U.S. Grant on December 17, 1862, which ordered the immediate expulsion of alleged Jewish black marketers in Tennessee, Kentucky and Mississippi (see pages 121 and 216). Eventually Lincoln rescinded this Order, but only after a firestorm of protest from Jews and fair-minded Christians. Leeser warned about a double standard in judging Jews and Christians: "We know well enough that it may be said with justice, that men of all persuasions seek their gain from the results of the war; but while Christians can commit the most monstrous frauds, almost with impunity, mere suspicion of an unproved wrong is enough to bring misery on Israelites, in general, not to mention the one who is the guilty party" (p. 544).

NEW YORK – 1849
The Asmonean

Robert Lyon (b. 1810; d. 1858), a London-born businessman with no previous journalistic experience, started this New York City weekly in 1849. It was published until 1858. Like most nineteenth newspapers, *The Asmonean* was basically a one man enterprise, and it ceased publication upon Lyon's death. The most colorful part of this newspaper was its masthead which displayed the American flag on a shield with the Star of David, three animals associated with Hebrew tribes

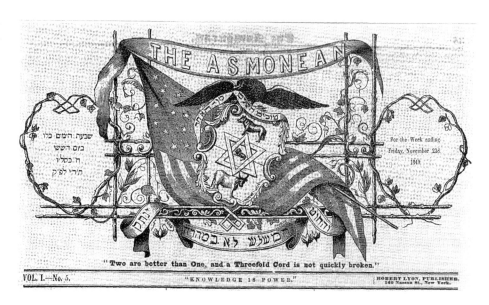

(the lion of Judah, the wolf of Benjamin, the bull of Manasseh), and a quote from *Ecclesiastes*, "Two are better than One, and a Threefold Cord is not quickly broken." The message of this quote was the value of unity for American Jewry.

In terms of layout, the newspaper had a three column front page and four columns on the other eleven pages. Half of the inside pages were taken up with advertisements. Conceptually, *The Asmonean* tried to pass on the Jewish heritage and prevent the assimilation of its largely immigrant readership, while helping them to navigate life in their new country. When Jews were challenged in the general press, Lyon rose to their defense. The newspaper reprinted editorials from other newspapers as well as guest columns by prominent Jews. Lyon was involved with the Democratic Party, and this publication made political endorsements such as supporting James Buchanan in the 1856 presidential election. For a while, Isaac Mayer Wise, the Reform Rabbi, served as Lyon's co-editor.

CINCINNATI – 1854
The Israelite

Rabbi Isaac Mayer Wise (b. Moravia, 1819; d. Cincinnati, 1900), began publishing America's third Jewish periodical, *The Israelite,* in Cincinnati, Ohio in 1854. Called *The American Israelite* since 1874, it is the nation's longest still-running Jewish periodical, available today in a more attractive print format and in an electronic version at americanisraelite.com.

Wise had two purposes in mind for editing *The Israelite*: first, to establish a voice for the new Reform Jewish movement he is credited with starting in the United States; and second, to provide news information to especially small Jewish communities.

In his *Reminiscences* Wise wrote, "I promised Judaism a sharp weapon. I promised progress, enlightenment, spiritual striving, a fearless organ." In the beginning the newspaper's motto, carried on the front page, was *"Yehe Or – Let There Be Light."* As did the Rev. Isaac Leeser, Rabbi Wise tried to end the spiritual anarchy in the American Jewish community by establishing a national Jewish federation. While this goal was only accomplished during Wise's lifetime on a rudimentary level, he, more than any other Jewish American of the day, was responsible for the launching of Hebrew Union College in 1875 and spreading the message of Reform Judaism in frontier America through *The Israelite's* editorial and news pages.

SAN FRANCISCO – 1857
The Weekly Gleaner

Rabbi Julius Eckman (b. Prussia, 1805; d. San Francisco, 1874) studied in Berlin and immigrated to Mobile, Alabama in 1846. After a number of disappointments in the pulpit, he accepted a rabbinic post at San Francisco's Temple Emanu-El in 1854. After this position also did not work out, Eckman devoted the rest of his life to running a Jewish day school in that city, and to publishing *The Weekly Gleaner*, the newspaper he founded in 1857. Though it also covered Jewish-related national and international news, the paper's unique focus was on western Jewry, an area extending between Oregon and Nevada. The newspaper was in English, but Eckman printed certain Hebrew words such as *kosher* in Hebrew type. The newspaper, under Eckman's editorship, lasted until 1863. It is considered a very reliable source of information about Jews in the early West.

Chapter #5

Jews in the American Marketplace

CHARLES WATKINS, Merchant, intending soon for England, desires all Persons indebted to him, to make speedy Payment, and those that have any Demands, to bring in their Accounts, that they may be settled. The said Charles Watkins has to sell a Sortment of sundry European and East-India Goods lately imported, viz. Oznaburgs, Lubecks, Checks, Silk Grograms, printed Callicoes and Chints, Cambricks, clear Lawns, Bandannoes, and strip'd and colour'd Ginghams, very cheap for ready Money, at his Store near the Merchant's Coffee-House, New-York, 4th November, 1745.

ALL Persons that have any Demands on the Estate of Capt. Michael Thody, late of the City of New-York, deceased, are desired to bring in their Accounts and receive Satisfaction; and all those who are indebted to the said Estate, are hereby requested forthwith to pay off the same, in order to prevent further Trouble. Elizabeth Thody, Executrix.

ALL Persons that have any Demands on the Estate of Thomas Cox, late of this City, Butcher, deceased, are desired to bring in their Accounts to Mr. Peter De Lancey, Administrator; and all those indebted to the said Estate, are desired speedily to pay off the same, and prevent Trouble.

ALL Persons who have any Demands on the Estate of Larans Garner, late of the Bow'ry-Lane, deceased, are desired to bring in their Accounts to Benjamin Nicoll, Attorney at Law in New-York, Administrator to the said Estate; and all those who are indebted to the same, are desired to pay the several Sums due without further Notice.

To be SOLD,
ALL Sorts of Dry Goods and Houshold-Stuff, at reasonable Rates for ready Money, at Mr. Solomon Hays's, in the Broad Way, opposite the Post-Office: All Persons indebted to the said Solomon Hays, are desired to pay off the same, to prevent further Trouble.

A CHOICE Parcel of Turpentine, to be Sold either by Wholesale or Retail, by ANDREW FRESNEAU.

WHEREAS on the Nineteenth Day of October, 1744, Partition was made of part of that Tract of Land in Dutchess County, known and called by the name of the Second Nine partners Tract, pursuant to the Acts of Assembly in that Case made: And whereas, by that Partition, One Ninth of the said Tract was set out for Sampson Shelton Broughton, or his Heirs or Assigns, in Severalty; and his or their part of the Charge thereof is found to be Thirty five Pounds eleven Shillings: And One other Ninth of the said Tract was set out for Thomas Wenham, or his Heirs or Assigns, in Severalty; and his or their part of the Charge thereof is found to be other Thirty five Pounds eleven Shillings: One other Ninth Part of the said Tract was set out for Richard Sacket, or his Heirs or Assigns, in Severalty; and his or their part of the Charge thereof was found to be Thirty seven Pounds eight Shillings and eleven Pence. Two Thirds of One other Ninth part of the said Tract were set out for Rip Van Dam, or his Heirs or Assigns, in Severalty; and his or their part of the Charge thereof was found to be Twenty three Pounds fourteen Shillings: These are to give Notice, that the Judge of the Inferior Court of Dutchess County, and the Sheriff of the same County, will sell so much of the said Persons Lands set out as aforesaid, as shall be sufficient to satisfy and pay their said Parts of the Charges of Partition and their respective Parts of the Charges of such Sales, with lawful Interest for the said Moneys from the Twenty fifth Day of April, 1744, to the Day of Sale; which Sales are to be at public Vendue to the highest Bidder or Bidders, at the Court-House of the said County of Dutchess, on the first Day of the Meeting of the Judge and Justices, to hold the next Inferior Court of Common Pleas in and for the said County of Dutchess, which is in the Month of May next. Witness our Hands the Seventeenth Day of October 1745.
JACOBUS SWARTWOUT, Judge.
HENRY FILKIN, Sheriff.

THE Cargo of the French Prize Snow lately brought in here by the Privateer Brig. Dolphin, Capt. Richard Langdon Commander, consisting of both White and Brown Sugars, some Coffee, Elephants-Teeth, with other Effects not yet known; will continue to be sold at publick Vendue from Day to Day, at the House of Capt. James Coden, near the Ferry Stairs, till the Whole, together with the Vessel is Sold.

To be SOLD,
A Good Plantation in the County of Orange, a little above the High-Lands, containing two Hundred Acres of Land, forty Acres whereof is clear and in very good Fence, all the rest is well timber'd and water'd, with Abundance of Wallnut or Hickory Wood intermixed; fifty Acres of it is choice good low Land, fit for either Grain or Meadow: There is on it a good Dwelling house and a small well bearing Orchard; On the back of it is a lasting Outlet or Range for raising Stock; It is situate about a Mile and Quarter from the North River near Goshen Landing, and is near to both a Saw-Mill and Grist-Mill, with several other Conveniencies too tedious here to mention. Whoever inclines to purchase the said Plantation, may apply to Samuel Wickham, Taylor, opposite to Mr. Jacob Goelet's, near the Old Slip Market, and agree on reasonable Terms.

To be SOLD,
A Likely stout Negro Fellow about 21 Years of Age, fit for either Town or Country Business, and has had the Small pox. Enquire of Thomas Stokes, Blacksmith, on the New Dock in New York.

THIS is to give Notice, That the Ferry from Westchester to Nassau-Island, will, on the first Tuesday in November next, be let out to the highest Bidder at Vendue for the Term of five Years, and the Vendue will be opened at Ten o'Clock in the Forenoon of the same Day, at the Court-house. Dated October 2d, 1745.
ISAAC WILLET, Mayor of the Corporation.

THE Partnership of Jeremiah Lattouch and Joseph Haynes, being expired; This is to give Notice to all Persons indebted to them, to make speedy Payment, to prevent Trouble; and those that have any Demands, to bring in their Accounts that they may be settled.

THIS is to give Notice to all Persons whatsoever, That William Grant, Stone-Cutter, and Samuel Hunterdon, Quarrier, of Newark, lately arrived from England, carves and cuts all Manner of Stones in the neatest and most curious Fashions ever done in America. The said Grant is to be spoke with at Mr. Welsh's, Sexton to Trinity Church, in New-York.

For LONDON directly,
The Ship Albany, WILLIAM BRYANT, Commander, Burthen about 200 Tons, mounts 14 Carriage Guns, and to carry Men in proportion;
FOR Freight or Passage, agree with the said Commander. ALSO,
The Ship Four Brothers, ABRAHAM BRASHER, Master.
FOR Freight or Passage, agree with CORNELIUS VAN HORNE, or said Master.
Both Vessels are near full, and will sail in a few Days.

CHoice good SAFFRON, at 40 s. per lb. to be sold by the Printer hereof, or cheaper by the Quantity. Just published, and Sold by the Printer hereof, Wholesale and Retail, The American Country Almanack, For the Year of Christian Account, 1746. Calculated from Caroline Tables according to Art, and fitted for the Province of New-York. By Thomas More, Philodespot.

To be SOLD,
A Likely Negro Boy, about seven Years old, this Country born, and a good plain Gold Watch: Also a Lot of Ground in the City of New-Brunswick, adjoining to the River. Enquire of Samuel Farmar, Merchant, near the Fly-Market in New-York.

NEW-YORK: Printed by James Parker, at the New Printing-Office in Beaver-Street, Where Advertisements are taken in, and all Persons may be supplied with this Paper.

NEW YORK CITY – 1745
"TO BE SOLD. ALL SORTS OF DRY GOODS…"
The New-York Weekly Post-Boy, p. 2 (col 1)
November 4, 1745

In this advertisement, Solomon Hays announces the sale of "all sorts of dry goods and household stuff at his Broad way shop opposite the post office:" and continues, "All Persons indebted to said Solomon Hays, are desired to pay off the same, to prevent further Trouble."

Hays, one of four brothers who emigrated to New York from Holland, was made a freeman of New York in 1742. Hays was considered to be a disputatious figure. In October 1756, the *hazzan* of the congregation read a public proclamation announcing that synagogue members were forbidden to have any "conversation, correspondence or community" with Hays and his family, effectively putting them into excommunication.

This ban was precipitated by Hays having gone to secular court in an action against fellow congregants for allegedly assaulting him in a dispute over whether or not a window should be opened in the women's gallery where his wife was seated during prayers. This incident, known as "The Yom Kippur Balcony Window Battle," marked the first time in the colonies that a Jew had sought to involve Christians in seeking to settle an inter-congregational dispute. Similarly, Hays placed an ad in *The New York Weekly Post-Boy* newspaper (September 6, 1756) offering to pay one hundred pistoles to anyone who revealed the identity of "several; scandalous Jews" who were "defaming his character and hurting his credit."

According to William Pencak, *Jews and Gentiles in Early America 1654–1800* (The University of Michigan Press, 2005, p.55), the Hays experience was among the main factors showing that "whatever their behavior toward non-Jews, the members of New York's small Jewish community had little love for each other and, it seemed, could not agree on anything."

PHILADELPHIA – 1747
TO BE SOLD TO HIGHEST BIDDER
The Pennsylvania Gazette, p. 2 (col 2)
September 14, 1747

In this advertisement, Joseph Marks announces the auction, to be held "on Tuesday, the 20th of October next," of a site consisting of a stone house, several other buildings, orchards and eleven lots located at the lower end of Germantown. Marks was among the organizers of the City Dancing Society founded in 1748, consisting of the elite of Philadelphia Jewry. He was the largest ship owner in the Middle Atlantic States among Jewish merchants of that era.

Philadelphia, Sept. 24. 1747.

On Tuesday, the 20th of October next, at the house where Bernard Refer lately lived, at the lower end of Germantown, wil lbe fold to the higheft bidder,

THe faid ftone-houfe, and feverai other buildings, a barn, and eleven lots of land; 3 of the faid lots fronting Germantown main ftreet, on one whereof the ftone-houfe (of 2 ftories high, and 40 feet front) ftands, having 3 perches and 12 feet front, and 20 perches and 12 feet back, adjoining all the way to a 40 feet ftreet, having fome other large buildings thereon. The other 2 front lots, having each 3 perches and one foot front, and 20 perches and twelve feet deep, with fome ftone buildings on one of them. The other 8 lots are all a young thriving orchard of the beft fruit, fronting the faid 40 feet ftreet, having each 4 perches front, and ten perches and ten feet deep; all of them being conveniently fituate for any tradefman or publick bufinefs. The fale will begin at ten o'clock, and reafonable credit will be given by the owner   *Jofeph Marks.*

Above: Germantown in the mid-1700s. Credit is given to the Bushong United Project website.
http://www.belizebreeze.com/bushongunited/images/Germantown_Sower_house_and%20publishing.jpg

NEW YORK CITY – 1758 PROMINENT JEWISH MERCHANTS

New York Mercury, p. 4 (col. 1, 3)
February 27, 1758

In 1758, the British-ruled Colony of New York consisted of 13,000 inhabitants, including some 200 Jews. According to the *Jewish Encyclopedia* (1909), the ties that these New York Jews had with brethren all over the world, based on "language, blood and mutual confidence," made it easier for them to enter the ranks of merchants.

This issue features advertisements from two of New York City's most prominent Jewish merchants. Samuel Judah (b. 1728; d. 1781) advertises "a large assortment of European and India goods" in addition to sundry items including muskets, perfumery and regimental buckles. Judah became a freeman of New York in 1769 and a year later signed the Non-Importation agreement adopted by the colonists to pressure the British on taxation. His brother, Hillel (b. ca. 1740; d. ca. 1815), was a *shochet* (Jewish ritual slaughterer) in Newport, Connecticut.

Hayman Levy (see page 27), another leading New York merchant who would also sign the Non-Importation agreement in 1770, advertises a variety of "ready-made" shirts at his Bayard Street store in this issue.

Imported in the WILLIAM, Capt. GLASGOW, from LONDON,
And, TO BE SOLD

By Samuel Judah,

At his STORE, oppofite to JOHN CRUGER, ESQ; Mayor;

A Large Affortment of *European* and *India* Goods, fuitable for both SEASONS.

N. B. HE has LIKEWISE, blue,--- fcarlet,--buff, and green CLOTHS,--*Manchefter* Velvets,--ditto Shags,--and Plufhes ditto.--Ruffia fheetings,--Ravens Duck,--Ozenbrigs,...Dowlafs,...Hollands,...fheetings,...Yarn ftockings,...Regimental fhoe-Buckles and Buttons, Gold and filver-lac'd Hatts, Caftors,....Lace,...Peruke-Makers Hairs,....Perfumery,... Pewter,...Hard Ware,...fttationary,...Mufkets,...fwivels,...Piftols,... Hangers,...Cutlaffes,...Blunderbuffes,...fhot,...Cannon Balls,....&c. &c. &c.   J9n†

TO BE SOLD,

By Hayman Levy,

At his STORE, in BAYARD-STREET;

A Quantity of ready-made fhirts, of different prices ; corded dimity flocks ; Englifh and American made fhoes ; mill'd and yarn flockings ; Raven's duck, and Ruffia fheeting ; hair cockades ; blankets ; gold and filver lace ; with a great variety of goods fit for the army, or other gentlemen. Likewife, An affortment of ftationary ; fpermacetæ candles, and beft green TEA.   J23¶

PHILADELPHIA – 1762
"LEVY MARKS, TAYLOR"

The Pennsylvania Gazette, p. 3 (col 3) – August 19, 1762

In this advertisement, "Levy Marks, Taylor" notifies the public that he has "removed" from Chestnut Street to Front Street.

Marks was one of the Jewish merchants of Philadelphia who were patriots of the American Revolution. One example of Levy's espousal of the patriot cause was his taking of the "Oath of Allegiance to the State of Pennsylvania" on January 5, 1779. In this oath, Levy and the others declared:

We whose names are hereunto Subscribed. Do solemnly and sincerely Declare and Swear, (or affirm). That the State of Pennsylvania is and of right ought to be a free Sovereign and Independent State – and I do forever renounce all Allegiance, Subjection, and Obedience to the King or Crown of Great Britain, and I do further swear, (or solemnly, sincerely and truly declare and affirm), that I never have since the declaration of Independence, directly or indirectly aided, assisted, abetted, or in any wise countenanced the King of Great Britain, his Generals, fleets, or armies; or their adherents in their claims upon these United States, and that I have ever since the Declaration of Independence thereof demeaned myself as a faithful citizen and subject of this or some one of the United States, and that I will at all times maintain and support the freedom, sovereignty, and Independence thereof.

During the Revolutionary War, Levy, together with other prominent Pennsylvania Jewish merchants such as Barnard Gratz and Joseph Simon, subscribed to a fund for the hiring of "one or more proper persons to ride between Lancaster and General Washington's Army with and for intelligence."

Marks moved to Lancaster, Pennsylvania, later in his life.

NAMES OF PERSONS

WHO TOOK THE

Oath of Allegiance to the State of Pennsylvania.

BETWEEN THE YEARS 1777 AND 1789.

WITH

A HISTORY OF THE "TEST LAWS" OF PENNSYLVANIA.

BY

THOMPSON WESTCOTT.

PHILADELPHIA:
JOHN CAMPBELL.
MDCCLXV.

1779.
Jan. 1, FREDERICK SEEGEZ, Shopkeeper.
SAMUEL LYON, Commissary.
JAMES DUNLAP, Philada., Physician.
2, PETER CRISPIN, Roxbury.
JOHN TIBIN, JR., do.
JOSEPH LEAMAN (his mark), do.
MICHAEL SMITH (his mark), Merrion. Farmer.
WILLIAM KIDD, Schoolmaster.
4, PHILIP RUMBLE (his mark), Labourer.
MICHAEL METZINGER (his mark), Weaver.
5, NICHOLAS JACOBS, Cordwainer.
WILLIAM LAWRENCE, Hatter. Affirmed.
PHILIP TRUCKENMILLER, Taylor.
JONATHAN DRAPER, Cordwainer.
JOHN GARDNER, do.
MARTIN BENNER (his mark).
PETER SUTTER, Hatter.
GEORGE ATTKINSON, Ship Captain.
ADAM MYRTELUS, Blacksmith.
JACOB ERINGER, of Philada., Hosier.
MILES HILLBORN, Mercht. Affirmed.
ANDREW TERRY, Hatter.
LEVY MARKS, Taylor.

[THURSDAY, JANUARY 21, 1768.]   THE   [NUMB. 1307.]

NEW-YORK   JOURNAL;
OR,   THE
GENERAL   ADVERTISER.

Containing the freshest Advices,   both FOREIGN and DOMESTICK.

Imperious Death demands a Royal Prey.   of the Judges of the Supreme Court of Judicature for the Province of New-York, upon the Petition of Joseph Marschalk and John

*NEW YORK – 1768
"TO BE SOLD…"
The New-York
Journal, or
The General
Advertiser,
p. 4 (col 3)
January 21, 1768*

To be sold cheap for ready Money, or short Credit,
At SIMSON'S in Stone-Street,
BEAVER coating, plain cloth colour'd, and napt blue and green ; 7, 8. 9, and 10 quarter rose blankets, Worrendorps and Silesia linens, fine copper plate chintzs, beautiful figures of lace work, ribbons, &c. silk and worsted breeches patterns, white and black silk mitts, Russia duck and colour'd drillings, low priced stone rings, rhubarb, cotton, indigo, and some choice picked beaver, beaver coat, foxes, racoons, &c. vermillion, black and white wampum, Swedes iron. Also Lisbon salt, clean and large, on board
The Snow R E S O L U T I O N,
Charles Chevalier, Master, now lying at Cruger's-Wharf.

Choice Carolina PINK ROOT,
TO BE SOLD, By
ISAAC PINTO,
In BAYARD-STREET,

TO BE SOLD,
The New BRIGANTINE
THREE SISTERS,
Now lying at Byvanck's Wharf, burthen 110 Tons.—Inquire of
SAMUEL VERPLANK.
New-York, 23d December, 1767.   3—

Salt Petre,
TO BE SOLD, By
Thomas Doughty,
In DOCK-STREET.

Choice Carolina PINK ROOT,
TO BE SOLD, By
ISAAC PINTO,
In BAYARD-STREET,

To the PUBLICK,
PETER VIANEY,
Music, Fencing, and Dancing-Master ;
WHO keeps a private and public school opposite to the Hon. John Watts's, at Mrs. Hayes's, near the exchange: heard that a report has been spread, that he asks two guineas a quarter, and two guineas entrance, for teaching young ladies and gentlemen to dance, finds it necessary to contradict publickly a report certainly publish'd to prevent him from getting scholars.—His demand was no more than one guinea a quarter and a guinea entrance, however at the desire of some gentlemen and ladies, he will for the future teach at a pistole a quarter, and a pistole entrance, and will wait on any ladies or gentlemen that choose to be taught, at their own houses.——He will teach French country dances, either at home or abroad.

TO BE SOLD,
THE House wherein ANDREW ELLIOT, Esq; now lives, if not sold before the first of February, then it will be Let : For Particulars, inquire of   92   NICHOLAS BAYARD.

Remsen and Van Alstyne,
Will expire on the first Day of May next :
ALL Persons therefore whose Debts have been or will become due, either on Bond, Note or Book, by the first Day of January next, are desired to make Payment, or give undoubted Security for the same by that Day, or they will be put in Suit.

They have now by them, a general Assortment of Ironmongery, Cutlery, and Sadlery, which will be sold for the Cash, at prime Cost.   98 2

To be sold cheap for ready Money, or short Credit,
At SIMSON'S in Stone-Street,
BEAVER coating, plain cloth colour'd, and napt blue and green ; 7, 8. 9, and 10 quarter rose blankets, Worrendorps and Silesia linens, fine copper plate chintzs, beautiful figures of lace work, ribbons, &c. silk and worsted breeches patterns, white and black silk mitts, Russia duck and colour'd drillings, low priced stone rings, rhubarb, cotton, indigo, and some choice picked beaver, beaver coat, foxes, racoons, &c. vermillion, black and white wampum, Swedes iron. Also Lisbon salt, clean and large, on board
The Snow R E S O L U T I O N,
Charles Chevalier, Master, now lying at Cruger's-Wharf.
M. PHILIPS,
Has just imported in the Ship New-York, Captain Lawrence, from London :
A Large Assortment of MILLINERY of the newest and genteelest Taste ; also a great Variety of new fancied Goods too tedious to mention, at her Store in Smith-Street.   95

This issue of the *Journal / Advertiser* contains separate merchandising advertisements from two scholarly Jews.

(1) The ad placed by Isaac Pinto (b.1720; d. New York City, 1791) — selling raw vegetables from his Bayard Street home — provides a revealing insight into the life of this Jewish merchant and translator. Ezra Stiles, president of Yale College and a prominent colonial Hebraist (see page 63), mentions Pinto in his *Diary* as "a learned Jew from New York." The two carried on a correspondence.

Pinto published the first English translation of a Hebrew prayer book in 1766. It contained the prayers for the Sabbath, the Jewish New Year, and the Day of Atonement conforming to the Spanish and Portuguese ritual. Significantly, Pinto authored this work when the colony of New York numbered only a few hundred Jews, whereas no such English translation had yet been undertaken for London's ten-thousand-member Jewish community.

Who would expect that such an erudite gentleman would sell food in the marketplace? This advertisement, where Pinto advertises "Choice Carolina Pink Root" for sale, clearly indicates that Pinto emulated the commercial spirit of ancient Talmudic sages in venturing into the marketplace and shows how merchandising did not deter Jewish scholarship.

(2) Joseph Simson (b. 1686; d. New York City, 1787) was another New York Jew holding scholarly credentials. He carried on a correspondence with Dr. Kennicott of Oxford and Dr. Cooper, president of King's (later Columbia) College on issues relating to the Hebrew language. In his advertisement he invites the public to his Stone-Street store where he is selling beaver coating, Silesia linens, raccoons, indigo, and foxes.

NEW-YORK : Printed by JOHN HOLT, at the Printing-Office near the Exchange, in Broad-Street, where all Sorts of Printing Work is done in the neatest Manner, with Care and Expedition. Advertisements of no more Length than Breadth are inserted for Five Shillings, four Weeks, and One Shilling for each Week after, and larger Advertisements in the same Proportion.

HETTY HAYS is removed from *Bea-ver-Street*, into her House in *Carman-Street*, near *Mr. Samuel Deals*, and continues to fell the beft of pickl'd Peppers, Walnuts, Cucumbers, and Mangoes.---Can furnifh any Quantity for Shipping of the beft Quality.---Alfo Cherry, and Currant Sweetmeats. And fundry other fmall Articles.

NEW YORK – 1768
"HETTY HAYS..."
The New-York Gazette; The Weekly Post-Boy,
p. 4 (col 3)
September 5, 1768

The Hays family, consisting of six brothers of Dutch descent, first settled in New Rochelle, New York in 1720. They were one of the families that held on to Jewish observance after coming to America. Jacob, the eldest of the brothers, was a merchant, and one of the earliest members of Congregation Shearith Israel in New York City.

In this advertisement, Jacob's wife, Hetty, notifies the public that she has moved from her Beaver Street house to one on Carman Street. She "continues to sell the best of pickl'd Peppers, Walnuts, Cucumbers and Mangoes.... And sundry other small Articles."

The family was known for its patriotism especially because they lived in New York's Tory-favored Westchester County. They were also known, in later generations, for its colorful history which includes Jacob and Hetty's grandson, another Jacob Hays, who served as New York City's High Constable (the equivalent of today's Chief of Police) for almost a half century. High Constable Hays was well known for his expertise as a detective and for some of the techniques he developed. He was the first to shadow a suspect and the first to administer the first degree. He served in his position until his death in 1850.

TO BE LET, that large convenient INN, where the subscriber lives, lately occupied by Robert Mullan, pleasantly situated on the banks of the river Schuylkill, about four miles from the city of Philadelphia, together with the lot of ground thereto belonging, containing about two acres, on which are erected a good barn, stables, sheds, &c. Also another house and lot near the abovementioned premises, containing about six acres of well improved land. Likewise to be let on reasonable terms, upon a long lease or leases, about twelve hundred acres of good, rich, unimproved land, well watered, and divided into four tracts, situate on Wiconesco creek, in Hoffman's valley, Lancaster county. Any person inclinable to rent any part of the said premises may know the terms, by applying to

LEVY MARKS.

As the said Levy Marks intends to leave the province by the first of April next, all persons who have any demands against him, are desired to bring in their accounts, and receive their respective balances; and those who are indebted to him, are hereby desired to make immediate payment to William Lewis, of the city of Philadelphia, attorney at law, in whose hands the subscriber's books are lodged, with directions to bring actions against those who do not comply herewith.   March 6.

PHILADELPHIA: Printed by BENJAMIN TOWNE, in Front-street, near the London Coffee-House.

PHILADELPHIA – 1776
"TO BE LET"
The Pennsylvania Post, p. 4, (col 1)
March 7, 1776

In this publication, Levy Marks, merchant and patriot, advertises that "that large convenient INN" on the banks of the river Schuylkill, four miles from Philadelphia, is available to be rented. With the immanence of the American Revolution, Marks notes that he will be departing his dwelling. He requests that those with any "demands" against him should bring in their accounts, and that those who are indebted to him should make "immediate payment."

Marks and other prominent Philadelphia Jewish merchants subscribed in 1777 to an account for the hiring of "one or more proper persons to ride between Lancaster and General Washington's Army with and for intelligence." In 1779, Marks took an oath of allegiance to the State of Pennsylvania, thereby pledging himself to maintain the sovereignty of the United States.

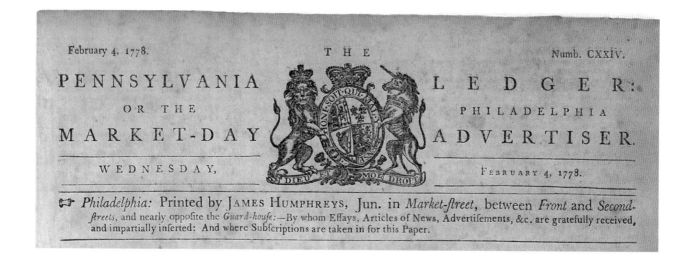

PHILADELPHIA – 1778
WANTED FOR SELLING RUM
WITHOUT PERMISSION

The Pennsylvania Ledger; or the
Philadelphia Market-Day Advertiser,
p. 2 (col 3)
February 4, 1778

This was a strongly Tory newspaper which began in 1775 and closed shop in May 1778 as the British prepared to evacuate Philadelphia. In this rarely found newspaper, on page 2, is a fascinating report on how Barnard Solomon, "a Jew of this city," ran afoul of the law by selling rum without official permission and subsequently absconded from the law.

The wanted notice, signed by "Enoch Story, Inspector of prohibited goods," reads "BARNARD SOLOMON, a Jew of this

Philadelphia, February 3, 1778.

BARNARD SOLOMON, a Jew of this city, having lately purchased several hogsheads of rum, for sale, under the regulations made by the Superintendent-General, in pursuance of the proclamation of the Commander in Chief, &c. HAS IN DEFIANCE OF THE SAID REGULATIONS, sold several small quantities of rum, without first obtaining permission for so doing. And not only refused to give the necessary information respecting the storing, or vending this rum, but has withdrawn from his last place of abode, in Front-street, near Union-street. NOW, in order to bring the said Solomon before the Magistrates of the Police, to answer for his conduct aforesaid, I do hereby offer a reward of FIVE GUINEAS to any person or persons who will give such sufficient information of his present residence, that he may be brought to justice.

ENOCH STORY,
Inspector of prohibited goods.

N. B. A reward of one fifth part the value shall be paid to any person who will give information and make discovery, of any rum stored, being the property of said Solomon, or of any quantity sold by him, (and now in possession of any person or persons) without permission for so doing.

city, having lately purchased several hogsheads of rum, for sale, under the regulations made by the Superintendent-General, in pursuance of the proclamation of the Commander in Chief &c. HAS IN DEFIANCE OF THE SAID REGULATIONS sold several small quantities of rum without first obtaining permission for so doing. And not only refused to give the necessary information respecting the storing, or vending of this rum, but has withdrawn from his last place of abode in Front-Street near Union-Street."

The notice then offers a five guinea reward to anyone helping to bring Solomon to justice and adds that "N.B. [i.e., note well] A reward of one fifth part the value" is also offered to any individual who actually provides the actual rum which Solomon is accused of unlawfully selling.

T O   EE   S O L D,
A NEGRO MAN, ftout and healthy, aged 29 years, has had the fmall-pox, is a good farmer, can do all manner of work upon a plantation, honeft a d fober, can be well recommended, is fold only for want of employ, and his own choice to live rather in the country than in a city, will be fold at a reafonable price. Apply to
ISAAC FRANKS, Broker, in Second-ftreet.   Aug. 15.

PHILADELPHIA – 1778
"TO BE SOLD, A NEGRO MAN... FOR WANT OF EMPLOY"
The Pennsylvania Packet or, The General Advertiser, p. 3 (col 3)
August 17, 1778

Slave advertisements were far from uncommon in late eighteenth century Philadelphia newspapers. In this particular advertisement "a negro man, stout and healthy, aged 29 years" is being "sold only for want of employ, and his own choice to live rather in the country than in a city … at a reasonable price." The ad lists the man's attributes, noting that he "has had the small pox, is a good farmer, can do all manner of work upon a plantation, [is] honest and sober, [and] can be well recommended."

The ad was placed by Isaac Franks (b. New York City, 1759; d. Philadelphia, 1822), a "Broker, in Second Street." Franks was among the more than one hundred Jews who fought in the Revolutionary War. He began his military career at the age of seventeen, taking part in the Battle of Long Island under the direct command of George Washington. He was jailed as a prisoner by the British for three months. Following his escape in 1777, he became a quartermaster, and later a forage-master, and was stationed at West Point until 1781. After his honorable discharge, he settled in Philadelphia and became a merchant and broker. In 1784 he associated with Dr. Benjamin Rush, a Founding Father of the United States and civic leader in Philadelphia, to purchase tracts of land. In 1789, he was appointed a Notary Public by Governor Mifflin of Pennsylvania. And in 1793, during the yellow fever epidemic, he hosted President George Washington at his home in Germantown.

PHILADELPHIA – 1782
JEWISH MERCHANTS AND FINANCIERS
The Independent Gazetteer; or, the Chronicle of Freedom,
p. 4 (col 3)
October 11, 1782

At the top of column 3 in this issue are separate advertisements for three Philadelphia Jewish brokers, each an important Jewish figure in early American history – Isaac Franks (see page 91), Haym Salomons (see page 94), and Nones and Cohen (see pages 29 and 141). In his advertisement, Salomons notes his credentials as a broker to the Office of Finance of the Consul General of France and to the Treasurer of the French Army.

The fourth advertisement in the column, bearing the name Jonas Phillips, notes products which have "just come to hand by the last vessels from France," to be sold "at his store in Market Street, between Front and Second Streets." The variety of items include goose, ducks and pigeons which were "shot," linens, dishes, blankets, lace ruffles, and "a few Kegs of green, soft Swedish Soap, for Family Use, equally as good as Castille Soap."

Phillips (b. Germany, 1736; d. Philadelphia, 1803), a patriot, merchant and congregational leader, was among the most prominent Jews both in the colonial period and the early days of the republic. He was founder of the Phillips family in America. Arriving in Charleston, South Carolina in 1756, he soon moved to Albany, New York, and several years later to New York City. In 1759, Phillips was made a freeman of the State of New York.

Phillips was one of the signers of the Nonimportation Agreement (1770), a protest against British taxation. When the Revolutionary War broke out, he urged members of Congregation Shearith Israel to close its doors in response to the British occupation of New York City. Phillips himself abandoned the city, moving to Philadelphia. In response to a call to join the ranks of the Continental Army, Phillips terminated his business activities and enlisted in October, 1778 in a company of the Philadelphia militia.

He was one of the active founders of Congregation Mikveh Israel in Philadelphia, serving as the synagogue's president in 1782. The letter from the congregation asking George Washington to attend the congregation's dedication ceremonies bears Phillip's signature. Among his grandsons were such Jewish notables as Mordecai M. Noah (see Chapter 8) and Uriah P. Levy (see page 26).

1

BROKER's OFFICE, by
ISAAC FRANKS,

In Second Street, between Market and Chesnut-Streets,
Who is acquainted with every Species of the Broker's Business,
and is conversant in the Laws of Exchange and Barter :
At his OFFICE
*Daily Attendance is given; Secrecy and the utmost Punctuality
are observed, in transacting every Kind of Business
incident to this Office.*

BILLS of EXCHANGE, &c.

FOREIGN Bills of Exchange, either upon France, Spain,
Holland, Gottenburgh, or any Part of Europe; also Inland Bills, Notes and Certificates are negotiated, discounted, or
sold with the greatest Attention to the Interest of the Party
concerned.

OFFICER's NOTES and CERTIFICATES, LOAN-OF-
FICE CERTIFICATES, and NEW-YORK
DEPRECIATION NOTES,

Are negotiated on the best Terms --Cash will be given, at a
very reasonable Discount, for Officer's Notes.

MONEY PUT OUT,

From Time to Time, upon such Security, Interest, or Allowance, as shall be agreeable to the Parties, either for a Week,
Month, or Year.

MERCHANDISE

Of every Sort, where Money is wanted to be raised immediately by Strangers or others, is received, and sold upon Commission; in the Transacting of which Business, Fidelity may be
depended on.

HOUSES and LANDS

May be bought or sold by applying to this Office, held either
in fee simple, for Life, or Years, in the Disposal of which, due
Regard will be paid to the Legality of Title and the Right of
Persons to transfer.

N. B. As the Business of his Office is become very extensive, and greatly exceeds his most sanguine Expectations, it will
be transacted upon such easy Terms as cannot fail to ensure a
Continuance of Business.

ISAAC FRANKS, BROKER,

Hath for Sale, several very valuable Tracts of Land, twelve
Lots of Ground in the City, a House and Lot in Walnut-
street, between Front and Second-streets, and a Variety of Dry Goods.

2

HAYM SALOMONS,

Broker to the Office of Finance, to the Consul General of
France, and to the Treasurer of the French Army,

AT his Office in Front-Street, between Market and Arch-
Streets, buys and sells on commission, BANK STOCK,
BILLS of EXCHANGE on France, Spain, Holland, and
other parts of Europe, the West-Indies, and Inland Bills, at
the usual commissions.

He buys and sells LOAN OFFICE Certificates, CONTI-
NENTAL and STATE MONEY, of this or any other State,

Pay-Master and Quarter-Master General's Notes; these, and
every other kind of Paper Transactions (Bills of Exchange excepted) he will charge his Employers no more than ONE HALF
PER CENT for his Commission.

He procures MONEY on LOAN for a short Time, and gets
Notes and Bills discounted.

Gentlemen and others, residing in this State, or any of the
United States, by sending their Orders to this Office, may depend on having their Business transacted with as much Fidelity
and Expedition as if they were themselves present.

He receives Tobacco, Sugars, Tea, and every other Sort of
Goods, to sell on Commission, for which Purpose he has provided proper Stores.

He flatters himself his Assiduity, Punctuality, and extensive
Connections in his Business, as a Broker, is well established in
various Parts of Europe, and in the United States in particular.

All Persons who shall please to favour him with their Business, may depend upon his utmost Exertion for their Interest,
and PART of the MONEY ADVANCED, if desired.

15---

3

NONES and COHEN,
BROKERS.

*At their Office in Front-Street, two Doors below the Coffee-House,
in the House occupied by the Widow Laboyteaux,*

TRANSACT every Kind of Business as Brokers,
such as buying and selling Bills of Exchange on France,
Spain, Holland, and other Parts; likewise Loan-Office and
other Certificates, State Money of this and other of the United States: They will also receive and sell on Commission all
Kinds of Dry and other Goods.

Their Employers may be assured of having their Business
done on the most equitable Terms, Dispatch, and Punctuality
of Payments.

Constant Attendance will be given at their Office aforesaid,
and at the Coffee-House, at the usual Hours of transacting Business there.   14

4

Just came to Hand by the last Vessels from France, and to be
Sold by
JONAS PHILLIPS,
At his Store in Market-Street, between Front and Second-
Streets,

A Quantity of Goose, Duck, and Pigeon Shot; China
Dishes and Plates, Tureens and Soup Dishes, Blankets
and Rugs, Broad Cloths, Coatings, Naps and Flannels, coarse
and Britannia Linens, Chintzes and Calicoes, Hair Colour and
red imaged Bed Furniture Calicoes, Writing Paper, Worsted fit
for knitting Stockings, ready made Shirts, fine Lace Ruffles,
and Edgings, with sundry other Dry Goods; likewise a few
Kegs of green, soft, Sweedish Soap, for Family Use, equally as
good as Castile Soap, with sundry Dry Goods of various Kinds.

A vacant Lot of Ground, in Race-street, near Third-street.
Inquire as above.

August 13, 1782.   19

PHILADELPHIA – 1784
HAYM SALOMON ADVERTISEMENTS
Pennsylvania Packet and Daily Advertiser, p. 4 (col 1) December 24, 1784

Haym Salomon (b. Lisa, Poland, 1740; d. Philadelphia, 1785) has a series of advertisements in this issue publicizing the various services he offers, including "Factor, Auctioneer & Broker," publicizing his services in both English and French.

Salomon, known in history books of the United States as the financier of the American Revolution, was already thirty two years old when he came to the U.S. He would live only another thirteen years on American soil. In that short time, he opened an office in New York as a broker and commission merchant, fled to Philadelphia after the British captured New York, was captured twice and sentenced to be hung

The Pennſylvania Packet, and Daily Advertiſer.

Price Four Pence.]   FRIDAY, DECEMBER 24, 1784.   [No. 1836.

Haym Salomon,

Authoriſed Broker to the Office of Finance, &c. has now to diſpoſe of at his OFFICE in Front-ſtreet (where he tranſacts, in the moſt extenſive manners every branch of Buſineſs relative to his profeſſion.)

BANK STOCK.

THE various ſorts of Certificates, Notes, &c. iſſued by the public; Bills of Exchange upon France, Spain, Holland, England, Denmark, Hamburgh, &c. and the principal Weſt-India iſlands; and can draw bills upon moſt of the principal places on this continent.

He receives every ſpecies of Merchandize to ſell upon Commiſſion; for which purpoſe he has provided proper Stores; and procures freight for veſſels. Any perſon reſiding in this or any of the United States, who will ſend their orders to his office, may depend on having their buſineſs tranſacted with as much fidelity as if they were themſelves preſent.

He flatters himſelf his aſſiduity, punctuality and extenſive connections in his buſineſs, as a broker, are well eſtabliſhed in ſeveral parts of Europe, and the United States in particular.

All thoſe who ſhall pleaſe to favor him with their buſineſs, may depend upon his utmoſt exertions for their intereſt, and part of the money advanced, if deſired.

Haym Salomon, BROKER

To the Office of Finance.

HAVING procured a licence for exerciſing the employment of an AUCTIONEER in the city of New-York, has now opened, for the reception of every ſpecies of Merchandize, his Houſe, No. 22, Wall-ſtreet, lately occupied by Mr. *Anthony L. Blecker,* (one of the beſt ſtands in that city) and every branch of buſineſs, which in the ſmalleſt degree appertains to the profeſſions of

Factor, Auctioneer & Broker.

will be tranſacted in it with that fidelity, diſpatch and punctuality which has hitherto characteriſed his dealings. The houſe, in point of convenience and ſituation, is exceedingly well calculated for the different kinds of buſineſs abovementioned; and he thinks it almoſt unneceſſary to aſſure thoſe who may favor it with their orders, that the ſtricteſt attention ſhall be paid to them, and the utmoſt care and ſolicitude employed to promote their intereſt.

The nature of his buſineſs enables him to make remittances to any part of the world with peculiar facility, and this he hopes will operate conſiderably in his favor with thoſe who live at a diſtance.

A deſire of being more extenſively uſeful, and of giving univerſal ſatisfaction to the Public, are among his principal motives for opening this houſe, and ſhall be the great leading principle of all its tranſactions. By being Broker to the Office of Finance, and honored with

its confidence, all thoſe firms have paſſed through his hands which the generoſity of the French Monarch, and the affection of the Merchants of the United Provinces, promoted them to furniſh us with, to enable us to ſupport the expence of the war, and which have ſo much contributed to its ſucceſsful and happy termination; this is a circumſtance which has eſtabliſhed his credit and reputation, and procured him the confidence of the Public, a confidence which it ſhall be his ſtudy and ambition to merit and encreaſe, by ſacredly performing all his engagements. The Buſineſs will be conducted upon the moſt liberal and extenſive plan, under the Firm of HAYM SALOMON and JACOB MORDECAI.   Philadelphia, May 7, 1784.

Haym Salomon,

Courtier de Change & du Bureau des Finances,

AYANT obtenu la permiſſion d'exercer la charge de Maitre d'Encan dans la ville de New-York, vient d'ouvrir les magazines pour la reception de toutes ſortes de merchandiſes, dans la maiſon ci devant occupe par Mr. *Anth ny Bleeker,* ſituee dans Wall-ſtreet, No. 22, une des meilleurs ſituations de la ville pour les affaires, ou il exerce es emplois et profeſſions de FACTEUR, MAITRE D'ENCAN et COURTIER, et tranſige avet la fidelite, la promptitude & la ponctualite, qui ont juſqu'ici caracteriſe ſes operations, & qui ont etabli ſa reputation tant en Europe qu'en Amerique toutes ſortes d'affaires ayant le moindre raport avec les differentes branches.

Sa maiſon par ſa ſituation et par ſa commodite eſt extremement propre aux differens genres d'affairs ci deſſus mentionnés, et il croit qu'il et preſque inutile d'aſſurer ceux qui voudront bien l'employer, qu'il donnara tous ſes ſoins et toute ſou attention a leurs affairs et a l'avancement de leurs interets.

La nature & l'etendue de ſes affaires, le mettent dan le cas de pouvoir faire des envois et des retours dans toutes les parties au monde, avec une facilite particuliere, ce qu'il croit devoir operer en ſa faveur avec les perſonnes qui demeuren, dans des lieux eloignes.

Le deſir de ſe rendre de la plus grande utilite et de donner au public toute eſpece de ſatisfaction ſont les principaux motife qui l'induiſent a ouvrir cette nouvelle maiſon, & ce mems deſir ſera toujours le grand principe qui dirigera toutes ſes operations.

Etant depuis longtems honore de la confiance de Meſſieurs les Chefs du Bureau des Finances, dont il eſt le Courtier, il u eu entre ſes mains toutes les ſommes que la generoſite du Monarque de France, et l'affection des Negociants des Province Unies les ont engage a avancer aux Etats Unis, qui nous ont aides a ſoutenir les depenſes de la guerre et qui ont contribue a ſon ſucces & a ſon heureuſe fin—C eſt cette circonſtance qui a etabli ſon creait & ſa reputation & qui lui a procure la confiance du public, confiance qu'il s'efforcera de meriter de plus en plus, en rempliſſant fidelement tout ſes engagemens.

Les affaires de la dite maiſon ſe conduiront ſur le plan, le plus liberal & le plus etendu ſous la raiſon de HAYM SALOMON & JACOB MORDECAI.
a Philadelphie, le 7 May, 1784

by the British, escaped twice, and rose to become one of the main financiers of the day, specializing in complicated transactions involving French and Dutch securities.

During the war, Salomon contributed the enormous sum of over $200,000 which proved indispensable to the military campaign. He assisted the Continental Congress's Department of Finance, and his key role was referred to often in Chairman Robert Morris's *Diary.*

Salomon also gave money to many of the personally indebted public leaders of this young nation, including Jefferson, Madison and Monroe. And he helped finance Armand's French legion following the disastrous Battle of Camden.

Salomon was a trustee of Philadelphia's first synagogue, Congregation Mikveh Israel, and paid one fourth of this new congregation's building costs. He played a big role in lobbying against a provision in the Pennsylvania Constitution which upheld a religious test for public office.

The Pennſylvania Packet, *and Daily Advertiſer.*

Price Four-Pence.]   TUESDAY, APRIL 18, 1786.   [No. 2247.

PHILADEPHIA – 1786
"SAMUEL HAYS, BROKER"
*The Pennsylvania Packet and
Daily Advertiser, p. 1 (col 2)
April 18, 1786*

In this front-page advertisement, Samuel Hays (b. New York City, 1764; d. Philadelphia, 1839) announces that, as a broker, he "buys and sells, on commissions, bills of exchange" from abroad, and certificates from any state in the union. What is especially noteworthy is that the ad cites Hays' association with Haym Salomon (see page 94) in order to burnish his credentials: "By a long residence with the late Mr. Haym Salomon, he has acquired a perfect knowledge of this business."

Samuel Hays, Broker,
At his OFFICE, in Front ſtreet, oppoſite the Cuſtom Houſe,

BUYS and ſells, on commiſſion, bills of exehange upon France, Spain, Holland, England, and other parts of Europe, the Weſt-Indies, or any part of this Continent; alſo, final ſettlements, depreciation and loan-office certificates of this or any other ſtate in union; likewiſe, ſtate and continental money, houſes, lands, &c. and tranſacts, in general, all ſuch buſineſs as pertains to his profeſſion—By a long reſidence with the late Mr. Haym Salomon, he has acquired a perfect knowledge of this buſineſs; and he flatters himſelf, that his care, attention, ſecrecy and punctuality, will give entire ſatisfaction to thoſe who may favor him with their orders. Thoſe gentlemen tranſacting buſineſs with the land-office, may be ſupplied with certificates, receivable there. on the moſt moderate terms.

NEWPORT, RHODE ISLAND – 1789
JACOB RODRIGUES RIVERA, MERCHANT
*The Newport Herald, p. 3 (col 3)
February 26, 1789*

Jacob Rodrigues Rivera (b. Spain, 1717; d. Newport, R.I., 1789) was among the foremost Jews contributing to the flourishing commerce of eighteenth-century Newport, Rhode Island. He came from a family which was prominent in Spain for centuries and which became anusim (marranos) during the Inquisition. Among the ranks of Jewish entrepreneurs in Newport – second only to his son-in-law Aaron Lopez – Rivera was the first to introduce the sperm oil industry into America. He espoused the colonial cause during the Revolution and was among those who evacuated Newport following its capture by the British. At his death, he left a fortune of $100,000.

This obituary, recognizing Rivera's distinction, referred to him as "'an Israelite indeed.'" It notes that Rivera was "exemplary in his observance of the Jewish Ritual, intelligent and upright in commerce, and an ornament to all the social virtues."

[VOL. III.]   THE   [NUMB. 105.]

Newport Herald.

THURSDAY, FEBRUARY 26, 1789.

NEWPORT (RHODE-ISLAND) PRINTED BY PETER EDES, IN THAMES-STREET.

Thurſday laſt departed this life after a lingering illneſs, Mr. JACOB RODREGUEZ RIVERA merchant, in the 72d year of his age; "*an Iſraelite indeed.*" He was exemplary in his obſervance of the Jewiſh Ritual, intelligent and upright in commerce, and an ornament to all the ſocial virtues.

[SATURDAY, JULY 18, 1789.]   THE   [NUMBER 174.]

NEW-YORK DAILY GAZETTE.

PUBLISHED BY J. & A. M'LEAN, AT THEIR PRINTING-OFFICE, *FRANKLIN'S HEAD*, No. 41, HANOVER-SQUARE.

"Wall street with Bohemian Church" by Johann Georg-Rosenberg, 1776.

NEW YORK – 1789
"DRY GOODS"
The New York Daily Gazette,
p. 3 (col 3)
July 18, 1789

Sales at Auction,
By *Isaac Moses*,
On Tuesday, at the Auction-Room, No. 21, Wall-street,
A large assortment of
DRY GOODS.
Suitable to the season,
Also, a few dozen looking-glasses.

On Wednesday, opposite the Auction-Room, No. 21, Wall-street.
60 quarter casks port wine, of the first quality, approved notes at 90 days pay; in specie, will be received in payment.
At the same time,
5 ton best London ground white lead in casks containing 1-2 cwt. and 1-4 cwt. in each.
2 ton red lead,
6 hogsheads Malaga wine,
10 chests souchong tea.
50 dozen shovels and spades steel plate,

AT PRIVATE SALE,
Cassia in chests, Malaga raisins, Madeira wine, hyson and souchong teas, of the first quality, shot, nankeens, 6-4 and 4-4 book muslins, purple and stormont callicoes, fine cambricks, Irish linens, and a great variety of India goods, Russia duck, Holland quills, and a large assortment of Indigo.

In this advertisement Isaac Moses notifies the public of auctions of Dry Goods, "suitable to the season," he would be holding "at the Auction-Room, No. 21, Wall-street."

Moses (b. Germany, 1742; d. 1818), was a colonial merchant and patron of the American Revolution. The earliest reference to Isaac Moses is in the Boston records of May 18, 1762, where it stated, "The selectmen are informed that one Isaac Moses, a Jew, has lately come to town." Moses was one of fourteen Jews in the colonies who signed the Non-importation resolution of 1765, and records show he was one of the few New York City Jews who voted in the 1766, 1768, and 1769 elections.

In 1775, Moses was president of New York's Congregation Shearith Israel. Upon the occupation of New York by the British, Moses and other patriotic Jews fled the city. He took up residence in Philadelphia, where he remained during the war. In 1780, when funds were badly needed to provide necessities to the American army, Moses gave his personal bond for 3,000 pounds sterling and purchased bills of credit to support the Treasury. He also purchased bills in large amounts to raise funds for the French army.

In Philadelphia, he was the main organizer and first president of Congregation Mikveh Israel. When he returned to New York following the Revolution, Moses was among the founders of the Bank of New York.

PHILADELPHIA, PA – 1791
PAPER MONEY FOR SALE
Gazette of the United States, p. 4 (col 3) – April 6, 1791

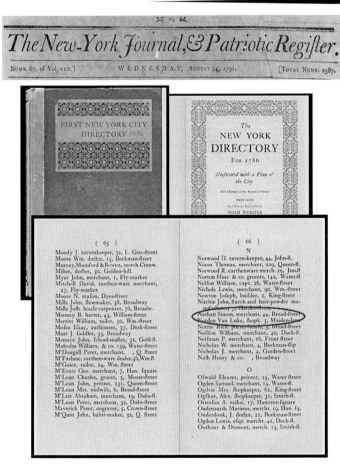

MANUEL NOAH,
BROKER,
No.91, Race-Street, between Second and Third-Streets,
BUYS and SELLS
Continental & State Certificates,
Pennfylvania and Jerfey Paper Money,
And all kinds of SECURITIES of the United States, or of any
particular State.

In an advertisement in this publication, Manuel Noah informs readers that he buys and sells Continental and State certificates from his office at 91 Race Street, between Second and Third Streets. Noah, who served in the Revolutionary War under George Washington, was the father of Mordecai Manuel Noah (see Chapter 8), the most prominent American Jew of the nineteenth century.

The New-York Journal, & Patriotic Register.
NUMB. 67, of Vol. XLV.]   WEDNESDAY, AUGUST 24, 1791.   [TOTAL NUMB. 2587.

NEW YORK – 1791
"TO THE PUBLIC . . . AVIS."
The New-York Journal & Patriotic Register, p. 5 (col 3)
August 24, 1791

Simon Nathan (b.1746; d. 1822) highlights his skills as an Auctioneer in this advertisement published in both English and French. Nathan, who was identified with the patriotic cause, fled New York City for Philadelphia after New York was captured by the British. He was president at different times of Congregation Shearith Israel in New York and Mikveh Israel in Philadelphia. During the Revolutionary War, he loaned vast sums of money to the state of Virginia which were not repaid. Nathan was listed in the first New York City Directory in 1786.

TO THE PUBLIC.

THE Subfcriber, having obtained a commiffion to tranfact the bufinefs of an Auctioneer, folicits his friends and the public for their favors, affuring them that he will ftudioufly endeavor to render perfect fatisfaction to all who may pleafe to employ him, and will at all times advance money (if required) on property depofited with him for fale. He has furnifhed himfelf with good and convenient ftores for the reception of all merchandize; and has alfo provided himfelf with a commodious Auction Room, at No. 9, Hanover-fquare, at prefent occupied by Mr. William Rhodes, where he will difpofe of, on every Tuefday after the 1ft of May next, to the higheft bidder, all kinds of Dry Goods; and at the Coffee-houfe will fell Weft-India produce, and fuch other articles as are ufually fold there. Alfo fuch public fecurities as may be entrufted to his difpofal. Captains of veffels and fuper-cargoes, who may pleafe to put their cargoes into his hands on their arriving, will have an immediate advance made them, if required.   SIMON NATHAN.
New-York, April 26, 1791.   87 2aw. 1y.

AVIS.

LE Soufcripteur, qui a obtenu le droit de vendre toutes fortes de marchandifes a vente publique, a l'honneur d'offrir fes fervices aux negocians, et de foliciter les faveurs de fes amis. Il affure les perfonnes qui voudront bien l'employer qu'il fera tout fon poffible pour leur donner une entiere fatisfaction, et qu'il fera toujours pret a faire des avances, fi on l'exige, fur les marchandifes deftinees a l'encan, qu'on remettra a fes foins.
Il s'eft procure de commodes et bons magazins pour la reception de toutes efpeces de denrees—auffi aut il engage une Salle tres convenable a ce genre de commerce, au No. 9, Hanover-fquare, maintenant occupee par Monf. Wm. Rhodes, ou il vendra tous les Mardis, apres le 1r, de Mai, toutes fortes de marchandifes fines au plus offrant. Il vendra de meme au cafe des productions des iles, et de tels autres articles qu'on y vend ordinairement, ainfi que les fecurites publiques qui lui feront confiees pour cet effet.
Il fera des avances, fi on l'exige, fur le champ, aux Capitaines et aux commis de vaiffeaux marchands qui voudront, bien a leur arrivee, mettre leurs cargaifons entre fes mains.
SIMON NATHAN.
New-York, Avril 26, 1791.   87 2aw. 1y.

Dunlap's American Daily Advertiſer.

> Juſt Arrived from Hamburgh,
> **ISAAC COHEN,**
> *Doctor* and *Surgeon,*
> WHO ſtudied in the Hoſpitals at Copenhagen ſeven years, moſt reſpectfully acquaints the Public in general, that he makes Truſſes of all ſorts and ſizes, for children as well as grown perſons on the ſhorteſt Notice ; cures Ruptures in children; the Venereal Diſeaſe without Mercury, with ſecrecy ; Rheumatiſm, Conſumptions; alſo, cures the Fiſtula, & Corns: he prepares the Balſam of Life, which he ſells at one quarter of a dollar each bottle, and will make a generous allowance to thoſe who take a quantity : it is a certain cure for the Cholic, and other complaints. Orders from the country, *poſt paid,* will be duly attended to.
> Poor people, coming properly recommended, cured gratis.
> He may be ſpoken with at Mr. *Moſes Hornberg's,* in Race ſtreet, the corner of Second ſtreet, Franklin's Head, Philadelphia.

PHILADELPHIA – 1791
"JUST ARRIVED FROM HAMBURGH"
Dunlap's American Daily Advertiser, p. 4 (col 5)
December 26, 1791

This advertisement announces that "Isaac Cohen, Doctor and Surgeon," who had studied for seven years in the hospitals of Copenhagen, has arrived from Hamburgh and taken up residence in Philadelphia. The skills listed by Dr. Cohen include the making of trusses and curing such ailments as "Ruptures in children; Venereal Disease without Mercury, with secrecy; Rheumatism, Consumptions" and more. He also makes the "Balsam of Life" and sells it for a quarter a bottle, less for "those who take a quantity."

"Poor people coming properly recommended," he advises, are "cured gratis."

The advertisement concludes with the notice that Dr. Cohen "may be spoken with" at the home of Mr. Moses Hornberg in Race Street. According to Henry Samuel Morais' *The Jews of Philadelphia* [1894], Hornberg was among the founders of Philadelphia's first synagogue, Congregation Mikveh Israel.

HUDSON, NEW YORK – 1803
CHEAP DRY GOODS STORE
The Bee, p. 4 (col 1)
September 6, 1803

Although Benjamin Gomez (see page 65) is known historically as New York City's first Jewish bookseller and as the publisher of titles under his own imprint, this advertisement reveals that when he was forced to flee the city as a result of a prevailing epidemic, he retooled himself commercially as a dry goods merchant in the town of Hudson, 120 miles north.

According to the advertisement, headlined "Cheap Dry Goods Store," "Benjamin Gomez having left the city of New York on account of the prevailing epidemic, respectfully informs the citizens of Hudson and the public, that he has taken the store of Mr. Pratt, in Warren (or Main) street lately occupied by Mr. McKinstry, where he has opened for sale wholesale or retail a general and well-chosen assortment of dry goods which he will sell at the lowest prices for cash." The advertisement also notes that Gomez is the proprietor of the "Fortunate Lottery Office," listing the prices and payouts of various priced tickets.

Cheap Dry Goods Store.

BENJAMIN GOMEZ,

HAVING left the city of New York on account of the prevailing epidemic, respectfully informs the citizens of Hudson and the public, that he has taken the store of Mr Pratt, in Warren (or Main) street, lately occupied by Mr. M'Kinstry, where he has opened for sale,

WHOLESALE OR RETAIL,

A general and well-chosen assortment

OF

DRY GOODS,

Which he will sell at the lowest prices for CASH.

☞ HE IS THE PROPRIETOR OF THE

FORTUNATE LOTTERY OFFICE,

Where 2 of 10.000$, 2 of 5.000, 1 of 3.000, 1 of 2,000 dollars, and other valuable prizes were sold in the late State Road Lotteries; and has for sale, Tickets in the *Lottery for the Relief of poor Widows with small Children*, either Whole or in Halves, Quarters, or Eighth parts. Persons wishing to become fortunate adventurers will do well by applying as above.

10,000 dollars for 7!

SCHEME.

1	prize of	10,000	First drawn number on		
1	of	5,000	the 1st day		500
1	of	2,000	4th	do.	1,000
1	of	1,000	7th	do.	1,000
13	of	500	10th	do.	2,000
40	of	200	13th	do.	1,000
100	of	100	16th	do.	5,000
150	of	50	19th	do.	1,000
300	of	20	22d	do.	1,000
4,500	of	10	25th	do.	500

5,116 prizes, 13.884 blanks.

*** The price of tickets is expected to rise soon to 7½ dollars.

157   Hudson, August 22.

AMERICAN CITIZEN.

[No. 1620]   WEDNESDAY, JUNE 5, 1805.

☞ *TO BE SOLD.*—The House and Lot of Ground, No. 71 Broad-street, directly opposite Beaver-street.

ALSO, the House and lot of Ground, No. 97 Broad-street, nearly opposite Pearl-street.—The said houses are replete with every convenience. The purchase money (a very small part excepted) may remain on mortgage, at the option of the purchaser. For terms apply to   S SIMSON.
May 11 tf   No. 97 Broad-street.

Columbia College's Park Place campus until 1857. Courtesy of University Archives, Rare Book and Manuscript Library, Columbia University Libraries.

NEW YORK – 1805
HOUSES FOR SALE BY "FATHER OF MOUNT SINAI"
American Citizen, p. 2 (col 1) - June 5, 1805

Sampson Simson, the first Jewish graduate of Columbia College, delivered his 1800 valedictory address – believed to have been authored by Rev. Gershom Mendes Seixas, his teacher at Congregation Shearith Israel – in Hebrew. Simson noted that "Jews throughout the Union have taken fate hands into their own hands by strengthening and supporting [the nation] together with their fellow citizens." Together with seven other Jewish philanthropists, Simson founded "Jew's Hospital." Eventually, the hospital's name was changed, and Simson is known historically as the father of New York City's Mount Sinai Hospital.

In this advertisement Simson offered properties at 71 and 97 Broad Street for sale. "The said houses," the ad says, "are replete with every convenience."

NEW YORK – 1805
"SALES BY AUCTION"
American Citizen, p. 3 (col 3)
September 6, 1805

SALES BY AUCTION.

BY NAPHTALI PHILLIPS.
This Day,
At 11 o'clock at no. 43 Water-street, a variety of household goods and kitchen furniture.

In this notice for an auction set for that day at 43 Water Street, Naphtali Phillips (see also page 73), one of the leading Jewish journalists of the time, seems to be advertising personal items for sale. For auction will be "a variety of household goods and kitchen furniture."

Phillips began his career in journalism in Philadelphia, where his family had fled when the British invaded New York in 1776. He worked at the city's leading newspaper, Claypole's *American Advertiser*. He moved to New York City in 1801 and for many years had a relationship as proprietor as well as publisher and editor of the *National Advocate*.

Phillips was active in Jewish community affairs, writing a historical sketch of Jewish life in New York and an account of Congregation Shearith Israel. He was prominent in politics as a member of the Tammany Society for nearly seventy years.

CHARLESTON COURIER.

CHARLESTON – 1807
"PRIME AFRICANS"

Charleston Courier, p. 3 (col 3)
June 17, 1807

In an advertisement titled "Prime Africans" Cohen & Moses announce a sale "TO-MORROW, the 18th… consisting of 4 Men, 3 Women, 8 Girls, 5 Boys…."

PRIME AFRICANS.

TO-MORROW, the 18th inst. at 11 o'clock, will be sold before our Vendue store, without reserve, 15 AFRICANS, consisting of—
4 Men, 3 Women, 8 Girls, 5 Boys.
Conditions—All sums under 300 Dollars, 60 days; all above, notes at 60, 90 and 120 days, with approved indorsers.

June 17.   **Cohen & Moses.**

These two items, both from 1807 issues of the Charleston Courier, *announce sales of slaves by Jews. This sketch of the Charleston Slave Market, originally featured in a November 1856 issue of* The London Illustrated News, *accompanies an article at iaamuseum.org, "Slavery in the Lowcountry," which notes, "Slavery in South Carolina was different from anywhere else in America • Almost half of all of the enslaved Africans who came to the U.S. first arrived in the port of Charleston • In Lowcountry, the proportion of enslaved Africans to whites could be as high as 9:1 • Enslaved people comprised nearly 50% of Charleston's population before the Civil War."*

CHARLESTON – 1807
"SALES OF AFRICANS."

Charleston Courier, p. 3 (col 4)
October 10, 1807

Jacob de Leon (b. Kingston, Jamaica, 1764; d. Columbia, S.C., 1828) fought in the Revolutionary War, probably in the special infantry corps, organized in Charleston in 1799, which was composed almost exclusively of Jews.

Sales of Africans.

On TUESDAY the 13th instant will be sold at ten o'clock before my store, without reserve, to close sales, 25 AFRICANS, consisting of men, women, boys and girls Conditions—for 1 Negro, 60 days; for 2 Negroes, 60 and 90 days; and for more, 1st January next—for notes with approved indorsers.

                                     Jacob De Leon.

☞ As the above Negroes must be sold, great bargains may be expected.   October 9.

He was also a Masonic officer and a merchant, with slaves among his wares. In this issue, de Leon advertises an upcoming auction of 25 Africans. "As the above Negroes must be sold," the advertisement ends, "great bargains can be expected."

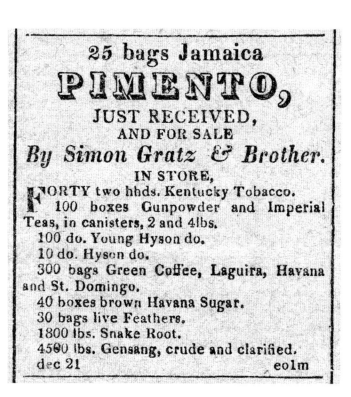

25 bags Jamaica
PIMENTO,
JUST RECEIVED,
AND FOR SALE
By Simon Gratz & Brother.
IN STORE,
FORTY two hhds. Kentucky Tobacco.
100 boxes Gunpowder and Imperial
Teas, in canisters, 2 and 4 lbs.
100 do. Young Hyson do.
10 do. Hyson do.
300 bags Green Coffee, Laguira, Havana
and St. Domingo.
40 boxes brown Havana Sugar.
30 bags live Feathers.
1800 lbs. Snake Root.
4500 lbs. Gensang, crude and clarified.
dec 21   eo1m

PHILADELPHIA, PA – 1820
SIMON GRATZ & BROTHER
Poulson's American Daily Advertiser, p. 1 (col 5)
December 23, 1820

When Simon Gratz (b. 1773; d. 1839) was three years old and his younger brother Hyman just an infant, Thomas Jefferson was renting quarters in the famous "Graff House" at 700–704 Market Street that would later be their home. It was during his stay at the Graff House that Jefferson, a delegate to the Second Continental Congress at the time, wrote drafts of the Declaration of Independence. Simon and Hyman's father, Michael Gratz, and Michael's brother, Barnard, were known as patriots, both having signed documents protesting the Stamp Act issued in 1765.

In the historical records, Simon and Hyman are far less known than their sister Rebecca (b. 1781; d. 1869), a distinguished educator and philanthropist who was secretary of the Philadelphia Orphan's Society for forty years and one of the founders of the first Jewish Sunday School in the United States. Sir Walter Scott modeled the Jewish heroine Rebecca in *Ivanhoe,* after her.

This front-page advertisement by Simon Gratz & Brother announces the sale of 25 bags of Jamaican pimento ("just received"), and other products including Kentucky tobacco, Havana sugar, snake root and live feathers.

Poulson's American Daily Advertiser.

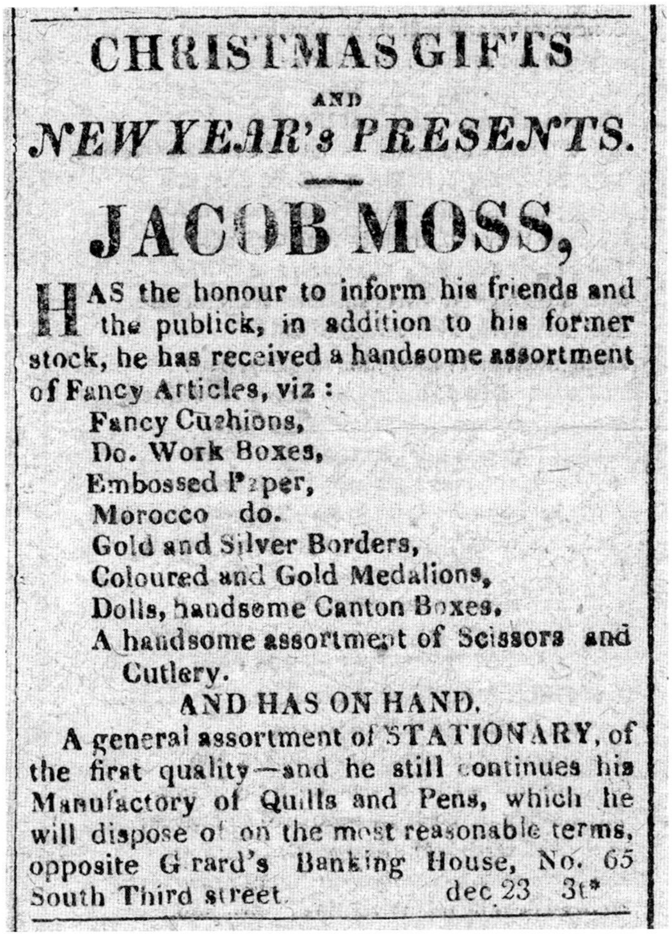

CHRISTMAS GIFTS
AND
NEW YEAR's PRESENTS.
—
JACOB MOSS,

HAS the honour to inform his friends and the publick, in addition to his former stock, he has received a handsome assortment of Fancy Articles, viz :

Fancy Cushions,
Do. Work Boxes,
Embossed Paper,
Morocco do.
Gold and Silver Borders,
Coloured and Gold Medalions,
Dolls, handsome Canton Boxes.
A handsome assortment of Scissors and Cutlery.

AND HAS ON HAND,

A general assortment of STATIONARY, of the first quality—and he still continues his Manufactory of Quills and Pens, which he will dispose of on the most reasonable terms, opposite Girard's Banking House, No. 65 South Third street.   dec 23 3t*

PHILADELPHIA – 1820
"CHRISTMAS GIFTS AND NEW YEAR'S PRESENTS"
Poulson's American Daily Advertiser, p. 1 (col 3)
December 27, 1820

Though Jacob Moss (b. London, 1793; d. 1830) would be one of the signatories of Congregation Mikveh Israel's 1824 Constitution, he apparently did not face any inner conflict in publicly advertising the sale of Christmas gifts from his South Street store. In addition to being the first Jewish bookseller in Philadelphia, Moss was a quill manufacturer, pen cutter and fancy stationer. His water color supplies were sought after by young ladies of Philadelphia.

In this front-page advertisement headlined "Christmas Gifts and New Year Presents," Moss announces that in addition to his regular stock, he has received a "handsome assortment" of such items as fancy cushions, embossed paper, gold and silver borders, scissors and cutlery.

WE, the undersigned, give notice, that we have this day been appointed by Nathan Williams, Esq. a Commissioner, to perform certain duties of a Judge of the Supreme Court, Trustees for all the creditors of *Cephas Wood*, late of the town of Springfield, in the county of Otsego, an absconding debtor, and we require all persons indebted to the said absconding debtor, by the first day of January next, to pay all debts and sums of money which they owe to such debtor, and deliver all property of such debtor which they have in possession to us the said trustees: and we desire all creditors of the said debtor, by the first day of January next, to deliver to us or one of us, their respective accounts and demands against such debtor. Dated the 26th day of November, 1822.

DAVID P. HOYT,
NICHS. N. WEAVER, } Trustees
EPHRAIM HART,

nov 29—clawtjl

NEW YORK CITY – 1823
TRUSTEE FOR ABSCONDING DEBTOR
New-York American, p. 4 (col 1)
January 4, 1823

Ephraim Hart (b. Bavaria, Germany, 1747; d. New York City, 1825), fled to Philadelphia together with other patriotic New York City Jews when the city was occupied by the British during the Revolutionary War. While residing as a merchant in Philadelphia, he was a member of Congregation Mikveh Israel. In 1782 he married Frances Noah, sister of Manuel Noah and aunt of the noted Mordecai Manuel Noah. Returning to New York in 1787, Hart went into business as a stockbroker, becoming one of the wealthiest merchants in the city. He was one of the twenty two original members of the Board of Stock Brokers, forerunner of the New York Stock Exchange, organized in 1792. Communally, he was among the founders in 1802 of the Hebra Hesed VeEmet, a benevolent society of Congregation Shearith Israel. He was a member of the New York State Senate in 1810.

Hart was one of three trustees appointed by the Supreme Court to deal with the finances of Cephas Wood, an "absconding debtor" of the town of Springfield. In this notice the Trustees request that those owed money to or from Wood should deliver summaries of their accounts by January 1, 1823.

NEW YORK – 1824
PRINTER, BROKER & TAX RECEIVER
The National Advocate, p. 1 (cols 3 and 5) – March 26, 1824

The front page of the March 26 issue of *The National Advocate* included the following items pertaining to Jews. The first is an announcement by a Jew; the second refers to a Jew.

REDEMPTION OF ILLINOIS LANDS

In "Redemption of Illinois Lands," Mordecai Myers informs the public that individuals who sold their land for taxes in that state may redeem them at his Military and General Agency Office, located at 107 Water Street. Myers (b. 1776; d. 1871), served as a Captain in the War of 1812, represented a New York City district in the state Assembly between 1831 and 1834, and later moved to Schenectady where he served as Mayor between 1851 and 1854.

A NOTICE FROM THE
"Southern District of New York, ss.
(L.S.) BE IT REMEMBERED"

This item refers to Solomon Henry Jackson (b. England; d. 1847), the first Jewish printer in New York (see also page 72). In the years 1824 and 1825, Jackson edited and published the first Jewish periodical in America, *The Jew: being a defence of Judaism against all adversaries, and particularly against the insidious attacks of Israel's Advocate.*

Jackson's purpose in establishing his periodical was to counter the perceived missionizing of *Israel's Advocate,* a periodical carrying a misleading name, published by the American Society for Meliorating the Condition of the Jews, a missionary organization. Among Jackson's main themes in his periodical was his right, as an American, to defend his faith.

In this front page, column 5, announcement in the *National Advocate,* James Dill, Clerk of the Southern District of New York, attests to Jackson's registration of the publication cited above.

What is especially unique in the notice is the reproduction – in the actual Hebrew type plus its English translation – of a quote carried on the masthead of Jackson's periodical. Consisting of two verses from "Psalm cix" [sic; it is actually Psalm 119], the quote reads: "T'is time to work for the Lord; they make void thy Law. And I will answer the blasphemers of thy word, for I depend on thy words." This was among the first usages of a Hebrew type in a general circulation American newspaper.

REDEMPTION OF ILLINOIS LANDS.
THOSE whose lands have been sold for taxes, may redeem them at this office As only one year is allowed for redemption, no time should be lost. An official list of the whole sale is received at this office. Any person in doubt of their lands being sold to not, may obtain correct information, by applying at this office, and paying a small fee for the examination. Those who are in arrears for 1823, should apply immediately and settle up their taxes. Our books are written up, and we are ready to receive the taxes for 1824, for lands in Missouri, Arkansas, Illinois, and Ohio. Our fees shall be as low as any other regular agency in the United States. All errors arising at the public offices, on settlement of taxes paid at this office, will be rectified free of loss or chorge by us.
Military & General Agency Office,
    107 Water-street, N. York.
    mh 18   M. MYERS & CO.

Southern District of New-York, ss.
    (L. S.) BE IT REMEMBERED, that on the twelfth day of February, in the forty-eighth year of the Independence of the United States of America, S. H. Jackson, of the said district, hath deposited in this office the title of a book, the right whereof he claims as proprietor, in the words following, to wit:
    The Jew: being a defence of Judaism against all adversaries, and particularly against the insidious attacks of Israel's Advocate.

עת לעשות לה׳ הפרו תורתך :
ואענה חרפי דבר כי בטחתי בדברך :

    "'Tis time to work for the Lord: they make void thy law. And I will answer the blasphemers of thy word, for I depend on thy words."
                    Psalm cix.
        Edited by S. H. Jackson.
    In conformity to the Act of Congress of the United States, entitled, " An Act for the encouragement of Learning, by securing the copies of Maps, Charts, and Books, to the authors and proprietors of such copies, during the time therein mentioned;" and also to an Act entitled, " An Act, supplementary to an Act, entitled, an Act for the encouragement of Learning, by securing the copies of Maps, Charts, and Books, to the authors and proprietors of such copies, during the time therein mentioned, and extending the benefits thereof to the arts of designing, engraving and etching historical and other prints.
                    JAMES DILL,
    Clerk of the Southern District of New-York.
    mh23—1m

THE NATIONAL ADVOCATE.

VOL. XII.   NEW-YORK, WEDNESDAY MORNING, JUNE 2, 1824.   NO. 3262.

NEW YORK – 1824
"SMALL'S PLANET"
The National Advocate, p. 1 (col 7)
June 2, 1824

Hendricks Brothers, a family metals business founded by Uriah Hendricks (b. Amsterdam, 1737; d. New York City, 1798), was the oldest continuous Jewish business in the United States when it closed in 1938. Based on the firm's revenues, Uriah's son, Harmon (b. 1771; d.1838), was most likely the wealthiest Jewish man in New York City in his day. Together with his brother-in-law Solomon I. Isaacs, Harmon established the first copper-rolling mill in the United States, playing a major role in the country's economic and military growth.

Like his father, Harmon Hendricks was active in the Sephardic Jewish community affairs and served as *parnas* (president) of Congregation Shearith Israel from 1824 to 1827. During the war of 1812, he subscribed $40.000 towards a government loan.

In this five-inch-long front-page advertisement, Harmon Hendricks and his partner, E. Tibbits, announced the auction of two properties bordering New York State in nearby Canada. One property, with an "inexhaustible bed of iron ore upon the lake shore," contained about 5,000 acres, and the other, in Ontario, about 6,000. Accompanying the description of the second property was a chart listing the acreage for 45 potential lots.

SMALL'S PATENT.

WILL be sold at auction, at the Tontine Coffee House, in the city of New York, at 12 o'clock, on the 15th day of July next, by Franklin & Minturn, the tract of Land known as Small's Patent, situate on the shores of Lake Champlain, in the County of Essex, and town of Moria, about 9 miles from Crown Point, containing about 5,600 acres. Those Lands are advantageously situated, having by means of the Canal, a water communication to New York. They are well covered with valuable timber, and have an inexhaustible bed of Iron Ore upon the Lake shore.

Also, at the same time and place, all that certain piece or parcel of LAND, situate, lying and being in township No. 11, in the 5th range of Phelps and Gorham's purchase, in the county of Ontario, beginning at the north-west corner of said township, and running east on the north line thereof, to the west line of lands of Wm. Walker, or Wm. Wadsworth; running thence south, bounded on said Walker or Wadsworth's lands east and west on the west line of said town, far enough to make 6000 acres, the same having been laid out in lots, and numbered from 1 to 45, inclusive, and supposed to contain as follows:

No.	Acres	Qrs.	Rods.	No.	Acres	Qrs.	Rods.	No.	Acres	Qrs.	Rods.
1	103	1	21	16	87	1	12	31	172	3	13
2	107	2	19	17	118	0	26	32	144	2	26
3	107	3	30	18	37		23	33	160	0	00
4	116	0	16	19	111	3	49	34	157	2	25
5	100	0	17	20	104	0	12	35	162	0	22
6	106	0	10	21	150	1	1	36	168	1	34
7	108	1	00	22	151	0	36	37	116	3	4
8	103	3	31	23	154	2	26	38	148	2	32
9	107	3	31	24	160	2	22	39	147	1	3
10	110	0	29	25	163	3	28	40	121	1	18
11	128	2	24	26	158	1	11	41	156	0	16
12	128	2	4	27	160	2	3	42	132	2	23
13	127	1	30	28	148	3	3	43	175	2	00
14	127	2	15	29	103	2	14	44	173	2	5
15	90	1	4	30	130	0	00	45	163	2	23

Being held by the subscribers in trust, a quit claim deed will be given. For further particulars, apply to either of the subscribers. The sale will be positive, and for cash on delivery of the deeds.   E. TIBBITS.

may 28 –tjy15   H. HENDRICKS.

CHARLESTON – 1856
"SOUTHERN CLOTHING EMPORIUM"
The Charleston Mercury, p. 1 (cols 5–6)
February 11, 1856

A front page two column drawing advertises the Southern Clothing Emporium of D. J. and C. J. Levy, manufacturers of men's, youths and boys clothing – both wholesale and retail – at 288 King St. in Charleston, S.C.

Estate Sale of Lands, Negroes, Provisions, Horses Mules, Sheep, Hogs, Oxen, Cattle, Furniture, &c.

BY JACOB COHEN & SON.

On TUESDAY, 19th January, 1864, at 11 o'clock, we will sell, in front of the Court House, in the city of Columbia, S. C., by order of the Executor of the Estate of Mrs. P. W. B. Eustis,

The following PROPERTY, viz:

All that valuable and well known SEA ISLAND COTTON PLANTATION, situated on Ladies' Island, St. Helena Parish, three miles from the town of Beaufort, containing one thousand and thirty (1,030) acres, of which there are five hundred and four acres in fine tilt, ninety-six of well wooded land, and four hundred and thirty acres of reclaimable marsh land. The place is settled in the best style. Its celebrity requires no further description, it being notorious for producing the finest Sea Island cotton on the continent.

ALSO,

All that tract of well wooded PINE LAND, containing two hundred and fifteen acres, situated on Port Royal Island, St. Helena Parish, five miles from the town of Beaufort, on the road leading to the town.

ALSO,

All that well known RICE AND COTTON PLANTATION, in Prince William's Parish, called "Tomothey," five miles from the Pocotaligo Depot, on the Charleston and Savannah Railroad, containing twelve hundred and fifty (1250) acres, of which two hundred and forty (240) acres of prime rice land are cleared and in a fine state of cultivation, with never-failing reserves and an ample supply of water; three hundred and fifty acres of superior cotton and provision land; the balance well wooded. On this place there is a fine Dwelling House, with all outbuildings necessary to an elegant establishment, quarters for one hundred and fifty negroes, Rice Thresher, Barns, Stables, &c.

ALSO,

Five hundred acres of well-timbered PINE LAND, called BLUNTSVILLE, three miles from the Pocotaligo Depot, on which there is a FAMILY RESIDENCE, celebrated for its salubrity, and to which the neighborhood resort for health.

ALSO,

A remarkably prime GANG OF FIFTY-EIGHT NEGROES, among which there are three superior Carpenters, Teamsters, Ploughmen, &c.

Terms cash; purchasers to pay for papers.

January 5   tuths

CHARLESTON, S.C. – 1864
ESTATE SALE
The Charleston Mercury, p. 2 (col 4)
January 14, 1864

By 1864, newspapers in the beleaguered state of South Carolina were printed in limited size due to economic privations stemming from the war. In this two-page issue, Jacob Cohen & Son notified the public of a forthcoming estate sale to be held on January 19th, 1864 in front of the Court House in Columbia. The advertisement's headline lists the items for sale: "Lands, Negroes, Provisions, Horses, Mules, Sheep, Oxen, Cattle, Furniture." After describing the plantation for sale, the advertisement concluded, "Also, A remarkably prime GANG OF FIFTY-EIGHT NEGROES, among which there are three superior Carpenters, Teamsters, Ploughmen, &c."

Chapter #6

Jews in Politics

The Maſſachuſetts CENTINEL.

PUBLISHED ON WEDNESDAYS AND SATURDAYS.   Uninfluenced by Party, we aim to be JUST.

WEDNESDAY, JULY 26, 1786.   [12s. pr. ann.]   NUMBER 37, of VOL. V.   Price Two Pence.

CHALESTON, [S. C.] May 10.

WHEN Lord Charles Greville Montague raiſed his regiment in this ſtate, to induce General Moultrie to accept of the command, and enter the Britiſh ſervice, he wrote him the following letter :

March 11, 1781.

"SIR,

"A ſincere wiſh to promote what may be to your advantage, induces me now to write. The freedom with which we have often converſed, makes me hope you will not take amiſs what I ſay.

"My own principles reſpecting the commencement of this unfortunate war, are well known to you, of courſe you can alſo conceive what I mention is of friendſhip. You have now fought bravely in the cauſe of your country for many years, and, in my opinion, fulfilled the duty every individual owes it: You have had your ſhare of hardſhips and difficulties; and, if the conteſt is ſtill to be continued, younger hands ſhould now take the tour from you. You have now a fair opening of quitting that ſervice with honour and reputation to yourſelf, by going to Jamaica with me. The world will readily attribute it to the known friendſhip that has ſubſiſted between us, and by quitting this country for a ſhort time, you would avoid any diſagreeable converſations, and might return at your own leiſure, to take poſſeſſion of your eſtates for yourſelf and family. The regiment I am going with, I am to command ; the only proof I can give you of my ſincerity is, that I will quit that command to you with pleaſure, and ſerve under you. I earneſtly wiſh I could be the inſtrument to effect what I propoſe, as I think it would be a great means towards promoting that reconciliation we all wiſh for. A thouſand circumſtances concur to make this a proper period for you to embrace ; our old acquaintance, my having been formerly Governour in this province, &c. &c. the intereſt I have with the preſent commander.

I give you my honour what I write is entirely unknown to the commander, or to any one elſe, and ſo ſhall your anſwer be, if you favour me with one. Yours ſincerely,

CHARLES MONTAGUE.
To Brigadier-Gen. Moultrie."

To this Brigadier-General Moultrie returned the following anſwer:

Haddrell's Point, March 12, 1781.

"My Lord,

"I received yours this morning. I thank you for your wiſh to promote my advantage, but am much ſurpriſed at your propoſition. I flattered myſelf I ſtood in a more favourable light with you. I ſhall write with the ſame freedom with which we uſed to converſe, and doubt not you will receive it with the ſame candour. I have often heard you expreſs your ſentiments reſpecting this unfortunate war, when you thought the Americans injured, but am now aſtoniſhed to find you taking an active part againſt them, though not fighting particularly on the continent; yet the ſeducing their ſoldiers away, to inliſt in the Britiſh ſervice, is nearly ſimilar.

My Lord, you are pleaſed to compliment me with having fought bravely in my country's cauſe for many years, and in your opinion fulfilled the duty every individual owes to it: But I differ widely with you in thinking that I have diſcharged my duty to my country, while it is ſtill deluged in blood, and overrun by Britiſh troops, who exerciſe the moſt ſavage cruelties. When I entered into this conteſt, I did it with the moſt mature deliberation, with a determined reſolution to riſk my life and fortune in the cauſe. The hardſhips I have gone through, I look back upon with the greateſt pleaſure and honour to myſelf. I ſhall continue to go on as I have begun, that my example may encourage the youths of America, to ſtand forth in defence of their rights and liberties. You call upon me now, and tell me I have a fair opening of quitting that ſervice with honour and reputation to myſelf by going with you to Jamaica. Good God ! is it poſſible that ſuch an idea could ariſe in the breaſt of a man of honour. I am ſorry you ſhould imagine I have ſo little regard for my own reputation as to liſten to ſuch diſhonourable propoſals. Would you wiſh to have that man, whom you have honoured with your friendſhip, to play the traitor ? Surely not. You ſay, by quitting this country for a time, I might avoid diſagreeable converſations; and might return at my own leiſure, and take poſſeſſion of my eſtates for myſelf and family ; but you have forgot to tell me how I am to get rid of the feelings of an injured, honeſt heart, and where to hide myſelf from myſelf. Could I be guilty of ſo much baſeneſs, I ſhould hate myſelf and ſhun mankind. This would be a fatal exchange for my preſent ſituation, with an eaſy and approving conſcience, of having done my duty, and conducted myſelf as a man of honour.

"My Lord, I am ſorry to obſerve, that I feel your friendſhip much abated, or you would not endeavour to prevail upon me to act ſo baſe a part. You earneſtly wiſh you could bring it about as you think it will be the means of bringing about that reconciliation we all wiſh for. I wiſh for a reconciliation as much as any man, but only upon honourable terms. The re-poſſeſſing my eſtates, the offer of the command of your regiment, and the honour you propoſe of ſerving under me, are paltry conſiderations to the loſs of reputation. No, not the fee ſimple of that valuable iſland of Jamaica, ſhould induce me to part with my integrity.

"My Lord, as you have made one propoſal, give me leave to make another, which will be more honourable to us both. As you have an intereſt with your commanders, I would have you propoſe the withdrawing the Britiſh troops from the continent of America, allowing Independence, and propoſe a peace. This being done, I will uſe my intereſt with my command to accept of the terms, and allow Great-Britain a free trade with America.

"My Lord, I could make one more propoſal; but my ſituation as a priſoner, circumſcribes me within certain bounds, I muſt therefore conclude with allowing you the free liberty to make what uſe of this you may think proper. Think better of me. I am, my Lord, your Lordſhip's moſt humble ſervant.

WILLIAM MOULTRIE.
To Lord Charles Montague.

MISCELLANY.

On the real Value of one's native Country.

WE ſhall content ourſelves, ſays M. Voltaire on the ſubject, with our uſual cuſtom of propoſing ſome queſtions which we cannot reſolve.

Has a Jew then any country ? If he is born at Coimbra, he is born among a ſet of ignorant wretches, who will peſter him with abſurd arguments, to which he will anſwer in terms as abſurd, if he durſt anſwer at all. He is watched by the inquiſitors, who will burn him for refuſing to eat bacon, and by that means become maſters of his property. Is Coimbra then his country ? Can he be ſo paſſionately fond of Coimbra ?

Is Jeruſalem his country ? He has heard from ſome vague report that his anceſtors, ſuch as they were, inhabited that barren rocky region, which borders on a miſerable deſert, and is now inhabited by the Turks who got nothing by it. Jeruſalem is not his country ?

The Geber more ancient and more reſpectable than the Jew, the ſlave of the Turk, or the Perſian, or the Mogul, can he call a few piles of ſtones which he has erected ſecretly on the mountains his country.

The Banian, the Armenian, who paſs their lives in wandering over the eaſt, in the capacity of brokers, have theſe any country peculiarly dear to them ? Their purſe and their pocketbook is all the country they have.

In the European nations, all thoſe murderers, by trade, who let out their ſervices, and ſell their blood to the firſt prince that will pay them, have they any country ?—Not ſo much, ſurely, as the bird of prey, that returns at night to the hole in the rock, where her mother built her neſt. Shall the Monks preſume to ſay, that they have any country ? Their country, they tell you, is in Heaven. And I am convinced I never knew any they had on earth.

With what propriety could a Greek make uſe of this term, country, who is ignorant that there ever were ſuch perſons as Miltiades and Ageſilaus, and who knows only that he is the ſlave of a Baſhaw, who is the ſlave of a Viſir, who is the ſlave of a being whom he calls the Grand Turk. What is it then that a man can properly call his country ? Is it not a good eſtate, with a good houſe upon it, of which the poſſeſſor can ſay, theſe fields, that I cultivate, and this houſe which I have built, are my own. I live under the protection of laws, which no tyrant can infringe. When thoſe who like me, are poſſeſſed of lands and houſes, aſſemble for their common intereſt,— I am a part of the whole—a part of the community—a part of the ſovereignty.—This is my country. All elſe loſes the idea of an habitation of men, and may more properly be termed a ſtable of horſes, that, at the pleaſure of the keepers, undergo the diſcipline of the whip.

Such is M. Voltaire's explanation of the words "Native Country."—An explanation which will, no doubt, be particularly agreeable to Americans.

GLEANINGS from HISTORY.

LIBERTY cannot be preſerved, if the manners of the people are corrupted ; nor abſolute monarchy introduced, where they are ſincere, ſays Sidney on government.

When Antigonus, and Archaians, reſtored liberty to the Spartans, they could not keep it ; the ſpirit of liberty was gone.

When Thraſybulus delivered Athens from the thirty tyrants, liberty came too late ; the manners of the Athenians were too far gone into licentiouſneſs, avarice, and debauchery. There is a time, when a people are no longer worthy ſaving.

Pluto calls virtue the health of the mind, and vice its diſeaſe and diſorder. The nation is in a dreadful way, in which almoſt every mind is diſeaſed and diſordered.

The Athenians conſidered, that in a republick purity of manners was above all things neceſſary. "It is of great conſequence (ſays Solon in his letter to Epimenides) of what diſpoſition thoſe are, who influence the common people."

It was impoſſible for any man at Athens to live a diſſolute life unreproved ; for every man was liable to be ſent for by the Areopagites, to be examined and puniſhed if guilty. At Rome the Cenſors had the ſame power. We Chriſtians may be as wicked as we pleaſe.

Every page of the hiſtory of the great revolution of Rome ſhews ſome inſtance of the degeneracy of the Roman virtue, and of the impoſſibility of a nation's continuing free after its virtue is gone.

William Tant

INFORMS his Friends and the Public, That he has removed his Tavern (formerly *Vernon's Head*) in State-Street, nearly oppoſite, in ſaid Street, to that elegant Houſe, formerly the property of Mr. *Wheatly*, where he has opened

The *Eaſtern Coffee-Houſe,*

Gentlemen may be accommodated with genteel Lodgings, beſt of Liquors, and good Stabling for Horſes.

All favours conferred on him will be gratefully acknowledged by
The Publick's humble ſervant,
June 12, 1786.   WM. TANT.

MISCELLANY.

On the real Value of one's native Country.

WE shall content ourselves, says M. Voltaire on the subject, with our usual custom of proposing some questions which we cannot resolve.

Has a Jew then any country? If he is born at Coimbra, he is born among a set of ignorant wretches, who will pester him with absurd arguments, to which he will answer in terms as absurd, if he durst answer at all. He is watched by the inquisitors, who will burn him for refusing to eat bacon, and by that means become masters of his property. Is Coimbra then his country? Can he be so passionately fond of Coimbra?

Is Jerusalem his country? He has heard from some vague report that his ancestors, such as they were, inhabited that barren rocky region, which borders on a miserable desert, and is now inhabited by the Turks who got nothing by it. Jerusalem is not his country?

The Geber more ancient and more respectable than the Jew, the slave of the Turk, or the Persian, or the Mogul, can he call a few piles of stones which he has erected secretly on the mountains his country.

The Banian, the Armenian, who pass their lives in wandering over the east, in the capacity of brokers, have these any country peculiarly dear to them? Their purse and their pocketbook is all the country they have.

In the European nations, all those murderers, by trade, who let out their services, and sell their blood to the first prince that will pay them, have they any country?—Not so much, surely, as the bird of prey, that returns at night to the hole in the rock, where her mother built her nest. Shall the Monks presume to say, that they have any country? Their country, they tell you, is in Heaven. And I am convinced I never knew any they had on earth.

With what propriety could a Greek make use of this term, country, who is ignorant that there ever were such persons as Miltiades and Agesilaus, and who knows only that he is the slave of a Bashaw, who is the slave of a Visir, who is the slave of a being whom he calls the Grand Turk. What is it then that a man can properly call his country? Is it not a good estate, with a good house upon it, of which the possessor can say, these fields, that I cultivate, and this house which I have built, are my own. I live under the protection of laws, which no tyrant can infringe. When those who like me, are possessed of lands and houses, assemble for their common interest,—I am a part of the whole—a part of the community—a part of the sovereignty.—This is my country. All else loses the idea of an habitation of men, and may more properly be termed a stable of horses, that, at the pleasure of the keepers, undergo the discipline of the whip.

Such is M. Voltaire's explanation of the words "Native Country."—An explanation which will, no doubt, be particularly agreeable to Americans.

MASSACHUSETTS – 1786
"ON THE REAL VALUE OF ONE'S NATIVE COUNTRY"
The Massachusetts Centinel, p. 1 (col 2–3)
July 26, 1786

Voltaire's notions on the elusive nature of nationalism are discussed in this front page article. In the end, concluded the French philosopher, "When those who like me, are possessed of lands and houses, assemble for their common interest,—I am part of the whole—a part of the community—a part of the sovereignty.—This is my country…."

As proof of statelessness, Voltaire's first example is the Jew:

Has a Jew then any country? If he is born at Coimbra, he is born among a set of ignorant wretches, who will pester him with absurd arguments, to which he will answer in terms as absurd, if he durst answer at all. He is watched by the inquisitors, who will burn him for refusing to eat bacon, and by that means become masters of his property. Is Coimbra then his country? Can he be so passionately fond of Coimbra?

Is Jerusalem his country? He has heard from some vague report that his ancestors, such as they were, inhabited that barren rocky region, which borders on a miserable desert, and is now inhabited by the Turks who got nothing by it. Jerusalem is not his country?

The Massachusetts CENTINEL.

PUBLISHED ON WEDNESDAYS AND SATURDAYS.   Uninfluenced *by* Party, *we* aim *to be* JUST.

GRATITUDE.

SEVERAL German news-papers have published the following anecdote which we shall entitle

Practical Lecture on CHRISTIAN CHARITY, *by a* JEW.

Our illiberal prejudices have, in a manner stigmatised with infamy the followers of Moses, and the appellation of Jew has been used ungenerously to denote an usurious money lender, who rejoices at other people's misfortunes, and lives on the plunder of the unfortunate, who are compelled to seek assistance from him. A thousand instances might be adduced to convince us of our injustice, and to prove that, in the interpretation we are pleased to give to CHRISTIANS, now are the worst Jews. The fact we intend to record does the highest honour to human nature : And be the hero Turk, Jew, or Infidel, his action will find amongst us more admirers than persons ready to emulate his noble conduct in a similar situation.

The scene lies in Poland, and the story related as follows :—" A considerable Polish family, by some broils which had brought that country very near the brink of ruin, had been plunged from rank and affluence into obscurity and wretchedness. An only son was left, whom necessity had compelled to enter into the service of a polish nobleman, and change his name. As the latter was taking an airing in the country, his good fortune led him to a cabaret, or small inn, kept as all these houses of publick accommodation are, by a Jew. The good Israelite having surveyed the youth with attention, civilly craved his name, which the other told him freely. But, said the host, though you go by that name, it is not your real one. Be sincere with me, I can trace in your face, features which I am ever bound to revere. If I mistake not, you are the son of the late worthy, but unfortunate Prince Woboniefki. I own it, said the youth, but unable to support the title with proper splendour, I thought it prudent to conceal my birth. Heaven, I thank thee for the favour, exclaimed the Jew, now I have it in my power to requite on the son, part of my obligations to his parents. Yes, Sir, to your noble family I owe my very existence. I long subsisted on their benevolence : Providence has blest my endeavours, and I have in a few years, amassed a considerable fortune, which it is my duty to share with the representative of my benefactor. To-morrow your Excellency will be placed in a proper sphere. A state of servitude becomes you not ; I should be a slave myself, had I not other means left to release you from bondage. The next morning a coach and six, with a suitable number of servants were provided and having received from the grateful Israelite, a purse of 1000 ducates, the Prince set off for Warsaw, where having made himself known, he was in a few days honoured by the King in Council with the badge of the first order of Knighthood. The Prince returned to the friendly Jew, who could not refrain shedding those tears, which are the effusions of sensibility. He had, during the Prince's absence, negociated a marriage between his Excellency and a rich German heirefs, which was consumated a few weeks afterwards, when the parents paid down 100,000 florins, with a promise of as much more, on the birth of their first son. It would be a difficult matter to match such an instance of gratitude. " Go then, Christian, and do thou likewise."

MASSACHUSETTS – 1786
ANECDOTE ON A JEW'S GRATITUDE
The Massachusetts Centinel, p. 2 (col 1)
August 12, 1786

In an anonymous fable previously published in German newspapers – and which the *Centinel* entitled "Practical Lecture on CHRISTIAN CHARITY, by a Jew" – a Polish Jew is portrayed in a compassionate and grateful light.

The Jew, an innkeeper, asked a young Pole his name and then challenged the name the youth gave saying, "I can trace in your face, features which I am ever bound to revere." He recognized that the young man was actually a prince who was concealing his identity because of his poverty. The Jew, who had become wealthy, confessed to the young Pole that he "owes his very existence" to the prince's late father. "The grateful Israelite," the fable continues, gave the youth a purse of 1,000 ducats enabling him to set off to Warsaw. There, the king restored the youth to his princely role. In the meantime, the Jew arranges a marriage between the newly identified prince and a "rich German heiress." The fable concludes, "It would be a difficult matter to match such an influence of gratitude. 'Go then, Christian, and do thou likewise.'"

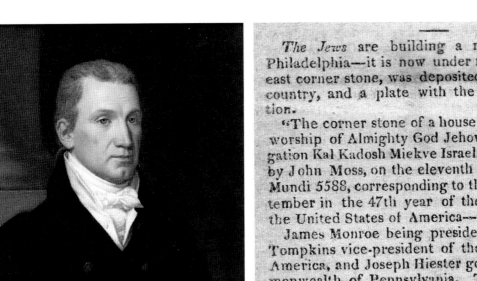

NILES' REGISTER---JANUARY 4, 1823---FOREIGN NEWS.   275

The Jews are building a new synagogue at Philadelphia—it is now under roof. In the south east corner stone, was deposited the coins of the country, and a plate with the following inscription.

"The corner stone of a house consecrated to the worship of Almighty God Jehovah, by the congregation Kal Kadosh Miekve Israel, is placed in its bed by John Moss, on the eleventh day of Tisri, Anno Mundi 5588, corresponding to the 26th day of September in the 47th year of the independence of the United States of America—

James Monroe being president, and Daniel D. Tompkins vice-president of the United States of America, and Joseph Hiester governor of the commonwealth of Pennsylvania. This happy country in which religious and civil liberty is secured to its inhabitants, is now at peace with the whole world; may that enjoyment long endure, and the integrity of this government, and the reign of "virtue, liberty and independence" be triumphant until "the wreck of matter and the crush of worlds."

After this follows the names of the building committee, &c.

Reference is made to "James Monroe being president ... of the United States" in the corner stone placed at Mikveh Israel, always a bastion of nationalism.

[Black and white reproduction of oil on canvas portrait of James Monroe by John Vanderlyn, 1816, courtesy of the National Portrait Gallery, Smithsonian Institution.]

PHILADELPHIA – 1823
CONGREGATION'S NATIONALISM
Niles' Weekly Register, p. 275 (col 1)
January 4, 1823

Congregation Mikveh Israel, Philadelphia's oldest synagogue, was always a bastion of nationalism. An example of this leaning was the speech of dedication on September 23, 1782, given by the Rev. Gershom Mendes Seixas, who had fled his own New York City synagogue, Congregation Shearith Israel, after the British captured that city during the Revolutionary War.

The continuing nationalism of Congregation Mikveh Israel is shown in this article's description of the contents of the cornerstone of the synagogue's new structure: "In the southeast corner stone, was deposited the coins of the country," and a plate indicating the ceremony took place on "the 26th day of September in the 47th year of the independence of the United States of America—James Monroe being president and Daniel D. Tompkins vice-president of the United States of America…".

The inscription continues, "This happy country in which religious and civil liberty is secured to its inhabitants, is now at peace with the whole world; may that enjoyment long endure, and the integrity of this government, and the reign of 'virtue, liberty and independence' be triumphant until 'the wreck of matter and the crush of worlds.'"

ballot Mr. Rochester had 103 votes. Messrs. Sanford, Savage and Thompson had been spoken of—but they declined a nomination.

Mr. Rochester is the secretary of the Panama mission, and a decided friend of the administration. The

THE JEWS. Though a little paragraph complimentary to ourselves, as citizens of Baltimore, was prepared for the press last week, it was accidently omitted. We intended to have said, that, at the late election for members of our city council, two gentlemen of the Jewish persuasion were chosen by the suffrages of a large part of the citizens of their several wards, Messrs. S. Etting and J. I. Cohen. They are such as we would (in the language of Henry the IV.) introduce either to the friends or the enemies of our city. They are the first Jews ever elected by the people to office in Maryland, being until lately denied the rights of citizens, by the constitution of the state. Mr. Etting has been elected president of the first branch of the city council.

pared for the press last week, it was accidently omitted. We intended to have said, that, at the late election for members of our city council, two gentlemen of the Jewish persuasion were chosen by the suffrages of a large part of the citizens of their several wards, Messrs. S. Etting and J. I. Cohen. They are such as we would (in the language of Henry the IV.) introduce either to the friends or the enemies of our city. They are the first Jews ever elected by the people to office in Maryland, being until lately denied the rights of citizens, by the constitution of the state. Mr. Etting has been elected president of the first branch of the city council.

THE DEBATES IN CONGRESS, at the last session, were thus spoken of in a late French paper. The remarks are rather severe and too general; but it must be confessed we have been rendered liable to them—

"Violent language, gestures, personalities, threats, a total disregard of all good breeding and ordinary courtesy, have changed the aspect which the congress of the United States formerly wore."

HISTORY! The British Annual Register, generally received as one of the most authentic works that issues from the European press, under head of "United States, 1825," has the following false and ridiculous statement: every point of it is untrue:

"In the United States, the public attention was occupied by the election of a president, more than by any other event. The candidates were John Quincy Adams, secretary of state; Mr. Clay, speaker of the house of representatives; Mr. Crawford, secretary of the treasury, and general Jackson, distinguished by the cheap renown of being the only American general, who in the last war, had been engaged with British troops, and yet had escaped the disgrace of total defeat. * * * * * Mr. Clay, it was understood, transferred his votes to Mr. Adams, upon an agreement that, if Mr. Adams obtained the presidency, Mr. Clay should be secretary of state; and by this union of strength Mr. Adams was enabled to triumph. * * * As Jackson counted among his partizans the whole rabble of the country, their rage at their defeat was extreme; and it was the more violent because their candidate had unquestionably had a vast majority of the people on his side," &c.

A BANK! The commissioners appointed to take charge of the property and concerns of the Greene county (N. Y.) bank, have made a report, in which they state that in their opinion a great proportion of the debts due the bank are doubtful, and a very considerable part of them bad. It appears that the debts due and property belonging to the bank, consisting of notes discounted, bonds and mortgages, balances due from others banks for stock, value of banking house, cash on hand, counterfeit notes do. besides $20,000, of the New-Hope Delaware Bridge Company, held as collateral security, overdrawings, &c. amount to $216,409 70. The claims against the bank consist of stock $72,083 33, bills in circulation $123,713 50, and due to depositors, &c. $20,585 80—total $216,380 63.

[What excuse can be offered for exhibits like this? and yet the Greene county bank must have been honestly and prudently conducted—compared with many others that have blown up! Laws must be made that will reach such cases, and equally punish fraudulent persons within, as they do fraudulent persons without the banks.]

The account from the Rochester Album, that a verdict of guilty had been pronounced against Messrs. Wells and Forward, for a conspiracy to defraud the Niagara bank, is "a gross mistake, or unpardonably false." They are indicted, it is true, but have not been tried. Mr. Wells declares that the first intimation that he had in relation to the subject, was by a publication

BALTIMORE – 1826
FIRST JEWS ELECTED IN MARYLAND
Niles' Weekly Register, p. 102
October 14, 1826

In the first election following the passage of the Jew Bill in Maryland, allowing Jews to hold public office, two Jews were elected to the Baltimore City Council. Solomon Etting (b. 1764; d. 1847), who was elected president of the first branch of the city council at the time, and Jacob I. Cohen, Jr. (b. 1789; d. 1869), who would serve for several more terms and be elected first branch president from 1849 to 1851, had been instrumental in getting the Jew Bill passed. Cohen would later also serve as secretary-treasurer of the Baltimore City Board of School Commissioners for eight years after helping get it established.

According to the article, Etting and Cohen were "such as we would (in the language of Henry IV) introduce either to the friends or the enemies of our city."

(Cohen's business acumen is described in a "City of Washington – 1824" article on page 199.)

curiously preserved paper, I recognized it as an old acquaintance.

THE JEWS. Though a little paragraph complimentary to ourselves, as citizens of Baltimore, was pre-

NEW YORK – 1849
"DEFEAT OF [ENGLAND'S] JEWS' BILL"
New-York Weekly Tribune, p. 1 (col 2)
July 21, 1849

In a front-page article in the "From the Old World" column, the Tribune's London correspondent reports the defeat of England's Jews' Bill by the House of Lords. This act, which would allow Jews to take seats in Parliament, was previously approved by the House of Commons. Among the casualties of this defeat was the prevention of Baron Lionel Rothschild from entering Parliament. The correspondent, who regards this defeat as an example of the prejudices of the House of Lords, argues that it is only a matter of "time and labor" before this outdated view would be completely rejected. Moreover, he notes, "in a nation whose scepter extends over nations of Mohommedeans and Hindoos, it were to be wished that all restrictions upon opinion as marking legislative fitness were done away with."

The city of London election took place on Wednesday, and resulted in the re-election of Baron Rothschild, by an overwhelming majority. The event is regarded as an unmistakeable sign of the determination of the citizens to secure what is termed full religious liberty. The opposing candidate was Lord John Manners, who was beaten by a majority of over 3,000.

NEW YORK – 1849
ENGLAND
The New York Herald, p. 1 (col 1)
July 22, 1849

Though Baron Lionel de Rothschild was elected to Parliament as an MP from the City of London in 1847 – and re-elected in 1849, 1852 and 1857 – he refused to take his seat because of a required oath to the Christian faith. It wasn't until 1858, after the provision of Christian affirmation was removed, that he finally entered the House of Commons.

Rothschild's struggle was reported in the American press and carefully followed by American Jews. This item regarding Rothschild's 1849 re-election was reported in the "England" section of the Herald's "News from Europe" column. It noted that Rothschild was reelected "by an overwhelming majority" and that "the event is regarded as an unmistakable sign of the determination of the citizens to secure what is termed full religious liberty."

Religious restrictions for holding *any* political office in the United States was finally removed by the passage of the Fourteenth Amendment in 1868, ten years after England removed its restrictions.

FOR THE NEW-YORK TRIBUNE.

ENGLAND.
Defeat of the Jews' Bill—Political Progress in England — Queen's Visit to Ireland — Cholera—Mesmerism—Social Doctrines.
London Correspondence of The Tribune.

LONDON, Friday afternoon, June 29, 1849.

The principal event of the past week has been the rejection, by the House of Lords, of the claims of the Jews to sit in Parliament. The Parliamentary Oaths bill has been defeated. This, it was foreseen, would happen. Whenever an important measure, carrying with it the heart of the British people, goes up from the Commons to the Lords, the latter body, taught by abundant schooling, lets it pass with more or less important modifications. That which is carried in the Commons by reasoning and argumentation, runs through the Lords by the impetus received from below—by a kind of moral-physical force; for our hereditary legislators have had fearful experience, in the agonies of the Reform Bill, of what would occur were they to offer a passive resistance, which only calls for a sufficient push to give way. In revenge, however, for this permanent defeat in substantials, which all Conservative powers must undergo, their Lordships gallantly destroy small and uncared for measures of a popular kind, meanly nipping and tweaking where they dare not show open fight against the people. So it is with the Jew's bill. It is now defeated once more, though coming before them with an increased pressure from the House of Commons. But the subject begins to excite wider sympathies: the City of London—whose representative, Baron Lionel Rothschild, is deprived of his seat in Parliament by this vote of the Peers—is fairly *up*. The Baron has resigned his seat, and comes forward again for reëlection, and it is supposed will walk over the course. Moreover, the question has somewhat shifted; in the first instance it was a question of religious toleration, but it is now regarded as involving the matter, whether the City shall be dictated to in the choice of its representative; and this by a body which has no Constitutional right to interfere in the election of members for the Commons House of Parliament. Still, no one denies that the House of Lords has the privilege of doing what it has done; and it is curious to mark the strictly pacific and Constitutional tone which pervades the agitation. The successes of the People against the Lords, during the past twenty-five years, have taught them the science of political warfare which is adapted to this country; and future reforms are regarded as problems of time and labor, just as the taking of strongholds is at present a calculation of men and time.— There is no spite or brawling necessary, but such and such measures, so many sessions fo Parliament, so many favorable votes of the Commons, so many votes of the Lords, an extension of the interest involved to so many large towns; and then the matter is done.— Such is the tedious, cautious, thorough manner in which our people bear, forbear and triumph in their political career. There is no brilliancy here, but only the grandeur and solemnity of a passionless, but resistless, march. It may be years, but it will not be many, before the Jews are not only Commoners but Peers in our Legislature. And in a country whose scepter extends over nations of Mahommedans and Hindoos, it were to be wished that all restriction upon opinion as marking legislative fitness were done away with and that the door of permission were opened in the Constitution to men of every creed.

National Intelligencer.

WASHINGTON: TUESDAY, NOVEMBER 3, 1857.

FOR THE NATIONAL INTELLIGENCER.

A CARD. (2.)

In a recent political address General PILLOW charged that Mr. TRIST, with my assistance, had, in Mexico, administered a bribe to President or General Santa Anna, &c. By a card in the National Intelligencer I promptly replied that I was morally certain Mr. T. had not paid a cent, in the way of a bribe, to any body whatever in Mexico, and I solemnly added that I was personally totally ignorant of any bribe of any sort whatever, great or small, being paid to that high functionary, (Santa Anna,) or to any other, directly or indirectly, for his use or benefit, by or on account of any American officer or agent, civil or military. My denial Gen. Pillow calls (in a rejoinder) "evasive," "a mere quibble," and he affects to support his first assertion by extracts from "the sworn statements of Generals QUITMAN and SHIELDS," which, he says, he has "procured from the record of the War Department."

Entertaining for those Generals (Q. & S.) high admiration and respect, I was in haste—not that there was any thing material in the extracts—to learn from the War Department the character of the (to me) unknown "record" quoted by General Pillow. I have but now received a copy of the document, and in some of its other aspects it shall, presently, receive a passing notice. Suffice it to say, in this connexion, that neither of the statements produced by General Pillow, with so much gravity, contradicts me in the least on the only point in question, viz. the ten thousand dollar bribe; for neither of those Generals pretends to know to whom the bribe was paid, nor did any other American ever hear me whisper the name or names of the receivers, until confidentially disclosed on the final settlement, at the War Office, of my secret disbursements. General Pillow, however—"most ignorant of what he's most assur'd"—first assumes that he has had confided to him a great secret, and next betrays it by way of letting the world know that he had the honor of being trusted! The Mexican newspapers, I learn, have recently been filled with notices of General Pillow's denunciation of General Santa Anna, mixed up with the inquiry, *Who is the more infamous? He who receives a bribe*, or *the functionary who, in violation of his own and his country's honor, discloses the name of the traitor?"*

But this case, bad as it is, does not stand alone in our *recent* annals, (and, of course, nothing so base could have occurred in our earlier history;) for, January 30, 1857, a pliant Executive was made, by the plastic hand of a malignant Secretary, to communicate to the Senate, for *publication*—without any conceivable purpose but, at the expense of national faith and honor, to give me annoyance—the entire account I had confidentially rendered to the War Department of my secret disbursements in the Mexican war! It is true that *names* had been suppressed, by me, in the written items; but many entries were rendered, and now stand so published in this manner: "Paid messenger of the — Consul, $50;" "Paid an Englishman to report violations of the armistice, $200;" "Paid a member of the municipality, $162.50," &c., &c., &c. Already, in consequence of this publication, five highly respectable residents of Mexico—utterly guiltless of bribery, but liable to suspicion under those designations—have, through a distinguished channel, made application to me for exoneration.

Gen. Pillow speaks feelingly of "the great and patriotic statesman who was [in 1846] Chief Magistrate of the nation," his some time law partner, who had made him a major-general; the same who, early in the war, sent for me, and in the kindest and most beseeching manner solicited my personal sympathy as well as professional aid in conquering a peace, promising me his entire confidence and support; the same who, before I had reached Mexico, endeavored, first, to appoint a lieutenant general to supersede me; and, failing in that, next thought of placing me under the same party, appointed a major-general, (and of course) my junior; the

FROM THE CITY OF NEW YORK.

NEW YORK, OCTOBER 31.

The State election, to be held on Tuesday next, begins to engross more and more of the public attention, in spite of the money question. It being for State officers exclusively, no questions of national policy are properly involved in it; yet politicians find it difficult to divest themselves of extraneous influences. The choice of good men to fill seats on the bench is a paramount duty. In each of the tickets for this branch of the public service there are nine names, to wit: one Judge of the Court of Appeals, two Judges of the Supreme Court, two Judges of the Superior Court, one Judge of the Court of Common Pleas, one Judge of the Marine Court, the Surrogate and Recorder. It is but fair to say that the candidates of all the parties are men of high character and qualifications.

The Express thinks the death of a man like CRAWFORD, the sculptor, "so eminent in his profession, with friends and admirers in both hemispheres, and a fame that will live as long as that of the distinguished artists of ancient Greece and Rome," ought to receive more than the mere passing newspaper notices of the day and hour. It thinks the artists of New York, the city which gave him birth, ought to unite in some fitting memorial or remembrance.

There seems to be a concurrence of opinion amongst sagacious men every where that the merchants and banks of the East should co-operate in efforts to forward the produce of the West to market, thus relieving the East from its embarrassment in a great degree, and at the same time enabling Western merchants to pay their debts. In some instances there is a disposition to hold back for better prices, but the loss of interest for three or four months will more than counterbalance any supposed advantage by delay.

The Asia, which sailed on Wednesday for Liverpool, took out one hundred thousand dollars, chiefly in certificates of deposites on the Bank of England, in which shape a considerable amount of the reported specie arrivals by the Persia and Baltic were sent to this country.

The feeling in business circles appears to be more confident and cheerful. There is a disposition amongst many of the Banks to accommodate, at least so far as renewals are concerned. No new enterprises are undertaken, and a spirit of economy is beginning to rule. Considerable anxiety is felt to hear the effect in England of the news of our suspensions. The next steamer is, therefore, looked for with great interest.

The total amount of importations of specie and bullion into England for the first nine months of 1857 is stated as follows: From Australia, £8,472,300; from the United States, £6,182,400; from West Indies, Mexico, &c. £4,858,600; total £20,865,800—about one million greater than for the same period of the preceding year.

The Evening Post thus discourses on the policy of relieving the community by throwing the teeming crops of the country into market:

"The necessity of some measures for bringing forward the grain and produce of the West is daily more pressing. In the presnt state of financial affairs, the crops are the only means of liquidating the indebtedness of the West to the seaboard cities. There is scarcely money enough in the West for the daily transaction of their own business. In a little more than a month, at the longest, the means of transportation in any quantity commensurate with the requirements of commerce will be seriously impeded, if not rendered impossible. Last year, in the months of August, September, and October, millions of dollars worth of produce were forwarded from the West to the seaboard. This year, October has nearly passed and we have as yet comparatively nothing. Not a third so much has been received at the seaboard this year as last, while the demand during the coming winter is likely to be greater than ever before."

It seems that the indefatigable ERICSSON has never despaired of the success of his caloric motive power, and that he is now likely to prove its merit beyond a doubt. One of his engines, occupying less than a cubic foot of

THE SWISS TREATY.—THE HEBREW COMMITTEE AND THE PRESIDENT.

On Wednesday last a National Hebrew Convention was held in the city of Baltimore, represented by delegates appointed from Charleston, (S. C.) St. Louis, Chicago, Cincinnati, Maryland, and the District of Columbia. One of the principal subjects discussed was the recent treaty between the United States and Switzerland. Before adjourning a committee was appointed to draw up a memorial to the President of the United States and present it in person.

The committee thus appointed, after having performed the first portion of their labors, proceeded to this city, and on Saturday, by appointment, waited upon the President.

The memorial was presented by Col. P. PHILLIPS, late of Alabama, in a brief and appropriate speech. The President, in replying, said he would do all in his power to carry out the objects of the memorial and to abrogate the obnoxious clause of the treaty, and that instructions had already been forwarded to our representative at Berne to that effect.

Capt. J. P. LEVY then presented a similar memorial on the part of the Hebrews of the District of Columbia, and another was presented from the Hebrews of Charleston, of the same tenor, with a long list of influential names appended. To these the President replied that it afforded him great pleasure in being able to assure them that it would be one of his happiest moments to see throughout, not in only our own country, but the whole world, free religious toleration.

After a pleasant conversational intercourse of half an hour the committee withdrew, much pleased with the result which had attended the performance of their duties. They then waited upon the Secretary of State, who assured them that he would co-operate with the President in his endeavors to remove the cause of their complaint.

DEFENSIVE MEASURES.

The people of Philadelphia have taken the initiative in resisting and remedying the extortionate prices of subsistence to which city consumers on the whole Atlantic seaboard have been long subjected. Here in Washington, in the midst of the great wheat-growing States of Virginia and Maryland, the best quality flour is still kept up to *nine dollars* a barrel. A large meeting was held in Philadelphia on Tuesday night, at which the following preamble and resolutions were reported:

Whereas, in the present prostrate condition of the commercial and manufacturing interest of the community, involving the suspension of many of our leading merchants and the closing of our workshops and manufactories, whereby thousands whose sole dependence is their daily labor have been thrown out of employment:

And whereas, in consequence of this unusual and distressing state of affairs, a rapid depreciation in the value of merchandise, of labor, and of property generally has been and is now being experienced, which depreciation appears not up to the present time—contrary to all reasonable expectation, in view of the vast resources of the country—to have extended to the necessaries of life:

And whereas it is evident that, at the present high prices of provisions, it will soon be impossible for a large portion of our people to procure the comforts of life, and that many are threatened with actual starvation unless speedy relief be obtained: Therefore, be it

Resolved, That it is alike the duty and interest of all to unite their efforts in resisting the present extravagant prices of the leading articles of food, and to secure a reduction in the cost of living corresponding with the decreased value of other merchandise and labor.

2. *Resolved*, That, in the judgment of this meeting, a material reduction in the price of the leading articles of food may be made, and still leave to the producer a fair return for his labor and capital, to demand more than which is neither just nor wise.

3. *Resolved*, That, in order to bring the prices of provisions to a fair standard, we pledge ourselves not to pay more than the annexed prices for the following articles, viz:

Butter, per pound ....25 cents.
Beef, " ....12 cents.

WASHINGTON, D.C. – 1857
PROTESTING THE SWISS TREATY
National Intelligencer, p. 1 (col 3)
November 30, 1857

Beginning with the administration of Millard Fillmore, problems arose for American Jews regarding a commercial treaty with Switzerland that gave full rights to American Christians working or traveling there but allowed Swiss cantons to deny entry to American Jews. As a result of protests by American Jews, Fillmore refused to sign the treaty. But in 1855, the Senate approved a second draft of the treaty which, although less overtly, still enabled Swiss cantons to discriminate. This became clear in 1857 after an American, Mr. A. H. Gootman, was forced to leave the Swiss canton of Neuchatel – after five years of conducting business there – simply because he was a Jew.

This front page article, prominently displayed on the top half of the page, details one of many protests organized by American Jews, whom the article referred to as "Hebrews," against this Swiss-American treaty. At a National Hebrew Convention in Baltimore, delegates from Charleston, St. Louis, Chicago, Maryland and the District of Columbia drew up a Memorial addressed to President James Buchanan stating their objections. According to the article, the sympathetic Buchanan assured the petitioners that "it would be one of his happiest moments to see throughout, not only in our own country, but the whole world, free religious toleration."

Despite the president's acquiescence with the Jewish delegation, these anti-Jewish provisions were not removed until 1866 – and full civil rights for Jews in Switzerland were not guaranteed until a new Swiss Constitution was passed in 1874.

THE SWISS TREATY.—THE HEBREW COMMITTEE AND THE PRESIDENT.

On Wednesday last a National Hebrew Convention was held in the city of Baltimore, represented by delegates appointed from Charleston, (S. C.) St. Louis, Chicago, Cincinnati, Maryland, and the District of Columbia. One of the principal subjects discussed was the recent treaty between the United States and Switzerland. Before adjourning a committee was appointed to draw up a memorial to the President of the United States and present it in person.

The committee thus appointed, after having performed the first portion of their labors, proceeded to this city, and on Saturday, by appointment, waited upon the President.

The memorial was presented by Col. P. PHILLIPS, late of Alabama, in a brief and appropriate speech. The President, in replying, said he would do all in his power to carry out the objects of the memorial and to abrogate the obnoxious clause of the treaty, and that instructions had already been forwarded to our representative at Berne to that effect.

Capt. J. P. LEVY then presented a similar memorial on the part of the Hebrews of the District of Columbia, and another was presented from the Hebrews of Charleston, of the same tenor, with a long list of influential names appended. To these the President replied that it afforded him great pleasure in being able to assure them that it would be one of his happiest moments to see throughout, not in only our own country, but the whole world, free religious toleration.

After a pleasant conversational intercourse of half an hour the committee withdrew, much pleased with the result which had attended the performance of their duties. They then waited upon the Secretary of State, who assured them that he would co-operate with the President in his endeavors to remove the cause of their complaint.

CHARLESTON – 1863 "DISMISSAL OF THE BRITISH CONSUL…"

The Charleston Mercury,
p. 1 (col 2)
June 16, 1863

Judah P. Benjamin (b. St. Thomas, Virgin Islands, 1811; d. Paris, 1884) was Secretary of State of the Confederate States of America and the highest-ranking Jew in the Confederacy. A letter to Mr. Mason, the Confederate Commissioner to England, expressing his ill feelings about the refusal of Great Britain to recognize the Confederacy diplomatically was reprinted "from the Richmond

---

DISMISSAL OF THE BRITISH CONSUL AT RICHMOND—A STATE PAPER.

We give below, from the Richmond *Sentinel* of yesterday, a despatch of the Secretary of State of the Confederate States to Mr. MASON, our Commissioner to England. It makes known the causes of the late revocation of the exequatur of the British Consul at the port of Rich mond, and in doing so takes occasion to explain the general grounds of the President's action, and the views which govern the policy which he is pursuing:

CONFEDERATE STATES OF AMERICA,
DEPARTMENT OF STATE,
RICHMOND, 6th June, 1863.

SIR:—Herewith you will receive copies of the following papers:

A. Letter of George Moore, Esq., H. B. M.'s Consul in Richmond, to this Department, dated 16th February, 1863.

B. Letter of the Secretary of State to Consul Moore, 20th February, 1863.

C. Letters patent by the President, revoking the exequatur of Consul Moore, 5th June, 1863.

D. Letter enclosing to Consul Moore a copy of the letters patent revoking his exequatur.

It is deemed proper to inform you that this action of the President was influenced in no small degree by the communication to him of an unofficial letter of Consul Moore, to which I shall presently refer.

It appears that two persons, named Molony and Farrell, who were enrolled as conscripts in our service, claimed exemption on the ground that they were British subjects, and Consul Moore, in order to avoid the difficulty which prevented his corresponding with this Department as set forth in the paper B, addressed himself directly to the Secretary of War, who was ignorant of the request made by this Department for the production of the Consul's commission. The Secretary of War ordered an investigation of the facts, when it became apparent that the two men had exercised the right of suffrage in this State, thus debarring themselves of all pretext for denying their citizenship; that both had resided here for eight years, and had settled on and were cultivating farms owned by themselves. You will find annexed the report of Lt. Col. Edgar, marked E, and it is difficult to conceive a case presenting stronger proofs of the renunciation of native allegiance, and of the acquisition of *de facto* citizenship, than are found in that report. It is in relation to such a case that it has seemed proper to Consul Moore to denounce the Government of the Confederate States to one of its own citizens as being indifferent "to cases of the most atrocious cruelty." A copy of his letter to the counsel of the two men is annexed, marked F.

The earnest desire of this Government is to entertain amicable relations with all nations, and with none do its interests invite the formation of closer ties than with Great Britain. Although feeling aggrieved that the Government of Her Majesty has pursued a policy which, according to the confessions of Earl Russell himself, has increased the disparity of strength which he considered to exist between the belligerents, and has conferred signal advantage on our enemies in a war in which Great Britain announces herself to be really and not nominally neutral, the President has not deemed it necessary to interpose any obstacle to the continued residence of British Consuls with in the Confederacy, by virtue of exequaturs granted by the former Government. His course has been consistently guided by the principles which underlie the whole structure. The State of Virginia having

of our Government. The State of Virginia having delegated to the Government of the United States by the Constitution of 1787 the power of controlling its foreign relations, became bound by the action of that Government in its grant of an exequatur to Consul Moore. When Virginia seceded, withdrew the powers delegated to the Government of the United States and conferred them on this Government, the exequatur granted to Consul Moore was not thereby invalidated. An act done by an agent, while duly authorized, continues to bind the principal after the revocation of the agent's authority. On these grounds the President has hitherto steadily resisted all influences which have been exerted to induce him to exact of foreign consuls that they should ask for an exequatur from this Government as a condition of the continued exercise of their functions. It was not deemed compatible with the dignity of the Government to extort, by enforcing the withdrawal of national protection from neutral residents, such inferential recognition of its independence as might be supposed to be implied in the request for an exequatur. The consuls of foreign nations, therefore, established within the Confederacy, who were in possession of an exequatur issued by the Government of the United States prior to the formation of the Confederacy, have been maintained and respected in the exercise of their legitimate functions, and the same protection and respect will be accorded to them in future, so long as they confine themselves to the sphere of their duties, and seek neither to evade nor defy the legitimate authority of this Government within its own jurisdiction.

There has grown up an abuse, however, the result of this tolerance on the part of the President, which is too serious to be longer allowed. Great Britain has deemed it for her interest to refuse acknowledging the patent fact of the existence of this Confederacy as an independent nation. It can scarcely be expected that we should, by our own conduct, simply assent to the justice or propriety of that refusal. Now that the British Minister accredited to the Government of our enemies assumes the power to issue instructions and exercise authority over the Consuls of Great Britain residing within this country; nay, even of appointing agents to supervise British interests in the Confederate States—this course of conduct plainly ignores the existence of this Government, and implies the continuance of the relations between that Minister and the Consuls of Her Majesty resident within the Confederacy which existed prior to the withdrawal of these States from the Union. It is further the assertion of a right, on the part of Lord Lyons, by virtue of his credentials as Her Majesty's Minister at Washington, to exercise the power and authority of a Minister accredited to Richmond, and officially received as such by the President. Under these circumstances, and because of similar action by other Ministers, the President has felt it his duty to order that no direct communication be permitted between the Consuls of neutral nations in the Confederacy and the functionaries of those nations residing within the enemy's country. All communications, therefore, between Her Majesty's Consuls, or Consular Agents, in the Confederacy and foreign countries, whether neutral or hostile, will hereafter be restricted to vessels arriving from or dispatched for neutral ports. The President has the less reluctance in imposing this restriction because of the ample facilities for correspondence which are now afforded by the fleets of Confederate and neutral steamships engaged in regular trade between neutral countries and the Confederate ports. This trade is daily increasing in spite of the paper blockade, which is upheld by Her Majesty's Government, in disregard, as the President conceives, of the rights of this Confederacy, of the dictates of public law, and of the duties of impartial neutrality.

You are instructed by the President to furnish a copy of this despatch, with a copy of the papers appended, to Her Majesty's Secretary of State for Foreign Affairs.

I am, very respectfully,
Your obedient servant,
J. P. BENJAMIN,
Secretary of State.

Hon. JAMES M. MASON,
Commissioner, &c., &c., London.

Sentinel of yesterday," on the front page of this abbreviated two-page issue of the *Mercury*. Benjamin wrote: "Great Britain has deemed it for her interest to refuse acknowledging the patent fact of the existence of this Confederacy as an independent nation. It can be scarcely expected that we should, by our own conduct, simply assent to the justice or propriety of that refusal." He went on to detail the limitations placed by "the President" of the Confederacy on communications and correspondence, restricting communications "to vessels arriving from or dispatched for neutral points [because this] trade is daily increasing in spite of the paper blockade, which is upheld by Her Majesty's Government…."

THE ARTICLES on the next three pages discuss the political ramifications of Grant's notorious Order No. 11. The Order itself is discussed in greater detail in *Chapter 10: The Civil War (see page 216).*

Photograph of Ulysses S. Grant from the Brady-Handy Collection courtesy of the Library of Congress, Prints & Photographs Division, [LC-BH826- 3703]

MANCHESTER, NEW HAMPSHIRE – 1868
"GRANT AND THE JEWS."
The Union Democrat, p. 1 (col 1)
June 30, 1868

Grant and the Jews.

The following is Grant's famous order issued at Memphis in 1862:

The Jews, as a class, violating every regulation of trade established by the Treasury Department, also department orders, are hereby expelled from the depart ment within twenty-four hours from the receipt of this order by post commanders.

They will see that this class of people are furnished with passes and required to leave, and any one returning after such notification will be arrested and held in confinement until an opportunity occurs of sending them out as prisoners, unless furnished with permits from these headquarters.

No passes will be given this people to visit headquarters for the purpose of making personal application for trade permits.

There can be no apology for such an order. Men should be punished for violations of laws and orders, not for being of this or the other party or sect. The Jews take this view of it, and we have before us a denunciation of Grant signed by 2000 Jewish voters in St. Louis. They say:

"Worse than Gen. Grant none in the nineteenth century in civilized countries has abused the Jews, officially, in broad daylight and most barbarously. If there are any among us who lick the feet that kick them about, and like dogs, run after him who has whipped them; if there are persons small enough to receive indecencies and outrages without resentment, and creep about their tormentors for selfish purposes, we hope their number is small, and we know it is too small to be counted in comparison to those who will not vote for a man and oppose him who outraged the Jews in a manner as Gen. Grant did."

The presidential candidacy of General U.S. Grant drew strong front-page condemnation from this New England newspaper, published in a city where very few Jews lived, based on the notorious General Order No. 11 he issued in 1862. The Order required Jews in the states of Tennessee, Mississippi and Kentucky to leave within 24 hours – as punishment for their alleged black market activities – or face arrest.

"There could be no apology for such an order," claimed the article entitled *Grant and the Jews*. "Men should be punished for violation of laws and orders, not for being of this or the other party or sect."

The last paragraph of the article cites a petition signed by 2,000 St. Louis Jewish voters claiming that none in civilized countries in the nineteenth century has abused the Jews more than General Grant.

The New-York Times.

Hebrew Grant and Colfax Campaign Club.

The Hebrew Grant and Colfax Campaign Club was organized on the 22d of August, and has its headquarters at No. 7 Delancey-street. It held its first regular meeting last evening, and will continue to hold them every Tuesday throughout the campaign. The President is Dr. ABRAM G. SEVY; the Vice-Presidents, S. LANG and H. WATERMAN; the Secretary, H. D. KALINSKI, and the Treasurer, M. FLOERSHEIM. This claims to be the first Jewish political club organized in this country. According to its circular it was formed to demonstrate that the Hebrews of this City, as a body, have no affinity with traitors, smugglers or repudiators. The Club will endeavor to remove the prejudice against Gen. GRANT still lingering in the minds of a few of their race, on account of his old order excluding a few Hebrew sutlers from his army in the West. The assemblage last evening was exclusively for business purposes, and plans were laid for a thorough canvass of the Hebrew population of this City. Sixty names were added to the roll, and great interest was manifested in the proceedings. Rev. WOLF SCHREIER, Mr. ABRAM D. LEVY and Mr. S. LANG made short addresses. Mr. LEVY made allusion to a Democratic Club of Hebrews, about forming in St. Louis, which will make Gen. GRANT's anti-Hebrew army order a leading feature of its opposition to him. The Grant and Colfax Hebrew Club would do its best, he said, by publications, to neutralize the effect of the St. Louis Club among the Hebrews in the South and West.

NEW YORK CITY – 1868
"HEBREW GRANT AND COLFAX CAMPAIGN CLUB"
The New-York Times, p. 1 (col 7)
September 9, 1868

Despite the anti-Semitic cloud attached to General Grant that stemmed from Order No. 11 requiring Jews to immediately exit the three Border States under his command in the Civil War, certain New York City Jews supported his Republican presidential candidacy. A front-page item reported the formation of the "Hebrew Grant and Colfax Campaign Club … the first Jewish political club organized in this country."

This debut announcement indirectly supported Grant's charge of treasonous Jewish traders which precipitated his expulsion order. "Hebrews of this city, as a body, have no affinity with traitors, smugglers or repudiators. The Club will endeavor to remove the prejudice against Gen. Grant still lingering in the minds of a few of their race on account of his old order."

In addition, this new club would seek to "neutralize" the influence of a "Democratic Club of Hebrews" in St. Louis that planned on making "Gen. GRANT's anti-Hebrew army order a leading feature of its opposition to him" (see page 119).

The New-York Times.

VOL. XVIII......NO. 5362.   NEW-YORK, MONDAY, NOVEMBER 30, 1868.   PRICE FOUR CENTS.

GEN. GRANT'S JEW ORDER.

Why It Was Issued—A Statement of the Circumstances of the Case.

From the Israelite.

We cheerfully give place to the following distinguished correspondence, which will, beyond all doubt, be read with pleasure by all of our readers who, like ourselves, desire to see justice done to Gen. GRANT, now the incoming Executive head of the Government:

LETTER FROM HON. I. N. MORRIS, OF ILLINOIS.

QUINCY, Ill., Nov. 15, 1868.

Dr. Isaac M. Wise, Editor of the Israelite:

I send you inclosed a copy of a letter in my possession from Gen. GRANT, together with one from Mr. MOSES, written to Gen. GRANT, and to which this is a reply. Few men have the moral greatness of character to write such a letter. Its publication during the pendency of the election would have cast suspicion on the motive which prompted it. No such suspicion can arise now.

I am aware that you and many of you have conceived that Gen. GRANT did you great injustice in promulgating Order No. 11. His frank denial of any such intention proves not only the magnanimity of his character, but that he is incapable of entertaining against the Jews, or any other people, as a sect or race, an unkind feeling. He is too great and good for that. Will you, therefore, do the General the justice to publish his letter in your widely-extended paper? I assume the liberty of sending it to you for that purpose. I remain, Sir, yours respectfully,

I. N. MORRIS.

ADOLPH MOSES TO GEN. GRANT.

QUINCY, Ill., Sept. 3, 1868.

Gen. U. S. Grant, Washington, D. C.:

SIR: I address you at the earnest solicitation of your friend, Hon. I. N. MORRIS, in relation to the matter now generally known as Order No. 11. It will hardly surprise you that we, as a people, already over-sensitive through former oppression and contumely, should lament the issuance of that order, whatever the immediate causes might have dictated. I am assured by high authority, some of which I might call Jewish, that no idea of special dislike to the Jews prompted you; on the contrary, that you regret the sweeping effect of the order.

However generous this avowal may be on your part, yet you are well aware that a word spoken or a sentence written ceases to be the property of the speaker or writer, and passes into the domain of history, particularly when spoken or written by a man of super-eminent position and worth. I regret that our people, who love to enjoy the quiet retreat of private life, should be so prominently paraded in this campaign, but the instinct of self-defence presses utterance, however welcome the task. Our demands are simply to be judged like other people, and not to have the vices and shortcoming of our bad men illuminated at the expense of the many virtues and excellent qualities of our good men.

Whatever the issue of this campaign may be, Mr. MORRIS assures me that you bear no ill-will to the Jewish people, and if they feel the severe compulsion to cast their suffrages against you in this campaign, they do so, in many instances, under protest, for with them their long-assailed reputation demands the greatest sacrifices, even at the risk of being misunderstood by the judgment of the hour. Excuse the liberty of addressing you. I have the encouragement of one of your friends.

Very respectfully,   ADOLPH MOSES.

GEN. GRANT TO HON. I. N. MORRIS.

GALENA, Ill., Sept. 14, 1868.

Hon. I. N. Morris:

DEAR SIR—I am in receipt of a letter of Mr. A. MOSES, of the 3d inst., inclosing one from you, bearing same date. My first inclination was to answer Mr. MOSES, because you desired it; then I thought it would be better to adhere to the rule of silence as to all letters. Were I once to commence answering all political questions asked of me, there would not be time between now and the 3d of November to get through. Mr. MOSES, I think, will readily understand this. In regard to Order No. 11, hundreds of letters have been written to me about it, by persons of the faith affected by it. I do or did not answer any of the writers, but permitted a statement of the facts concerning the origin of the order to be made out and given to some one of them for publication. *I do not pretend to sustain the order.*

At the time of its publication I was incensed by a reprimand received from Washington for permitting acts which Jews within my lines were engaged in. There were many other persons within my lines equally bad with the worst of them, but the difference was that the Jews could pass with impunity from our army to the other, and gold, in violation of orders, was being smuggled through the lines, at least so it was reported. The order was issued and sent without any reflection and without thinking of the Jews as a sect or race to themselves, but simply as persons who had successfully (I say successfully, instead of persistently, because there were plenty of ——— ——— ——— ——— ——— ——— who violated an order, which greatly inured to the help of the rebels.

Give Mr. MOSES assurance that I have no prejudice against sect or race, but want each individual to be judged by his own merit. Order No. 11 does not sustain this statement, I admit, but then I do not sustain that order. It never would have been issued if it had not been telegraphed the moment it was penned, and without reflection.

Yours, truly,   U. S. GRANT.

NEW YORK –
1868
"GEN. GRANT'S JEW ORDER"
The New-York Times, p. 2 (col 7) November 30, 1868

Following Grant's election to the presidency, this article, originally published in *The Israelite,* appeared. The article consisted of correspondence two months preceding the election between Adolph Moses (b. 1837; d. 1905) and Grant. Moses began the Civil War as a member of the Louisiana military, but after capture and parole built a new life in Chicago.

Rather than expressing a tone of victimhood, Moses apologetically queries Grant about the notorious Order No.11 he issued which expelled Jews from three states under his command on 24 hours' notice. "I regret," wrote Moses, "that our people who love to enjoy the quiet retreat of private life, should be so prominently paraded in the campaign."

Grant replied that although there were smugglers of various ethnicities, Jews were the only ones who seemed to move with "impunity" between both military lines. "The order," he notes, "was written and sent without reflection and without thinking of the Jews as a sect or race to themselves." Grant added that he himself bears no prejudice to any sect or race, and that he believed that people "should be judged by their own merit."

Chapter #7

Images of "The Jews"

VANDALISM of Jewish burial grounds in the mid-eighteenth century represented a subtle but real form of anti-Semitism. Prominent Jews such as New York's Jacob Franks and Philadelphia's Nathan Levy turned to newspapers when the cemeteries of their respective Jewish communities were attacked. Notices offering rewards were placed by each to seek help in finding the perpetrators in order to bring them to justice.

According to William Pencak *(Jews and Gentiles in Early America, 1654-1800,* Ann Arbor, 2005), these incidents of violence against Jews were attributable to what he terms "populist" anti-Semitism. Because a good number of Pennsylvania's early Jews [for example] were wealthy, cosmopolitans "easily accepted as members of [and by] anglicized Philadelphia elite to which Quakers, Anglicans, and Presbyterians all belonged," the common people resented them all the more. Pencak maintains that Benjamin Franklin set the tone for this elite form of philo-Semitism – leading to the "populist" anti-Semitism – when he made the following complimentary reference to Jews in *The Pennsylvania Packet* (September 15, 1737), around the same time that the Levy brothers first settled in Philadelphia: "The Jews were acquainted with the several Arts and Sciences long e're the Romans became a People, or the Greeks were known among the Nations."

WHEREAS some malicious and evil-minded Persons, have lately been guilty of doing very considerable Damage, both to the Walls and Tombs of the Jewish Burying-place, near this City : This is therefore to give Notice, that if any Person or Persons, shall discover the Offender or Offenders, so that he or they may be brought to Justice, they shall receive a Reward of *Five Pounds,* paid by   JACOB FRANKS.

NEW YORK – 1746
REWARD OF FIVE POUNDS OFFERED
New York Gazette or Weekly Post-Boy, p. 2 (col 2)
July 21, 1746

Long before Congregation Shearith Israel built its first synagogue at Mill Street – the first such building in New York City – the congregation had established a Jewish cemetery. In fact, the congregation's cemetery had already been moved to a second location, in what is today Chinatown, more than 40 years before the 1730 consecration of their Mill Street Synagogue.

Serving a Jewish population of some one hundred at the time, the Jewish burial ground was situated outside the city limits. It required a deliberate trip to get to, yet vandals went out of their way to do so and to do "very considerable Damage, both to the Walls and Tombs of the Jewish Burying-place." In this advertisement, Jacob Franks – the city's wealthiest Jewish merchant and a learned and observant Jew – offered to personally finance a "Reward of *Five Pounds*" to anyone discovering the "malicious and evil-minded persons . . . so he or they may be brought to Justice." Franks (b. Germany, 1688; d. New York, 1769) was closely involved in both the synagogue and cemetery and had served as Shearith Israel's president when the Mill Street synagogue's cornerstone was laid.

Portrait of Jacob Franks by Gerardus Duyckinck I, Crystal Bridges Museum of American Art, Bentonville, AR.

WHereas many unthinking people have fet up marks, and fir'd feveral fhot againft the fence of the Jewifh Burying-ground, which not only deftroyed the faid fence, but alfo a tomb-ftone inclofed in it; there being a brick-wall now erected, I muft defire thofe fportfmen to forbear (for the future) firing againft the faid wall: If they do, whoever will inform, fo that the offender be convicted thereof before a magiftrate, fhall have Twenty Shillings reward, paid by   NATHAN LEVY.

PHILADELPHIA – 1751
REWARD OFFERED
The Pennsylvania Gazette, p. 2 (col 2)
August 29, 1751

The earliest public presence of Philadelphia's small Jewish community was a grave. Arriving from New York, Philadelphia's first permanent Jewish settlers were the Levy brothers, Nathan (b. 1704; d. 1753) and Isaac (b. 1706; d. 1777). When one of Nathan's children died in 1738, he applied to John Penn for "a small piece of ground" to be used as a family cemetery. The grave, originally located on Walnut Street, was moved two years later to Spruce Street, where Levy secured a larger plot, several blocks west of the built-up city, to be used as a permanent burial ground for the entire Jewish community.

Still on the same site, the cemetery is the resting place for several historically prominent members of Philadelphia's colonial and Revolutionary eras. A plaque at the entrance notes a common, though erroneous, belief about Nathan Levy, that the Liberty Bell was brought to America on his ship, the Myrtilla. However, the ship is reported to have docked at the end of September 1752 while the bell had already been reported as having "recently arrived" in a September 1, 1752 report by Isaac Norris, the man responsible for the bell.

Until Philadelphia's first synagogue, Mikveh Israel, was built in 1771, Levy's small graveyard remained the only institutional sign of the Jewish community's presence. And although it was rather remote at the time, just like the one in New York, this cemetery was also vandalized, forcing Levy to place his notice in the *Gazette.*

June 14. 1750.

NUMB. 1122.

The Pennsylvania GAZETTE.

Containing the freſheſt Ad-   vices, foreign and domeſtick.

Extract of a private letter from Liſbon, March 1.

I MUST not conclude without informing you of a very unfair proceeding of the Portugueſe, in regard to Capt. Veal, of the Queen of Portugal, employed in this trade.——Some time ago this gentleman carried over to England a very rich cargo: I mean a knot of Jews, who had feather'd their neſts here, and thought it time to withdraw with the fruits of their induſtry. But it ſeems thoſe Jews were good chriſtians, or good catholicks, as many profeſs to be, for the ſake of making their fortunes in this country: So that by their flight, thoſe *locuſts* [the inquiſition] whoſe origin is, doubtleſs, from the *bottomleſs pit,* have been deprived of a good fat prey; for a Jewiſh convert, if he becomes rich, has all his words and actions watch'd by the informers and familiars of that infernal tribunal, that they may find occaſion to take him into their clutches, from whence he never gets looſe without the loſs of goods or life, or both. So that you need not be ſurprized when I tell you that poor Capt. Veal, upon his return hither, has been clapp'd up in priſon, for no other reaſon, that I can learn, than that he was inſtrumental in balking the expectations of the holy office; a crime for which others have ſuffer'd before him, whenever thoſe *ſatanical Harpies* could come at the knowledge of it, and had an opportunity to wreak their revenge. After going through ſome forms of law, he may get his liberty, but never any ſatisfaction for loſs of time and expence, &c."

An Extract of a letter from Amſterdam, March 8.

" Affairs grow every day more quiet in Holland than other; but it appears that the ſyſtem for levying of taxes by way of collection, will not continue long, eſpecially if what has been publiſhed be true, that the Prince Stadtholder (whom certain people had impoſed upon by feigning ſo well to be in the true intereſt of their country, that his ſerene highneſs was perſuaded there were not more zealous patriots in it) begins now to ſee that he has been deceived. Some of theſe pretenders have taken off the maſk, and his ſerene highneſs has diſcovered that they are ſecret abettors in the faction of the old magiſtrates, have been always bitter enemies to his houſe, are ſo ſtill, and are conſtantly labouring to alienate the affections of the people from, and even to ſtir up their hatred to his ſerene highneſs; wherein they have but too well ſucceeded, by cauſing the proviſional tax to paſs, and in levying the other taxes by collection, which were accompanied by placarts without number, and almoſt all of them exacting dreadful oaths from all degrees of people, which occaſioned ſome body to tell a magiſtrate, ' That it looked as if the government had a mind to people hell with the Dutch.' To the breach of theſe oaths large penalties are added, which is rarely practiſed in any other ſtate; but where there is none, 'tis generally heavy. 'Tis aſſured, however, theſe pretended patriots are upon the point of being diſgraced; but as this is to be done at once, great pains are taken to diſcover all thoſe who are of the ſame ſtamp, in order to get rid of them all at the ſame time,

and to ſend them by an exceſs of goodneſs, to plant cabages in their places of retreat, inſtead of puniſhing them as they deſerve. 'Tis propoſed that honeſter men will be put in their places, in caſe ſuch can be found; for private intereſt has made the Dutchmen, who were heretofore honeſt and ſimple, ſuch knaves, that they are not inferior in roguery to the moſt determined Machiavels."

Extract of a letter from Stockholm, March 20.

" Baron Rhode, envoy extraordinary from the king of Pruſſia, has declared to our miniſtry, that his Pruſſian majeſty will punctually perform his engagements with this crown, as ſoon as Ruſſia ſhall commence hoſtilities againſt us. According to treaty, Pruſſia is bound to furniſh 6000 foot and 3000 horſe, with a ſuitable train of artillery. The ſuccours which France is alſo obliged to furniſh to Sweden, are to conſiſt of ſhips of war and land-forces. But as thoſe ſuccours may not be ſufficient to put us in a condition to cope with Ruſſia, there is a clauſe in the treaties, importing, that farther aſſiſtance ſhall be given, as occaſion may require. According to a liſt of our forces, which is about, and is ſaid to be very exact, they conſiſt of 54,000 men, all well diſciplined: A breakfaſt indeed for the forces of our over-grown neighbour; but with the aſſiſtance of France and Pruſſia, and a diverſion on the ſide of the Ukrain and Hungary, we hope to cut out work enough for the Ruſſians."

Hague, March 13 There hath been an inſurrection at Heldey, a burgh on the territory of the Texel, on occaſion of collecting the taxes. The rioters carried things ſo far as to oblige the magiſtrates to lay down their office, and leave the town. The ſtadtholder, being informed of it, ſent thither the fiſcal, two commiſſaries, and a party of ſoldiers, to enquire into the affair, and ſeize the ringleaders.

The proclamation iſſued by the ſtates general for a faſt on the 25th inſt. N. S. has theſe remarkable words in the preamble, *viz.* " Whereas the ſtates are not entirely without diſquietude on the ſubject of the late peace, on account of its not being ſo firmly eſtabliſhed as that they can abſolutely depend on its laſting, eſpecially when they reflect on the ſituation of affairs in the North, which are ſtill very far from being adjuſted in the manner to be wiſhed, and which would not fail, if unhappily they ſhould come to a rupture, to embroil the ſtate in a new war; for theſe cauſes, &c."

Leghorn, March 21. The maſter of an Engliſh merchant ſhip arrived here from Port-Mahon reports, that at his departure from thence a great number of workmen were employed in repairing the fortifications, and that a large convoy of all kinds of ammunition was daily expected from England. This news appears to us, as if the negotiations at Madrid did not go to the liking of the Britiſh court.

Hambourg, April 6. According to all the accounts we now receive, there is great reaſon to fear that a war will ſpeedily break out in the North, notwithſtanding all the pains which moſt of the courts of Europe ſeem to have taken to preſerve its repoſe.

PUBLICK AFFAIRS, March 31.

As to the affairs of the Dutch, and their reflections on what paſſes in the reſt of Europe, we have nothing better concerning them than what is contained in the following extract of a letter from Amſterdam, dated March 10.

" Our merchants now begin to hope that their grievances, which are without number, will be redreſſed, ſince the Prince Stadtholder has laid open the conduct of the financiers, and has begun to cauſe report to be made to the ſtates general, of the petitions which have been preſented to him by different bodies of tradeſmen and manufacturers, and are more than 500 in number.

" Our affairs in France go on but very indifferently, the miniſters there ſhowing great backwardneſs to revive the tariff of 1739, as we have been made to hope they would, in order to lull us aſleep as uſual. They now make our ſhips pay 50 ſols per ton, and 4 ſols per cent. They moreover prohibit the entry of our dry'd herrings. What can we do in theſe affairs? We muſt ſubmit, at leaſt for a time, not being in a condition of doing ourſelves juſtice. People here are much ſurprized, that the court of France defers ſo long, under frivolous pretences of ceremony, to ſend its ambaſſadors to Vienna and the Hague, and that theſe two courts have ſhown no impatience to ſend theirs to Paris; whereas the courts of Madrid, Verſailles and London, have already made each other this compliment."

LONDON, March 12.

The ſhock of the earthquake which was felt on the 8th inſtant, was very ſenſibly felt in Eſſex, as far as Epping, and at the following places, *viz.* Bromley, as far as Chriſlehurſt, Beckenham, and Croydon; at the two laſt mentioned places it occaſioned the hammers of the clocks to ſtrike upon the bells; it alſo threw down a ſtack of chimnies on Saffron-hill, two other ſtacks, and part of a building in Bermondſey-ſtreet; at Iſlington it was ſo violent that the bells at ſeveral gentlemens doors rang as if pulled by a ſudden jerk. It was judged to roll along from weſt to eaſt, like the waves of the ſea, when driven by the wind in a great ſtorm.

The biſhop of London, in his letter this day addreſſed to the clergy and inhabitants of the city of London, takes notice, that it is every man's duty to give attention to all the warnings which God in his mercy affords to a ſinful people: Such warnings we have had by two great ſhocks of an earthquake; tho' leſs or hardened ſinners may be deaf to theſe calls; and little philoſophers, who ſee a little, and but very little, into natural cauſes, may think they ſee enough to account for what happens, without calling in the aid of a ſpecial providence. But, be their imaginations to themſelves, the ſubject is too ſerious for trifling, and calls us off to other views.

His lordſhip, to inforce the ſerious conſideration of this warning, takes notice of the general corruption of the times: " While I was writing this, ſays he, I caſt my eye upon the newſpaper of the day, and counted no leſs than fifteen advertiſements for plays, opera's, muſick and dancing, for meetings at gardens, for cockfighting, prize fighting, &c. Should this paper go on, what an idea muſt it give to the church-

PENNSYLVANIA – 1750
"...PRIVATE LETTER FROM LISBON"

The Pennsylvania Gazette, p. 1 (col 1)
June 14, 1750

Reflecting Benjamin Franklin's opposition to religious coercion, the front page of his *Gazette* includes an "Extract of a private letter from Lisbon." The letter described the "very unfair proceeding of the Portuguese," in regard to certain "Capt. Veal, of the Queen of Portugal, employed in this trade."

During the Portuguese Inquisition, when Jews faced a death sentence for practicing their faith, many secretly observed Jewish rites but publicly pretended to be Christian converts in order to thrive. Veal was put in prison because "some time ago [he] carried over to England a very rich cargo: I mean a knot of Jews, who had feather'd their nests here, and thought it time to withdraw with the fruits of their industry."

Extract of a private letter from Lisbon, March 1.

I MUST not conclude without informing you of a very unfair proceeding of the Portuguese, in regard to Capt. Veal, of the Queen of Portugal, employed in this trade.——Some time ago this gentleman carried over to England a very rich cargo: I mean a knot of Jews, who had feather'd their nests here, and thought it time to withdraw with the fruits of their industry. But it seems those Jews were good christians, or good catholicks, as many profess to be, for the sake of making their fortunes in this country : So that by their flight, those *locusts* [the inquisition] whose origin is, doubtless, from the *bottomless pit*, have been deprived of a good fat prey ; for a Jewish convert, if he becomes rich, has all his words and actions watch'd by the informers and familiars of that infernal tribunal, that they may find occasion to take him into their clutches, from whence he never gets loose without the loss of goods or life, or both. So that you need not be surprized when I tell you that poor Capt. Veal, upon his return hither, has been clapp'd up in prison, for no other reason, that I can learn, than that he was instrumental in balking the expectations of the holy office ; a crime for which others have suffer'd before him, whenever those *satanical Harpies* could come at the knowledge of it, and had an opportunity to wreak their revenge. After going through some forms of law, he may get his liberty, but never any satisfaction for loss of time and expence, &c."

The unidentified writer of the letter goes on to explain how great a problem what Veal did was to the Portuguese: "But it seems those Jews were good Christians, or good catholics, as many profess to be, for the sake of making their fortunes in this country: So that by their flight, those *locusts* [the inquisition] whose origin is, doubtless, from the *bottomless pit,* have been deprived of a good *fat prey;* for a Jewish convert, if he becomes rich, has all his words and actions watch'd by the informers of that infernal tribunal, that they may find occasion to take him into their clutches, from whence he may never get loose without the loss of goods or life, or both."

The extract ends with information about Veal's status, reporting "...that poor Capt. Veal, upon his return hither, has been clapp'd up in prison, for no other reason, that I can learn, than that he was instrumental in balking the expectations of the holy office ; a crime for which others have suffer'd before him, whenever *those satanical Harpies* could come at the knowledge of it.... After going through some forms of law, he may get his liberty, but never any satisfaction for loss of time and expense &c."

November 1, 1753. NUMB. 1297.

The PENNSYLVANIA   GAZETTE.

Containing the Freſheſt Ad-   *vices, Foreign and Domeſtick.*

PHILADELPHIPHIA – 1753
FRANKLIN'S "GAZETTE" ON THE JEW BILL OF 1753
The Pennsylvania Gazette, p. 1 (col 2)
November 1, 1753

Benjamin Franklin's philo-Semitism was shown by the front-page prominence he gave in his paper to a description of the "Jew Bill of 1753," whose purpose was to allow for Jewish naturalization. Nearly half the front page is taken up with a defense of this legislation which would have permitted foreign born Jews to obtain English citizenship without being required to swear loyalty to the Church of England (native born Jews were citizens from birth). Ultimately, however, popular opposition to this bill was so strong, that it was repealed.

As precedent, the Bill noted that in 1740 in the American colonies, several hundred Jews who had either lived there for at least seven years, or had served as mariners during the war, were allowed to become naturalized without taking the sacrament.

But, in truth, the arguments for this Bill were more self-serving than humanitarian. The Bill aimed to attract "rich Jews," in particular, who might instead have immigrated to either France or Holland. The article points out that the English version was superior to the French, because both rich and poor were eligible to enter France, while eligibility for citizenship in England was limited to the "rich."

Moreover, Jews "support their own poor," and "their having no country of their own to retire to, after acquiring estates here," meant that England had nothing to fear about wealthy Jews possibly moving elsewhere. Given these positive features, concludes the author, opposition to the legislation was based on nothing more than "ignorance or folly."

From the GENTLEMAN's MAGAZINE *for* June, 1753.

The following Paper which is written by a Gentleman who ſigns J. S. did not come to our hands time enough to be inſerted in our Magazine of laſt month. It has been ſince publiſhed in the *London* papers, and from thence copied into thoſe publiſhed in other parts of the kingdom; but we think there is ſtill ſufficient reaſon to take it into our collection, as it is an excellent compendium of the ſtatute, and an irrefragable anſwer to all that has been or can be ſaid againſt it.

The BILL, *permitting the Jews to be Naturalized by Parliament, having been miſrepreſented in the* London Gazetteer, *of Friday the 18th of May; and probably having never been read either by the Author of that Paper, or by ſeveral others who have ſince ſigned a Petition, which that paper was calculated to ſupport: To remove thoſe falſe Impreſſions, the following ſhort, but true, State of Facts, is ſubmitted to the Conſideration of the Public.*

IN 1610, an act of parliament paſſed, requiring perſons, who ſhould apply to be naturalized, *to take the Sacrament, and the Oaths of Allegiance and Supremacy* --•- The objects of this law, at the time it was made, were the *Roman* Catholics --- there were no *Jews* at that time in *England.*

All that is intended by the preſent bill, is a *partial* repeal of this law, with reſpect to the *Jews*; and, for that purpoſe, the bill enacts, that the parliament may, if they think proper, naturalize *Jews*, without their taking the ſacrament.

This proviſion goes only to *Jews* born *abroad*; all *Jews* born here are to every intent, natural born ſubjects; and, as ſuch, without the aid of this bill, have, at this time, as they had five hundred years ago, a right by law to purchaſe real eſtates, to them and their heirs; in like manner as any other ſubject ---This will not be diſputed ---The public records from King *Henry* II. prove it beyond a doubt.

As therefore the bill gives to the *Jew*, to be naturalized, no *new or greater privileges* than what every *Jew* born in *England*, at preſent, by law enjoys, it ſeems hard to aſſign a good reaſon, why the parliament may not be ſafely intruſted with the power of naturalizing foreign *Jews*, if they ſhall think proper.

This is all the bill does in favour of the *Jews*; but it goes farther, and, *per contra*, abridges the natural right of every *Jew* born here; for the bill very prudently declares all *Jews*, for the future, incapable of purchaſing, or inheriting any advowſons, or rights of patronage, or preſentation to any benefice, prebend or other eccleſiaſtical living or promotion, ſchool, hoſpital, or do-native.

What is propoſed by the former part of the bill, is not *new*; it being leſs than what has been done by the legiſlature on ſeveral former occaſions, without any clamour made againſt it, or any bad effects attending it.

In 1740, an act paſſed, in conſequence whereof ſeveral hundred *Jews*, who have reſided ſeven years in the *American* colonies, or who ſerved as mariners, during the war, two years in *Britiſh*

(continued)

ships, are become natural born subjects of *Great-Britain*, without taking the sacrament.

It is the spirit and intention, and, I make no doubt it will be the certain consequence and effects, of the present bill, to encourage rich *Jews*, who live in foreign countries, to remove, with their substance, and settle here, instead of *France* or *Holland*.

In thus naturalizing foreign *Jews*, we do what the prudence of the *French* nation hath done for more than two centuries; with this only difference, that the *French* extend it to all that come, to the poor equally with the rich, without distinction; whereas the object of the present bill is confined to persons of substance and property only.

Henry II. of *France*, in 1550, by his letters patents, declared the *Jews* capable to purchase, inherit, and enjoy, real estates in *France*, *comme de* vrais regnicoles, *et sujets de Roi*. [as true inhabitants of the realm, and subjects of the king.] *Henry* III. in 1574, *Louis* XIV. in 1656, and *Louis* XV. in 1723, and 1728, renewed and confirmed this privilege, *sans que les Juifs soient tenus de prendre aucunes Lettres de Naturalite*. [without which the *Jews* are restrained from taking letters of naturalization.

The share foreigners, and, among them, the *Jews*, have in the public debt of this kingdom, is very considerable; the dividends whereof are either annually remitted to foreigners abroad, who contribute nothing to the expence of this government, or are laid out in increasing their mortgage upon us----Good policy, therefore, directs us to put every honest and prudent expedient in practice, that may induce or allure the foreign proprietors of this large debt to follow their property, and expend the dividends and income of it here.

There are other considerations, that make the naturalization of *Jews* preferable to that of most other foreigners---Such as, their supporting their own poor; their having no country of their own to retire to, after acquiring estates here, or in favour of which they might be induced to carry on their trade under the umbrage of naturalization.

Under these circumstances, when a small part only of the traders of this great metropolis (and many of them, probably, through mistake, imposition, or misrepresentation) have been prevailed on to sign a petition to parliament, against the bill in question, it must be decisive as to the point --- *What is the Opinion and judgment of merchants and traders in general concerning the utility of the bill*---- when it shall appear, that the petitions, in favour of the bill are signed by the greatest number of the most eminent and extensive merchants, traders and manufacturers, that hath been known on any former occasion; and the reasons they give why they hope the bill may pass, are, " That it will encourage persons of wealth and substance to remove, with their effects, from foreign parts into this kingdom; the greatest part of which, agreeable to the experience of former times, will be employed by them in foreign trade and commerce, in increasing the shipping, and encouraging the exportation of the woollen and other manufactures of this kingdom; of which the *Jews* have, for many years, exported great quantities."

J. S.

Extract of a Letter from a M------ *of* P------ *on the foregoing Subject.*

"The bill has, indeed, with great impropriety, whether by accident or design, been called a *naturalization* bill, and this word is the foundation of all the clamour that it has produced. It is only intended to render foreign *Jews* capable of *naturalization*, principally with a view to excuse them from payment of the aliens duty at the customs, and by such encouragement to invite over some very great traders from foreign parts; for tho' they will have a right after naturalization to purchase lands of inheritance as well as *Jews* born here, yet, by this act they are even then disabled from sitting in either house of parliament, and from holding any office or place of trust civil or military."

---Such is the act which has been represented as tending to subvert our liberty and religion as *Englishmen* and Christians; and, with yet greater absurdity, as frustrating the designs of providence, and falsifying the predictions of eternal truth.

---The extreme ignorance and folly which have appeared in some publick transactions upon this occasion, will for ever stigmatize the present age of moral philosophy, in which every one boasts to detect the frauds of superstition, and to determine all questions by right reason.

---If events which have been predicted do not happen, the prophet was an impostor; so that if the prophecies concerning the *Jews* are not fulfilled, Christianity is not true; and if Christianity is true, these prophecies cannot but be fulfilled. So obvious are truths which appear to have been utterly unknown to the literati, who have lately obliged the world with theological and political remarks; who have preached sermons, written books, talked in coffee-houses, and made interest for members of parliament.

Benjamin Franklin

to wit, when pulling, after rippling, and when lifting it off the grafs, the confequence of which neglect is, that very different kinds being mixed together, it can neither be watered, graffed, nor fcutched equally. They neither prepare proper canals nor water. They make the beets for watering a great deal too large, bind them very hard, and comprefs all their flax fo clofe together in the water, trampling it down to the bottom, and putting large ftones, feals, or logs above it, that the hearts of the beets cannot be half watered, or not at all, when fome of it is perhaps too much done. They frequently take it out of the water after it has been there a certain time, without examining whether it be underdone or overdone. They lay it too thick upon the grafs, and upon long grafsy meadows, by which means fome of it is tendered and rotted. In taking it off the field, they lay root-ends and crop-ends together. Flax fo managed muft come out very ill in the dreffing; and the fault is generally, but very unjuftly, laid to the flax-mill, which muft deftroy what is well watered before it can clean the ill-watered part of the fame handful. And thus it happens, that the ends are frequently beat away in the fcutching, when the middle is not well cleaned, the ends of a beet being well watered, perhaps too much fo, when the heart of a beet has fcarce felt the water. Such inequality in the watering of the flax appears very remarkable as it lies upon the field, the middle of the rows then generally appearing of an higher colour then either of the ends.

Meffrs. MEIN and FLEEMING.

If you think the following ftory worthy of a place in your Chronicle, pleafe infert it.

A CERTAIN Governour of *Egypt* having occafion for a fum of money, fell upon the following moft extraordinary method to raife it.

He iffued out an order, commanding the Chiefs of all the * *Jews* fettled in *Egypt* to appear before him on a certain day; on their being conducted into his prefence, they found him furrounded with his divan or council and the Pentateuch in his hand—he then afked them if they believed the whole that was written in that book, to which they replied they did, faying that it contained the precepts of their religion on which he turned to and reading the xi. and xii. *chapters* of *Exodus* in which is recorded the account of the *Jews*, juft before their departure from *Egypt*, borrowing of the *Egyptians* their jewels of filver and gold &c.

When he had finifhed, he told them

* Great numbers of Jews have been fettled in Egypt, for upwards of 2000 years, and Dr. Pocock informs us, that when he was in that country in the year 1737 they had no lefs than 37 fynagogues in the fingle city of the Grand Cairo, the prefent capital of Egypt.

that fince they had confeffed that their *forefathers* had about 3000 years ago borrowed of the *forefathers* of the *Egyptians* their jewels &c. he fent for them to know if thefe things had ever been returned, or fatisfaction made for them; if not, he added, it was now high time payment fhould be made, and that he being the political father of that people, he was in duty bound to fee that they had juftice done them.

The poor aftonifhed *Jews* ftood filent and knew not what to fay, though they immediately faw through the drift of the avaricious Governour, he, after waiting fome time for an anfwer, difmiffed them; but ordered them again before him in a few weeks, telling them that he gave them that time to fearch their records and fee whether or not they had ever returned or made fatisfaction to the *Egyptians* for the jewels they borrowed.

When the *Jews* had retired, they, after confulting among themfelves how to ward off the blow, came to the refolution of raifing a large fum of money, with which, on the day appointed they waited on the Governor, and told him, that fince the time their forefathers had borrowed thefe things of the *Egyptians*, their nation had undergone various revolutions, their temple had been burnt and their records deftroyed, fo that it was impoffible for them now to tell whether or not the *Egyptians* had received fatisfaction for their jewels, and prefenting him with the money added they hoped he would not make them, who were but a few, accountable for what the whole nation did fo many thoufand years ago.

This being all the Governor wanted, he took their money for which he gave them (in the name of the *Egyptians*) a receipt in part payment of the borrowed jewels, and fo left the fame door open to any of his fucceffors who may think proper to take the fame fteps to fqueeze that poor unfortunate people.

By this ftory we may fee how wicked men may pervert the beft things to the very worft purpofes.

Dr *WATKINSON*'s *family-medicine*

THE following Medicine has long been adminiftered with great fuccefs, it is now publifhed by the ingenious and humane Dr. Edward Watkinfon, rector of Chard in Kent, as being efficacious in the under-mentioned diforders. The dofe is a tea-fpoonful night and morning, guarding againft cold.

If prepared and made up ready (for it will keep many years) it may always be had recourfe to: and what will recommend this medicine is, that it is equally *fafe* when given to infants, as *efficacious* when given to adults.

To Infants. Habitual coftivenefs, whooping cough, convulfions, worms, breeding

of teeth, gripings with green ftools, eruptions, with all kinds of fwellings.

To Adults. Jaundice, dropfy, cholic, fcurvy; Obftructions to which the fex are fubjects when *fhort breathed*; pain at the ftomach, &c.

R. Senna, one pound fix ounces; jalap-root, one pound; fix ounces; cream of tartar one pound; ginger, one pound; falt of fteel (by which is meant green copper-as dried before the fire till it becomes white), one pound four ounces each of thefe to be reduced into very fine powder. Mix them well together, incorporating into the fame half an ounce of chymical oil of cloves- The vehicle is fyrup of orange-peel, or treacle.

From the LONDON GAZETTE, *Jan.* 27.
War-office, January 29.

SECOND troop of horfe-guards, Adjutant and Lieutenant Richard Timms is appointed to be Exempt and Captain, vice John Siveright, deceafed.

Ditto, Sub-Brigadier and Cornet, John Wyche, to be Adjutant and Lieutenant, vice Richard Timms.

Ditto, Dodington Egerton, Gent. to be Sub-Brigadier and Cornet, vice John Wyche.

36th. regiment of foot, Samuel Griffiths (Clerk) to be chaplain, vice John Pearfall, who retires.

1ft troop of horfe-guards, Cornet and Major James Dunn to be fecond Lieutenant and Lieutenant Colonel, vice Thomas Twyfden, who retires.

Ditto, Guidon and Major John Shore, to be Cornet and Major, vice James Dun. Exempt, Ditto, and Captain James Rolt to be Guidon and Major, vice John Shore.

Ditto, Brigadier and Lieutenant Thomas Dufour Eaton, to be Exempt and Captain, vice James Rolt.

Ditto, Sub-Brigadier and Cornet, the Hon. Richard Howard to be Brigadier and Lieut. vice Thomas Dufour Eaton.

Ditto, Henry Reid, Gent. to be Sub-Brigadier and Cornet, vice the Hon. Richard Howard.

Henry Shirdley, Efq; to be Commiffary General of ftores and provifions in Eaft-Florida, vice Thomas Shirdley, deceafed.

War-Office, Feb. 9. 4th reg. dragoons, Lieut. Gen. the Right Hon. Henry Seymour Conway is appointed to be Colonel, in the room of Field Marfhal Sir Robert Rich, Bart. deceafed.

13th reg. foot, Lient. George Henderfon to be Captain Lieutenant, vice John Raleigh, who retires.

Late Capt. Lieutenant John Raleigh, of 13th regiment of foot, to be Secretary to the Governor of the garrifon of Gibralter, in the room of John Braithwaite, removed.

Sir James Dunbar, Bart. to be deputy Judge Advocate and Clerk of the Court Martial to North Britain, in the room of Alexander Agnew, deceafed.

Meſſrs. MEIN and FLEEMING.
If you think the following ſtory worthy of a place in your Chronicle, pleaſe inſert it.

A CERTAIN Governour of *Egypt* having occaſion for a ſum of money, fell upon the following moſt extraordinary method to raiſe it.

He iſſued out an order, commanding the Chiefs of all the * *Jews* ſettled in *Egypt* to appear before him on a certain day; on their being conducted into his preſence, they found him ſurrounded with his divan or council and the Pentateuch in his hand—he then aſked them if they believed the whole that was written in that book, to which they replied they did, ſaying that it contained the precepts of their religion on which he turned to and reading the xi. and xii. *chapters* of *Exodus* in which is recorded the account of the *Jews*, juſt before their departure from *Egypt*, borrowing of the *Egyptians* their jewels of ſilver and gold &c.

When he had finiſhed, he told them

* Great numbers of Jews have been ſettled in Egypt, for upwards of 2000 years, and Dr. Pocock informs us, that when he was in that country in the year 1737 they had no leſs than 37 ſynagogues in the ſingle city of the Grand Cairo, the preſent capital of Egypt.

that ſince they had confeſſed that their *forefathers* had about 3000 years ago borrowed of the *forefathers* of the *Egyptians* their jewels &c. he ſent for them to know if theſe things had ever been returned, or ſatisfaction made for them: if not, he added, it was now high time payment ſhould be made, and that he being the political father of that people, he was in duty bound to ſee that they had juſtice done them.

The poor aſtoniſhed *Jews* ſtood ſilent and knew not what to ſay, though they immediately ſaw through the drift of the avaricious Governour, he, after waiting ſome time for an anſwer, diſmiſſed them; but ordered them again before him in a few weeks, telling them that he gave them that time to ſearch their records and ſee whether or not they had ever returned or made ſatisfaction to the *Egyptians* for the jewels they borrowed.

When the *Jews* had retired, they, after conſulting among themſelves how to ward off the blow, came to the reſolution of raiſing a large ſum of money, with which, on the day appointed they waited on the Governor, and told him, that ſince the time their forefathers had borrowed theſe things of the *Egyptians*, their nation had undergone various revolutions, their temple had been burnt and their records deſtroyed, ſo that it was impoſſible for them now to tell whether or not the *Egyptians* had received ſatisfaction for their jewels, and preſenting him with the money added they hoped he would not make them, who were but a few, accountable for what the whole nation did ſo many thouſand years ago.

This being all the Governor wanted, he took their money for which he gave them (in the name of the *Egyptians*) a receipt in part payment of the borrowed jewels, and ſo left the ſame door open to any of his ſucceſſors who may think proper to take the ſame ſteps to ſqueeze that poor unfortunate people.

By this ſtory we may ſee how wicked men may pervert the beſt things to the very worſt purpoſes.

BOSTON – 1768
A PERVERSION OF THE BIBLE
The Boston Chronicle, p. 176 (cols 2–3)
May 2, 1768

With seeming innocence, this article turns on its head the Biblical account in the Book of Exodus of the Jews' departure from Egypt. The article represents a parable on the injustice of Jewish persecution.

The contemporary Governor of Egypt calls the leading Jews to his palace and cites the Biblical account of the Jews leaving Egypt, some 2,000 years ago, carrying jewels and other riches they supposedly "borrowed." Had this wealth been repaid, asked the Governor of the "poor astonished Jews."

Omitted in the Governor's description was that this wealth, according to the Bible, was intended as payment for the 210 years of slavery and suffering endured by the Jews. Though the Jews "immediately saw through the drift of this avaricious Governor," they realized they had little bargaining power to counter his charge. In a defeated posture, they decide to raise a large sum in order to repay this fictional debt. In giving these Jews a receipt for "part payment" he "left the same door open to any of his successors who may think proper to take the same steps to squeeze that poor unfortunate people."

PHILADELPHIA
− 1784
RESPONSE TO AN
ANTI-SEMITIC
ATTACK
*The Independent
Gazetteer / The
Chronicle of
Freedom
March 13, 1784*

"The Great Triumvirate of Patriots Monument" in Chicago features Haym Salomon on the right with George Washington (center) and Robert Morris (left). Inscribed on the front of the base is Washington's address to the Hebrew Congregation in Newport Rhode Island.

Haym Salomon, considered the financier of the American Revolution (see page 94), passionately defends his Jewishness and asserts his commitment to the new American nation in this public letter responding to an anti-Semitic attack by Quaker lawyer Miers Fisher (b. 1748; d. 1819). Fisher, a loyalist, had been sent to a Virginia detention camp for his royal sympathies. Subsequently, he tried to persuade the Pennsylvania legislature to abolish the Bank of North America headed by Robert Morris, a colleague of Salomon's, and to replace it with another institution. Fisher argued that stock in the bank was held by Jewish merchants in Holland, and by Salomon, thereby forcing the main bank of the United States to be dependent on "foreign" investments.

He lambasts Fisher for his *"odious"* character – known for "Toryism and disaffection" – and for launching a "wanton" attack on an entire "religious persuasion." Attempting to turn the tables on Fisher, he refers to a stereotype, accusing members of Fisher's Quaker religion as being worse than *"heathens, pagans or idolaters"* who were "unwilling to venture money in trade during the war." Rather than his own name, Salomon signed his letter with "A Jew Broker."

To MIERS FISHER, ESQUIRE.

I Muſt addreſs you, in this manner, although you do not deſerve it. Unaccuſtomed as you are to receive any mark of reſpect from the public, it will be expected that I ſhould make an apology for introducing a character, fetid and infamous, like yours, to general notice and attention. Your conſpicuous *toryiſm* and *diſaffection* long ſince buried you in the ſilent grave of *popular* oblivion and contempt; and your extraordinary conduct and deportment, in ſeveral other reſpects, has brought and reduced you to that dreary dungeon of inſignificance, to that gulph of defeated ſpirits, from which even the powers of *hope* " that comes to all," cannot relieve or better you.

In this moſt miſerable of all ſituations, principally ariſing from an obſtinate, inflexible perſeverance in your political *hereſy* and *ſchiſm* (ſo deteſtable in itſelf, ſo ruinous and deſtructive to our country, and obnoxious

to all around us) you are now left quite deſtitute and forlorn!--Unhappy and diſappointed man! Once exiled and excommunicated by the ſtate, *as a ſly, inſiduous enemy*; ſevered and detached from the generous boſom of *patriotiſm* and *public virtue*: Shunned and deſerted by *faithful friends*, in whom you once ſo ſafely truſted: Since, debarred and prevented from *your practice* by rule of court, as an attorney at the bar; and *excluded* from every other eſſential and dignified privilege of which the *reſt of citizens* can boaſt,--with the wretched remains of a *wrecked* reputation,--you exhibit ſo complete a ſpectacle of diſtreſs and wretchedneſs, as rather excites one's tenderneſs than vengeance, and would ſoften and melt down diſpoſitions more relentleſs and unforgiving than mine!

But whatever claims of mercy you may demand, on theſe accounts: Whatever I ſhould think, were I to judge of you as your *perſonal* enemy in *private reſpects*: Yet the *forward* and unexampled advances and ſteps you have lately taken in the concert of *public* affairs: The high-cockaded air of *fancied* importance you now aſſume: The petulant, diſcontented humor you have manifeſted for eſtabliſhing *a new Bank*: Your longings and pantings to approach our *political vineyard*, and blaſt the fruits of thoſe labors for which you neither *toiled nor ſpun*; and more particularly, the indecent, unjuſt, inhumane aſperſions, you caſt ſo indiſcriminately on the *Jews* of this city at large, in your arguments of Wedneſday week, before the honorable Legiſlature of the commonwealth: Theſe circumſtances, if my apprehenſions are right, preclude you from any lenity or favor, and preſent you a fair victim and offering to the ſacred altar of public juſtice. You are not therefore to expect any indulgence, becauſe you merit none. I dare ſay you experience it not in your own feelings ; nor have you any right whatever to hope for the leaſt tenderneſs from me. You ſhall not have it ; and if you are cut and ſmarted with the whip and laſhes of my reproach and reſentments, if I lay my talons and point out the *ingrate*, if my tongue is clamorous of you and *your odious confederates*, and I ſhould pain the tendereſt veins of their breaſts,--remember you firſt gave birth to all yourſelf, that it aroſe entirely from you ; and in tracing of events hereafter, to the ſource, you will perhaps find to your ſorrow and coſt, that you are only blameable for whatever conſequences have or may ariſe, on the occaſion.

You not only endeavoured to injure me by your unwarrantable expreſſions, but every other perſon of the ſame *religious* perſuaſion I hold, and which the laws of the country, and the glorious toleration and *liberty of conſcience* have allowed me to indulge and adopt. The injury is highly crimſoned and aggravated, as there was no proper reaſon or ground for your invectives. The attack on the *Jews* ſeemed wanton, and could only have been premeditated by ſuch a baſe and degenerate mind as your's. It was not owing to the ſudden ſallies of paſſion, or to the warmth of a diſconcerted and haſty imagination. I cannot, therefore, place it to the account of meer human frailties, in which your *will* and underſtanding had no concern, and for which I am always diſpoſed to make every compaſſionate allowance. And though an individual is not obliged to avenge the injuries of particular ſocieties and ſectaries of men, he is nevertheleſs called upon, by every dear and ſerious conſideration, to ſpeak his mind freely and independently of public tranſactions and general events, to aſſert his own ſhare in the public conſequence, and to act his part fairly on the ſocial theatre.

Permit me, then, with this view of things, to take notice of theſe terms of reproach and invective, which, conſidering you as a friend to good manners and decorum, you have heaped on our nation and profeſſion with ſo liberal and unſparing a hand. I am a Jew ; it is my own nation and profeſſion. I also ſubſcribe myſelf a Broker, and a Broker too whoſe opportunities and knowledge, along with other Brokers of his intimate acquaintance, in a great courſe of buſineſs, has made him very familiar and privy to every minute deſign and arti-

(continued)

fice of your *wiley colleagues* and associates. I exult and glory in reflecting that we have the honour to reside in a free country where, as a people, we have met with the most generous countenance and protection; and I do not at all despair, notwithstanding former obstacles, that we shall still obtain every other privilege that we aspire to enjoy along with our fellow-citizens. It also affords me unspeakable satisfaction, and is indeed one of the most pleasing employments of my thoughtful moments, to contemplate that we have in general been early uniform, decisive whigs, and were second to none in our patriotism and attachment to our country!

What but *Erinnys* itself could have thus tempted you to wander from the common path of things, and go astray among *thorns and briars?* What were your motives and inducements for introducing the Jews so disrespectfully into your unhallowed and polluted lips? Who are you, or what are you (a meer *tenant at sufferance,* of your liberty) that in a *free* country, you dare to trample on any sectary whatever of people? Did you expect to serve yourself, or your friends and confederates,--those serpents in our bosom, whose poisonous stings have been darted into every *patriot* character among us?

In any other place, in managing another cause, you might have had patience to attend to the consequences of such unpardonable rashness and temerity. But here you thought yourself safe, and at full leave to take the most unlicensed liberties with characters, in regard of whom you can in no respect pretend to vie! You shall yet repent even in *sackcloth and ashes,* for the foul language in which you have expressed yourself. And neither the interposition of some well meant though mistaken whigs who, I am sorry to think, have joined you, " nor even the sacred shield of cowardice shall protect you," for your transgressions. Who knows but the beams of that very denomination whom you have traduced, may, on one day, perhaps, not very remote, warm you into the most abject servility, and make you penitentially solemnize what you have done?

An error is easily remedied, and there may be some compensation for actual injuries. But a downright insult can neither be forgiven or forgot; and seldom admits of atonement or reparation. It is our happiness to live in the times of enlightened liberty, when the human mind, liberated from the restraints and fetters of superstition and authority, hath been taught to conceive just sentiments of its own; and when mankind, in matters of *religion,* are quite charitable and benevolent in their opinions of each other.

Individuals may act improperly, and sometimes deserve censure; but it is no less unjust than ungenerous to condemn all for the faults of a few, and reflect generally on a whole community, for the indiscretion of some particular persons. There is no body of people but have some exceptionable characters with them; and even your own religious sectary, whom you have compelled me to dissect in the course of this address, are not destitute of *very proper objects of criticism and animadversion.*

Good citizens who nauseate, and the public who contemn, have heard your invectives against the Jews. Unhappily for you, a long series of enormities, have proved you more your own enemy than I am. To you, then, my worthy friends and fellow-citizens (characters teeming with strict candor and disinterestedness) do I turn myself with pleasure from that steril field--from that *Grampian* desart, which hath hitherto employed me.---It is your candor I seek--it is your disinterestedness I solicit----The opinions of *Fisher* and his adherents, whether wilful in their malignity, or sincere in their ignorance, are no longer worthy of my notice.--His observations are low--his intentions are too discernable.---His whole endeavours centre in one point, namely to create a *new Bank.*

To effect this end, he has spared neither pains or labours. He has said every thing that artifice could dictate, or malice invent. He has betrayed himself in a thousand inconsistencies, and adopted absurdities, which suppofing him a man of sense and observation, would have disgraced the lips of an idiot.

And for whom is the new Bank meant and intended? For the benefit of men like himself, who have been in

general averse, and opposed to the war and common cause: for the insurgents against our liberty and independence: for *mercenary* and *artful* citizens, where selfish views are totally incompatible with the happiness of the people: for bifronted political *Janus's,* the meer weather-cocks of every breeze and gale that blows.

Who traded with the enemy? Who first depreciated the public currency? Who lent our enemies money to carry on the war? Who were spies and pilots to the British? Who prolonged the war? Who was the cause of so many valuable men losing their lives in the field and *prison-ships?* Who did not pay any taxes? Who has now the public securities in hand? Who would not receive our continental money? Who has purchased *Burgoyne's* convention bills? Who depreciated the French bills? Who depreciated the bills of the *United States* on Paris? Who slandered the institution of the *Bank of North-America?* Who refused taking *Bank-Notes* when they first issued? Who discouraged the people from lodging money in the Bank? And are these the characters who talk of instituting a Bank for *the good of the public?* Are these the people who want a charter from our Legislature? Shall such a bastard, progeny of freedom, such jests and phantoms of patriotism and the social virtues be indulged in their wishes? For shame! for shame! Surrender the puerile, the fruitless pretensions! Public honor and public gratitude cry aloud against you, and says, or seems to say, as earnest as your endeavors have been, you shall not have your charter.

From such a *medley* and *group* of characters (an impure nest of vipers, the very *blood-hounds* of our lives and liberties) we have every thing to hazard, and nothing to expect. Suspicion shakes her wary head against them, and experience suggests that the sly, insinuating intrigues and combinations of these persons are to be watched and guarded against as much as possible. Though the *proposals* are generous and captivating, their practices, I will venture to affirm, cannot correspond; and however *fascinating* they may be *in appearance,* their designs are *deep* and *wiley.*--With the soft and soothing *voice* of *Jacob* they may exercise the *hand,* the *hairy* hand of *Esau!*

I shall not inquire whether twoBanks in a commercial country would not clash with each other, and prove exceeding detrimental and injurious to the community. Having only ventured to give an account of the leading characters who compose the new Bank, allow me in conclusion to rectify an error of Mr. Fisher's, who publicly declared, " the Jews were the authors of high and unusual interest." No! the Jews can acquit themselves of this artful imputation, and turn your own batteries on yourself. It was neither the *Jews* or *Christians* that founded the practice; but, *Quakers,*--and *Quakers* worse than *Heathens, Pagans* or *Idolaters*; men, though not Jews in *faith,* are yet Jews in *traffic*; men abounding with avarice, *who neither fear God, nor regard man.*

These very persons who are now flattering themselves with the idea of a new Bank, first invented the practice of discounting notes at five per cent. I have retained an alphabetical list of names as well as the other Brokers, and can specify persons, if necessary. In the language of *Naphtali* to *David,* I have it in my power to point at the very *would-be* Directors, and say, " *Thou art the man.*" I can prove, that it were these people, unwilling to venture money in trade during the war, who first declined letting out money on the best mortgage and bond security.

Were they now gratified in their expectations, would they not display the same undue spirit, and degrade the dignity of a Bank with practices unbecoming a common Broker? Is it not in their power to finesse at the Bank, and refuse discounting notes on purpose to gripe the necessitous part of the people, and extort improper premiums out of doors? And have we not reason to expect this would be the case?

A JEW BROKER.

LONDON–1789 "DR. FRANKLIN'S ADDRESS…"

The Gentleman's Magazine, pp. 95 (cover)–97 February, 1789

In this remarkable message, "the celebrated Dr. Benjamin Franklin" com-

THE

Gentleman's Magazine:

For FEBRUARY, 1789.

Mr. URBAN,   London, Feb. 10.

IF the following addrefs to the inhabitants of the United States of America, by the celebrated Dr. Benjamin Franklin, on the difaffection that has prevailed towards the new fyftem of government introduced in that country, is thought worth a place in your ufeful Repofitory, the immediate infertion of it will oblige   J. B.

A ZEALOUS advocate for the propofed Federal Conftitution, in a certain public affembly, faid, that ' the repugnance of a great

pared the factionalism in the young republic following the 1787 adoption of the Consti-tution to the divisions among the Israelites following their exodus from Egypt. Franklin's footnotes from the Biblical books of *Exodus* and *Numbers*, some of which are included, revealed his familiarity with *Old Testament* sources.

Franklin criticized those Israelites who failed to appreciate the leadership of both Moses and Aaron, saying "One would have thought that the appointment of men who had distinguished themselves in procuring the liberty of their nation ... might have been ... a grateful people ... yet there were, in every one of the *thirteen tribes,* some discontented, restless spirits...."

Significantly, Franklin in order to strengthen his metaphor with the republic's thirteen states, establishes the number of Israelite tribes at thirteen, though the Old Testament refers to the number as twelve. Franklin, perhaps in taking poetic license, added the Levites as tribe number thirteen.

Franklin cited the rebellion of Corah (i.e., Korach) and his followers as showing the self-interest of the unappreciative Israelites. "Thus though Corah's real motive was the supplanting of Aaron, he persuaded the people that he meant only the *public good."* Franklin claimed that though the Israelites actually desired liberty, "artful men" motivated by nothing more than "private interest" persuaded them to oppose the establishment of the *"new constitution."* As a result, they brought upon themselves "much inconvenience and misfortune."

In conclusion, noted Franklin, he had so much faith "in the governance of the world by PROVIDENCE," that he could not avoid concluding that an "omnipotent, *omnipresent* and beneficent Ruler" exercised at least some role in the birth of this new nation.

' part of mankind to good government was ' fuch, that he believed, that if an angel from ' heaven was to bring down a conftitution ' formed there for our ufe, it would never- ' thelefs meet with violent oppofition.' He was reproved for the fuppofed extravagance of the fentiment; *and he did not juftify it.* Probably it might not have immediately occurred to him that the experiment had been tried, and that the event was recorded in the moft faithful of all hiftories, the Holy Bible; otherwife he might, as it feems to me, have fupported his opinion by that unexceptionable authority.

The Supreme Being had been pleafed to nourifh up a fingle family, by continued acts of his attentive providence, till it became a great people; and having refcued them from bondage by many miracles performed by his fervant Mofes, he perfonally delivered to that chofen fervant, in prefence of the whole nation, a *conftitution* and code of laws for their obfervance, accompanied and fanctioned with promifes of great rewards, and threats of fevere punifhments, as the confequence of their obedience or difobedience.

This conftitution, though the Deity himfelf was to be at its head, and it is therefore called by political writers a *Theocracy,* could not be carried into execution but by the means of his minifters; Aaron and his fons were therefore commiffioned to be, with Mofes, the firft eftablifhed miniftry of the new government.

One would have thought, that the appointment of men who had diftinguifhed themfelves in procuring the liberty of their nation, and had hazarded their lives in openly oppofing the will of a powerful monarch who would have retained that nation in flavery, might have been an appointment acceptable to a grateful people; and that a conftitution framed for them by the Deity himfelf, might, on that account, have been fecure of an univerfal welcome reception; yet there were, in every one of the *thirteen tribes,* fome difcontented, reftlefs fpirits, who were continually exciting them to reject the propofed new government, and this from various motives.

Many ftill retained an affection for Egypt, the land of their nativity; and thefe, whenever they felt any inconvenience or hardfhip, though the natural and unavoidable effect of their change of fituation, exclaimed againft their leaders as the authors of their trouble, and were not only for returning into Egypt, but for ftoning their deliverers. Thofe inclined to idolatry were difpleafed that their *golden caif* was deftroyed. Many of the chiefs thought the new conftruction might be injurious to their particular interefts, that the *profitable places* would be engrossed by the families and friends of Moses and Aaron, and others equally well-born excluded *. In Josephus, and the Talmud, we learn some particulars, not so fully narrated in the Scripture. We are there told, that Corah was ambitious of the priesthood, and offended that it was conferred on Aaron, and this, as he said, by the authority of Moses only, *without the consent of the people.* He accused Moses of having, by various artifices, fraudulently obtained the government, and deprived the people of *their liberties*; and of CONSPIRING with Aaron to perpetuate the tyranny in their family. Thus though Corah's real motive was the supplanting of Aaron, he persuaded the people that he meant only the *public good*; and they, moved by his insinuations, began to cry out, " let us maintain the *common liberty* of our *respective tribes*; we have freed ourselves from the slavery imposed upon us by the Egyptians, and shall we suffer ourselves to be made slaves by Moses? If we must have a master, it were better to return to Pharaoh, who at least fed us with bread and onions, than to serve this new tyrant, who by his operations has brought us into danger of famine."—Then they called in question the reality of his conference with God, and objected the *privacy of the meetings*, and the *preventing any of the people from being present* at the colloquies, or even approaching the place, as grounds of great suspicion. They accused Moses also of *peculation*, as embezzling part of the golden spoons and the silver chargers that the princes had offered at the dedication of the altar †, and the offerings of gold by the common people ‡, as well as most of the poll-tax ‖; and Aaron they accused of pocketing much of the gold of which he pretended to have made a molten calf. Besides *peculation*, they charged Moses with *ambition*; to gratify which passion, he had, they said, deceived the people, by promising to bring them *to a* land flowing with milk and honey; instead of doing which, he had brought them *from* such a land; and that he thought light of all this mischief, provided he could make himself an *absolute prince* §. That to support the new dignity with splendor in his family, the partial poll tax, already levied and given to Aaron *, was to be followed by a general one †, which would probably be augmented from time to time, if he were suffered to go on promulgating new laws, on pretence of new occasional revelations of the divine will, till their whole fortunes were devoured by that aristocracy.

Moses denied the charge of *peculation*; and his accusers were destitute of proofs to support it; though *facts*, if real, are in their nature capable of proof. " I have not," said he (with holy confidence in the presence of God), " I have not taken from this people the value of an ass, nor done them any other injury." But his enemies had made the charge, and with some success among the populace; for *no kind of accusation is so readily made, or easily believed, by KNAVES, as the accusation of knavery.*

In fine, no less than two hundred and fifty of the principal men, " famous in the congregation, men of renown ‡," heading and exciting the mob, worked them up to such a pitch of phrenzy, that they called out, Stone 'em, stone 'em, and thereby *secure our liberties*; and let us choose other captains that may lead us back into Egypt, in case we do not succeed in reducing the Canaanites.

On the whole it appears, that the Israelites were a people jealous of their newly-acquired liberty, which jealousy was in itself no fault; but that, when they suffered it to be worked upon by artful men, pretending public good, with nothing really in view but private interest, they were led to oppose the establishment of the *new constitution*, whereby they brought upon themselves much inconvenience and misfortune. It farther appears from the same inestimable history, that when, after many ages, that constitution was become old and much abused, and an amendment of it was proposed, the populace, as they had accused Moses of the ambition of making himself a *prince*, and cried out, *stone him, stone him*; so, excited by their high priests and SCRIBES, they exclaimed against the Messiah, that he aimed at becoming *king* of the Jews, and cried out, *crucify him, crucify him!* From all which we may gather, that popular opposition to a public measure is no proof of its impropriety, even though the opposition be excited and headed by men of distinction.

To conclude, I beg I may not be understood to infer, that our General Convention was divinely inspired when it formed the new federal constitution, merely because that constitution has been unreasonably and vehemently opposed; yet I must own I have so much faith in the general government of the world by PROVIDENCE, that I can hardly conceive a transaction of such momentous importance to the welfare of millions now existing, and to exist in the posterity of a great nation, should be suffered to pass without being in some degree influenced, guided, and governed by that omnipotent, omnipresent, and beneficent Ruler, in whom all inferior spirits live and move and have their being.   B. F.

* Numbers, chap. xiv.

* Numbers iii.   † Exodus xxx.
‡ Numbers xvi.

The following news items contained short, but by no means sweet, digs against Jews.

> Monday evening laſt, the coroner's inqueſt ſat upon the body of a Mr. Ward, who was knocked overboard, and loſt his life, on Thurſday laſt, by a blow from one Levi, a Jew, when *wilful murder* was brought in as their verdict. Levi, and his accomplices, are ſafely lodged in the goal of this city.

MASSACHUSETTS – 1787
"LEVI, A JEW"
The Massachusetts Centinel, p. 3 (col 3)
September 19, 1787

This news item reports how a coroner's inquest brought in the verdict that a Mr. Ward, who was "knocked overboard, and lost his life" was willfully murdered "by a blow from one Levi, a Jew." It is doubtful that had the murderer been a Christian it would have pointed it out.

> An Italian Jew in this city, who is remarkable for nothing but a moderate ſhare of low cunning has within the preſent year cleared upwards of fifty thouſand pounds by his ſpeculations on the war—he always ſaid, *by gad dare can be no var.*

PHILADELPHIA – 1791
"LONDON, OCT. 14"
Gazette of the United States
January 12, 1791

Five news items reaching the United States from London were included in this issue of the *Gazette*. Amidst the items is thrown in one which appears to be of the sole purpose of promoting anti-Semitism – with a stereotypical report of a Jew's "low cunning" and a disparaging reference made to his accent: "... he always said, *by gad dare can be no var*" [i.e., by God there can be no war].

Gazette of the United States.

PUBLISHED WEDNESDAYS AND SATURDAYS BY *JOHN FENNO*, No. 69, *HIGH-STREET*, BETWEEN *SECOND* AND *THIRD STREETS*, PHILADELPHIA.

[No. 29, of Vol. III.]   SATURDAY, AUGUST 6, 1791.   [Whole No. 237.]

JEWISH ECONOMY.

TWO criminals, a Chriſtian and a Jew,
    Who'd been to honeſt feelings rather callous,
Were on a platform once expos'd to view,
    Or come, as ſome folks call it, to the gallows;
Or, as of late, as quainter phraſe prevails,
To try their weight upon the city ſcales.

In dreadful form, the conſtable and ſhrieve,
    The prieſt, and ord'nary, and croud, attended,
Till fix'd the nooſe, and all had taken leave,
    When the poor Iſraelite, befriended,
Heard, by expreſs from officer of ſtate,
A gracious pardon quite reverſe his fate.

Unmov'd he ſeem'd, and to the ſpot cloſe ſticking,
    Ne'er offers, tho' he's bid, to quit the place,
Till in the air, the other fellow kicking,
    The ſheriff thought that ſome peculiar grace,
Some Hebrew form of ſilent deep devotion,
Had for a while depriv'd him of his motion.

But being queſtion'd, by the ſheriff's orders,
    Why not with proper officer retiring,
In tone of voice that on the marv'lous borders,
    While that his looks were to the beam aſpiring,
" I only vait," ſaid he, " before I coes,
" Ov Miſter Catch to puy the *ted man's clothes*."

The logo of the Federalist Party

PHILADELPHIA – 1791 "JEWISH ECONOMY"

*Gazette of the United States,
p. 1 (col 2)
Augusts 6, 1791*

When John Fenno, editor of the *Gazette of the United States*, denigrated "the revolutionary vermin of foreign countries" for opposing the policies of the Federalist Party (November 12, 1798), it was easy to scapegoat Jews among this despicable cohort.

According to William Pencak, Fenno was among "the most virulent anti-Semites" of the colonial era. Pencak argued that Fenno projected his own "rootlessness and questionable devotion to revolutionary principles onto Jews who were, for the most part, well established in American society and who had vigorously supported the Revolution," (William Pencak, *Jews and Gentiles in Early America, 1654–1800,* University of Michigan Press, p. 240).

The poem "Jewish Economy," placed prominently on the front page of Fenno's newspaper, describes how a Christian and a Jew waited to be executed on the gallows. Though this Israelite received a "gracious pardon," he stayed around at the site awaiting the hanging of the Christian. The poem's conclusion not only underscores the Jew's love of money, but also mocks his foreign accent, 'I only vait before I coes, Ov Mister Catch to puy the ted man's clothes."

WARSAW, June 12.

The Diet are busy relative to a plan proposed in favour of the Jews, who are very numerous in this country, amounting to from 5 to 700,000 individuals, and they they will probably experience the effects of that wisdom which governs all the deliberations of our Senate.

PHILADELPHIA – 1791
"WARSAW, JUNE 12"
Gazette of the United States, p. 1 (col 3)
September 21, 1791

This front-page report from Warsaw, dated June 12, notes that the Diet was busy "relative to a plan proposed in favour of the Jews, who are very numerous in this country, amounting to from 5 to 700,000 individuals, and they will probably experience the effects of that wisdom which governs all the deliberations of our Senate."

Legal interest has been five, the real interest has sometimes been seven. Indeed the interest of money depends on such a combination of circumstances, as the scarcity of money, the demand in market, and the hazard, that an attempt to find and fix a permanent rate, is one of the most visionary schemes that a public body can undertake. To prove the impossibility of such a scheme I would only mention the continual practice of violating laws against usury; which would not be the case, if the real value of money had been ascertained and fixed.† If legislatures had found the true value of the use of money, there would have been fewer violations of their laws: If they have, in any case, fixed a rate of interest lower than the real value, they have violated the rights of their subjects. This is a serious consideration; and perhaps in no instance are the laws of England and America more strongly marked with the traces of ancient prejudice and barbarity, than in the prohibition which prevents a man from using his money as he pleases, while he may demand any sum whatever for the use of his other property.

The only power, I conceive, a legislature has to determine what interest shall arise on the use of money, or property, is where the parties had not determined it by agreement. Thus when a man has taken up goods upon credit, or where, by any other legal means, a man becomes possessed of another's money or estate, without a specific stipulation for interest, the law very properly steps in and ascertains the sum which the debtor shall pay for the use of that money. But to make a law that a man shall not take but six per cent. for the use of money, when the borrower is willing to give more, and the lender cannot part with his money at that rate of interest, is a daring violation of private rights, an injury often to both parties, and productive of innumerable embarrassments to commerce.

We are told that such laws are necessary to guard men from the oppression of the rich. What an error! Was a monied man ever compelled to assist a distressed neighbor by the forfeitures incurred by such laws? Is not his money his own? Will he lend at all, if it should not be for his benefit? Besides, cannot a man in necessity alienate his property for one fourth of its value? Are not such bona fide contracts

made every day to raise money to answer a temporary purpose? Nay, have not the laws of all commercial states authorized sales by auction, where any man may part with his property for a fourth of its value? Is there any remedy in law against such a sacrifice of a man's estate? Where in then consists a security of laws against usury?

The Jewish prohibition, not to take interest except of strangers, first gave rise to doubts in the minds of our pious christian forefathers, with respect to the legality of any interest at all. This produced, in the dark ages, severe ecclesiastical laws against taking any thing for the use of money; and these laws originated a general prejudice against it, through the Christian world.

In the twelfth and thirteenth centuries, commerce began to revive; but there was but little money, and trade was lucrative, because in few hands; money bore a very high interest. In some parts of Europe, the interest was forty per cent. Even with this interest, certain Italian traders could make an annual profit, and therefore it was for their benefit to give it. It however rendered them very unpopular.*

The Jews for their infidelity, had been considered by the Christians as outcasts on earth. Severe laws were enacted against them in almost every country; depriving them of the rights of citizens, and forbidding them to hold real estates. Proscribed and insulted, the poor Jews were compelled to turn their hand against every man in their own defence. They commenced strolling traders and bankers, and by these means commanded a large share of the money in every kingdom.

With this command of cash, the Jews very justly compensated themselves for the injuries they suffered from the tyrannical laws which existed against them. They loaned money at the highest rate of interest they could obtain. Hence the general character of the Jews, and the prejudice against them that survives to this enlightened period.

It is very probable, that before the discovery of the American mines, money was so scarce in Europe, that a few brokers in each kingdom might engross such a share, as to have it in their power to oppress people. This was evidently the case in England, about the reign of Edward I, and the parliament thought proper to interfere and restrain

the evil. Laws against usury were doubtless necessary and useful at that time. But since the world has been filled with gold and silver from South America, and nations have opened an intercourse with each other, there can never be a want of specie, where a country can supply produce enough to exchange for it. It has become a mere fluid in the commercial world; and in order to obtain a supply, in a country abounding with produce and manufactures, the legislature has nothing to do, but let it bear its own price; let it command its own value, either at interest, or in exchange for commodities.

Laws against usury therefore, I consider as originating either in the necessity of the times, which long ago ceased, or in a bigoted prejudice against the Jews, which was as barbarous formerly, as it is now infamous. *Laws restraining the interest of money I now consider in the same light as I do laws against freedom of conscience.* [I believe that the legal fixing of a permanent interest rate] will be answerable for more frauds, perjuries, treachery and expensive litigations, than proceed from any other single cause in society.

I am so firmly persuaded of the truth of these principles, that I venture to predict, the opinions of men will be changed in less than half a century, and posterity will wonder that their forefathers could think of maintaining a position so absurd and contradictory, as that men have no right to make more than six per cent. on the loan of money, while they have an indefeasible right to make unlimited profit on their money in any other manner. They will view laws against usury in the same light that we do the inquisition in Spain, the execution of gypsies and witches in the last century, or those laws of England which make 100l. annual income necessary to qualify a man for killing a partridge, while they allow forty shillings only to qualify him for electing a knight of the shire.

* Blackstone, Vol. II. 462.
† What are marine insurances, bottomry, loans or respondentia and annuities for life, but exceptions to the general law against usury? The necessity of higher interest than common is pleaded for these exceptions. Very good: but they prove the absurdity of attempting to fix that, which the laws of nature and commerce require should be fluctuating. Such laws are partial and iniquitous.

* Robertson's Charles V. Vol. I. 280.

NEW YORK – 1795
USURY
The Herald,
A Gazette for the Country, p. 2 (col 1–3)
February 4, 1795

In 1793 Noah Webster, the famous lexicographer, moved from Connecticut to New York where he founded two newspapers, one of which was the semi-weekly, *The Herald.* In this "Extra" issue he discussed the ills of usury and raised the role of Jews in this practice.

Webster sympathized with the plight of Jews which forced them to become money lenders. "Proscribed and insulted, the poor Jews were compelled to turn their hand against every man in their own defense.... Hence the general character of the Jews and the prejudice against them that survives to this enlightened period."

PHILADELPHIA – 1800
RESPONSE TO THE FEDERALIST
PARTY

Aurora General Advertiser, p. 2 (col 1–2)
August 13, 1800

"BENJAMIN NONES, 1757–1826, Patriotic Frenchman who served in the Revolutionary army, Philadelphia's President, for years, of the Sephardic congregation."

In this bold and defiant message, Benjamin Nones (b. Bordeaux, France, 1757; d. Philadelphia, 1826; see also page 29) proudly defends his Jewish religion and his Republican Party political affiliation, and he insists that carrying a "poor" label brings him no dishonor. What brought about Nones's moving piece was the Federalist Party's use of anti-Semitism in a letter published in the August 5, 1800 issue of the Federalist-oriented *Gazette of the United States*. Nones's letter "To the Printer of the *Gazette...,*" as published in the *Aurora*, is preceded by a letter "To The Editor" in which he announces that the *Gazette's* printer, Mr. Wayne, neglected to print the reply despite having promised in front of witnesses that he would.

Though the nation's Jews numbered a miniscule 1,600 out of an overall American population of 5,300,000, the Federalists tried to promote the candidacy of John Adams over Thomas Jefferson in the presidential race of 1800 by casting aspersions on Jews supporting Jefferson.

The Federalists attacked the Republican sympathizers in the Democratic Society of Philadelphia as "composed of the very refuse and filth of society." After denigrating a black man known as "Citizen Sambo," the Observer described the presence of "Citizen N . . .the Jew," whose speech in dialect notes his being bankrupt. Clearly, this reference meant Nones, who was closely involved in the Republican Party.

For these Federalists, anti-Semitism trumped the bravery of Nones in the Revolutionary War. Though his family originally settled in Savannah following their arrival from France, Nones moved to Philadelphia in 1777 after the British captured Georgia. He enlisted as a private in Captain Verdier's regiment under General Pulaski, and his bravery quickly stood out. He fought in almost every battle in the Carolinas and was commended by Verdier for his heroism in the siege of Savannah: "His behavior under fire in all the bloody actions we fought has been marked by the bravery and courage which a military

man is expected to show for the liberties of his country." He became the first Jewish major in the United States army.

After the war, Nones returned to Philadelphia, worked as both an interpreter and notary public, and was a prominent member of the Jewish community. He served as president of Mikveh Israel congregation between 1791 and 1799.

Nones's feisty reply in this *Gazette* begins with a request that since the paper inserted "calumnies against individuals, for the amusement of your readers," they then permit the slandered party to use "the same channel ... to appeal to the public in self defense."

He notes that in the slanderous article he is "accused of being a *Jew*: of being a *Republican*: and of being *Poor*" and continues his defense by beginning the next several paragraphs:

I am a Jew. I glory in belonging to that persuasion, which even its opponents, whether Christian, or Mahomedan, allow to be of divine origin ...

But I am a Jew. I am so—and so were Abraham, and Isaac, and Moses and the prophets, and so too were Christ and his apostles ...

I am a Republican! Thank God, I have not been so heedless, and so ignorant ... so proud or so prejudiced to renounce the cause for which I have fought, as an American ... more than my religious principles...

I am a Jew, and if for no other reason, I am a republican. ... In republics, we have rights, in monarchies we live but to experience wrongs....

How then can a Jew but be a Republican? in America particularly. Unfeeling & ungrateful would he be, if he were callous to the glorious and benevolent cause of the difference between his situation in this land of freedom, and among the proud and privileged law givers of Europe. But I am poor*, I am so, my family also is large, but soberly and decently brought up....*

Nones then writes about his bankruptcy, noting that although he was discharged from all his debts, he went on to repay them all when his situation improved, offering "interest which was refused by my creditors," who later, on their own, wrote testimonials to Nones's "honor and honesty." The letter ends:

This is a long defense... The Public will now judge who is the proper object of ridicule and contempt, your facetious reporter or
Your Humble Servant,
BENJAMIN NONES

the door against justification. I need not say more:
    I am &c.   B. NONES.
Philadelphia Aug. 11, 1800.

——————

To the Printer of the Gazette of the U. S.
    SIR,
    I hope, if you take the liberty of inserting calumnies against individuals, for the amusement of your readers, you will at least have so much regard to justice, as to permit the injured through the same channel that conveyed the slander, to appeal to the public in self defence.——I expect of you therefore, to insert this reply to your ironical reporter of the proceedings at the meeting of the republican citizens of Philadelphia, contained in your gazette of the fifth instant; so far as I am concerned in that statement.——I am no enemy Mr. Wayne to wit; nor do I think the political parties have much right to complain, if they enable the public to laugh at each others expence, provided it be managed with the same degree of ingenuity, and some attention to truth and candour. But your reporter of the proceedings at that meeting, is as destitute of truth and candour, as he is of ingenuity, and I think, I can shew, that the want of prudence of this Mr. Marplot, in his slander upon me, is equally glaring with his want of wit, his want of veracity, his want of decency, and his want of humanity.
    I am accused of being a *Jew*: of being a *Republican*: and of being *Poor*.
    I am a *Jew*. I glory in belonging to that persuasion, which even its opponents, whether Christian, or Mahomedan, allow to be of divine origin—of that persuasion on which christianity itself was originally founded, and must ultimately rest—which has preserved its faith secure and undefiled, for near three thousand years—whose votaries have never murdered each other in religious wars, or cherished the theological hatred so general, so unextinguishable among those who revile them. A persuasion, whose patient followers, have endured for ages the pious cruelties of Pa-

continued ⟶

gans, and of christians, and persevered in the unoffending practice of their rites and ceremonies, amidst poverties and privations—amidst pains, penalties, confiscations banishments, tortures, and deaths, beyond the example of any other sect, which the page of history has hitherto recorded.

To of be such a persuasion, is to me no disgrace; though I well understand the inhuman language, of bigotted contempt, in which your reporter by attempting to make me ridiculous, as a Jew, has made himself detestable, whatever religious persuasion may be dishonored by his adherence.

But I am a Jew. I am so—and so were Abraham, and Isaac, and Moses and the prophets, and so too were Christ and his apostles, I feel no disgrace in ranking with such society, however, it may be subject to the illiberal buffoonery of such men as your correspondents.

I am a *Republican!* Thank God, I have not been so heedless, and so ignorant of what has passed, and is now passing in the political world. I have not been so proud or so prejudiced as to renounce the cause for which I have *fought*, as an American throughout the whole of the revolutionary war, in the militia of Charleston, and in Polasky's legion, I fought in almost every action which took place in Carolina, and in the disastrous affair of Savannah, shared the hardships of that sanguinary day, and for three and twenty years I felt no disposition to change my political, any more than my religious principles.—— And which in spite of the witling scriblers of aristocracy, I shall hold sacred until death—as not to feel the ardour of republicanism,—Your correspondent, Mr. Wayne cannot have known what it is to serve his country from principle in time of danger and difficulties, at the expence of his health and his peace, of his pocket and his person, as I have done; or he would not be as he is, a pert reviler of those who have so done—as I do not suspect you Mr. Wayne, of being the author of the attack on me; I shall not enquire what share you or your relations had in establishing the liberties of your country. On religious grounds I am a republican. Kingly government was first conceded to the foolish complaints, of the Jewish peo-

ple, as a punishment and a curse; and so it was to them until their dispersion, and so it has been to every nation, who have been as foolishly tempted to submit to it. Great Britain has a king, and her enemies need not wish her the sword, the pestilence, and the famine.

In the history of the Jews, are contained the earliest warnings against kingly government, as any one may know who has read the table of Abimelick, or the exhortations of Samuel. But I do not recommend them to your reporter, Mr. Wayne. To him the language of truth and soberness would be unintelligible.

I am a Jew. and if for no other reason, for that reason am I a republican. Among the pious priesthood of church establishments, we are compassionately ranked with Turks, Infidels, and Heretics. In the *monarchies* of Europe, we are hunted from society—stigmatized as unworthy of common civility, thrust out as it were from the converse of men; objects of mockery and insult to froward children, the buts of vulgar wit, and low buffonery, such as your correspondent Mr. Wayne is not ashamed to set us an example of. Among the nations of Europe, we are inhabitants indeed every where—but Citizens no where *unless in Republics*. Here, in France, and in the Batavian Republic alone, are we treated as men, and as brethren. In republics we have *rights*, in monarchies we live but to experience *wrongs*. And why? because we and our forefathers have *not* sacrificed our principles to our interest, or earned an exemption from pain and poverty, by the dereliction of our religious duties, no wonder we are objects of derision to those, who have no principles, moral or religious to guide their conduct.

How then can a Jew but be a Republican? in America particularly. Unfeeling so ungrateful would he be, if he were callous to the glorious and benevolent cause of the difference between his situation in this land of freedom, and among the proud and privileged law givers of Europe.

But I am *poor*, I am so, my family also

is large, but foberly and decently brought up. They have not been taught to revile a chriftian, becaufe his religion is not *so old* as theirs. They have not been taught to mock even at the errors of good intention, and confcientious belief. I hope they will always leave this to men as unlike themfelves, as I hope I am to your scurrilous correspondent.

I know that to purfe proud ariftocracy poverty is a crime, but it may fometimes be accompanied with honefty even in a Jew. I was a Bankrupt fome years ago. I obtained my certificate, and I was discharged from my debts. Having been more fuccessful afterwards, I called my creditors together, and eight years afterwards unfolicited I difcharged all my old debts, I offered intereft which was refufed by my creditors, and they gave me under their hands without any folicitations of mine, as a teftimonial of the fact (to use their own language) as a tribute due to my honor and honefty. This teftimonial was figned by Meffrs. J. Ball, W. Wifter, George Meade, J. Philips, C. G. Paleske, J. Bispham, J. Cohen, Robert Smith, J. H. Leuffer, A. Kuhn, John Stille, S. Pleasants, M. Woodhouse, Thomas Harrifon, M. Boraef, E. Laskey, and Thomas Allibone, &c.

I was discharged by the infolvent act, true. becaufe having the amount of my debts owing to me from the French Republic, the differences between France and America have prevented the recovery of what was due to me, in time to difcharge what was due to my creditors. Hitherto it has been the fault of the political fituation of the two countries, that my creditors are not paid ; when peace fhall enable me to receive what I am entitled to, it will be my fault if they are not fully paid.

This is a long defence Mr. Wayne. but you have called it forth, and therefore I hope you at leaft will not object to it. The Public will now judge who is the proper object of ridicule and contempt, your facetious reporter or

Your Humble Servant.
BENJAMIN NONES.

Following Benjamin Nones's letter was a commentary about "Master *Wayne*" that indicates *Aurora*'s apparent lack of respect for the man.

Master *Wayne* wifhes to learn where we came by the *Morning Chronicle* of the twenty-fifth of June?——Why did he not afk where we got *Timothy* Pickering's accounts— Jonathan Dayton's pretty tricks—Lord Hawksbury's declaration of a Britifh party being formed in America America—Mr. Adams's declaration that Britifh influence was employed with effect in our cabinet—Lifton's letters found on Sweazy—the account of the Caucusus at Binghams, and other caucuses—the Tribunitial Bill of Mr. Rofs—John Quincy Adams's late curious treaty with Pruffia, in which the rights of neutrals are facrificed—Timothy Pickering's converfations about John Adams—the proceedings of the notables at Trenton in 1798—the fquabble at Trenton in 1799—the tea-table talk of Mrs. Adams, about Ige Denny—the tricks of the *illuminati* of Connecticut, &c. he might have afked where we got thefe, as well as the other—but if he or any of his friends chufe to fee the Morning Chronicle of June 25, it may be feen in fmall pieces at the office of the Aurora, merely to oblige them.

260   NILES' WEEKLY REGISTER—SATURDAY, DECEMBER 14, 1816.

The Jews.—It appears by a late magazine, that about five hundred thousand dollars have been assessed on the public in one form or other for the last five years, and expended—with what result?— The convertion, real or supposed, of *five Jews.*— This is at the rate of one hundred thousand dollars per Jew—"a pretty round sum for Christendom to make a purchase of the scattered nation." We grant it: but whether Jews convert Christians or Christians convince Jews, what is it to us in this land of civil and religious liberty?   Col.

BALTIMORE – 1816
"THE JEWS" – TO CONVERT OR NOT
Niles' Weekly Register, p. 260 (col 1)
December 14, 1816

"The Jews" relays information from a "late magazine" that an expenditure assessed on the public of some five hundred thousand dollars resulted in the "convertion" of five Jews to Christianity – "a pretty round sum for Christendom to make [such a] purchase…." The blurb then asks the question, "Whether Jews convert Christians or Christians convince Jews, what is it to us in this land of civil and religious liberty?"

THURSDAY, SEPTEMBER 14, 1818.

BOSTON, (Massachusetts) Printed by ADAMS & RHOADES, Publishers of the Laws of the United States.

VOLUME XLVII.—NUM

BOSTON – 1818
"TOLERATION"

Independent Chronicle, p. 1 (col 3) September 14, 1818

A front-page article, "TOLERATION" confronts the issue of anti-Semitism from the perspective that it violates American principles of decency and places Jews in a negative light, which they do not deserve. The specific section pointed to discusses the symbiotic relationship between this country and its Jews.

TOLERATION.

Several letters (says the National Advocate) addressed to the Jews, under the signature of JOSEPHUS, have been published in N. York in the Commercial Advertiser, and generally republished throughout the union. These letters are written with ability, and with a spirit of liberality and great benevolence: they confirm the belief as to the origin, the providential care and protection, as well as the final restoration of the nation.— A writer, however, in Richmond, has combatted the grounds assumed by Josephus, and declares the impossibility of restoring the Jews to their ancient possession, in consequence of their character. The editor of the *Virginia Patriot*, in declining to publish his communication, gives the following liberal and just reasons, as contained in the article below. There is, unquestionably, no part of the world where invidious distinctions in consequence of religion are so little known or encouraged as in this country. The *people* indulge themselves in no hostile feelings against *any* sect, and the true spirit of christianity, which combines faith with mildness and tolerance, is better understood and manifested here than in any other part of christendom. Our prosperity has resulted from this liberality of sentiment—and to say that this country is an *asylum* for the Jews who are in it, would go to make them *aliens* in the American family, mere dependents, not partners in the national compact. The existence of the Jews in the United States is cotemporaneous with its first establishments. The first *settlers* and active *improvers* in the state of Georgia, under Gov. Ogelthorpe, were Jews. There are in their burial ground in this city tombs near 150 years old.— There were certain exclusive, civil, as well as ecclesiastical privileges granted by Great-Britain at the first settlement of some of the colonies, to the Jews in this country. From the commencement of the revolutionary war until the present time, they have, by their devotion to the interests of the union, and the active part taken in defence of our rights, rendered themselves worthy of the equal liberty which they enjoy, and which no disposition exists to deprive them of.— To say that they should possess no religious toleration, would go to break down the barriers which we oppose to bigotry and superstition, and to deprive them of civil rights, or render them ineligible for office, would violate the genius and spirit of our constitution. To say that there are no men of talent and integrity among them, would be untrue—to condemn the whole for the faults or crimes of a few, would be unjust—to deny them a participation in the lawful commerce of the country, would be ungenerous —and to declare them all usurers, would be FALSE.

From the Virginia Patriot, Richmond Sept. 4.

"A CONSTANT READER" is received but we must decline publishing it. We shall give our reasons with some remarks on the subject.

The letters to the Jews are republished in the Patriot, to gratify the wishes of some of our subscribers. They are open to remark; but the Constant Reader, in endeavoring to show that the Jews could not live, if in possession of the Holy Land, has given a severe philippic on the Jews who reside among us. We give him credit for the vigor of his pen; but he should recollect that the same argument and sarcasm may be applied with equal propriety to some Christians as well as Jews.

They could not live, says the Constant Reader, because they never labor—"I never knew one of them to plough, dig or sow; raise a flock for meat, milk or butter, or follow any mechanical trade or manufacture." To how many Christians will this apply. They have the same right to obtain a living without manual labor that Christians have.— There are no *paupers* among them. They are "pedlars, shopkeepers and money dealers." Are they the only ones? They shave and have various prices for their goods. Do not Christians do the same? Who encourages their shaving? Jews or not, they have a right to trade with their money. Shall one man, not a Jew, make 100 per cent. a month with his money, by speculating, and a Jew, or other Christian not be allowed his one or two per cent. by a direct bargain for the use of his money? They would not lend if no one borrowed. Are there no men of integrity and honor among them as well as among other various sects of religion? Is it fair to speak of them in the gross in such terms as the Constant Reader uses? Would it not be equally fair to term the Methodists enthusiasts, the Baptists hypocrites, the Episcopalians haughty aristocrats, &c. as thus to condemn the Jews? Are they violaters of the laws more than Christians? Are they disturbers of society? If they are able to live without labor, Christians give them the ability so to live, as they give it to one another.

If the Constant Reader had only combatted the possibility of their obtaining a living should they be restored, because they do not labor, it would have been fair; but we cannot admit such denunciations, in such language, against any religious sect, denunciations which, while they apply to a few Jews, apply to such greater numbers of Christians. What are all our Bank Directors and Stock holders but money dealers, who, if they could, would receive and be glad of two per cent per month, for their money.

We cannot notice at all the historical remarks of the Constant Reader, without entering too wide a field. The Constant Reader ought, however, to remember, that the errors or crimes of the ancient Jews are not the errors and crimes of the *Jews in the United States.*

As to America's being an Asylum for the Jews, so is it for the Quakers, Baptists, Presbyterians, Mahomedans, Papists and Gentoos, if they choose to come here, and all others. It is no more the asylum of one, than the others. Jews have been here almost as long as any religious sect.

JEWS IN MARYLAND. From an agitation of the subject in the papers, we presume that another attempt will be made at the ensuing session of the legislature of Maryland, to exonerate this persecuted sect from the odious restrictions which our *incomprehensible* constitution imposes on them. The principle is worth contending for, though the number of such persons, who are residents in the state, is very small.

It is truly wonderful, if not miraculous, that this people are almost every where denied some part of those rights which belong to other men in similar locations. There must be some moral cause to produce this effect. In general, their interests do not appear identified with those of the communities in which they live, though there are some honorable exceptions to this remark. But they will not sit down and labor like other people—they create nothing, and are mere consumers. They will not cultivate the earth, nor work at mechanical trades, preferring to live by their wit in dealing, and acting as if they had a home no where. It is to this cause, no doubt, that an hostility to them exists so extensively; and that hostility is again, perhaps, a cause why they do not think and act like other people, and assume the character and feelings of the nations in which they live. But all this has nothing to do with their rights as men;—let us do our duty and place them upon an equality with ourselves, or renounce the great Christian obligation, "to do unto others as we would that they should do unto us." It is not the business of the state to judge them—their religion is an affair between them and their Maker. If we believe them to be wrong—"let them

stand as monuments of the safety with which error of opinion may be tolerated, when reason is left free to combat it." It cannot do harm to invest them with the enjoyment of every political right which we possess. It is time that the *spirit* of those days when fire and faggot were brought in furious aid of the meek doctrines of Christ, should be banished from the earth, as repugnant to all that is reasonable, all that is rightful, all that is just. It is in opposition to those principles, that some persons in England affect to be alarmed at the arrival of a few *Jesuits* in that country, and are striving to raise up a call on parliament to send them away. It is true, the ethics of this sect—"that the end justifies the means," are not very acceptable; and they are apt to meddle with things which do not belong to them. Hence they have been bandied about in the Christian world pretty much like the Jews. They may freely come to the United States, and no danger would be apprehended from them—yet we would rather receive one Irish ditcher or a German farmer than a dozen of them; we want workers, but have consumers enough already—We mean, if workmen had employment, which is not the case at present.

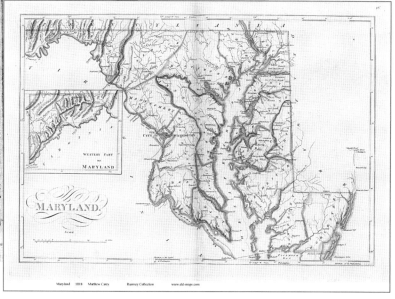

Maryland 1818   Mathew Carey   Ramsey Collection   www.old-maps.com

BALTIMORE, MARYLAND – 1820
"JEWS IN MARYLAND"
Niles' Weekly Register, p. 114 – October 21, 1820

Maryland's first Constitution, adopted in 1776, retained a colonial provision requiring public officials to uphold the Christian faith. It was not until the adoption of the Fourteenth Amendment in 1868 that Jews in every state were accorded full political equality. As early as 1797, Maryland Jews protested this inferior political status. It was not until 1826 that the Maryland legislature removed these political disabilities.

This article, "Jews in Maryland," argues the case for the Maryland legislature "to exonerate this persecuted sect from the odious restrictions which our incomprehensible Constitution imposes on them. The principle is worth contending for, though the number of such persons who are residents in our state is very small. ...let us do our duty and place them upon equality with ourselves, or renounce the great Christian obligation 'to do unto others as we would that they should do unto us.' It is not the business of the state to judge them – their religion is an affair between them and their Maker."

BOSTON –
1822
"VISIT TO A
JEWISH
SYNAGOGUE
IN INDIA"
*Boston Recorder,
p. 1 (col 4)
March 16, 1822*

VISIT TO A JEWISH SYNAGOGUE IN INDIA.

Extracted from a work lately published, entitled, Sketches of India.

" From this Chapel (Armenian) scene, I was led by my conductor, the very same morning, to one greatly and most affectingly contrasted with it.

" I followed him down a narrow back street, through a dark and dirty entrance, and up a staircase, the lower half of worn brick, that above, of broken ladder, like wooden steps, into an antichamber, filled with slippers; from whence after rapping at a half closed door, we were admitted into a dismal looking room, where such daylight as found its way was broken and obscured by the dull and feeble light of several mean lamps of oil.

" Round this chamber, sat about fifty venerable looking figures, in large robes of white, with turbans, out of the centre of whose muslin folds, the short top of a crimson cap was just visible.

" One of them stood up at a raised reading-table near the entrance, and opposite him, was fixed against the wall, a sort of plain wooden press, like a half book case.

" Of those seated round the room, some were aged, with long silver beards, some middle aged, with beards black or red, and curling or bushy; their complexions differed from olive even to fresh, and they were in general, very handsome. Although their dress and style of sitting, save that they used a broad raised bench, was Asiatic, still they appeared totally unlike, not only the Mahometans of India, but also those from Asia Minor, who visit our Indian ports. At the sounding of a small bell, he at the table began reading to them from an ancient manuscript volume, and the eye of every one was immediately rivetted on small written or printed books, with which each, even a boy among them, was provided.

" Here, without a temple, and without altar, giving mournful evidence of the truths of those very prophecies, the divine interpreter of which their fathers rejected, and the past accomplishment of which they still deny, here was a stray flock of the house of the lost sheep of Israel. Unhappy race! Cursed be the man who, believing your origin and history, should, in a bigot's zeal, look on you with that insulting pity which partakes of scorn. Ye were, ye are, our elder brethren. We know, that arm which scattered you with fury, will gather you with great mercy.

Is this mean chamber, your temple? Do these dull lamps supply the mystick branches of your golden candlestick? Your tabernacle and ark of the covenant, is it thus poorly you possess them? The alter of incense, the mercy seat, are they gone? And do ye, whose forefathers went up in open state, through the gate Beautiful, into that temple so familiar to you by description, so clear in cherished recollections of it,—do ye steal thro' yon dark entrance to your degraded worship? Dry up your tears; still press the law and the prophets to your bosoms. Seventy years before the destruction of your second temple, the foundation stone of your third was laid; was laid in the sepulchre of a crucified Saviour: he too is the key-stone of its loftiest arch, where he sitteth on high a King of glory, triumphant over sin and death; a prince of peace, making intercession for you, a God of mercy, waiting to be gracious.

This front-page article, "Visit to a Jewish Synagogue in India," expresses both admiration for the integrity of the prayer service – "a stray flock of the house of the lost sheep of Israel" – but disappointment in the failure of these Jews to understand the religious progression based on the crucifixion of the Savior seventy years before the destruction of the Second Temple in Jerusalem.

NEW YORK – 1822
"CONSTANTINOPLE AND THE
BOSPHORUS: THE JEWS"
*New-York American, p. 4 (col 2)
November 20, 1822*

The section about "The Jews" in "Constantinople and the Bosphorus," in an undated *London Magazine*, ends with the statement, "No wonder, therefore, that the Jews form the dregs of the [Constantinople] population: they are mostly Caraites." The information leading up to that conclusion shows how much heavier "the curse of reprobation with which this nation [the Jews] has been more or less smitten" was in Constantinople than elsewhere in the world, so much so "that a Jew who wishes to turn Moslem, is never received immediately into the faith of Islam, but must first get baptized by the Christians."

THE JEWS.

The curse of reprobation with which this nation has more or less been smitten the whole world through, lies no where so heavy upon them as in the Turkish empire, where they are not only exposed to the ill usage of the domineering party, but also to the scorn and insult of Christian slaves. Christian boys tease the Jews with impunity, especially in the holy week, when they no more dare show themselves than a Sunei in Persia during the anniversary of Hutsein's funeral. An idea may be formed of the low estimation in which Jews are held from this circumstance, that a Jew who wishes to turn Moslem, is never received immediately into the faith of Islam, but must first get baptized by the Christians, and is thence admitted, as from a higher degree of nobility, into the honours of the true faith. No wonder, therefore, that the Jews form the dregs of the population: they are mostly Caraites.

CHRISTIAN REGISTER.

AND WHY EVEN OF YOURSELVES JUDGE YE NOT WHAT IS RIGHT?—LUKE XII. 57.

VOL. III.   BOSTON, FRIDAY EVENING, MARCH 26, 1824.   No. 33.

RABBI JUDAH MONIS.

The following account of Judah Monis is from Dr Dwight's Travels, vol. i. p. 324. It has come to us through the London Jewish Expositor for January:

"In the cemetery of Northboro' is the grave of a Mr Monis, originally a Jewish Rabbi, afterwards converted to Christianity, and established in Harvard College as an instructor of the Hebrew language, the first who held this office in that seminary. Upon the loss of his wife he resigned his place, in the year 1761, and spent his remaining days with his brother-in-law, the Rev. Mr Martyn, minister of Northboro'. Mr Monis was well skilled in the Hebrew language, and had made considerable progress in other branches of learning. He left one volume of religious discourses, which I have seen, addressed chiefly to the people of his own nation.— They are solemn, impressive, and, when considered as written by a man originally a Jew, affecting. At his death he left between five and six hundred dollars for charitable uses, a principal part of which was destined as a fund for the relief of the widows of poor clergymen.

"The following epitaph is inscribed on his tombstone—

Here lie the remains of
Rabbi JUDAH MONIS, M. A.
Late Hebrew Instructor
at Harvard College, in Cambridge;
in which office he continued forty years.
He was by birth and religion a Jew,
but embraced the Christian faith;
and was publickly baptized
at Cambridge, A. D. 1722;
and departed this life April 25, 1764,

aged eighty-one years, two months, and twenty-one days.

—

A native branch of Jacob see,
Which once from off its olive broke;
Regrafted from the living tree,*
Of the reviving sap partook.

From teeming Zion's fertile womb,†
As dewy drops in early morn;‡
Or rising bodies from the tomb,§
At once be Israel's nation born.

"Mr Monis is a very uncommon, if not a singular instance of conversion from Judaism to Christianity; of candour yielding in spite of the prejudices of a bigoted education, and the powerful influence of bigotry to the light of evidence and the force of truth. Several Jews have embraced Christianity in this country and elsewhere, but Mr Monis was a man of learning, distinguished among his own people, and possessed of the honourable character of Rabbi. His mind, therefore, was obliged, in its progress towards Christianity, to encounter and overcome that unchanging enemy to truth, that prime auxiliary of error, the pride of self-consistency. Of the sincerity of his conversion there is no doubt. Beside the proof exhibited by an unblemished Christian life, both Christians and Jews agreed in acknowledging his sincerity; the Christians by their general respect for him, and the Jews by their hatred and obloquy."

* Rom. xi. 17, 24.   † Isa. lxv. 8.
‡ Ps. cx. 3.   § John v. 28, 29.

BOSTON – 1824
"RABBI JUDAH MONIS"
Christian Register, p. 1 (col 3) – March 26, 1824

Judah Monis (b. Algiers, 1683; d. 1764), author of the first Hebrew grammar printed in the New World, served as Harvard College's first instructor in this required subject for some forty years. Having graduated from Harvard, he is also considered as the first Jewish college graduate in American history. But in order to join the Harvard faculty, he had to convert to Christianity, which he did publicly.

The theme of this article on the front page of this Christian publication is the enlightened judgment of this scholar in converting to Christianity. His tombstone contains the image of a grafted tree symbolizing his conversion. The article notes "Of the sincerity of his conversion there is no doubt. Beside the proof exhibited by an unblemished Christian life, both Christians and Jews agreed in acknowledging his sincerity; the Christians by their general respect for him, and the Jews by their hatred and obloquy."

CHRISTIAN REGISTER.

AND WHY EVEN OF YOURSELVES JUDGE YE NOT WHAT IS RIGHT?——LUKE XII. 57.

THE JEWS.

The Existence and present Circumstances of the Jews, a proof of the authenticity of their history. From Wakefield's answer to the second part of Paine's Age of Reason.

A numerous race of men during a period of *three thousand three hundred years*, amidst the revolutions of empires, and the vicisitudes of time, during a transient sun-shine of national prosperity, and a long storm of exile, poverty, and persecution, have adhered with unshaken steadfastness to a system of religious polity, which they pretend was delivered to their legislator in the days of their fore-fathers, from the Divinity himself. The notoriety and renown of this people with the celebrated nations of antiquity, does not depend for credibility on the solitary evidence of their own annals, but is attested by a long series of ancient writers high in reputation, neither connected with their religion, nor friendly to their race. Many of these curious and striking testimonies, whose en tire existence has been long lost in the darkness of oblivion, are now found only in the bodies of these works, which are indeed devoted to the cause of revelation; but whose fidelity is assured, not only by the acknowledged survival of the writings under contemplation, at the time when these extracts were exhibited in confirmation of the points in question, but is most satisfactorily ascertained by the accuracy of these quotations, preserved in the same repositories, from authors still in being, and become thereby standing vouchers for the general sincerity of these advocates of revealed truth. The preservation of such a host of people to a system of faith, with inseparable association, under such circumstances, and for such duration, is a fact unparalleled in the history of the human race; and as it is perfectly unaccountable, I trust, by any wit of man, upon any principles of analogy, philosophy, or tradition, without some original authentication, proportionate to such a consequence, and therefore it should seem an authentication from divine interference; this union and perseverance may be reasonably regarded as an earnest of some important dispensation in reserve for the consolidation of this people in one united body; a consolidation rendered practicable at any time, by the most extraordinary preservation of the same customs, the same detatchment from extraneous connection, and the transmission of the same language. This subject is in truth pregnant with curiosity and wonder.—Should you say (for what will you not say?) that this pertinacity in their superstitions is the mere result of early education and rooted prejudice, without any respect to a providential economy, in their former aggregation, and their future disposal; I would ask, where these ten tribes of Israel, who had imbibed the same prejudices of education, are existing at this day? *They* are no more known; though abundant in number above the chosen tribes, they are long since dissolved and lost in the vast ocean of mankind; whilst this slender rivulet, conducted by the hand of God, has transmitted, like the fabled river of poetical antiquity, a pure and unmingled current, through the stream of time, and the torrent of revolutions, to the present age.

Protestant Dissenter's Mag. vol. iii. p. 140.

BOSTON – 1824
"THE JEWS"
Christian Register, p. 1 (col 3) – July 16, 1824

This front-page article, quoted from *"Protestant Dissenter's Mag,* vol. iii, p. 140,*"* praises the steadfastness of "The Jews."

According to this praiseworthy piece, "The notoriety and renown of this people with the celebrated nations of antiquity, does not depend for credibility on the solitary evidence of their own annals, but is attested by a long series of ancient writers high in reputation, neither connected to their religion nor friendly to their race."

taxes" as probably "taxes will, in a short time, be entirely dispensed with." What a comment upon the doctrine of internal improvement.

PROJECTED ROADS IN MEXICO. One of the most singular spectacles presented to the world in the present age, is the influence extended by wealthy individuals of Great Britain to some of the new states, which are rising so fast in physical strength and moral improvement. The French have repeatedly accused their own government of inactivity and short-sightedness in permitting the British ministry to seize the favorable moment for declaring themselves the friends of Colombia, the provinces of La Plata. and more recently of Greece; and truly the advantages which they promise to the nations who act towards them with judgment and promptitude are great and important. Since the revolution in the Mexican government, which, about a year ago, left the control of the state in the hands of the natives, and thus secured the country against the interference of Ferdinand, the English, as well as our own countrymen, have been very active in forming connections with the people, and have not only loaned them large sums of money, but are introducing many great improvements, calculated to bring into action the natural sources of wealth with which that country so wonderfully abounds.

The house of Barclay, Herring, Richardson & Co. of London, have largely embarked in Mexican connections, and their agents, Messrs. Manning & Marshall, reside permanently in the capital of that country. The following is a brief statement of their operations:—

"The house of Messrs. Barclay, Herring, Richardson and Co." the agents remark, "have indentified themselves with the fate of this republic, by the advances they have made, on its account, of five hundred thousand dollars to the treasury, at the most urgent and important juncture, of two millions and a half to defray the expense of ships and munitions of war, of five millions for the formation of the great mining company, and of an additional sum, subsequently offered on the 19th and 29th of May, when the country was imminently threatened by the designs of Iturbide against this country."

The same house, through their agents, have lately proposed the construction of a great and most valuable national work, which will form a fine counterpart to the road proposed to the congress of the United States, from Arkansas to Santa Fee. The agents have had a correspondence with the government on the subject, which is published in the Mexican Sun. It is the repairing or rather the renovation of the road from the capital to Vera Cruz, which, it is well known, has been left in a most miserable condition. They propose to choose some new routes, by which a firmer soil will be obtained, as well as many circuits avoided, and great advantages furnished, by the lake of Tazcoco. The road is to be made convenient for carriages; and will prove of the highest importance to the commerce of the interior states of Michoacan, Queretara, Guanajuaso and Jalisco, as well as that of Mexico, and the principal ports on the Gulf, Vera Cruz and Alvarado. It is proposed, also, to open a cross road to Puebla, which will avoid the circuit of the great Salt Lake, and the places that become miry when the water rises. To show the advantages the company expect from the execution of this plan, they offer, when it shall have been executed, to manage the courier department, between Mexico and Vera Cruz, at an abatement of one quarter of its present expenses, and to carry flour to the coast for the price of two dollars a barrel.

Thus, the same plan for the introduction of internal improvements, is likely to be adopted in Mexico, which the Colombian government has some time since put in practice; and we may expect to see the country derive from them those advantages which they are calculated to bestow; and to find her new system of government established and improved by the physical and moral effects they can scarcely fail to produce.   [Daily Advertiser.

THE ISRAELITES. The pope has lately issued an edict for the conversion of the Jews of which the following is an extract:—"In order the better to spread the light of the gospel amongst the Israelites, the measures taken during the time, of pope Clement VIII to compel Jews to attend Catholic sermons, and which was only interrupted by the recent political events to which Italy has been a prey, are re-established from the date of 1st March last." The edict afterwards orders "300 Jews to attend sermon every Saturday evening, and that, according to their turn, their shall be amongst them 100 individuals aged from 12 to 13 years, and 50 girls and women of the same age. Each time that a Jew misses sermon, when it is his turn to attend, he shall pay a fine of 5 paoli; no excuse will be admitted, if the oldest Jews do not denounce the defaulters, they shall be fined 30 soudi.

CHRISTENINGS AND BURIALS IN LONDON. During the year ending 14th December, 1824, the total number of christenings in the whole parishes, within and without the walls, and in Westminister, was 25,758; the total number of burials was 20,237; being a decrease of the burials, in those of the year, of 350. The mortality has been—of those under two years of age, 6,476; between two and five, 2,103; between five, and twenty, about 770, of an average from twenty up to seventy, 1,800 to 1,750; ninety to a hundred and three, 1; one hundred and seven, 1.

TREASURY DEPARTMENT, March 14, 1825.

Whereas, on the 3d of March, 1825, a law was passed by the congress of the United States, of which the 3d, 4th and 5th sections, are in the words following, viz:

"Sec. 3. And be it further enacted, That a subscription, to the amount of twelve millions of dollars, of the six per cent. stock, of the year eighteen hundred and thirteen, be, and the same is hereby, proposed; for which purpose, books shall be opened at the treasury of the United States, and at the several loan offices, on the first of April next, to continue open until the first day of October thereafter, for such parts of the above-mentioned description of stock, as shall, on the day of subscription, stand on the books of the treasury, and on those of the several loan offices, respectively; which subscription shall be effected by a transfer to the United States, in the manner provided, by law, for such transfers, of the credit or credits standing on the said books, and by a surrender of the certificates of the stock so subscribed: Provided, that all subscription, by such transfer of stock, shall be considered as a part of the said twelve millions of dollars, authorized to be borrowed by the first section of this act.

"Sec. 4. And be it further enacted, That, for the whole or any part of any sum which shall be thus subscribed, credits shall be entered to the respective subscribers, who shall be entitled to a certificate or certificates, purporting that the United States owe to the holder or holders thereof, his, her, or their assigns, a sum to be expressed therein, equal to the amount of the principal stock thus subscribed, bearing and interest not exceeding four and one half per centum per annum, payable quarterly, from the thirty-first day of December, one thousand eight hundred and twenty-five; transferrable in the same manner as is provided by law for the transfer of the stock subscribed, and subject to redemption at the pleasure of the United States, as follows: one half at

THE ISRAELITES. The pope has lately issued an edict for the conversion of the Jews of which the following is an extract:—"In order the better to spread the light of the gospel amongst the Israelites, the measures taken during the time, of pope Clemant VIII to compel Jews to attend Catholic sermons, and which was only interrupted by the recent political events to which Italy has been a prey, are re-established from the date of 1st March last." The edict afterwards orders "300 Jews to attend sermon every Saturday evening, and that, according to their turn, their shall be amongst them 100 individuals aged from 12 to 13 years, and 50 girls and women of the same age. Each time that a Jew misses sermon, when it is his turn to attend, he shall pay a fine of 5 paoli; no excuse will be admitted, if the oldest Jews do not denounce the defaulters, they shall be fined 30 soudi.

BALTIMORE – 1825
"THE ISRAELITES"
Niles' Weekly Register, p. 39 (col 2)
March 19, 1825

This issue of the *Nile's Register* included a report that the pope "lately issued an edict for the conversion of the Jews…."

"In order the better to spread the light of the gospels among the Israelites," an extract from the edict reads, "the measures taken during the time, of pope Clemant [sic]VIII to compel Jews to attend Catholic sermons … are re-established…." The edict ordered 300 Jews, by turn, to attend sermon every Saturday evening or face the punishment of fines. Among the 300 Jews were to be 100 (boys) from 12 to 13 years, and 50 "girls and women" of the same age – possibly targeting Jewish youth on the cusp of their coming of age religiously.

Christian Register.

AND WHY EVEN OF YOURSELVES JUDGE YE NOT WHAT IS RIGHT?—LUKE XII. 57.

PRINTED BY FRANCIS Y. CARLILE, No. 4 SPEAR'S BUILDINGS, CONGRESS-STREET, FOR DAVID REED, EDITOR AND PROPRIETOR.

VOL. IV.   BOSTON, SATURDAY, NOVEMBER 5, 1825.   No. 44

BOSTON – 1825
"THE JEWS"
Christian Register, p. 2 (col 1–2)
November 5, 1825

The article titled "The Jews" refers to Jewish population data based on a speech by the eminent Jewish public figure Mordecai M. Noah (see Chapter 8). Some highlights of the article are Noah's indications that: The Jews in Jerusalem are "poor and dreadfully oppressed [yet] they are the great sentinels and guardians of the law and religion" amidst the severest privations . . . there is a "large colony" of white and black Jews in Cochin, China; and . . . because of their quickness and intelligence the upwards of one and one half million Jews in the Ottoman Empire enjoy commercial success even though they are "severely taxed and treated with utmost severity."

CHRISTIAN REGISTER.

THE JEWS.

In Mr. Noah's late speech, to which we have before alluded, he gives the following account of the number and situation of the Jews, in different parts of the world.

There are several hundred families in Jerusalem, Hebron, and Tiberias, three of the most ancient congregations in the world, and the number in the Holy Land may be computed at one hundred thousand.— Those on the borders of the Mediterranean are engaged in trade and manufactures ; those in the interior, and particularly in Jerusalem, are poor and dreadfully oppressed. They are the great sentinels and guardians of the law and religion, and amidst the severest privations and the most intense sufferings, they have for centuries kept their eye upon the ruined site of the temple and said, " the time will come, the day will be accomplished." The Samaritan Jews who formerly were numerous and scattered over Egypt, Damascus, Ascalon, and Cæsarea, are now reduced to a few hundred poor inoffensive persons, principally residents of Jaffa and Naplouse. As there is no essential difference between their doctrines and the rest of our brethren, the distinction between them should cease. The Baraite Jews, who are numerous, are principally residents of the Crimea and the Ukraine, and are a respectable body of men. They reject the Talmud and rabbinical doctrines, adhering closely to the precepts of our divine law. On the borders of Cochin China we have a large colony of white and black Jews. Their numbers are computed at ten thousand. The white Jews reside on the sea coast and the blacks in the interior. The blacks, who call themselves *Beni Israel*, must have existed at the time of the first temple. The researches in the interior of Africa may, at some future period, give us immense colonies of Jews, which emigrated at an early period from Egypt. There are on the coast of Malabar and Coromandel, and the interior of India, a considerable number of wealthy and enterprising Israelites. Measures will be adopted to ascertain their force and condition. Upwards of a million and a half of Jews, reside in the dominions of the Ottoman Porte, including the Barbary States. In Constantinople and Salonichi there cannot be less than one hundred thousand. They suffer much from the oppression of the Turks—are severely taxed, and treated with undisguised severity ; but their skill in trade and their general quickness and intelligence as bankers, brokers, and merchants, give them the entire control of commerce and the command of important confidential stations in the empire. The same character and condition may be likewise attributed to those numerous Jews residing in Egypt and in Persia ; they have many wealthy men in Alexandria, Cairo, Ispahan, and the numerous cities beyond the Euphrates.

From countries yet uncivilized, we turn to those which, still withholding the rights of man from the descendants of the patriarchs, are, nevertheless, more mild and tolerant in their measures, more liberal and generous to an afflicted people.

WASHINGTON, D.C. – 1826
"A RELIC OF THOMAS JEFFERSON"
National Intelligencer, p. 3 (col 4)
August 29, 1826

Thomas Jefferson, despite his having authored the Virginia Statute of Religious Freedom, singled out Jews for special censure. Jefferson held this surprisingly low estimate of Jews even though he knew Jews who made enormous sacrifices during the Revolution such as Haym Salomon, and their having refuted stereotypes about their alleged ethnic insularity as a result of substantial contributions they made to Christian churches and other civic causes. William Pencak, in *Jews and Gentiles in Early America, 1654–1800* (The University of Michigan Press, 2005, p. 10) cites Jefferson's opinion of Jews as "repulsive and anti-social as respecting other nations," their ideas of God as "degrading and injurious," and their "ethics ... often irreconcilable with the sound dictates of religion and morality."

In this "never before been published" letter Jefferson wrote to the Hon. George Thatcher of Newburyport, Massachusetts on January 26, 1824 – published in this issue a month following Jefferson's death on July 4, 1826 – Jefferson praised religions that inculcate the "love of mankind" in contrast with "the anti-social spirit with which Jews viewed all other nations."

A RELIC OF THOMAS JEFFERSON.

A highly respected friend has placed in our hands the original of the following letter from Mr. JEFFERSON to the late Honorable GEORGE THATCHER, of Newburyport, which has never before been published. It will, we doubt not, be read with interest.—*Eastern Argus.*

MONTICELLO, *Jan.* 26, 1824.

SIR: I have read with much satisfaction the sermon of Mr. Pierpont, which you have been so kind as to send me, and am much pleased with the spirit of brotherly forbearance in matters of religion which it breathes, and the sound distinction it inculcates between the things which belong to us to judge, and those which do not. If all Christian sects would rally to the Sermon in the Mount, make that the central point of union in religion, and the stamp of genuine Christianity, (since it gives us all the precepts of our duties to one another) why should we further ask, with the text of our Sermon, 'What think ye of Christ?' and if one should answer 'he is a member of the Godhead,' another 'he is a being of eternal pre-existence,' a third 'he was a man divinely inspired,' a fourth 'he was the Herald of truths reformatory of the religions of mankind in general, but more immediately of that of his own countrymen, impressing them with more sublime, and more worthy ideas of the Supreme being, teaching them the doctrine of a future state of rewards and punishments, and inculcating the love of mankind, instead of the anti-social spirit with which the Jews viewed all other nations,' what right, or what interest has either of these respondents to claim pre eminence for his dogma, and, usurping the judgment-seat of God, to condemn all the others to his wrath? In this case I say, with the wiser heathen, 'deorum injuriæ diis curæ.'

You press me to consent to the publication of my sentiments, and suppose they might have effect even on Sectarian bigotry. But have they not the Gospel? If they hear not that, and the charities it teacheth, neither will they be persuaded though one rose from the dead. Such is the malignity of religious antipathies that, although the laws will no longer permit them, with Calvin, to burn those who are not exactly of their creed, they raise the hue and cry of heresy against them, place them under the ban of public opinion, and shut them out from all the kind affections of society. I must pray permission, therefore, to continue in quiet during the short time remaining to me; and, at a time of life when the afflictions of the body weigh heavily enough, not to superadd those which corrode the spirit also, and might weaken its resignation to continue in a joyless state of being, which Providence may yet destine. With these sentiments, accept those of good will and respect to yourself.

TH JEFFERSON.

CHRISTIAN REGISTER

AND WHY EVEN OF YOURSELVES JUDGE YE NOT WHAT IS RIGHT?—LUKE xii. 57.

PUBLISHED BY THE AMERICAN UNITARIAN ASSOCIATION, AT 81 WASHINGTON STREET.—PRINTED BY ISAAC R. BUTTS &

VOL. V.   BOSTON, SATURDAY, NOVEMBER 11, 1826.

RELIGIOUS INTELLIGENCE.

FOREIGN.

In the last number of the Asiatic Journal, there is an interesting article respecting the Jews in China. They were settled in that country, as well as in other parts of Asia, many centuries prior to the Christian era; even as early as one thousand years before. They migrated from Persia, by way of Khorasan. They say themselves that they came from the west, or from Siyu. They have a manuscript copy of the Pentateuch; and they long kept up an intercourse with other Jews in Persia, and the more western parts of Asia; It is said they received some additions soon after the destruction of Jerusalem by Titus in 70. Some of them have become Mahometans.—They have a tradition, that Abraham, who they say was the nineteenth from Adam, was the author of their law, and that Moses derived it from him. There is a great similarity between the laws of Abraham or Moses, and those of the Chinese. Their calculation makes Abraham to have lived 2000 years before our era; whereas our account places him about 1850 before. The period between Abraham and Moses, is not very different in the two accounts. In the ancient Chinese laws, which originated with Abraham, as they pretend, are traces of a holy Sabbath. In their more ancient writings, they say Adam was the first man—that Abraham was the real author of the law, which was afterwards published by Moses. They inculcate *adoration of heaven*, by which is probably meant the *Invisible One* who inhabits the heavens and all worlds.—Hence in time, mankind, who worshipped the God of heaven, were led to fix their thoughts upon and to adore heavenly bodies, as the sun, moon, and stars; and *fire*, as the emblem of these. Abraham, they say, worshipped Heaven, but not under any figure or image.

These Jews are said to be honest and industrious, and esteemed by the Chinese.—They have a synagogue 350 feet long and 150 wide, and dedicated to " the Creator and Preserver of all things." There is this inscription also on a tablet in the synagogue,—" Hear, O Israel, Jehovah, our God, is the only Jehovah."

When the people enter the temple, they shake off their shoes, and when they pray they turn towards the west. The person who reads the law covers his face with a thin veil. They believe in a judgment, in a paradise and place of punishment. The Sabbath is kept strictly by them.—But they do not attempt to make proselytes, nor even to go into the temple where an idol is worshipped. Besides the pentateuch, they have only parts of Isaiah, Daniel and Jeremiah.—*Boston Gaz.*

BOSTON, 1826
"RELIGIOUS INTELLIGENCE:
FOREIGN"

Christian Register, p. 1 (col 1)
November 11, 1826

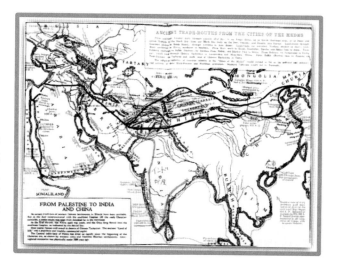

FROM PALESTINE TO INDIA AND CHINA

Taken from "an interesting article respecting the Jews in China" in a recent *Asiatic Journal*, this front-page column speaks about the Jews who originally came from Persia via Khorasan about 1,000 years "prior to the Christian era." Some of the unique aspects of their traditions are cited. For instance, they believed that Abraham "was the author of their law and that Moses derived it from him." They "strictly" observed the Sabbath; their synagogue is 300 feet long and 150 feet wide; and they "seem to be honest, industrious and esteemed by the Chinese."

THE SUN.

IT SHINES FOR ALL

NUMBER 547.]   NEW YORK, SATURDAY MORNING, JUNE 6, 1835.   [PRICE ONE CENT.

THE NEW YORK SUN.

SATURDAY MORNING, JUNE 6, 1835.

Jewing.—The Northampton Courier states that the good people of that town have been famously gulled during the past week. A couple of Jews from New York, with porcelain ware, have been all about there, trafficking their trumpery for old clothes.— Their speculations have been principally carried on among the ladies, and they, as a matter of course, have been fleeced, some of them, most outrageously. Husbands' coats and brothers' pantaloons and daughters' gowns—old vests, threadbare trousers and frocks with tattered linings—have all been swept in one heterogeneous mass into the bags of these travelling pawn brokers. But the bargains they have made! aye! there's the rub! For various old garments worth say ten or fifteen dollars, why, they would "trade away" a pair of vases or a flip-mug worth not one third that sum. "De men" they did'nt want to see, but "de women," aye, they liked to trade with "de women." They could *jew* them and in the absence of the men, they accomplished their object most successfully.

NEW YORK, 1835
"JEWING"
The New York Sun, p. 2 (col 2)
June 6, 1835

Although America's 10,000 Jews had by this date successfully established themselves legally and commercially, they were still regularly scoffed at in the press. Anti-Semitic references such as "Jewing" often appeared. It reported that "a couple of Jews from New York with porcelain ware" appeared in Northampton aiming to deceitfully exchange their cheap merchandise for the more expensive second hand clothing. These Jews were "trafficking their trumpery" on gullible women. Making fun of the accents of these European Jews, the article added that they were more inclined to 'jew" "de women" and not "de men."

THE OLEAN ADVOCATE.

PUBLISHED EVERY SATURDAY MORNING, AT OLEAN, CATTARAUGUS COUNTY, N.Y. AT TWO DOLLARS PER ANNUM, IN ADVANCE, TWO FIFTY AT THE END OF SIX MONTHS, OR THREE DOLLARS AT THE END OF THE YEAR.

BY RUFUS W. GRISWOLD.   SATURDAY MORNING, APRIL 15, 1837.   VOLUME I, NUMBER 35.

AMERICAN INDIANS.

The origin of the American Indians, is at present a subject receiving a good share of attention in our literary circles. The editor of the Evening Star not long since delivered an instructive lecture upon this subject, and at present an intelligent Indian of the Mohawk tribe is delivering a course of Lectures upon the history of the red men of America. In reference to this subject, a correspondent of the New London Gazette, writes as follows from Fort Gibson, Arkansas;

It has been supposed that the Indians are of Jewish origin, which appears somewhat confirmed by their late emigration, nine men have gone before the emigrants ever since they left the old nation, and one of them Covenant, or the tables which Moses bro't from the Mount. White men are not allowed to see them, but an old negro says, that they have two brass plates about 18 by 6, with letters engraved on them: probably the commandments. The man carrying it has not been known to speak to any one upon the road; and in his manners he has been as solemn as the grave. It is said that the plates are cleaned once a year by a person who attends to no other business. I shall endeavor to obtain further information on this highly interesting subject."

THE OLEAN ADVOCATE.

JEWS IN CHINA.

There is a colony of Jews in China, at Kae-fooling-foo, of whom Mr. Cavis in his work on the Chineese, gives some interesting particulars. They are said to have reached China as early as 200 years before Christ. There is a place reserved in its synagogue for its chief, who never enters there except with profound respect. They say that their ancestors came from the Kingdom of the West, called the kingdom of Judea, which Joshua conquered after having departed from Egypt, and passed the Red Sea and the Desert, and that the number of Jews who emigrated from Egypt was about 500,000. They say their alphabet has twenty-seven letters, but they commonly make use of twelve, which accords with the declaration of St. Jerome, that the Hebrew has twenty-two letters, five of which are double. When they read the bible in their synagogue, they cover their face with a transparent veil, in memory of Moses, who descended from the mountain with his face covered, and who thus published the decalogue and the law of God to his people; they read a section every sabbath. Thus the Jews of China, like the Jews of Europe, read all the law in the course of the year.

OLEAN, NEW YORK – 1837
"AMERICAN INDIANS" & "JEWS IN CHINA"
The Olean Advocate, p. 1 (col 4), p. 2 (col 4)
April 15, 1837

This issue features two rather exotic reports relating to Jews. In a front page story relating to the origins of American Indians, the author cites evidence that they may come from Jewish stock. The evidence noted is that certain Indians carry two brass plates … "the Covenant, or the tables which Moses bro't from the Mount." The correspondent indicated that he "shall endeavor to obtain further information on this highly interesting subject."

A page two article, "Jews in China," describes a colony of Jews in "Kae-fooling-foo" [Kai-fung-foo] that had "reached China as early as 200 years before Christ … [from] the Kingdom of the West, called the Kingdom of Judea, which Joshua conquered after having departed from Egypt." The article speaks of their alphabet, the reading of the Bible in synagogue, their covering of their faces with transparent veils in memory of Moses who descended the Mount with his face covered, and more.

CHURCH CHRONICLE AND RECORD.

"WHAT THOU SEEST, WRITE IN A BOOK."—"EVANGELICAL TRUTH—APOSTOLIC ORDER."

VOL. VII.   NEW HAVEN, CONN, FRIDAY, AUGUST 25, 1843.   NO. 346.

The East.—From the Boston Recorder we extract the following, in relation to the doings of the London Jews Society in the East, and the condition of the mission of the Church in that quarter ;

'By the last report of the London Jews Society, we perceive that a larger number of Jews were baptized during the past year than any former year, within the space of that Society's labors. Three new missionary stations have been occupied during the year in the East, and five missionaries sent forth from the Hebrew College in London. Safet, the place which it is believed our Lord had in view when he spoke of "a city set on a hill;" Hebron the residence of Abraham, and of Isaac, and of Jacob ; and Beyroot, the emporium of Palestine, have all Jewish missions established in them. In Jeruselem, the work seems to be in successful progress, under the labors of the new bishop, Alexander, who is a converted Jew, and from all accounts a truly evangelical man. The obstacles which have arisen to the building of a Church there, it is thought, will be temporary, and Jerusalem may soon be the great centre of missionary operations among the Jews.'

NEW HAVEN, CONNECTICUT – 1843
MISSIONARY ACTIVITY IN THE EAST
Church Chronicle and Record, p. 267 (col 1)
August 25, 1843

This newspaper's blurb, extracted "from the Boston Recorder," boasts about successful missionary activity in the Holy Land in converting Jews. Based on reports from the London Jews Society in the East, more Jews in the Society's realm were baptized that year than in any other. Five missionaries were sent forth to the East from the Hebrew College in London and new missionary stations were set up in Hebron, Safet and Beyroot. Jerusalem, the thought is, will become "the great centre of missionary operations among the Jews" because of "the labors of the new bishop, Alexander, who is a converted Jew, and … a truly evangelical man."

Michael Solomon Alexander (b. 1799, King of Prussia; d. 1845, Jerusalem) served as the first bishop of Jerusalem.

"Grabstein Bischof Michael Salomo Alexanders auf dem Zionsfriedhof in Jerusalem" (Tombstone of Bishop Michael Salomo Alexander at the Zion Cemetery in Jerusalem): Photo by Ulf Heinsohn – https://commons. wikimedia.org/wiki/File:Alexander,_Michael_Salomo_2_ Zionsfriedhof_Jerusalem.jpg

162   NILES' NATIONAL REGISTER—NOV. 6, 1844—MISCELLANEOUS'

THE NATURALIZATION LAW OF MOSES.
Extract from Prof Wines on the Civil Government of the Hebrews

"I proceed to an exposition of the provisions of the Hebrew constitution, in reference to the admission of foreigners to the right of citizenship. And, if I mistake not, we shall find it characterised by the same wise and patriotic forecast which marks all the other enactments of this admirable code."

"I sympathise, most sincerely, with an eloquent rebuke, administered by a distinguished divine* but a few weeks ago, in one of the pulpits of this city, of that mercenary patriotism which would repel from our shores the friendless and the oppressed of other climes. I say emphatically, 'let them come!' Let every ship that enters our harbors pour them by hundreds upon our soil. The first civilized men who settled as permanent residents on this continent, sought, in the then howling wilderness, among savages and wild beasts, a refuge from tyranny and oppression; a home where they could breathe the air of freedom, where they could think without a master, and above all where they could worship God without asking a titled and purse proud hierarchy when,

Christianized America.—America blessed with free institutions, and embellished with the trophies of science and religion,—should be more hard-hearted than America peopled with the wolf, the panther, the buffalo, and the painted Indian! God forbid that my native country, whose boast it is to be free and happy herself, should ever cease to afford to the sons and daughters of sorrow, fleeing from the wrongs and miseries of European despotism, a hearty welcome and a happy home!

"But are we, therefore, to permit these foreign refugees to overturn our liberties, and render the government under which we live so happily, as little worth as any of the worn-out and tottering dynasties of Europe? Have they any of that attachment to our institutions, which would make them at once safe depositories of political power? Are they qualified either by their education, habits, or sympathies, to exercise the most precious of a freemen's franchises, and march to the ballot box almost within the first twenty four hours after their arrival upon our shores?

"In my opinion, our American law-makers might profitably go to school to Moses in this, as well as on several other questions of public policy; and if they should not carry the principle of his naturalization laws to the full extent that he did, it would at least be instructive to them to contemplate the procedure of a true patriot, and an able statesmen, and one, too, under the guidance of a divine wisdom.

"Admission to citizenship was denominated by Moses, "entering into the congregation of Jehovah." He ordained that this should never take place in the first or second generation. Some nations, the Ammonites and Moabites, for particular reasons, were not to be admitted to the tenth generation; that is, never. But the Edomites, Egyptians, and probably foreigners of other nations, could become Israelitish citizens in the third generation. That is to say, the grand-children of those who had immigrated into Judea from foreign climes, could be admitted to the privileges of natives of the soil. Why this jealousy of foreign influence? The reason is plain. Moses was an intelligent and devoted lover of his country's liberties, and he was not willing that they should be lightly subjected to the peril of destruction, through the ignorance and recklessness of foreign voters.— Hence, he required that foreigners should become, so to speak, naturalized in their sentiments, habits, sympathies, and manners, before by a legal naturalization they should be incorporated into the body politic and invested with the rights and dignities of citizens. And, certainly, the principle of this enactment must commend itself to every sober understanding, as founded in the wisest policy and the most true hearted patriotism; though, doubtless, the application of the principle need not, in all cases, be carried on to an equal degree of rigor."

WESTERN RIVER SNAG BOATS — *The St. Louis Rep.* says W. learn from Capt. Russell, superintendent

*Rev. Dr. Bethune, of Philadelphia.

BALTIMORE – 1844
"THE NATURALIZATION LAW OF MOSES"
Niles' Weekly Register, p. 162 (col 1)
November 16, 1844

In response to growing demands for restrictions on immigrants, this issue of the *Register* carries an article by Professor Enoch S. Wines, a Christian theologian, on the naturalization law of Moses. Professor Wines, clearly referring to prospects of future Jewish immigration, argued, "God forbid that any native country, whose boast is to be free and happy herself, should ever cease to afford to the sons and daughters of sorrow, fleeing from the wrongs and miseries of European despotism, a hearty welcome and a happy home!"

Yet he cited the naturalization policies of Moses as a guide for future American public policy. According to the Bible, certain nationalities – such as Ammonites and Moabites – were not to be admitted into the House of Israel "to the tenth generation; that is, never." But Egyptians, Edomites, "and probably foreigners of other nations could become Israelitish citizens in the third generation." American immigration policy, he maintained, should similarly follow the guideline that only the grandchildren of the new arrivals, after presumably absorbing the American cultural environment, "be incorporated into the body politic and invested with the rights and dignities of citizens."

THE DEMOCRAT.

JAMAICA, MAY 22, 1849.

JAMAICA, NEW YORK – 1849
"CONVERSION OF THE JEWS"

Long-Island Democrat, p. 2 (col 1)
May 22, 1849

In this page 2 article, taken from the "*N. Y. Mercury*," a columnist takes issue with a movement in the United States called the Society for the Conversion of the Jews. After pointing out that the enterprise is very expensive, with very little to report in the way of benefit, noting that "it cost the society a year's labor and $3000—all its contributions within a few dollars—to make one convert," he goes on to say why the Jews do not need to be converted in order to follow an honorable life:

> Now the truth of the matter is, that *the Jews are the only practical and moral Socialists of the day*.... They are loyal in all the relations of life; their women are proverbially virtuous, and they are peaceable, unobtrusive citizens. Who ever saw a Jew or a Jewish child, a beggar; In distress, in sickness, or in death, they help one another. Their religion seems to be based on the grand precepts of peace and goodwill to all mankind—do unto others as you would that others should do unto you—love your neighbor as yourself.

> We hardly think the Jews stand in need of any conversion—in fact, we rather opine that it is a pity the attempt should be made.

He closes with the statement, "Let the Jews alone."

CONVERSION OF THE JEWS.

Among other anniversaries in New York last week, was that of the 'Society for the Conversion of the Jews and Evangelization of Israel.'

We are told that a 'very encouraging and flattering report of the state and condition of the society' was read, wherein it appeared that the contributions amounted to over $3,000, fifi, and the *expenditures* came very near that sum—within a few dollars only of it, in fact. And then we learn, that 'no account was given of any prejudicial results, but hopes were held out of the benefits to be derived from specific action.'

In other words, it cost the society a year's labor and $3,000—all its contributions within a few dollars—to make one convert to christianity, a Mr. Sheinkoph, who is on the look-out for a berth in the church.

Of course, resolutions were passed regulative of future action, and in view of practical gullibility. It was 'resolved' that the 'present time is a time peculiarly favorable for the conversion of the Jews, and that the American people seem to be the people peculiarly designed by Providence to take the lead in evangelizing the Jews.'

Isn't this pretty cant? One of the speakers, a Dr. Bacon, all unconsciously gave a capital reason why those singular and most consistent people, the Jews, need no 'conversion:' their '*uninterrupted and ever preserved nationality.*' 'This,' said he, 'is a visible miracle not to be denied, but daily before the eyes of all the world and in all parts of the world. It has happened to no other people that ever existed.' But this 'same learned Theban' made one assertion which we must beg leave to doubt; namely, that the Jews were 'plunged in ignorance and superstition.'

Now the truth of the matter is, that *the Jews are the only practical and moral Socialists* of the day; hence their 'uninterrupted and ever preserved nationality.' They are loyal in all the relations of life; their women are proverbially virtuous, and they are peaceable, unobtrusive citizens. Who ever saw a Jew or a Jewish child, a beggar; In distress, in sickness, or in death, they help one another. Their religion seems to be based on the grand precepts of peace and good will to all mankind—do unto others as you would that others should do unto you—love your neighbor as yourself.

We hardly think the Jews stand in need of any conversion—in fact, we rather opine that it is a pity the attempt should be made. If the Jews are not Christians, or believers in Christ, they understand and carry out the true spirit of christianity—CHARITY—better than any other people. Let the Jews alone.—*N. Y. Mercury.*

Daily National Intelligencer.

VOL. XXXVII.   WASHINGTON: SATURDAY, NOVEMBER 24, 1849.   No. 11,

LETTERS TO THE HEBREWS.

The Hebrew Benevolent Society and the German Hebrew Benevolent Society of New York celebrated their Anniversary in conjunction, by a Dinner at the Apollo Saloon, in the city of New York, a few evenings ago.

After the Regular Toasts had been drank through, Major M. M. Noah (who presided on the occasion) informed the party that several prominent men in the Union having been invited to attend, and being unavoidably prevented from honoring the festival with their presence, had sent letters of sympathy and thanks to the Committee of Invitation, and he begged attention for a few moments while he read the following from the Hon. DANIEL WEBSTER and Hon. WM. H. SEWARD, among many others which had been received:

BOSTON, NOVEMBER 9, 1849.

MY DEAR SIR: I am afraid it will not be in my power to attend the anniversary of the "Hebrew Benevolent Society" and the "German Hebrew Benevolent Society" on the 13th of the present month. I am, however, grateful for having been remembered on this occasion, and desire to present my acknowledgments and thanks to the committee.

I feel and have ever felt respect and sympathy for all that remains of that extraordinary people, who preserved through the darkness and idolatry of so many centuries the knowledge of One Supreme Spiritual Being, the Maker of Heaven and Earth, and the Creator of Man in his own image; and whose canonical writings comprise such productions as the books of Moses and the Decalogue, the Prophecies of Isaiah, the Psalms of David, the Book of Job, and Solomon's prayer at the dedication of the Temple. The Hebrew Scriptures I regard as the fountain from which we draw all we know of the world around us, and of our own character and destiny as intelligent, moral, and responsible beings.

I wish, my dear sir, for the associated societies who have honored me with their invitation a gratifying anniversary, and am, with respect, your obedient servant,

DANIEL WEBSTER.

M. M. NOAH, Esq., New York.

AUBURN, NOVEMBER 6, 1849.

MY DEAR SIR: The letter of the managers, inviting me to the anniversary festival of the Hebrew Benevolent Society and the German Hebrew Benevolent Society, has been received, together with your note so kindly urging me to accept the invitation.

The day appointed for these festivities falls within the very brief period I have assigned for the preparation indispensable for an absence from home for a long season. I deeply regret that I am, therefore, obliged to deny myself the pleasure of becoming personally acquainted, under propitious circumstances, with so large and respectable a portion of the Hebrew nation dwelling among us.

Under any circumstances it would afford a rare pleasure to a person of generous sentiments to enjoy the conversation of representatives of that extraordinary people who alone of all the nations of antiquity have retained, among the vicissitudes of human affairs, their God and their religion; that only ancient people whose doctrines have commanded our unqualified belief through so many ages, whose songs constitute the devotional melody of their most relentless enemies, and whose very prophecies, after the lapse of thousands of years, are still regarded as the infallible oracles of the fate of Empires, States, and Men. But the gathering of the Hebrews, now contemplated, derives additional attractions from its design to welcome to our shores their brethren driven from Europe by fresh persecutions and by new and disastrous revolutions.

I pray you to tender to the societies assurances of my sincere respect, and of my cordial sympathy in their benevolent purposes, with my grateful acknowledgments for their kind remembrance of me, while I remain, with great respect and esteem, your friend and humble servant,

M. M. NOAH, Esq.   WM. H. SEWARD.

WASHINGTON, D.C. – 1849
"LETTERS TO THE HEBREWS"
Daily National Intelligencer, p. 3 (col 3) – November 24, 1849

Though New York City's Jewish population numbered only some 10,000, two of the nation's most prominent political leaders sent personal regrets when they were unable to attend the anniversary celebration of the Hebrew Benevolent Society held at the Apollo Saloon. In letters addressed to Mordecai M. Noah they revealed their great esteem for the Judaic contribution to civilization.

In a top of the page article, "Letters to the Hebrews," United States Senator (MA) Daniel Webster is quoted as having written, "I have and have ever felt respect and sympathy for all that remains of that extraordinary people, who preserved through the darkness and idolatry of so many centuries the knowledge of One Supreme Spiritual Being, the Maker of Heaven and Earth, and the Creator of Man in His own image…."

In a similar tribute, United States Senator (NY) William H. Seward's RSVP hailed "that extraordinary people who alone of all the nations of antiquity have retained, among the vicissitudes of human affairs, their God and their religion; that only ancient people whose doctrines have commanded our unqualified belief through so many ages, whose songs constitute the devotional melody of their most relentless enemies, and whose very prophecies, after the lapse of thousands of years, are still regarded as the infallible oracles of the fate of Empires, States, and Men…."

The Daily Advocate.

OFFICIAL PAPER FOR PUBLISHING THE JOURNALS AND DEBATES OF THE GENERAL ASSEMBLY OF THE STATE OF LOUISIANA.

VOL. 5.   BATON ROUGE, LA., WEDNESDAY EVENING, NOVEMBER 19, 1856.   NO. 111.

THE JEWS.—At the present moment a Jew stands at the head of nearly every walk in life throughout Europe. The Rothschilds command the money market of Europe, some in Paris, some in Vienna, some in London, and that family loaned immense sums to both Russia on the one hand, and the allies on the other in the late war in Europe. In literature, for centuries they have produced the ablest scholars, the subtlest of all thinkers, the foremost men of each age. In the dark ages, and amid the greatest persecution, they produced lights whose lustre still shines; and now in England, a Jew, D'Israeli, leads the House of Commons, and a Jew is Lord Mayor of London. In Germany at least half a dozen of the most distinguished professors are that race. The great Neander himself was one of them, and Mendelssohn, who was the envy of Goethe for his power of language. In Spain, men of this nation have, in former days, as professed Jesuits, while secretly retaining their own faith, obtained direction even of the Inqusition. In fact, there are few heights of power to which they have not attained, as there are no amounts of persecution they have not endured. No matter what they undertake, they seem to push it through with a vigor and an enterprise that they carry their point to the furthest attainable degree, and further than will be reached by any other. The ablest musician in London was a Jew, Braham, who retained his voice and his position till about eighty, forming his name out of Abraham, by the simple expedient of dropping the A, to disguise his origin. And so in like manner, the most distinguished actress of Paris, at this moment, is Rachel, the Jewess, In fact, no matter what they turn their hands to, philosophy or fine arts, money changing or old clothes, they uniformly push their occupations to an extent, and with a closeness of computation, that carries them beyond all competitors.—*Philadelphia Ledger.*

BATON ROUGE, 1856
"THE JEWS."
The Daily Advocate, p. 2 (col 4)
November 19, 1856

Telegraphed from the *Philadelphia Ledger,* "The Jews" speaks admirably about the many areas in which Jews have excelled throughout Europe. The article carries the following tribute: "In the dark ages, and amid the greatest persecution, they produced lights whose luster still shines…. .No matter what they undertake, they seem to push it through with vigor and an enterprise." The article identifies several distinguished Jews in Europe, including Benjamin Disraeli, the Rothschilds, French actress Rachel the Jewess and British opera singer Braham.

THE DAILY EVENING COURIER.

PUBLICATION OFFICE ON WEST STREET, A FEW DOORS NORTH OF THE MADISON INSURANCE CO. BANK.

VOL. 11.   MADISON INDIANA, TUESDAY EVENING, FEBRUARY 21, 1860.   NO. 251.

THE EVENING COURIER,
lished every evening (Sundays excepted) by
M. C. GARBER,
IN THE COURIER BUILDINGS, WEST STREET,
BETWEEN MAIN CROSS AND SECOND STS.
MADISON, INDIANA.
"And is delivered to City Subscribers at 10 cents per
week.   Single copies 5 cents.   Mail Subscribers, $5
per annum, in advance.
All letters on Business, to receive attention
must be addressed "Editor Courier."
THE WEEKLY COURIER,
Is published every Wednesday at $1 per annum in
advance.
No paper sent without the money, nor c
ed a longer time than paid for.

Jewish Women in Morocco.

The Mogadar Jewesses are not very strict to their faith. They will marry any well-to-do Christian gentleman who would make the offer seriously. They are singularly lovely in face, though stout in form. Both in Tangiers and Mogador I was fortunate enough to be acquainted with families who could boast of the most perfect and classic types of Jewish female loveliness. Alas that these beauties should be only charming animals, their minds and affections being left uncultivated, or bonverted into caves of unclean and tormenting passions. The Jewesses, in general, until they become enormously stout and weighed down with obesity, are of extreme beauty. Most of them have fair complexions their rose and jasmine faces, their pure wax like delicate features, and their exceedingly expressive and bewitching eyes, would fascinate the most fastideous of European connoisseurs of female beauty.

But these Israelitish ladies, recalling the fair image of Rachel in the patriarchal times of Holy Writ and worthy to serve as models for a Grecian sculptor, are treated with savage disdain by the churlish Moors, and some times are obliged to walk barefoot and prostrate themselves before their ugly negross concubines. The male infants of Jews are engaging and goodlooking when young; but, as they grow up, they become ordinary; and Jews of a certain age are decidedly and most disgustingly ugly. In former days Jewesses, as well as Jews, were obliged to take off the slippers or sandals in passing a mosque. But the predecessor of the present Emperor, a rigid Mussulman, considered it a great scandal that these fat enormous infidels should disturb the devotions of the faithful by showing their well conditioned ankles, so the order was rescinded, and the spirits of the Mussulmans left in peace.

[Richardson's Morocco.

MADISON, INDIANA – 1860
"JEWISH WOMEN IN MOROCCO"
The Daily Evening Courier, p. 1 (col 5)
February 21, 1860

The author of this front page article can't seem to make up his mind whether to flatter or insult the Mogador Jewesses he writes about. In the first paragraph he begins with the claim that they "are not very strict to their faith [and] will marry any well-to-do Christian gentleman who would make the offer seriously" and then speaks of their loveliness. "Their rose and jasmine faces, their pure wax like delicate features and their exceedingly expressive and bewitching eyes," he writes, "would fascinate the most fastidious connoisseurs of female beauty," but he precedes this comment with a note that their extreme beauty is only until they become "enormously stout and weighed down with obesity."

The second paragraph speaks about how the Jewish women in Morocco, though "recalling the fair image" of the biblical Rachel and "worthy to serve as models," were treated with disdain by the "churlish" Moors. Jewesses were sometimes "obliged to walk barefoot and prostrate themselves before [the Moors'] ugly negross [sic] concubines."

The Charleston Mercury.

CHARLESTON, S. C., SATURDAY, MAY 26, 1860.   NUMBER 10,866

FASHIONABLE WEDDINGS IN NEW YORK.—At six o'clock this evening there will take place a grand diamond wedding in the Fifth Avenue, the preparations for which have kept the aristocratic circles of the Hebrew community in a flutter of excitement for some time past. The fair bride is the daughter of an eminent broker, is quite young, and one of the most beautiful of "Israel's dark-eyed daughters;" and the fortunate groom is a scion of a Philadelphia family, honorably distinguished in the political history of the country. He is also youthful; and as both the parties are as wealthy as they can desire, of course the alliance is one of affection.

The nuptials will be performed with all the splendor of the Jewish Ritual. Three hundred guests, among whom are a number of Christians, will be present; and as it is Jewish etiquette to wear the most costly jewels that can be procured, the occasion will be one of great brilliancy. The bridal presents are superb. One single shawl cost one thousand dollars; and the bride's dress, which is a miracle of point lace, is said to be worth double the money.

Rev. Mr. Lyons, of the Nineteenth-street and Fifth Avenue Synagogue, will officiate, assisted by Rev. Mr. Leeser, of Philadelphia, Rev. Dr. Fischel, and other eminent Jewish ministers.

This morning Capt. George McClelland, late of the U. S. Army, was married to a daughter of Capt. R. B. Marcy, U. S. A.

New York Express, 22d inst.

CHARLESTON – 1860
"FASHIONABLE WEDDINGS IN NEW YORK"

The Charleston Mercury, p. 1 (col 7)
May 26, 1860

Two "fashionable" New York weddings received front page coverage in this issue of *The Charleston Mercury."*

The first, a Jewish wedding to be held "at six o'clock this evening" on Fifth Avenue, got top billing with a 27-line report, whereas the second simply stated in 3 lines that Capt. George McClelland had been married that morning to the daughter of another captain.

The article referred to the Jewish wedding as a "grand diamond wedding" and focused primarily on the wealth of the celebrants. References to such wealth, whether deliberate or not, no doubt helped further the stereotype of the rich Jew. The unnamed "fair bride" is described as the daughter of "an eminent broker" and "one of the most beautiful of 'Israel's dark-eyed beauties,'" and the groom is the scion of a Philadelphia family "honorably distinguished in the political history of the country." The article notes that since it is Jewish etiquette "to wear the most jewels that can be procured, the occasion will be one of great brilliancy."

Two of the most renowned American rabbis ("ministers") of the day, Rabbi Jacques Judah Lyons of the Spanish and Portuguese Synagogue (Congregation Shearith Israel) and Rabbi Isaac Leeser of Philadelphia's Mikveh Israel, were among those scheduled to officiate.

NEW YORK – 1863
"THE GOLD PANIC"
Harper's Weekly, p. 187 (col 3)
March 21, 1863

The Civil War gold panic is reported from the stereotypical perspective that Jews were the main speculators, and likely the main group to suffer from the crash in the value of gold. At the gold exchange on William Street, "there were frightened, panting Jews who were evidently holders of gold. And there were exultant, joyful Jews who had foreseen the crash and 'sold gold short.'"

The article quotes an earlier piece in *The New York Herald,* which also portrayed Jews in a disgusting light: "Most of the heavy speculators were Jews, and they cut miserable figures as they rushed to and fro, foaming at the mouth, cursing with impotent rage Old Abe and Secretary Chase, who had brought this ruin on the house of their fathers."

The page following the article (p. 188) contained a page-length cartoon, facing sideways, of the crowd – mostly stereotypical Jewish caricatures – attempting to sell their gold.

THE GOLD PANIC.

WE illustrate on page 188 the Gold Panic which occurred last week, when gold fell in Wall Street in two days from 173 to 149, ruining half the Jew speculators who had been buying specie, and improving the national currency some fifteen per cent. The scene on Thursday, at noon, in William Street, outside the new public Board, beggars description. The street was thronged from the houses on one side to the houses on the other. Half a dozen policemen endeavored vainly to keep order, and made arrests right and left without much judgment, discretion, or effect. Every body was raging to sell his gold. Hundreds of speculators who had bought gold within a week appeared with blanched faces and trembling gait, vainly offering their gold to every one they met. Among the crowd the Jew element rather preponderated. There were frightened, panting Jews, who were evidently holders of gold, and there were exultant joyful Jews, who had foreseen the crash and "sold gold short." There were New Testament Jews, too, by the score, with a bilious Southern aspect, who had bought gold in the belief and hope that the Northern finances would collapse, and who now saw that they and their funds were likely to anticipate the Government in that catastrophe. Fortunes were made and lost in a day in that seething caldron of speculation.

THE GOLD PANIC IN WALL STREET—ENTRANCE OF THE PUBLIC BOARD.—[SEE PAGE 187.]

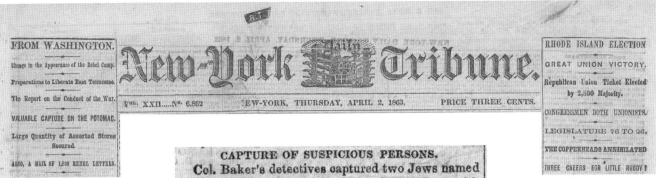

CAPTURE OF SUSPICIOUS PERSONS.

Col. Baker's detectives captured two Jews named Levy and Miller, up the Potomac, yesterday, with $10,000 or $12,000 of Confederate money upon their persons. A number of citizens of Fairfax County have been escorted to the Old Capitol within a few days, charged with being concerned in the recent raid into Fairfax Court-House, and for expressing disloyal sentiments.

LORD LYONS'S DISPATCH.

Lord Lyons's dispatch of Nov. 17 continues to be the leading topic of discussion in political and diplomatic circles. Equally intelligent and patriotic Americans differ widely in opinion as to its significance.

CAPTURE OF REBEL MAIL-CARRIERS.

Lieut. Wm. Smith and Joseph Coleman, private, in the Rebel army, left Richmond two weeks ago with a Rebel mail, reaching Matthews Court-House. They passed to Chesapeake Bay and crossed into Accomac County, Md., and thence proceeded to Baltimore. There Col. Baker heard of them, and his detectives were at once put on their track. From Baltimore they came to Washington, Lieut. Smith having a wife in Alexandria, and, finding it difficult to reach that place, sent for Mrs. Smith to meet him here, which she did yesterday.

After diligent search they were found this morning at 4 o'clock, and taken into custody. Meanwhile, Joseph had stolen a boat, in which with the mail he embarked for Alexandria, where he was met at the coal wharf by Col. Baker's men, who captured him and the mail.

NEW YORK – 1863
"CAPTURE OF SUSPICIOUS PERSONS"
New-York Daily Tribune, p. 1 (col 1)
April 2, 1863

A front-page report on the war included a notice with the sub headline, "Capture of Suspicious Persons," which notes that "Col. Baker's detectives captured two Jews named Levy and Miller, up the Potomac, yesterday, with $10,000 or $12,000 of Confederate money upon their persons."

It is not unexpected but revealing to note that in another notice just one blurb down – about another capture made by Baker's detectives – there was no indication as to the religion of "Lieut. Wm. Smith and Joseph Coleman, private."

The Jews in Dixie.
From The Richmond Dispatch, Feb. 22.

Johnny Hook, bawling "Beef" in the Revolution, seems to have had a prolific progeny. The Johnny Hooks abound in every city, village and cross-road. *If all the Johnny Hooks were in the ranks, and made such charges as they make upon their own countrymen, the Southern Confederacy would establish its independence in six months.* In sunshine or darkness, victory or defeat, they raise one eternal cry of "Beef! Beef!" He is not alone a Jew who is one outwardly. *If one of our modern speculators had been with the Jews in the wilderness he would have been up in the morning before they were awake, collected the manna, and sold it to the children of Israel at five dollars an ounce. If he had gone to spy out the promised land, he would have converted the grapes into wine and sold it at three hundred dollars a gallon.* If he had been a priest, he would have sold the sacrifices to the highest bidder. If he had a soul he would sell it for a nine pence, and, being acquainted with the market value of the article, would rightfully conclude he had made a good bargain.

NEW YORK – 1865
THE JEWS IN DIXIE
New-York Daily Tribune, p. 1
February 25, 1865

In a front page, three column round up of "Late Rebel News," taken from actual Confederate newspapers, the newspaper cites a piece that ran in *The Richmond Dispatch,* "The Jews in Dixie."

> *If one of our modern speculators had been with the Jews in the wilderness he would have been up in the morning before they were awake, collected the manna, and sold it to the children of Israel at five dollars an ounce. If he had gone to spy out the promised land he would have converted the grapes into wine and sold it at three hundred dollars a gallon.*

Chapter #8

Mordecai M. Noah

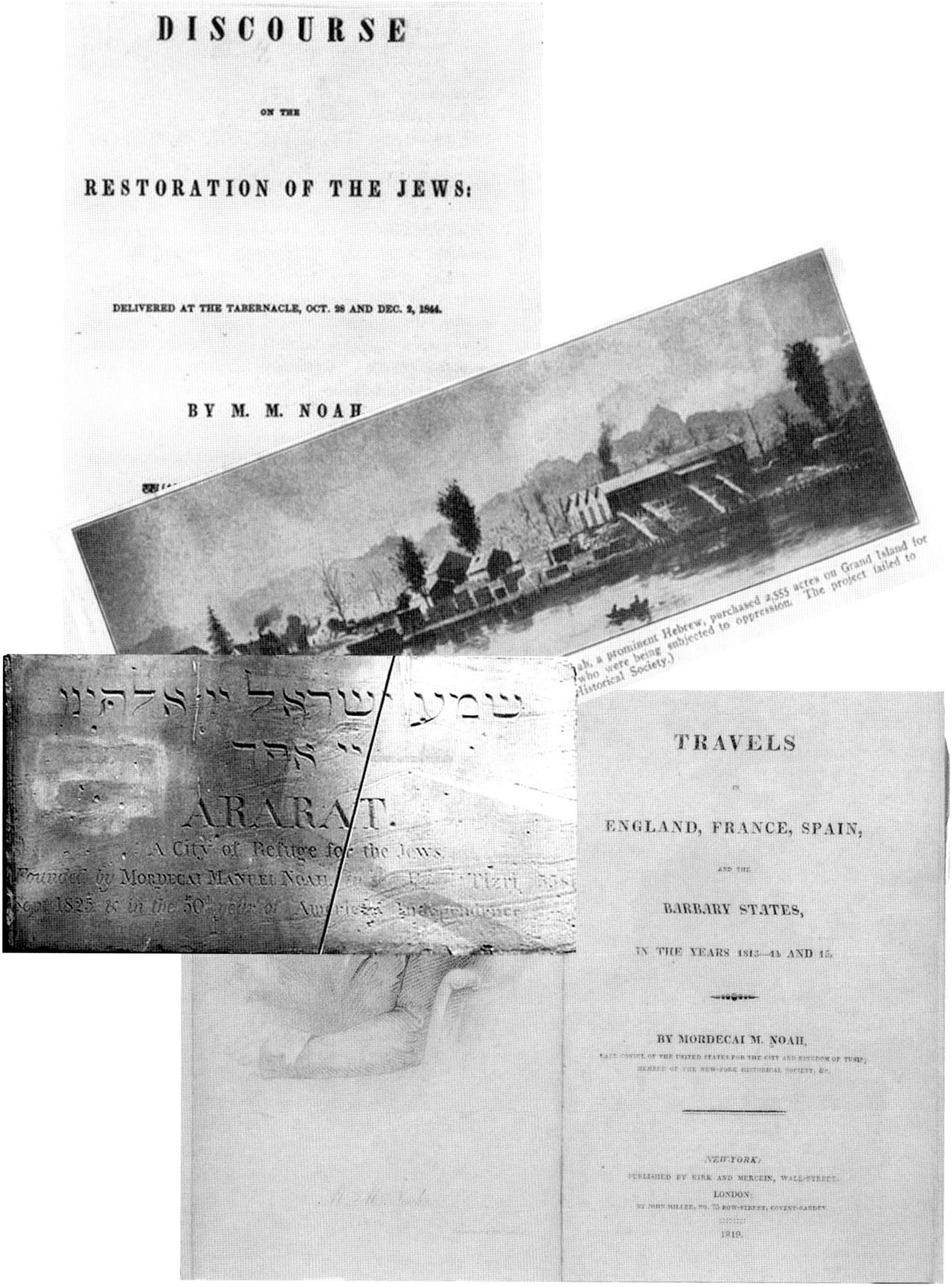

DISCOURSE

ON THE

RESTORATION OF THE JEWS:

DELIVERED AT THE TABERNACLE, OCT. 28 AND DEC. 2, 1844.

BY M. M. NOAH

ah, a prominent Hebrew, purchased 2,555 acres on Grand Island for
who were being subjected to oppression. The project failed to
Historical Society.)

שמע ישראל י'י א'להינו
י'י א'חד

ARARAT.

A City of Refuge for the Jews.

Founded by MORDECAI MANUEL NOAH in
Sept. 1825 & in the 50th year of American Independence

TRAVELS

IN

ENGLAND, FRANCE, SPAIN,

AND THE

BARBARY STATES,

IN THE YEARS 1813—14 AND 15.

BY MORDECAI M. NOAH,

LATE CONSUL OF THE UNITED STATES FOR THE CITY AND KINGDOM OF TUNIS;
MEMBER OF THE NEW-YORK HISTORICAL SOCIETY, &c.

NEW-YORK:
PUBLISHED BY KIRK AND MERCEIN, WALL-STREET.
LONDON:
BY JOHN MILLER, NO. 25 BOW-STREET, COVENT-GARDEN.

1819.

ABOUT MORDECAI M. NOAH

Mordecai Manual Noah, editor, Sheriff of New-York City, politician, diplomat and Zionist (b. Philadelphia, 1785; d. New York, 1851), was among the most colorful American Jews – and is considered the most important lay leader – of the post-Revolutionary era. His father was a Portuguese Sephardic Jew and Revolutionary War hero. His mother, who died when he was seven or ten, was of Ashkenazi and Portuguese Sephardic descent. After his mother died, he was raised by his maternal grandfather, Jonas Phillips, an immigrant from Germany and American patriot whose descendants include several historic names.

In 1801 Noah had the good fortune to see one of those descendants, his uncle Naphtali Phillips, become the proprietor of *The National Advocate.* This event would have a profound influence on him. Writing became one of his main pursuits and, as a young man, he received attention for the wit shown in his patriotic "Mulek" articles published in *The Charleston Times.*

As the new nation entered the War of 1812, Noah's support for the administration of James Madison won him admirers in the White House. In 1813, he was named United States Consul to the Kingdom of Tunis, the first American Jew appointed to a diplomatic post. But when his ransoming of US citizens enslaved by pirates became politically unpopular, his religion became the excuse used by Secretary of State James Monroe to sack Noah.

Upon his return to New York City, Noah worked for his uncle, taking over as editor of *The National Advocate* which was published there. At the outset, Noah continued the newspaper's pro-Tammany editorial policy. In 1826 his uncle sold the *Advocate*, and Noah shifted his political ground so soon resigned from the paper.

Among his posts was that of Sheriff of New York City.

Noah's quest for establishing a City of Refuge he would call Ararat, on Grand Island, near Buffalo, New York, led to much controversy and was the topic of many editorials and articles. While his Jewish commitments were undeniable, the self-promoting aspect in the way he tried to execute those commitments turned off many people. Thus, the September 25, 1825 dedication ceremony of Grand Island as "Ararat, the restored home of the Jews" – where cannons boomed and Noah, garbed in crimson judicial robes, proclaimed himself "Governor and Judge of Israel" – drew much criticism.

When his attempts at Grand Island failed, Noah recognized the need to push for a Jewish homeland – and the rebuilding of the Temple – in Israel. He is considered the first American proto-Zionist and in 1845 presented a "Discourse on the Restoration of the Jews" which was published by Harper & Brothers. An address he delivered in 1848 to raise funds for rebuilding the Temple on Mount Moriah received four columns of front page covered in the *New York Daily Tribune.*

Even five years after his death, Mordecai M. Noah, was receiving accolades in the American press.

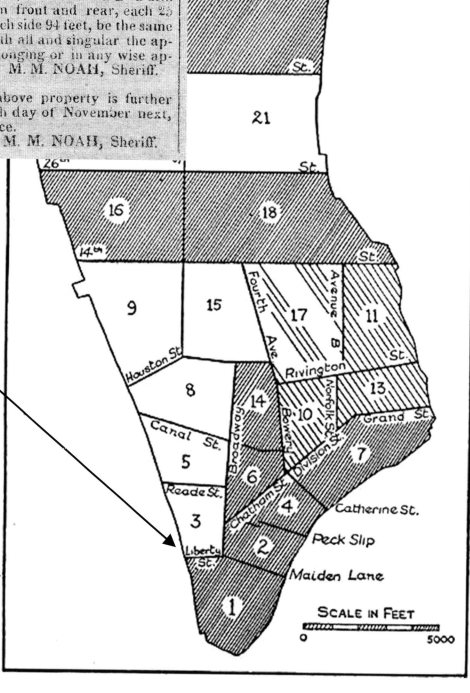

SHERIFF'S SALE.

By virtue of a writ of *fieri facias*, to me directed and delivered, I will expose to sale on the fourth day of October next, at 12 o'clock at noon, in front of the Tontine Coffee House, all the right, title and interest of Robert Patison, of, in and to all that certain lot, piece or parcel of ground, with the buildings thereon erected, situate, lying and being in Liberty-street, in the third ward of the city of New-York, on the south side of the said street; bounded in front by Liberty-street aforesaid; in the rear by a lot now or late belonging to Mary Brunton; easterly by a lot now or late belonging to George Cleland; and westerly by lots now or late belonging to the heirs of Wm. Walton, deceased, to James Anderson, to Abraham Brower, and to John B Dash. Containing in breadth, in front and rear, each 25 feet; and in length on each side 94 feet, be the same more or less, together with all and singular the appurtenances thereunto belonging or in any wise appertaining.   M. M. NOAH, Sheriff.

august 22

☞ The sale of the above property is further postponed until the fourth day of November next, at the same hour and place.

oct 5   M. M. NOAH, Sheriff.

NEW YORK – 1822
"SHERIFF'S SALE"
*New-York American,
p. 1 (col 2)
October 16, 1822*

In these front-page notices, Mordecai M. Noah ("M. M. Noah, Sheriff") announced the future sale of a certain property "in Liberty-street, in the third ward of the city of New-York."

Noah ran for the office of Sheriff in 1821, an election that was filled with anti-Semitic implications. His disparagers complained that it was not right to elect a Jew sheriff because he might be called upon to hang a Christian. Noah responded sarcastically, "Pretty sort of Christian that should require hanging at anyone's hands." Noah won the election.

A characteristic wish. —We do not oppose the election of Noah to the Sheriffalty, on the score of his religious opinions, but for his profligacy, his utter dishonesty, and his BLASPHEMIES! It is expected that the members of every religious denomination, Christians and Jews, will deliberately read his Grand Island proclamation, before they hand in a vote for him. We know several of our most respectable citizens, of the Jewish persuasion, who would not vote for Mr. Noah under any circumstances.— We have the following certificate to Mr. N.'s moral character, given by a relation of his, Mr. Myer Mo— —— Thursday evening.—" *I know Mr. Noah to be the most* UNPRINCIPLED POLITICIAN *in the world.*" So far the whole community will indorse Mr. Moses' observation. But he went on to say—" *I hope, notwithstanding my opinion of him, that he will be elected Sheriff, and that the first person he hangs will be a* CHRISTIAN !! " That such were the observations of Mr. Moses, is vouched for both in the National Advocate, and in the Courier of this morning.

NEW YORK CITY – 1828
MORDECAI M. NOAH'S POLITICAL PROBLEMS
New-York Spectator, p. 1 (col 5)
November 7, 1828

Mordecai M. Noah, the most important Jew in pre-Civil War New York City, encountered several anti-Semitic attacks during his political career. In 1815, Secretary of State James Monroe removed Noah as the United States Consul to the Kingdom of Tunis noting that Noah's religion served as an "obstacle" to his effectiveness. Similarly, Noah's Jewishness was used to attack him during his candidacy for New York City Sheriff.

Myer Moses (b. Charleston, SC, 1779; d. New York City, 1833), a relative of Noah's who is quoted in the article, served in the South Carolina legislature, fought in the War of 1812, and wrote *A History of the Revolution in France* (1830) after moving to New York City.

The front page excerpt illustrates the anti-Semitic campaign waged against Noah in his bid for Sheriff. Grand Island refers to the Jewish colony near Buffalo, New York, that Noah tried to launch in 1825. The paper claims to "have the following certification to Mr. Noah's moral character given by a relative of his, Mr. Myer Moses, last Thursday evening: '*I know Mr. Noah to be the most* UNPRINCIPLED POLITICIAN *in the world.*'"

A QUESTION STARTED! In a laborious examination of old papers, to gather facts for an interesting purpose,—I oftentimes meet with things that amuse, and some that astonish me—among them many queer sayings of my old friend, *Thomas Ritchie*—which are valuable, seeing that a file of his paper cannot be obtained for reference to his vagaries; and thus, as has been severely said of medical gentlemen, his *works are covered*—almost by oblivion. What a fate for the great autocrat of "orthodoxy?"

The following, however, amused me,—and I thought that it ought to have a renewed and full publication, for the benefit of all men, and the Hebrews in particular! But this "I, MORDECAI MANUEL NOAH," [I always thought his middle name was "Manassah"], now holds a high and responsible office under the United States—and I must needs think that the fact never occurred to president *Jackson* when he appointed him, that the said MORDECAI stands before us as a SOVEREIGN PRINCE, *in command of a whole nation, making laws and assessing taxes*, without the jurisdiction of the U. States, as well as within the same! The great question then is—is this *sovereign prince*, the said "MORDECAI" —deriving his title, as he gives us to understand, from "JEHOVAH," eligible to the office of *surveyor of the port of New York?* Will the judge of the United States court, (who lately volunteered an opinion that certain of the most important acts of congress were unconstitutional), examine this matter and give us his decision? If *Mordecai's* office as "judge of Israel," is valid—the title of gen. *Jackson* to the presidency would appear somewhat questionable!

Ceremonies at the laying of the corner stone of the city of Ararat!!

BY M. M. NOAH.

[Extract from the order of procession.]

"Rev. clergy, stewards with *corn, wine* and *oil*.

"Bible, square and compass, borne by a master mason, the JUDGE OF ISRAEL in black, wearing the *judicial robes of crimson silk, trimmed with ermine*, and a richly embossed gold medal suspended from the neck."

The procession enters the church. On the communion table lay the corner stone of ARARAT, with the following inscription in Hebrew:

"Hear, O Israel! the Lord *is* our God.—The Lord *is* ONE." Ararat, the Hebrew refuge, *founded by* MORDE-CAI MANUEL NOAH, in the month of Tisri, 5585, corresponding with September, 1825, and in the 50th of American Independence."

"PROCLAMATION."

[*Extracts.*]

"Whereas it has pleased ALMIGHTY GOD to manifest to his chosen people the approach of that period when, in fulfilment of the promises made to the race of Jacob, and as a reward for their pious constancy and triumphant fidelity, they are to be gathered from the four quarters of the globe, and to resume their rank and character among the governments of the earth."

"I, MORDECAI MANUEL NOAH, citizen of the United States of America, late consul of the said states for the city and kingdom of Tunis, high sheriff of New York, counsellor at law, and by the GRACE OF GOD, Governor AND JUDGE OF ISRAEL, have issued this MY proclamation."

"The desired spot in the state of New York, to which I hereby invite *my* beloved people throughout the world, in common with those of every religious denomination, is called GRAND ISLAND, and on which I shall lay the foundation of a city of refuge, to be called ARARAT."

"In His (JEHOVAH'S) *name do I revive*, renew and re-establish the government of the Jewish nation, under the auspices and protection of the constitution and laws of the United States of America. Confirming and perpetuating all our rights and privileges, our name, our rank, and our power, among the nations of the earth, as they existed and were recognized under the governments of the judges. And I HEREBY ENJOIN it upon all our pious and venerable rabbis; our presidents and elders of synagogues, chiefs of colleges, and brethren in authority, throughout the world, to circulate and make known this *my* proclamation, and to give it full publicity, credence, and effect.

"It is my *will*, that a census of the Jews throughout

the world be taken, and returns of persons together with their age and occupation, be registered in the archives of the synagogue where they are accustomed to worship."

"Those of our people who, from age, local attachments, or from any other cause, prefer remaining in the several parts of the world which they now respectively inhabit, and who are treated with liberality by the public authorities, *are permitted to do so*."

"Those Jews who are in the military employment of the different sovereigns of Europe, are enjoined to keep in their ranks *until further orders*, and conduct themselves with bravery and fidelity."

"I *command* that a strict neutrality be observed in the pending war between the *Greeks* and the *Turks*, enjoined by considerations of safety towards a numerous population of Jews now under the oppressive dominions of the Ottoman porte."

"I *abolish*, forever, polygamy among the Jews."

"I *prohibit* marriages or giving *Keduchim*, without both parties are of a suitable age, and can read and write the language of the country which they respectively inhabit."

"*Prayers shall forever be said in the Hebrew language*, but it is recommended that occasional discourses on the principles of the Jewish faith, and the doctrines of morality generally, be delivered in the language of the country, together with such reforms which, without departing from the ancient faith, may add greater solemnity to our worship."

"*A capitation tax of three shekels in silver per annum, or one Spanish dollar, is hereby levied upon each Jew throughout the world.*"

"I do hereby name as commissioners" [here follows a list of commissioners] "to aid and assist in carrying into effect the provisions of this *my proclamation*, with powers to appoint the necessary agents in the several parts of the world, and to establish emigrating societies, in order that the Jews may be concentrated and capacitated as a distinct body, having at the head of each kingdom or republic such presiding officers as *I shall*, upon their recommendations, *appoint*.

"*I entreat to be remembered in your prayer*, and lastly and most earnestly. I do enjoin you to—"keep the charge of the Lord thy God, to walk in His ways, to keep His statutes and His commandments and His judgments and His testimonies, as it is written in the laws of Moses, that thou mayest prosper in all thou doest, and whithersoever thou turnest thyself."

"Given at Buffalo, in the state of New York, this second day of Tisri, in the year of the world 5585, corresponding with the fifteenth day of September, 1825, and in the fiftieth year of American Independence.

By the judge "A. B. SEIXAS, *sec'y protem.*"

BALTIMORE – 1831
"JUDGE OF ISRAEL"
Niles' Weekly Register, pp. 239–240
November 25, 1831

While Mordecai M. Noah's Jewish commitments were undeniable, the self-promoting aspect in the way he tried to execute those commitments turned off many people. Thus, the dedication ceremony of Grand Island as Ararat, the restored home of the Jews, September 25, 1825, drew much criticism. Cannons boomed and Noah, garbed in crimson judicial robes proclaimed himself as "Governor and Judge of Israel." In this article the author wonders sarcastically whether President Andrew Jackson knew of Noah's pedigree when he appointed him to the post of surveyor of the Port of New York. "If Mordecai's office as 'judge of Israel' is valid–the title of gen. Jackson to the presidency would appear somewhat questionable!"

NEW YORK –
1842
"M. M.
NOAH"
*New York Herald,
p. 2 (col 2)
October 28, 1842*

Among Noah's ene-
mies was James
Gordon Bennett,
founder and editor
of the *New York
Herald.* In this arti-
cle Bennett fiercely
attacked Noah on a
number of counts.
He claimed Noah
bankrupted the vari-
ous newspapers he
(Noah) had owned.

Noah had previously
sued Bennett for
$100, and according
to Bennett, after the
judge ruled in
Bennett's favor with a
$200 offset, "What
did this Noah? What
did this honest Jew?
He set up the plea for
the statute of
limitations and won
his case."

Bennett further
asserts that Noah's
"grossness and inde-
cency are so great,
that this infamous
old scoundrel had
the meanness to
attack my wife."

NEW YORK HERALD.

New York, Friday, October 28, 1842.

M. M. Noah.

Noah has a much larger stock of impudence than he has of oysters in his cellar. He talks to us of his "advice and his example." What is his example in reference to newspapers?

Every newspaper that did not kick him out of the concern, ended in bankruptcy and ruin. He managed the "National Advocate," and it died in debt; he managed the "New York National Advocate," and it died in debt; he managed the "New York Enquirer," and if he had not sold it to Webb for more than it was worth, it would have died in debt also; he was associated in the management of the "New York Courier and Enquirer," and if Webb had not kicked him out, it would have ceased in debt long since. He started and managed the "Evening Star," and it died in debt, owing its paper maker, Persse & Brooks, several hundred dollars, who trusted it on the representations of Noah. He has now connected himself with Beach in the "Sun and Union," and before he leaves the concern he will serve it as he has done every paper he has been connected with. The Sun will go down under such a load as M. M. Noah.

Noah says, "*James Gordon Bennett was several years in our employment, and always behaved well.*" This is a confession of the truth that astonishes us, from such an old rascal—but it is correct. During the time that we were in his service, we did all the heavy work—we were at it night and day—he doing nothing but writing squibs, dosing away his time, or talking to the brokers. Yet in spite of this, Noah sued us for $100 which he swore we owed him. A jury gave us a verdict of nearly $200 as an offset, for services rendered. What did Noah? What did this honest Jew? He set up the plea of the statute of limitations, and won his cause. Mr. David Graham can tell the rest.

This is the man that dares to talk of our character—and to assert falsely that we are in debt. We owe no debts that we cannot pay in less than a fortnight. We value our whole establishment, real and personal estate, at $130,000—and it is well worth $150,000 of any man's money. All our debts are a mortgage on the building of $20,000—which we can pay off in two years—and our general business was never so profitable—our circulation larger—our advertising better than at this moment. Ask our paper makers Persse and Brooks—our type maker James Conner—or our pressmakers, Richard Hoe & Co., what we owe.

Yet this impudent fellow—this Noah—has the audacity to talk of personalities and abuse—a fellow who has been at the root of all the attempts made in this city to destroy us. He got up all the attacks on us —out of sheer jealousy of our success. He instigated

the moral war—he was at the bottom of the ridiculous indictments—he has renewed his old animosities—and his grossness and indecency are so great, that this infamous old scoundrel had the meanness to attack my wife, whose character, birth, reputation, talents, devotion, honor, and domestic affections, are equal to any lady of this or any other country. It is true she is a native of Dublin, the descendant of a respectable and chivalric Irish family—on the one side the Crean-Lynch of the West of Ireland—and on the other side the Warrens of Dublin. All her relatives were persons of the best family and the highest character. Her maternal grandfather was the well known Alderman Warren, who distinguished himself in the Irish troubles of 1798—afterwards he was Lord Mayor of Dublin. Her father was a Catholic liberal, and a particular friend of O'Connell's till the death of the former. Two of her uncles were of a high rank in the British army. Col. Nathaniel Warren, who served bravely and died in India, was knighted, and had a statue erected to his brave memory in Madras. Another uncle, also a Colonel in the army, is now in a high post in the government at Jamaica. She came to this country four years ago with her excellent and amiable mother, who now lives at my house; and before her marriage, she lived the greater part of the time with a relative and cousin, at Dayton, Ohio, Mrs. Browning, the worthy and accomplished lady of Lieutenant Browning, of the U. S. Navy.

This is the amiable and excellent young woman, now my wife, whose character has been assailed by that old scoundrel M. M. Noah, that villain in human shape. He had the audacity, miserable rascal as he is, to insinuate—merely to hurt my feelings, against the conduct of my wife during her visit to Rockaway last summer, for the benefit of sea-bathing. Now, it is well known to every lady and gentleman who were at the Marine Pavillion during last summer, that Mrs. James Gordon Bennett, during her stay there, was one of the most reserved —the most correct—the most lady-like—the most amiable of persons. It is true, there was an attempt made by a few weak, impudent, and silly creatures, whose names are known, to talk against her because she was my wife—and I was told that Henry Allen Wright had been impudent in this respect—but in a personal interview I had with him, he denied the report, and I believe he was innocent, and always behaved like a young gentleman of propriety and feeling. Among the families there were those of Charles Augustus Davis—Mr. James Otis, Mr. Campbell P. White, and many others of both sexes—and none can say aught against my wife or myself, during the seven weeks that we resorted there for the benefit of sea bathing.

I must beg pardon of my readers for introducing this subject, but the horrible conduct—the atrocious malice—the ineffable infamy of M. M. Noah, and his miserable broken down coadjutors, has compelled me to do so, and to name names. And yet this miserable, unprincipled old scoundrel, has the impudence to talk of giving me advice—out of the sight of man, ye poor bloated wretch! You ought to be hung on the same tree with your forefather, Barrabbas, the robber.

TIMES AND SEASONS.

"Truth will prevail."

Vol. V. No. 13.]   CITY OF NAUVOO, ILL. JULY, 15, 1844.   [Whole No. 97.

The following paragraph, and reply from the pen of *M. M. Noah*, is inserted in the Times and Seasons, to show the amount of Jewish population. Any information relative to the Jews, old Israel, Ephraim or the remnants, which God in his infinite wisdom, deigns to restore to a state of light, liberty, and gospel unity, must be a sweet morsel to the Saint that is watching for such important events. The belief of Mr. Noah, however, "that the greatest triumphs reserved for Christianity will be in their agency [and co-operation in restoring the Jews to their ancient heritage," is all wind: God will never ask Christendom to do what he has declared in the scripture, he will do himself. The 11th chapter of Isaiah says, he will "gather together the dispersed of Judah from the four corners of the earth;" and sundry other places, carries strong proof *that God*, not man, will show the Jews the "wounds he received in the house of his friends."

Letter of M. M. Noah, to the Bos. Mer. Journal.
New York, June 18th, 1844.

Mr. Editor:—a late number of your paper contained the following paragraph:—

Jews.—It is said that the total number of Jews throughout the world is estimated at 3,163,700, and it is said that this number has never materially varied from the time of David downwards.

It has always been a subject of interest, although not of general inquiry, to ascertain as nearly as possible, the numerical force of the Jewish people in every part of the world, and looking forward to the speedy fulfillment of all the promises made to that peculiar and favored race in their restoration to the land of their ancestors. I have been at considerable pains to obtain a census, accurate as far as every country in Europe is referred to, but depending upon estimates, always below the actual number, of those residing in Asia and Africa, from which it appears that the Jewish nation number full six millions of people, divided and located as follows:—

In all parts of ancient Poland, before the partition of 1772	1,000,000
In Russia, comprehending Woldavia and Wallachia	200,000
In the different states of Germany	750,000
In Holland and Belgium	80,000
Sweden and Denmark	6,000
France	75,000
England	60,000
Italian States	200,000
All North and South America and West Indies	100,000
In the Mahometan States of Europe, Asia and Africa	3,000,000
Persia, China and Hindoston	1,000,000
	6,471,000

The above includes all who are actually known as professing and following the religion of their forefathers. It is impossible to ascertain the number of those residing in Catholic countries and concealing their religion from motives. The number in Spain who preferred outwardly embracing the Catholic faith to avoid banishment under Ferdinand and Isabella, is several hundred thousands, and are at this day connected with the first families in Spain and Portugal. In Asia and the Turkish dominions, I have made an estimate rather below their actual number. They are powerful in China, and on the borders of Tartary; likewise in Persia and the countries bordering on the Indian Ocean. In Abyssinia and Ethiopa there are many communities of black Jews, and they have a separate congregation at Calcutta.

The number of the Jewish people dispersed in every part of the world will surprise no one who takes into consideration that for the last four hundred years they have been in a measure exempt from those persecutions which they suffered prior to the reformation; nor have they been included in the various wars which have for several hundred years desolated Europe and Asia. Naturally a pacific people, adhering at a very early age to their international marriages, exceedingly temperate in living, and constitutionally active and energetic, their self-augmenting population from these causes must greatly have increased their numbers, and warrant the belief that they are at this time as numerous as they were in the palmy days of David and Solomon.

There is another error in your paragraph which it may be well also to notice at this time. You state that the number of Jews has never materially varied from three millions, from the time of David downwards. Very nearly that number has been exterminated by wars and violence, from what may be considered the the commencement of their national troubles.

According to Josephus and cotemporary writers there were slaughtered

in Cæsaria, by the Syrians	20,000
In Jerusalem, occasioned by the insolence of a Roman soldier, under the reign of Claudius	20,000
At Scitipolis	13,000
At Alexandrin, in consequence of the rivalry of the Greeks and Egyptians	50,000
At Ascalon from the same cause	2,500
At Ptolemais	2,000
At Silueia, by the Syrians and Greeks	50,000
At the siege of Jerusalem by Pompey	12,000
By an earthquake in Judea, 42 or 43 years before Christ	30,000
In consequence of a revolt occasioned by breaking a Roman eagle placed in the portico of the Temple, in the reign of Augustus	13,000
In a sedition suppressed by Varus, Governor of Syria	2,000
In an ambuscade before Ascalon, in the beginning of the war against the Romans	18,000
At the capture of Jaffa by Titus	15,000
At the siege of Jotapat 13th of Nero	40,000
Taking of Tariche, and at the naval battle on the Lake Genserette	6,500
After this victory, Vespasian being in the tribunal at Tariche, sent 6000 to Nero, to work at the Isthmus of the Mores—30,400 were sold at public vendue, and 12,000 old men, unable to bear arms, were put to death	12,000
At the capture of Gamala by Titus	9,000
In a battle against Placidus, Lt. of Vespasian, near the village of Galara	15,000
At the seige of Jerusalem and destruction of the Temple by Titus	1,100,000
In the revolt of the false Messiah Barchechobas, and in the several revolts under Adrian, Trojan, and Justinian	600,000
Add to this, that from the time of the adoration of the Golden Calf, to the return of the ark, which had been captured by the Philistines, there were destroyed	239,000
Making	2,248,000

This amount does not include neither the losses they met with in the wars anterior to the Captivity, nor the persecutions and revolts in the time of the German Emperors and the Middle Ages, nor the massacres which followed the Crusades, nor the proscriptions *en masse* which were so frequently renewed in different parts of the world, in the times of the invasions by the barbarians, and since their establishment in the Roman provinces. Under all these calamities and oppressions, the Jews like those vivacious plants which can resist the intemperance of all seasons, have been by divine interposition, enabled to sustain themselves amidst so many appalling obstacles, and have found in the strength of their laws, new principles of existence.

In pursuing the inquiry as to their numerical force, much interesting information has been obtained as to their various pursuits; and it is gratifying to learn that agriculture, their original occupation, claims a great portion of their attention. The plains of Nineveh Greece, Persia, Egypt, Lithunia, Ukraine and Moldavia, are full of Jewish agriculturalists; they are, it is said, the best cultivators of the grape in Turkey; in all parts of the East they are dyers, workers in silk, weavers and blacksmiths; in Poland they are farmers, curriers, lace weavers, potters and silversmiths; and although the great body of the nation are still engaged in trade and commerce in every quarter of the world, with undiminished success, they are nevertheless receiving a more liberal education, are cultivating a taste for the arts, many are pursuing the more enlightened and scientific professions with reputation, and are instituting reforms in the ceremonial parts of their religion, without invading any of its cardinal principles.

Wealth is not generally or equally diffused among the Jews, but the aggregate of their possessions constitutes them by far the most wealthy people on earth, and the enormous proportions are so located as to secure a very decided influence in the movements of every nation, making them, in a measure, the arbitrators of very important movements.

Although the Jewish people are entirely passive in relation to their restoration, and waiting the great advent with the same patience and humility which they have evinced for the last eighteen hundred years, relying with unabated confidence on the promises and protection of that divine power which has ever been near them and with them, nevertheless there has been no period in their history in which Christians generally have taken more interest in their temporal and religious welfare, than they evince at the present time. This is the providential prelude to great events;—they know too little of each other; and a closer approximation, a mutual surrender of prejudices, and a greater reliance of Christians upon what constituted primitive Christianity, will at once show how slender is the line that divides us. I cannot avoid believing that the great triumphs reserved for Christianity will be in their agency and co-operation in restoring the Jews to their ancient heritage, for it cannot be politically accomplished without their aid, and if the second advent, so called, and so ardently desired by pious Christians is ever to come to pass, it cannot, I hardly conceive, take place until after the restoration is accomplished, and there is a throne to be occupied a nation to be governed, and the prophecies fulfilled.

I beg your pardon for thus occupying your space. I intended merely to correct the error in the census, but have been led into other matters.

Respectfully yours,

Portrait of Joseph Smith

NAUVOO, IL – 1844
M. M. NOAH & JOSEPH SMITH
Times and Seasons, pp. 587–589
July 15, 1844

Noah's quest for establishing his City of Refuge, Ararat, near Buffalo, New York, struck a responsive chord with Joseph Smith and his Church of Latter-Day Saints. Smith was also trying to set up a home for dispossessed Israelites. Both plans called for an ingathering of religiously minded settlers in theocracies built on virgin land. Each vision held messianic elements.

Rather than joining Noah, many Jews criticized him for setting himself up as a forerunner of the Messiah. Smith's followers awaited an imminent second coming of Christ at their planned city. Similarly, both Noah and the Mormon leader wanted these communities to be populated both by Israelites and American Indians. *The Book of Mormon* was written with this specific missionary aim in mind. Noah and Smith believed that these American Indians stemmed from the ten lost tribes of Israel.

According to Noah and Smith, these Indians, once gathered to the new cities of Zion, would be civilized and integrated into modern society. The Mormon leader expected the Indian converts to experience a skin color change and then essentially to become "white" people. Noah was content just to "cultivate their minds, soften their condition and finally re-unite them with their brethren the chosen people." Originally, Mormons considered taking over Noah's Ararat after it failed in 1826. But after President Andrew Jackson ordered the removal of various Indian tribes to sites west of the Missouri River, the Mormons followed them in the hope of converting them.

In this issue from the official newspaper of the Latter-Day Saints, four columns on pages 587–589 are devoted to Noah's views. Most of the text consists of a letter Noah wrote to the *Boston Mercantile Journal* on June 18, 1844 dealing with Jewish population figures. But the editor takes issue with Noah in an introductory note:

The belief of Mr. Noah, however, "that the greatest triumphs reserved for Christianity will be in their agency and co-operation in restoring the Jews to their ancestral heritage" is all wind. God will never ask Christendom to do what he declared in the scripture, he will do himself.

NEW-YORK SEMI-WEEKLY TRIBUNE.

BY GREELEY & McELRATH.   OFFICE TRIBUNE BUILDINGS.   THREE DOLLARS A YEAR.

VOL. IV. NO. 55.   NEW-YORK, SATURDAY DECEMBER 2, 1848.   WHOLE NO. 367.

M. M. NOAH'S ADDRESS,

DELIVERED AT THE HEBREW SYNAGOGUE IN CROSBY-ST. ON THANKSGIVING DAY, TO AID IN THE ERECTION OF THE TEMPLE AT JERUSALEM.

[Reported verbatim, for the New-York Tribune.]

About two years ago, a messenger arrived in this City from Jerusalem, having been commissioned from the Hebrew Congregation at Hebron to visit the United States, to collect aid for the suffering poor of that venerable city. He came from the neighborhood of the Cave of Macphelah, where Abraham and the founders of our faith lie buried, and he asked in their name, and by their immortal memory, charity for our poor brethren, who have for many centuries piously and carefully watched that sacred spot. Some questioned the expediency of allowing our charity to travel so far from home; many gave in the name of Him who said the poor shall never depart from the land; but he asked only the aid of his Brethren. The liberal of other faiths asked permission to add something to his store; but his authority to ask and to receive was limited to the house of Israel. The reception which he met with here, from members of the oldest Congregation in America, endorsed his mission to other cities, and the Pilgrim returned to the Holy City, bearing with him some remembrance from the land where the Jew and the Gentile are equally free. In a letter which I received from the American Consul at Jerusalem, he said that he had met the Rabbi, who stated that he had brought with him from this country $18,000 for the poor families of Hebron. The fidelity with which he discharged that duty, induced the Rabbis and Trustees of the Congregation of BETH EL, at Jerusalem, to send him again to this country on a mission of still greater interest.

It may not be generally known to our People that since the destruction of our Temple, upward of 1,800 years ago, Israel has been without a place of worship, dedicated with all the solemnities of our faith, and erected with suitable magnificence, to the Divine Architect of Heaven and Earth. The Jews, in their own land, on that land which God gave to them as an inheritance forever, by a deed consecrated and confirmed by ages, were not permitted to erect a Synagogue from that fatal moment of the destruction of the Temple, even to the present day.

The army of the Roman Conqueror captured and carried away the Nation to be sold as Slaves. A few only of the faithful, hid in tombs and caverns, secreting themselves beneath the fallen columns of the Temple, remained on a spot endeared to them by so many blisful reminiscences, and by the promises of the Great Hereafter. The Roman Centurions pursued them—the Greeks persecuted them—the Persians destroyed them, and, in after ages, the followers of Mahomet visited them with fire and sword, and the Crusaders trampled upon their necks—yet they refused, under these unprecedented calamities, to abandon the home of their fathers, and their ancient heritage, the rich gift of the Almighty. With the laws of Moses, which they had preserved; with the sacred rolls, written by Esdras, now in their possession, which they bore from the flaming ruins; they read the law in chambers—in caves—confined rooms, and deserted places—for, among their Pagan persecutors, they did not dare to worship openly that God whose protecting mercies the civilized world now unites to invoke. The Mosque of the Musselmen reared its domes and minarets on the site of our Temple—Christians erected magnificent Churches and rich-endowed chapels on our soil; while our People, the rightful inheritors of all that Land of Promise, crawled in abject submission to the walls of the Temple, to bewail their hard destiny—to pray for the peace of Jerusalem, and weep on the solitary banks of the Jordan. They never despaired of the fulfilment of those promises which God had made to them —that Still Small Voice continually whispered in their ears, in accents soft as the cherub's voice, "Fear not, Jacob, for I am with thee."

Centuries rolled on—Nations arose, flourished, decayed, and fell—yet the Jewish People still existed, increased in numbers, and under every privation and persecution, preserved their identity, their faith, and their nationality.

At length a sign is given; the thunders begin to roll all over Europe; the cry is everywhere heard in despotic Governments—to arms; the People are at war with their Kings, and the Kings are overthrown; Priestcraft and fanaticism are overthrown; the Sun of Liberty begins to rise; the chains of the Jews are unloosed, and they are elevated to the rank of men; the fires of superstition had burnt out, and the age of reason had revived. The Sultan of Turkey, following the march of Civilized Nations, says to the Jews in his dominions—"You are free; you have my permission to erect a Synagogue in Jerusalem; and messengers are dispatched, as they were in the days of Solomon, to ask for aid from their brethren throughout the world, to erect a magnificent place of worship, the first that has been erected in the Holy City since the advent of Christianity.

Friends and Brethren, do you understand that Sign? Is it not pregnant with great events? Is not this another Seal broken? We can erect a Synagogue, and build a Temple here, and it excites no attention; but when the trumpet sounds from Mount Zion, every ear is opened, every heart throbs. I know full well, that there are many Jews throughout the world, who look upon the restoration of their brethren to the Holy Land as a possible event in the great changes which may hereafter occur—but they take little interest in the signs of the times. Happy in the enjoyment of every comfort here, they only think of their brethren in the Holy Land when their charitable feelings are appealed to; but when the great events of the Restoration which are to fulfil the prophecies are talked of, they cling to the home of their birth, and the country of their adoption, and say, My destiny is here. Be it so. I do not blame them; for great sacrifices of life and treasure await the first movements of Restoration. We are safe, but let us feel for those brave hearts, who will not forsake their ancient heritage—who cling with ardent devotion to the sacred soil, and who turn their eyes of hope toward Zion, and say "The time will come, the hour will arrive." Let us furnish them with the means of living until the Trumpet again sounds on the walls of Jerusalem—let us aid to erect a Temple worthy of their faith, their devotion, and their constancy.

The Jews, I regret to say, know little of the Holy Land and of their brethren who reside in it. It is now the object of Christian research, of Christian veneration, and no learned, pious and liberal Christian visits that sacred spot, who does not feel that the Chosen People of God are at this day the greatest miracle on earth, and have ever been the constant uniform object of Divine Protection. The fate of a nation may depend on many causes: one becomes weakened by unjust and unnecessary wars—another falls from want of energy, character, good faith and industry; a third is without courage to sustain its rights; and a fourth is ignorant, imbecile and bigoted. The rise, progress and fate of the Jewish nation, exhibited no such defects of character. We sinned against God because it is the nature of Man to be sinful; he punished us as the parent does his child, but, in the midst of our stubbornness, our disobedience, and hardness of heart, we did not forget the Unity and Omnipotence of that Divine Architect of the Universe, and he pardoned us: his arm always has guided us, and amid the vicissitudes of 6,000 years, the nation never has been lost; from the day and the hour that God declared us to be his People, down to the present time, we have remained the same People—distinct from all others. Shepherds of the Land of Promise—Slaves in Egypt—a mighty power in Canaan—the revolted tribes captured at Samaria and blended with other nations, still Judah and Benjamin remained, and were still the chosen People. The whole world of Idolatry united to crush us, but the handful of God's chosen servants could not be subdued or won to apostacy. By the rivers of Babylon they wept in captivity, but could not forget Jerusalem nor the Songs of Zion; the fiery furnace could not subdue them, and Pagan Kings, awe-struck at their self-sacrificing piety and fidelity, set them free. After seventy years of bondage the faithful were restored to Zion. Punished for their sins thus severely, the Children of Israel reposed 400 years in their Land of Milk and Honey, waiting for that Prince which God promised to send them, to consolidate and rule over the nation as their temporal Sovereign. But their glory was again destined to be dimmed—their light extinguished, and darkness once more enshrouded the People. The ambitious, conquering Romans appeared in great force under the walls of Jerusalem, and summoned them to surrender.

We have heard of many wars and sieges—of gallant victories, and brilliant defences, of intense sufferings, and indomitable valor; but where does the page of history inscribe deeds of bravery and personal sacrifices equal to the siege of Jerusalem? Had the Jews been united at that siege—had not the embers of faction been fanned into a flame, and its defenders divided and at war with each other—Titus Vespasianus could never have entered the Holy City. The testimony of Josephus is not always free from impartiality when he treats of Vespasian and Titus; he described their triumphs after the destruction of his nation, with that cowardly complacency which characterized the courtier; he was a traitor and fought against his people in the ranks of the enemy; and yet he admits, that the Jews performed prodigies of valor. "They cried to their besiegers from walls crumbling to ruins, that they courted death which was preferable to a shameful slavery, and that they would exert themselves to the last to prove to the Romans, that no boundary was to be affixed to their determined resistance." The siege of Jerusalem lasted 146 days; and after unheard of sufferings, the flames of their Temple lighted the funeral pile of the nation, and 1,100,000 souls were buried in the ruins. From that day they have been in a perpetual state of martyrdom, suspended between life and death. What bloody vicissitudes, what scenes of grief, what barbarities, what ravages, what disasters, what injustice, have not been exercised by the different nations of the globe, against a people devoted to slavery and abandoned by fortune. Pagans, Mahometans and Christians have by turns occupied the Holy Land, and deluged it with blood. Still our people refused to abandon the country which God had given them. Sentinels on the ramparts, they watched for us, prayed for us. We were driven out among the nations of the earth; our home was nowhere; our people everywhere. Who has done this? Who brought Abram from Ur of the Chaldees? Who sent Joseph a slave into Egypt? Who authorized Moses to lead the people through the Red Sea? Who gave the law in thunder on Mount Sinai? Who raised a long line of prophets who poured forth a living stream of eloquence and divine song, which even the present age cannot hear unmoved? Who preserved Daniel in the lions' den? Shadrach, Meschech and Abednego in the fiery furnace? Our God, your God, who made bare His holy arm in the eyes of all the nations. Shall we not sustain each other when so divinely sustained and protected? Shall we turn a deaf ear to the supplications of our brethren at Jerusalem, who have stood by their faith so triumphantly? I hope not.

It has been said that the Jews at Jerusalem are indolent, are disinclined to labor, are only employed in studying the law, and devoting all their hours to prayer, and prefer leading a life of dependence and want to one of prosperous active industry. I thank them them that they do so. Amid our worldly cares, our pursuits of gain, our limited knowledge of our holy faith, our surrender of many cardinal points—probably from hard necessity, I am thankful that there is a holy band of brotherhood at Zion, whose nights and days are devoted to our sublime laws, our venerable institutions. I wish them to remain so, I think it our duty and our interest to share our means with them—to repay them with the bread of life, for aiding us with the bread of salvation. Jerusalem should ever be an object of the warmest attachment in our sight. To see the Holy Land sovereign and independent under its rightful proprietors; to know that the Temple will again be rebuilt; to hope to see the standard of Judah once more unfurled **on Mount Zion; to die on that spot, and to be buried near David and Solomon in the valley of Jehoshaphat, should be our highest ambition, our earnest hope, our incessant prayer.**

There are some who may consider the permission extended to the Jews in Jerusalem to build a Temple, or a magnificent Synagogue, a concession of little importance; but taken with other extraordinary signs of the times, it has a most important bearing. *We* may be unmindful and indifferent in relation to those signs, but there is a Divine hand which directs, a Divine agency which controls these movements; there are Divine promises yet to be fulfilled, Divine attributes which are yet to be made apparent to the unbeliever. Since the establishment of Christianity, the world has not seen a revolution equal to that existing at the present moment in Europe: one hundred millions of people are in arms against their sovereigns; it is a struggle indeed for Liberty and Human Rights, but Religious as well as Civil Liberty; the blow is equally aimed at Priestcraft, at that powerful union of Church and State, which for centuries has kept the world in bondage. The allied Sovereigns may succeed in overpowering the people and maintaining their Thrones and Sceptres, but great concessions will be made to the wishes of the people to avoid a hurricane of frightful outbreaks;—the People are no longer in chains. To the Jews, this great Revolution has been a wonderful manifestation of God's Providence and watchfulness; it has made them men, citizens, a people, a nation—it has given them rank, position, power,—it has elevated them to the highest offices. Look back 1800 years on Rome, the proud mistress of the world, and see the Jewish captives in chains following the triumphant car of the victorious Titus; see them sold in bondage, see them the architects of the Coliseum and the Pantheon, the servile laborers everywhere. When Rome fell, and Christianity arose, see them even more fiercely persecuted, the inmates of the dungeons of the Inquisition, and the victims of the *Auto de Fe*; see the chosen people, whose only sin was their belief in one God, locked up at night in the Ghetto, like animals in a cage, and look at them now in Rome: declared to be free by law, and possessing equal rights with their fellow-citizens. See them in France and Germany, and in every country in Europe, filling the highest situations in the governments, the proudest elevations on the benches of law and science, and diffusing everywhere the lights of their deep philosophy, and the fruits of their close and ardent study. And has this great advent been brought about by human agency? I believe it not;—it is part and parcel of those promises—the first step in the fulfilment of that great event which is to manifest to the whole world the power, the unity, the omnipotence of the Lord God of Israel, one God and the God of all Creation, and that he alone is the King of Kings, Redeemer of the World, and the Sole Judge of the Earth.

Other great revolutions are also in progress—quietly, slowly, but securely—the age of Reason and Philosophy among Christians. In every direction, there appear to me evidences of a progressive, but mighty change in the fundamental principles of that faith, which it is our duty and our interest to watch, as developments of the deepest importance to our future destiny as a nation. I have noticed the liberal feelings everywhere evinced toward the Jewish people, an interest in their spiritual character, as much as in their temporal welfare: I see everywhere a change manifested toward us as a Sect; there are closer affinities developing themselves among Christians. They are gradually unloosing the chains of a religious prejudice against us, and feel a deeper interest in our fate and final advent. Few adhere at the present day, to the spiritual restoration of the Jews, while the multitude admit that this restoration must be literal. The promises of God to the Chosen People are now more fully recognized, and evangelizing them is postponed until after the great events contingent on our Restoration as an Independent Power. Reason and Truth begin to resume their empire, as the shackles of ecclesiastical power become weakened, and man defends his right to think, to speak, and to act freely and openly, upon all matters appertaining to the Christian faith.

The result of this religious freedom, manifests itself in gradually withdrawing from the great Founder of the Christian faith, the divine attributes conceded to Him by his disciples and followers. Since the Reformation, this change has been gradually unfolding itself; but professing Christians did not dare to express their doubts even to themselves; they were unbelievers ever, but only in the deep recesses of the heart; but now Reformers, Socialists, Communists, Philosophers, openly express their doubts. All Germany is deeply tinctured with this belief, and other Luthers are springing up, declaring their unchanged belief in the sublime morality of Jesus of Nazareth—their entire confidence in Him as an eminent and illustrious reformer, teacher, prophet, brother; but denying his divine issue, his participation in the God-head, and his right to share with the Almighty the attributes of divinity. The Jews are deeply interested in the extension and preservation of Christian morals; to us and to the world, it would be a deep calamity to see *our* laws, *our* principles, *our* doctrines abrogated, which have been so beneficially spread throughout the world, under another name. If we were enfeebled and broken down, and had not the power to enforce and carry out the doctrines of our faith, still happily they have not been lost to the world, but flourish under another denomination. "Do unto others as you would desire others to do unto you,—love your neighbor as yourself"—deal justly to all men, honor your parents, be faithftl to the governments that protect you, be merciful, be charitable, and love God with all your heart and soul—these are *Jewish* precepts, advanced as such by a great Jewish reformer, and ingrafted upon the religion adopted by his followers and friends; but their divine origin is unchanged.

If it is asked why has not Judaism preached against Christianity, when Christianity has, for 1800 years, been incessantly preaching against Judaism, the answer is this: Our cause is in greater hands; in good time, the Lord will open the eyes of all who would confer on a mortal the attributes of His divinity; he will give to the world the unmistakeable evidence that He alone is the Great Redeemer, and that salvation is alone with Him. Our unwillingness to preach against Christianity grew out of the fact, that in pulling down the landmarks of that faith, we should assail and endanger many of our own cherished principles and doctrines; and although disbelieving the divine attributes claimed for Jesus of Nazareth, we could not deny or reject His principles, for they were our principles, and He always avowed the faith which we avow.

Without wishing to unsettle any of the principles which sustain the Christian religion, we have asked what would be the effect of separating from the character of Jesus of Nazareth the divine characteristics claimed for Him? The world would become Unitarian Christians, and we are the head of the Unitarians; men would openly become converts to that belief with sincerity, as their hearts would be thereby released from harassing and perplexing doubts, and Christianity would still be Christianity, in all its high moral attributes.—There is enough in the character of Jesus to give to Him a rank among the highest practical moralists, divested of all faith in His divine attributes; more, much more than in the character of Mahomet, who claimed none of those attributes. Jesus declared that "God was a spirit, and those who worshiped Him must worship Him in spirit and truth:" we declare no more.

We must watch these changes closely as they occur; whatever doubts may shake the faith of Christianity, those doubts can never reach us—we are now as we ever have been, as we ever hope to be, one God, one faith, one people. We have no mysteries, no revelations which are not natural and reasonable. In this position we have stood for ages, and it is a platform which will endure forever, and on which all religions can stand. We must seek, however, to take advantage of the times and the changes throughout the world, as they may relate to our temporal prosperity. We cannot at this moment tell what important results may grow out of this permission to build a magnificent Synagogue in Jerusalem. One right conferred, one prejudice removed, leads to the enjoyment of other rights, to the removal of other prejudices, and finally the nation begins to lift up its head; education completes the great work, and the Jews of Jerusalem, the great defenders and expounders of the law, become enlightened and liberal citizens, qualified to be intrusted with higher powers.

Let us not believe that, although our faith is admitted to have a divine origin, that salvation is for the Jews exclusively. Salvation for the Gentiles, is equally included; he who made the whole earth, will protect all his children in it. We are the altar of the Sanctuary, on which it is said, a fire shall burn which never shall be extinct; but that fire shall animate and revive all creation alike—the Gentile shall stand before its light, and rejoice in the warmth which it imparts. Had it not been for Christianity and Mahometanism, which sprung up upon the ruins of our nation, and raised aloft our prostrate banner, Paganism would still have flourished; every god would have been worshiped but the true and living one; the heathen would have triumphed at this very day, and all would have been darkness and desolation. From among a few of our own people God raised up a new sect, which, with the descendants of Joshua, maintained in part his divine attributes, and did not surrender his divine precepts. This intermediate power, though intolerant and persecuting, has still stood between us and utter destruction, and now eight millions of the chosen people—the same people who were at Sinai, at Babylon and at Zion, stand forth

(article continues next page)

NEW YORK – 1848
"M. M. NOAH'S ADDRESS"

New-York Semi-Weekly Tribune,
p. 1 (col 1–4) — December 2, 1848

Noah aimed to raise funds towards the erection of the Temple in Jerusalem in this address delivered on Thanksgiving Day at the "Hebrew Synagogue in Crosby Street" (i.e., Congregation Shearith Israel). The Temple he attempted to finance would be the third Temple built on the holy site of Mount Moriah.

Half of the front page of this seven-column newspaper was devoted to the text of Noah's speech, a tribute both to his prominence and his oratory. This was the speech of a Jew proud of his religion's teachings, proud of the resilience and survival of his people, and proud of the Jewish contribution to the emerging spirit of liberality in the world. While he recognized that most of his audience would not settle in the Holy Land, Noah argued that they have a responsibility to support their brethren who are fulfilling the Zionist mission, "including those whose nights and days are devoted to [studying] our sublime laws."

("MM Noah's Address," *continued from p. 171*)

in the presence of all the earth, the miracle of God's Providence; and Christian and Mussulman will march before them in the great advent of the Restoration, surrendering their trust, giving up their guardianship, and crying aloud, with our great prophet, "Prepare ye the way of the Lord, make straight in the desert, a highway for our God," and this advanced guard will bear on their banner, as they pass beneath the triple walls of Jerusalem, that verse from Scripture, which has ever been our guide, "Yet I am the Lord thy God, from the land of Egypt, and thou shalt know no God but me: *for there is no Saviour beside me.*" Oh, children of Israel, you know not the great destiny which is in store for you! Study to deserve it, study to meet it and to merit it, by the practice of many virtues, by toleration and good faith, mercy, charity and forgiveness.

The world call us a proud people. If there is a nobility on earth: if pure and unadulturated blood, descending from such ancestors as Abraham, Isaac and Jacob, Moses, David and Solomon, which courses through our veins, gives us a claim to national distinction, we have a right to be proud of such ancestry; but that pride should be limited to imitating their wisdom and cultivating among ourselves that nationality which alone embraces the elements of our restoration. The designs of the Almighty are brought about by human agency; He inclines the hearts of men to execute His great purposes on earth; wars, revolutions, changes in the political world, the dismemberment of nations, the downfall of kings, the elevation of the people, the light of knowledge, the march of science and the triumph of liberal opinions, are all His works, through His inscrutable decrees.

This permission to lay a corner stone once more in Jerusalem, to erect a magnificent temple to His honor and to His worship, by His ancient and faithful people, and which we are this day called upon to aid, is another great sign of His Divine power and will, foreshadowing the great promises hereafter,—the assurances that we shall yet be independent and worship Him on Zion in freedom and tranquillity.

But I have often heard my co-religionarians say, painfully heard them say, that the promises of restoration though repeatedly made, are surrounded with many difficulties; that the land so remote, would never repay the sacrifices in reässembling the people from the four quarters of the earth; and that when assembled, bringing with them the languages and usages of many countries, it would be greatly embarrassing to organize the government, and we should be subjected to neighboring wars and internal difficulties—in short, that we were content with our present condition, and required no change. Such sentiments I know do prevail, but not among all; it is the fruit of toleration, of comfort, of ease, of wealth; but there are hearts which are yet to be touched with the pure love of liberty, and hands strong enough and willing enough to strike a blow for that liberty, when the time arrives. But the work is not to be accomplished by us; our will, our wishes, our doubts, and our scruples, are empty and evanescent; there is a higher power, and a stronger arm, which will direct the movements of the great advent, which will show us the path; our cloud by day and our pillar by night. Are we not His chosen people, has He not blessed us, when shadowed beneath His protecting mantle, and punished when we sinned, separated and dispersed us when we forgot His holy ordinances, and do we not await his promises of final national regeneration? How can we doubt the future, in contemplating the past? Has He not said "ALL the house of Israel, even *all of it*, and the cities shall be inhabited, and the wastes shall be builded?" Has He not said, "I will settle you after your *old estates*, and will *do better* for you than at your *beginning*, and you shall know that I am the Lord?" Has He not said, "For I will take you from among the heathen, and gather you from all countries, and will bring you into your *own* land?" But you shrink from the desolation of Judea, and fear that the land will forever wither under its ancient curse. Even there we have been anticipated by the mercy of divine forgiveness. "I will multiply the fruit of the tree, and the increase of the field, that ye shall receive *no more* reproach of famine, and they shall say, this land that *was* desolate, is become like the Garden of Eden; I the Lord have spoken it, and I *will* do it." Shall we ourselves become infidels, and doubt the promises of the Almighty? God forbid. Let us therefore prepare for that great change, which will fill the whole world with wonder and astonishment. Other nations in breaking the yoke of the oppressors, and becoming rulers in their own land, bring with them their national characteristics; an ignorant people cannot make an enlightened government, but when the trumpet sounds for us on Zion, every country on earth will give up its great men among the Jewish people, and a combination of talent, wealth, enterprise, learning, skill, energy and bravery will be collected in Palestine, with all the lights of Science and Civilization, and once more elevate those laws which Moses had consecrated to Liberty and republican forms of government. Let us commence the great work, and leave its consummation to our great Shepherd and Redeemer.

I hope you will agree with me, that it is a privilege to be permitted to contribute our mite to the erection of this great Synagogue, near the site of the temple that all Israel should aid in its completion. It will possess one advantage—it will be orthodox. The Jewish religion should never change its original form or type; reforms create schisms, and promote divisions beside impairing the unity of our faith; religion is of the heart, there must be the seat of devotion forms and ceremonies are all empty without sincere piety.

I must confess that I should like to see some changes in our Ritual and Ceremonies: while admiring the beauty and sublimity of the Hebrew language, I should still be gratified, if we could introduce in our prayers a portion of the language of the country, in order that we may better comprehend the great responsibilities of our faith. We might also curtail many repetitions and introduce some beneficial changes; but where are the limitations and boundaries to these reforms, when we once introduce the pruning knife? Where is our authority to change or modify those forms and ceremonies, the native purity of our faith, which we have sustained for four thousand years through the severest sufferings and privations? There are great dangers in all innovations on an established Religion, and it is preferable to pursue the plain beaten paths so long adopted by our ancestors, than to venture upon unexplored regions, and carry out reforms, which finally efface the landmarks of our ancient faith. Yet if this is pursued by other Congregations, we shall be gratified to know, that there is one Congregation in Jerusalem which will never change its ancient laws and customs and therefore we can more cheerfully and more liberally extend our aid in the erection of this new Synagogue, under the conviction that it will be founded on a rock, which will last for ages. The accommodations to the pious, which a new and extensive place of worship will afford, will attract a greater number of our people to Jerusalem from the surrounding countries Admonished by the signs of the times, and by the expectation of important events, we find the aged Jews with some little means, coming down the Danube, from the Red Sea, and over the mountains of Circassia, journeying toward Jerusalem, there in holy meditation and prayer, to spend the remnant of their days, and to sit under the wall of the Temple, and pray for the peace of Israel, and when they die surrounded by the learned and pious, to be buried in the consecrated earth, near the ashes of the great Prophets, the sublime Psalmist, and the illustrious of our fathers and ancestors. If there is any consolation in the last hour **of life among the truly pious of our faith, it is in know**ing that they are to be buried under the shadow of Mount Zion; to be near when the Trumpet shall arouse the quick and the dead, at the day of the Great Atonement. I never hear the name of Jerusalem, without thinking of that mighty man, whose consecrated fingers struck the wires of his ravishing harp, and gave alarm to the hosts of Heaven—that beloved of God, that Warrior, Poet, King—stern in his friendships, sublime in his orisons, he whose whole heart melted in his love and adoration of the Lord—the good, the great, the illustrious David. Who can read his Psalms without feeling all the pride of religious faith in knowing that he too was a Jew? What a privilege it is to stand by his tomb—what a blessing to lie near him even in death!

I have said that the building of this new Synagogue in Jerusalem would be considered throughout the world as a remarkable sign, particularly among a People, who, though separated and dispersed in the four quarters of the world, are united by the most extraordinary bonds of sympathy; like the magnetic shock, it reaches every extremity like the flash of electricity which conveys intelligence in every direction, the Jews will hear of it and will see the handwriting on the wall. We have been preserved miraculously for great and startling events; God's dealings with his People have been most wonderful; we have passed through the promised punishments; shall we not enjoy the promised blessings? When and how this great advent is to be brought about, is still in the heart and hand of that great Spirit, who depresses and raises up, who breaks down thrones and elevates the oppressed and persecuted; as the great French Historian has said, "Providence moves through time, as the gods of Homer through space—it makes a step, and ages roll away."—To the Christian world, which has a common origin with us, and still clings to the Jewish nation as the favored and chosen People of God, this little expressive sign will not be without its impression—it is one blast of that silver trumpet, which at the dawn of day was sounded from the eastern portals of our Temple. Here is the Church of the Holy Sepulchre, in which Christians offer up their pious orisons to the memory of Him, who, while on earth, deserved all that the best feelings of the heart could bestow; there are the Minarets of the Mosque of Omar, built on the site of our Temple; and there in simple grandeur, in one corner of Mount Zion, is the new Synagogue of the Jews—the parent and his children, all were happy on the same spot, all wafting the orisons to that Heaven where sits in divine majesty the Lord of Hosts and the God of Israel.

It is not the least curious in the erection of this new edifice in Jerusalem, that we can direct the builders to the spot where all the materials of Herod's Temple yet lie in silent grandeur. Beneath the Mosque of El'Aksa, the great chambers, the immense granite pillars, the magnificent marble columns with exquisitely carved tops and bases, the richly ornamented gates, the reservoirs still filled with water, in which the Priests and Levites bathed, are at this day to be found, not crumbling in ruins, but erect and majestic, and have been explored within the last two years by one of our people, now a resident of this City, proving, beyond doubt, the error of that prediction, which declared that not one stone of that temple shall stand upon another. At this particular crisis of affairs in Europe, this small sign will arouse the Jews in every direction. They have been busy amid these revolutions. It was not to be expected that a people of their literary, political and commercial influence—the bankers of Europe, the merchants of England, the statesmen of France, the philosophers of Germany, the agriculturists of Poland, the poets of Italy, the artists, mechanics and soldiers everywhere, could see these mighty events developing themselves on the Continent, without participating actively in their progress and results. They too will hear the distant sound of that trumpet, whose notes will float around the horizon, and will know who is moving in the great work.

The laying of the corner-stone of the new temple will attract an immense number of the faithful to Jerusalem to witness the ceremony; it will not be built as the old one, on the return of our people from Babylon, with the sword in one hand and the trowel in the other. The building and the builders will be protected and assisted by all religious denominations. For many years I have cherished the hope that I might have it in my power to visit the Holy City—that my country would enable me to say to my people, with the prophet Isaiah, "Hail to the land, shadowing with wings which lies beyond the ruins of Ethiopia, which sendeth ambassadors by sea in vessels of bulrushes," hail to the house of the Jew, as well as the Gentile.

It would be to me the proudest day of my life, if I could be present at laying the corner-stone of the new Temple of Jerusalem—if I could realize all the associations which spring from the spot, where Daniel and Solomon lived—where Isaiah prophesied, and where the Maccabees conquered.

Friends and Brethren, will you not contribute a small portion of that wealth which God has blessed you with, to aid in the erection of the new building on Zion?—Will you not assist our poor Brethren in Jerusalem, who are looking to you for aid in this interesting project? Will you not give a trifle, that you might have the gratification of saying: "I assisted to erect this edi**fice dedicated to the Most High in his own—his cherished City of Jerusalem?" I know you will: when was an appeal made to the charitable feelings of the Jew to aid his Brethren, that it was not cheerfully, lib**erally responded to? All have an interest, an inheritance in Jerusalem; Jew and Gentile, all expect to unite in pious zeal, in holy charity, in mutual forgiveness, on that day, when the nation is to be gathered together.—The honored Messenger, now here, the Rabbi Echiel Cohen, who is to convey the fruits of your bounty to the Holy Land, will be, I hope, enabled to say, "I met my People in the Western World, with hands that had hearts in them—who felt and who prayed for the peace of Jerusalem, who gave me the gold of Ophir, as we gave Solomon of blessed memory to erect the Temple, which yet lives in our hearts, and the prayers and blessings of the faithful await them." Send him not away to the banks of the Jordan without purse and without scrip. Let us give our mite, no matter how small. I know full well, my friends, how many claims you have upon your bounty—strong and natural ones; engraft this one upon the rest; you will not feel its pressure; but it will be to you a grateful, pleasing remembrance, that when this contemplated edifice is completed, that you have had an interest in its erection, and your names will be impressed upon the hearts of a People whose lives are devoted to piety and whose prayers are offered for our temporal happiness and eternal salvation.

MAY 10, 1856.]   FRANK LESLIE'S ILLUSTRATED NEWSPAPER.   349

EDITORIAL PORTRAIT GALLERY, No. V.
MAJOR NOAH.

NEW YORK never possessed, among its editorial corps, a more pleasant writer or genuine man than this Mordecai Manuel Noah. He was born in Philadelphia July 19th, 1785. He was early apprenticed to a mechanical trade, but soon abandoned it for the law, at the same time mingling in politics and literature. Mr. Madison, in 1812, appointed him U. S. Consul to Morocco. The vessel in which he sailed from Charleston was taken by a British frigate, and he was carried to England, when he was allowed to proceed on his destination. After his return to America, in 1819, he published a volume of his travels in *England, France, Spain, and the Barbary States, from* 1813 *to* 1815. He now established himself in New York, and edited the *National Advocate*, a Democratic journal. As an evidence of his personal popularity, he was elected Sheriff of the city and county.

NEW YORK – 1856
"EDITORIAL PORTRAIT GALLERY, No. V:
MAJOR NOAH."
Frank Leslie's Illustrated Newspaper, p. 349 (cols 1–2)
May 10, 1856

Noah's impact was still felt in New York City five years after his death as evidenced in this feature description in Leslie's "Editorial Portrait Gallery." The opening tribute claims that "New York never possessed, among its editorial corps, a more pleasant writer or genuine man" than Noah. His political career as the first American Consul to Morocco and his book of travels to *England, France, Spain and the Barbary States* are cited.

Noah is acknowledged for the various New York City newspapers that he either edited or owned. In the last paragraph, Leslie calls attention to Noah's popularity among a wide circle of friends in many walks of life.

Significantly, this biographical portrait contains no reference to Noah's Jewishness, an identity for which he was often maligned or praised.

The *National Advocate* was discontinued in 1826, and Mr. Noah then commenced the publication of the *Enquirer*, which he conducted

MAJOR NOAH.
FROM AN AMBROTYPE BY BRADY.

for a while, until it was joined to the *Morning Courier*, which originated the present large commercial journal, the *Courier and Enquirer*. In 1834 he established the *Evening Star*, which attained a wide circulation from the ready pen of Major Noah, who was considered the most popular paragraphist of his day. The *Star* was wide circulation from the ready pen of Major Noah, who was considered the most popular paragraphist of his day. The *Star* was finally united with the *Times*, and both names were absorbed in the *Commercial Advertiser*. The Major finally established, in connection with Messrs. Deans and Howard, a Sunday paper called the *Times and Messenger*, for which he wrote until within a few days of his death, which occurred March 22d, 1851.

There was no man better known in his day in New York than Major Noah. His easy manner, fund of anecdote, fondness for biographical and historical memoirs, acquaintance with public men, political and social, for a half century, with whom his newspaper undertakings had brought him in contact; his sympathy with the amusements of the town, with actors, singers, and every class of performers, all of whom were severally promoted by his benevolent disposition, made his company everywhere sought and appreciated.

Chapter #9

Historic Events

May 7. 1752.   NUMB. 1221.

The PENNSYLVANIA GAZETTE.

Containing the Freſheſt Ad-   *vices, Foreign and Domeſtick.*

By the Hawke, Capt. Brown, *arrived at* New-Caſtle   Chamber-keepers, the Herald of Holland, the States

Hamburgh, March 3. The Jew who came to treat with the Court of Denmark about accommodating the Affair which occaſioned the arreſting M. de Longueville, is a very ſenſible Man: He ſays that two Cauſes may be aſſigned for the Diſguſt which was taken againſt M. de Longueville; firſt, becauſe there was counterfeit Jewels in ſome of the Preſents made by his Daniſh Majeſty to the Emperor of Morocco; and ſecondly, becauſe that Officer took too much upon him, in pretending to erect Forts in the Ports of Saffia and St. Croix, though the Contract made with him gave him no ſuch Authority. He ſays likewiſe, that his Power is very extenſive, and that he can do the Danes great Service. The Paſſports which he expected from the King of Denmark being arrived, he ſet out Yeſterday for Copenhagen.

PENNSYLVANIA – 1752
A VERY SENSIBLE MAN
The Pennsylvania Gazette, p. 1 (col 3)
May 7, 1752

A report from Hamburg advises the Gazette that "The Jew who came to treat with the Court of Denmark about accommodating the Affair which occasioned the arresting M. de Longueville, is a very sensible man." The report then relays what the unnamed Jew said – first about the "two causes [that] may be assigned for the Disgust which was taken against M. de Longueville" and then about his own extensive Power and the "great Service" he can do for the Danes.

Paris A-la-main, Feb. 28. Letters received from Genoa, of the 14th of this Month advise, that the Revolt, which lately happened in the Suburbs of Biſagno, was not yet appeaſed; but that there was ſome Likelihood of Things being brought to an Accommodation; becauſe the People ſhewed Signs of a general Diſcontent, and murmured exceedingly at the Rigour with which they were treated, for doing all they could to deliver the Republick from the Oppreſſion it laboured under.

Letters from Genoa of the 21ſt of laſt Month, advise, that by Letters from Baſtia, it appeared, that the Miſunderſtanding between the Marquis de Curſay, the French General, and M. Grimaldi, Commiſſary General of the Republick, was renewed; the latter was the Occaſion of it, having refuſed to deliver up two Deſerters of the King's Troops, and five Banditti, who had been baniſhed from the Iſland of Corſica, not to return upon Pain of Death.

Berlin, Feb. 21. The King has offered a Refuge to great Numbers of Piedmonteſe Families, living by the Silk Trade, who are deſirous of removing into Proteſtant Countries, and will immediately employ them in our Manufactures.

Paris, March 3. Orders are ſent to all the Intendants of the Kingdom to ſend up to Court exact Accounts of the State of the Militia in their reſpective Departments, and to complete forthwith every Battalion of the ſame.

Hamburgh, March 3. The Jew who came to treat with the Court of Denmark about accommodating the Affair which occaſioned the arreſting M. de Longueville, is a ſenſible Man: He ſays that two Cauſes may be aſſigned for the Diſguſt which was taken againſt M. de Longueville; firſt, becauſe there was counterfeit Jewels in ſome of the Preſents made by his Daniſh Majeſty to the Emperor of Morocco; and ſecondly, becauſe that Officer took too much upon him, in pretending to erect Forts in the Ports of Saffia and St. Croix, though the Contract made with him gave him no ſuch Authority. He ſays likewiſe, that his Power is very extenſive, and that he can do the Danes great Service. The Paſſports which he expected from the King of Denmark being arrived, he ſet out Yeſterday for Copenhagen.

Cadiz, Jan. 28. The dreadful Storms which began in theſe Parts the fifth of the laſt Month, as hath been already related, have continued with more or leſs Violence almoſt every Day ſince: The Damage done thereby is greater than we can exactly compute. Upwards of 100 Ships, large and ſmall, have been loſt on our Coaſt.

Peterſburgh, Feb. 15. The Reſtoration of a good Underſtanding between this Court and that of Berlin, ſeems to be more likely, as both Parties make Advances towards it; It is even pretended, that Things are ſo far advanced in this Reſpect, that nothing is wanting to compleat it, but ſending the reſpective Miniſters. The Court ſeems very well ſatiſfied with the Diſpatches ſent from time to time by the Imperial Miniſters at Stockholm, from which there is Reaſon to believe, that the States of that Kingdom will take ſuch Reſolutions as may contribute to ſtrengthen the good Underſtanding between her Imperial Majeſty and the Crown of Sweden.

Florence, Feb. 12. They write from Leghorn, that the Corſairs of Barbary continue to cruize along the Coaſt of Sardinia, and by that Means hinder Communication between Leghorn and other Parts of Italy; inſomuch that no Ship has arrived there for ſome Time paſt, but ſuch as belonged to the Powers reſpected by theſe Corſairs. This has occaſioned a Reſolution of ſending to Sea the three Imperial Ships, in order to take under their Protection the Chriſtian Veſſels that trade to Leghorn.

Cadiz, Feb. 20. Every Method is made Uſe of to recover the Effects of the Superbe Regiſter Ship lately loſt off our Coaſt, and 1400000 Piaſters have been already ſaved. Four other Regiſter Ships are hourly expected from the Weſt-Indies. Letters from the Havanna, dated the 8th of December laſt, adviſe, that the Men of War which were in that Port could not put to Sea for want of Sailors, moſt of thoſe who had been ſent from Old Spain, having fallen ſick, and near 600 of them dead.

Paris, March 6. It is pretended that the Imperial Court has conſented that the King of Sardinia ſhould be admitted as high contracting Party to the Treaty which is negociating at Madrid for eſtabliſhing the Repoſe of Italy, this being one of the Difficulties which hindered the Concluſion of that Treaty.

the Truncheon, the Coat of Armour, the mourning Horſe, the Order of the Garter, the Sword of Sovereignty, the Crown on a black Velvet Cuſhion with Silver Lace, the great Officers of his Highneſs's Houſhold, the Funeral Car, of a particular Invention, covered with Silver-laced black Velvet, and a magnificent Canopy; the eight Horſes of the Car in which the Corpſe is to be placed, led by ſix Majors, and two Lieutenant Colonels; the Pall to be borne by Count Maurice of Naſſau, General Prætorius, the Admirals Schryver and Reyniſt; the Corpſe to be carried by twenty-two Majors Generals, and two Commodores, and the Canopy to be ſupported by twenty-three Colonels, the Prince of Baden Dourlach, the Duke of Brunſwick; theſe are ſucceeded by eight Meſſengers of State bare headed, and without Cloaks, two Chamber-keepers, four Trumpeters, the Herald of the Generality in a Coat of Arms, the Houſekeeper to the State; the States-General, two a-breaſt, in long mourning Cloaks, without Bands or Swords, and followed by their Domeſticks in Livery, eight Meſſengers of State, eight State Uſhers, two

Hague, Feb. 27. By Letters from Batavia we have Advice, that the Dutch have gained two ſucceſſive Victories over the Bantam Rebels, who were advanced even to the Frontiers of Jacatra. In the laſt Engagement they were totally defeated, and the Dutch Company were in great Hopes that they ſhould be able to raiſe the Siege of Bantam. According to the ſame Advices, the Emperor of Java had promiſed to aſſiſt our Countrymen in putting an End to the War.

Vienna, Feb. 23. They write from Conſtantinople, that the Effects of the laſt dreadful Peſtilence are ſcarce felt in that Metropolis; the Number of the Inhabitants is conſiderably encreaſed, and they reckon that near 200,000 Labourers and Artiſans are come to ſettle there ſince the Contagion ceaſed: So that the Loſs falls on the Provinces of the Ottoman Empire.

Berlin, Feb. 29. A Treaty of Peace is ſaid to be on Foot, between this Court and that of Spain, which in all Likelihood will be greatly facilitated by the Tranſit lately granted thro' the United Provinces for Goods ſent from Germany to Spain.

The

PHILADELPHIA – 1758 "SUBSTANCE OF A REMARKABLE SERMON PREACHED … BY A J E W"

The American Magazine and Monthly Chronicle, pp. 441–445 June, 1758

The publication of the English translation of a sermon delivered by David Hirchel Franckel, Chief Rabbi of Berlin, on December 10, 1757, was the first time Jewish material was published in the United States. Franckel (b. Berlin, 1707; d. Berlin, 1762), a scholar of the Palestinian Talmud, offered praise in honor of the December 5, 1757 upset victory by Frederick the Great of Prussia in one of the main battles in the Seven Year' War (1756–63). Entitled, "Thanksgiving Sermon for the Important and Astonishing Victory Obtained on the fifth of December, 1757 by the Glorious King of Prussia over the united and far superior forces of the Austrians in Silesia," the address was subsequently translated into English and printed in London in ten editions.

Politically, Franckel's sermon, which was published in Boston and New York following its Philadelphia appearance, is given credit for promoting the notion that Jews, though previously regarded as outside the body politic, do indeed feel national loyalty to their host nations. Thus, in a 1763 American appearance of this sermon, the editor noted that Jews hold "patriotic sentiments and the warmest gratitude to princes who have wisdom and humanity to protect and defend them."

POETICAL ESSAYS, *June*, 1758.   441

Too much *Cunning's* fraudful art,
Too much *Firmnefs* want of heart
Too much *fparing* makes a knave ;
Thofe are *rafh* that are *too* brave ;
Too much *Wealth* like weight oppreffes ;
Too much *Fame* with care diftreffes ;
Too much *Pleafure* death will bring,
Too much *Wit's* a dang'rous thing ;
Too much *Truft* is folly's guide,
Too much *Spirit* is but pride ;
He's a dupe that is *too free*,
Too much *Bounty* weak muft be ;
Too much *Complaifance* a knave,
Too much *Zeal to pleafe* a flave.
This TOO MUCH, tho' bad it feem,
Chang'd with eafe to good you deem ;
N. B. This little poem is fold for 6 *d fterl.* in *London,* and 3 *d* here.

But in this you err my friend,
For on *Trifles* all depend.
Trifles great effects produce,
Both of pleafure and of ufe ;
Trifles often turn the fcale,
When in love or law we fail ;
Trifles to the great commend,
Trifles make proud beauty bend ;
Trifles prompt the poet's ftrain,
Trifles oft diftract the brain ;
Trifles, trifles more or lefs,
Give us, or withold fuccefs ;
Trifles, when we *hope*, can cheer,
Trifles fmite us when we *fear* :
All the flames that lover's know,
Trifles quench and trifles blow.

Subftance of a remarkable Sermon preached at Berlin, *by a* J E W.

A Remarkable fermon has lately made its appearance in *Europe,* firft printed in the *German* language at *Berlin,* entitled——" A *Thankf-* " giving SER MON for the important " and aftonifhing *Victory,* obtained on the " 5th of *December* 1757, by the glorious " KING of PRUSSIA, over the u- " nited forces of the AUSTRIANS " in *Silefia,* preached on the *Sabbath* of the " tenth of the faid month, at the fyna- " gogue of the JEWS, in *Berlin,* by " DAVID HIRCHEL FRANCKEL, " *Arch-Rabbi.*" As this fermon fhews the idea entertained of the *Pruffian Hero* by his own fubjects, we imagine that the following view of it, will not be unacceptable after the above P O E M. Excepting the quotation from *Gen.* XIV, which the reader may perufe in his bible, and a few lines of the comment, the fermon is here inferted entire.

PSALM XXII, v. 23, 24.

Ye that fear the Lord, praife him: All ye the Seed of Jacob, glorify him ; and fear him, all ye the Seed of Ifrael. For he hath not defpifed nor held in Scorn the Af- fliction of the afflicted: Neither hath he hid his Face from him ; but when he cried unto him, he heard.

LET us this day, my beloved, folemn- ly imprefs on our hearts thefe words of the royal prophet ; for we are the afflicted, who's Affliction the Lord hath not defpifed, nor held in Scorn. Join with me in a retrofpect on thofe calamitous times, when our fufferings were without any ap- parent iffue ; when the miferies of war, with a ftrong and outftretched arm, were

haftening to furround us on all fides when the exulting enemy boafted, *That the Lord was no longer our Helper. Selah.* Reflect what earthly power was able to difperfe the ftorm, which impended over our heads, or what human underftanding could have forefeen the plan, by which our deliverance was to be wrought ? Our ruin feemed inevitable. The ravenous na- tions of the earth had already made fpoil of us, in their proud imaginations. But *he who fitteth in heaven derides them ; the Lord laugheth them to fcorn.* He has tried us. He has caufed us to feel the rod of his chaftifements, that we fhould humble our- felves before him ; that, with contrite hearts, we fhould pour out our fupplica- tions to him. *This the Lord hath done, that he might be feared.*

He has not hid his Face from us. The dif- tinguifhing favour of the moft high to our fovereign, in being a fun and a fhield to him ; in protecting him under his wings ; is, to all loyal fubjects, a glad- fome ray of hope, under the moft gloomy circumftances. Truly, thought we, *our Redeemer liveth ; now the Lord hath not for- faken us.* The goodnefs of our creator had been our refuge. We appointed a day of publick prayer and humiliation. Who, my brethren, can, without emotion, without a fympathifing fadnefs, call to mind that SOLEMN DAY ; when, with one heart and voice, ye all proftrated yourfelves in this temple, before the lord ; when, the tears flowing from every eye, fpoke the tumult of your hearts ; and the fervour of the petitions then offered up for the prefervation of our fole hope, the wel- fare of our fovereign, and for the fuccefs of his righteous arms ? *The Lord hath not defpifed, nor held our Affliction in Scorn ; and when we cry unto him, he hears us.*

Behold, he infpired our gracious mo- narch, with a wifdom, which the pre-

The London Chronicle:

OR,

UNIVERSAL EVENING POST.

VOL. XV.   [105]   N° 111.

From TUESDAY, JANUARY 31, to THURSDAY, FEBRUARY 2, 1764.

WEDNESDAY, FEBRUARY 1.

The London Gazette. N°10386.

Venice, January 6.

 IT has been ordered by the Senate, that all such Levant goods, as are or can be shipped here on English vessels for England, shall be exempted from the export duties, with the restitution of those paid on importation.

Venice, Jan. 11. There are no further accounts from Spalatro, which gives reason to hope that the plague is subsiding there, through the unwearied diligence used by the General Michieli to prevent any communication with the infected.

Lord Chamberlain's Office, Jan. 31. Orders for the Court's change of mourning on Sunday next the 5th of February, for the late Elector of Saxony, viz.

The Ladies to wear black silk or velvet, coloured ribbons, fans, and tippets.

The Men to continue in black full trimmed, and to wear coloured swords and buckles.

And on Sunday the 12th of February the Court to go out of mourning.

BANKRUPTS.

Thomas Naylor, and James Walker, of London, Merchants and Partners.—To appear Feb. 2, 15, March 13, at Guildhall.

Richard Simpole, of Wolverhampton, Grocer.—To appear Feb. 27, 28, at the Saracen's Head in Bewdley, March 13, at the Bell in Wolverhampton.

Sarah Backhouse, of Lancaster, Linnendraper.—To appear Feb. 22, 23, at Harry's Coffee-house in Hull, March 13, at the King's Arms in Market Weighton, Yorkshire.

A Dividend fixed, Feb. 22.

Robert Sawyer, of Great Yarmouth, Baker.

Certificates to be granted, Feb. 20.

James Warburton, of Wapping, Slop-seller.

AMERICA.

New-York, Dec. 22. Friday last Captain Montresor, Engineer, arrived here from Detroit, in 26 days, and brought the agreeable news, that the Indians under the command of Pondiack, consisting of the Ottawas, Jibbyways, Wiandots, and Powtewattamies, being tired of the war (having lost in the different attacks of the fort, vessels and row-gallies, between 90 and 100 of their best warriors) and studying their present conveniency, being in want of ammunition, and the hunting season advancing, had applied to Col. Gladwin for PEACE; which he granted them, upon condition that it was agreeable to the Commander in Chief of North America, and that they should bring in all their prisoners, which the Indians immediately complied with, and directly sent into the fort 17 Englishmen.

The garrison at Detroit was well supplied with every thing necessary till the first of July next, and the soldiers, 212 in number, hearty and well; as they were also at all the posts on the road. Major Rogers is arrived at Niagara, with 250 men from Detroit.

The same day Major Moncrief arrived here from Niagara; he belonged to the detachment under the command of Major Wilkins, destined from Niagara for Detroit, by whom we learn, that on the 7th ult. at eleven o'clock at night, 18 of their boats foundered in Lake Erie, in a violent storm at S. E. which came on suddenly; by which accident 70 brave men were drowned; in which number was Lieut. Davidson, of the train, and 19 of his men; as also Lieutenant Paynter, and Doctor Williams, of the 80th, and a French Pilot. The whole detachment was in danger of being lost, as every battoe that reached the shore was more than half full of water; by which means 50 odd barrels of provisions, all the ammunition but two rounds a man (which the officers saved in their horns) and two small brass field-pieces, were lost; and that after holding a council of war, it was thought most prudent to return to Niagara.

Another Account.

That on the 12th of October last Wappocomogath, chief of the Mississaque Indians, came under a flag of truce, to Major Gladwin at Detroit, to let him know that none of his band had hitherto committed the least hostilities, and that he was using all his influence to restore the nations in arms to their senses, that he had prevailed on most of them to listen to his arguments, and that through him (their Mediator) the Chippawas, Outawaws, Wiandats, Pontiwatamies, sensible of their villainous behaviour, begged forgiveness of what was past, and desired to be admitted to council, to make their submission:

That Major Gladwin, not having at this time above 14 days provision in store, listened to their overtures, though he looked upon it as an artifice to lull him for the winter, and that it was their present necessity, in the article of ammunition, a desire to go on their hunting grounds for their winter subsistence, with the fear of Major Wilkins's detachment reaching Detroit, that induced them to those measures. In council he told them, if they convinced him of their sincerity, all might be well again; hostilities then ceased, and many of them went to their hunting grounds; Major Gladwin took that opportunity to get provisions in from the inhabitants, and wood for the winter.

On the 30th of October a courier arrived at Detroit, with a letter from the French officer commanding at Fort Chartres on the Mississippi, to all the Indians, advising them to be at peace with their brothers the English, as they were one people; at the same time it contained an invitation to them to remove, with their families, to the Western bank of the Mississippi, where they should have fine hunting-grounds, with an easy and flourishing commerce.

A large party of Indians went from Detroit early this fall, with great quantities of beaver, to purchase ammunition at New Orleans; and it is thought their future temper, in a great measure depends on the talk they may have

with the Governor, and the means they may fall upon to procure supplies. Major Gladwin continues upon his guard, and expects the renewal of hostilities in the spring.

The detachment under the command of Major Wilkins, in their passage over Lake Erie, met with great difficulties by contrary winds and bad weather. On the 7th of November, about ten o'clock at night, they were suddenly surprized with a violent gale of wind, within thirty leagues of Detroit, at a place called Point du Pin; in which they lost three officers, viz. Lieutenant Davidson one of the artillery, Lieutenant Painter of the platoons, and Mr. Williams, Surgeon to the 80th regiment; four Serjeants, sixty-three privates, and a Canadian pilot: All their ammunition, and great part of their provisions lost and destroyed. In these circumstances Major Wilkins ordered a council, to consider of the present situation of the detachment, who were of opinion, it was better for the service to return to Niagara, than proceed to Detroit without ammunition, and with very little provisions: That Major of Brigade Moncrieffe, who was carrying orders from the Commander in Chief to Major Gladwin, under the escort of this detachment, being acquainted by Major Wilkins of the resolution he had taken, wrote a letter to Major Gladwin to acquaint him of it, that he might take his measures accordingly. This letter he sent off the 12th of November by two Hurons of the village near Quebec, which they delivered with great fidelity the 18th, and in consequence Major Gladwin reduced his garrison to 212 men having provisions sufficient for that number, and sent away the detachment of the 55th regiment, Hopkins's independent company, and Rogers's volunteers. Captain Montresor left Detroit the 20th of November with these Corps; and though they had intelligence that a large body of Indians intended to way-lay them, they arrived safe at Niagara the 27th.

Newport, Dec. 5. Friday last, in the afternoon, was the dedication of the new synagogue in this town. It began by a handsome procession, in which were carried the books of the law, to be deposited in the ark. Several portions of Scripture, and of their service, with a prayer for the Royal family, were read, and finely sung by the priest and people. There were present many gentlemen and ladies. The order and decorum, the harmony and solemnity of the musick, together with a handsome assembly of people, in an edifice the most perfect of the temple kind perhaps in America, and splendidly illuminated, could not but raise in the mind a faint idea of the Majesty and grandeur of the antient Jewish worship mentioned in Scripture.

COUNTRY NEWS.

Portsmouth, Jan. 30. This morning arrived at Spithead, the Worcester and Norfolk East Indiamen, from London, bound to the East Indies.

Last Saturday night was interred in the King's

[Price Two-pence Halfpenny.]

LONDON – 1763-64
DEDICATION OF THE TOURO
SYNAGOGUE IN RHODE ISLAND
The London Chronicle, p. 1 (col 3)
January 31–February 2, 1764

This front-page article reports a landmark event in the story of American Jewry, the dedication of Congregation Yeshuat Israel of Newport, Rhode Island. This structure, more commonly known as the Touro Synagogue, is the oldest synagogue functioning in United States history and is today a National Historic Site. While the Massachusetts Bay Colony granted religious freedom to all who believed exactly as they did (i.e., Puritanism), Rhode Island granted religious freedom to all.

Newport, Dec. 5. Friday laft, in the afternoon, was the dedication of the new fynagogue in this town. It began by a handfome proceffion, in which were carried the books of the law, to be depofited in the ark. Several portions of Scripture, and of their fervice, with a prayer for the Royal family, were read, and finely fung by the prieft and people. There were prefent many gentlemen and ladies. The order and decorum, the harmony and folemnity of the mufick, together with a handfome affembly of people, in an edifice the moft perfect of the temple kind perhaps in America, and fplendidly illuminated, could not but raife in the mind a faint idea of the Majefty and grandeur of the antient Jewifh worfhip mentioned in Scripture.

According to Morris A. Gutstein's *The Story of the Jews of Newport,* there were sixty to seventy Jewish families in town at the time of the dedication. Rev. Isaac Touro, previously from Curacao, served as the congregation's *hazzan* (reader). Funds to build the historic synagogue were provided by Newport Jewry and by other Sephardic congregations including New York's Shearith Israel (the principal donor outside Newport), and congregations in London, Amsterdam, Curacao and Surinam.

Peter Harrison, a pupil of Sir Christopher Wren, was the synagogue's architect. The design – in the Georgian style with Harrison's modification known as "classic colonial" – was combined with the traditional synagogue architecture of Spanish-Portuguese Jews. Close similarities were apparent between the Newport congregation and Spanish-Portuguese synagogues both in Amsterdam and London. But the Newport synagogue contained a feature not found in Sephardic synagogues in Europe – stairs that led from the reading desk to a secret passage in the basement. According to Gutstein, "This is said to have been a relic of the Marrano traditions of providing a hiding place or a passage of escape in case of danger. This tradition, the Newport Jews, who were Marranos in the majority of cases, remembering the dread of the Inquisition and spies of the Holy Office, carried over into their land of freedom."

Following several years of construction and furnishing, the dedication took place Friday afternoon, December 2, 1763, corresponding with the first day of Chanukah which celebrates the date on which Judah Maccabee reconsecrated and dedicated the Jerusalem Holy Temple in 165 B.C.E. Among the notables present was Dr. Ezra Stiles, Minister of the Second Congregational Church, who would later become president of Yale College (see page 63). Dr. Stiles often discussed Biblical passages and theology with Rev. Touro, who taught the minister Hebrew.

The *London Chronicle* account of the dedication read: "It began by a handsome procession in which were carried the books of the law, to be deposited in the ark. Several portions of the scripture, and of their service, with a prayer for the Royal family, were read, and finely sung by the priest and people. There were present many gentlemen and ladies. The order and decorum, the harmony and solemnity of the musick, together with a handsome assembly of people, in an edifice the most perfect of the temple kind perhaps in America, and splendidly illuminated, could not but raise in the mind a faint idea of the Majesty and grandeur of the ancient Jewish worship mentioned in Scripture."

Some twenty-seven years later, President George Washington, following a visit to this synagogue in August, 1790, sent a letter to the "Hebrew Congregation in Newport," in which he wished that the "Children of the Stock of Abraham" who dwell in this land continue to enjoy the goodwill of other inhabitants, while the government of the United Stated will give "to bigotry no sanction, to persecution no assistance" (see page 191).

PHILADELPHIA – 1787
THE NEW "STAR OF ISRAEL"
The Pennsylvania Packet and Daily Advertiser,
p. 2 (col 3)
July 10, 1787

This article, which appeared while the Constitutional Convention was in session, reported a significant early bout in the career of Daniel Mendoza (b. London, 1763; d. London, 1836), the Jewish boxing great known as the new "Star of Israel." Mendoza revolutionized the sport of fighting in England, substituting a science of precise blows, footwork and quick thinking for its more blatant brutalities. He held England's boxing championship from 1792 to 1795 and is alleged to have been the first Jew to ever personally converse with King George. At the height of Mendoza's career, reports of his matches in the British press took precedence over news of the storming of the Bastille during the French Revolution.

Mendoza's victory over Martin, the Bath butcher, described in this article, was a turning point in the Jewish pugilist's career, as fans began to take notice of this five foot seven fighter who had remarkable chest development and extraordinary speed.

"At the onset of the match, odds were two to one in Martin's favor…. On stripping, Mendoza appeared to be the more muscular of the two. And when they had fought 28 minutes Martin gave up the battle. The Jew's stile of fighting was much the neatest and quickest… Among the amateurs, *the Jew was held to have fought as well as any of the gymnastic professors… – Humphries excepted."*

BOXING MATCH.

At twenty minutes past three the stage being ready on Barnet Common, Martin, with Ben his second, and Mendoza, with Johnson for his, mounted it, and prepared themselves for engaging. At the onset, the odds were two to one in favour of Martin, from an idea that he struck with more force. On stripping, Mendoza appeared to be the more muscular of the two. And when they had fought 28 minutes Martin gave up the battle. The Jew's stile of fighting was much the neatest and quickest; whenever Martin struck, Mendoza struck top, and having the longest arm, always reached his adversary first.

Amongst the *amateurs*, the Jew was held to have fought as well as any of the gymnastic professors have hitherto done—Humphries excepted.

He was so little hurt, that when the battle was declared in his favour, he leaped on the railing of the scaffold, which was nearly two yards from the ground. Martin was carried off by his friends, unable to stand.

Another battle succeeded this, of no note, but its being the object of nature—as the other was the effort of art.

This was betwixt Doyle a sailor, and Mutton a soldier, the last of whom was beat very thoroughly. During the latter part of the battle, the soldier was always falling, which gave a countryman the opportunity of observing, " on Mutton being down, that he was glad of it, it had been long enough *up* in that country." The spectators amounted to about five thousand—amongst whom were his royal highness the Prince of Wales, Messieurs Bradyll, Wyndham, Afton, lord Gage, &c &c &c.—And all who have long or lately been *amateurs* of this art.

The prince rode after the first battle.

If, according to an opinion of a celebrated poet, the knowledge of the pleasures of lunacy is limited exclusively to madmen, it may also follow, that boxing administers to the mind a delight which only the chosen few, the happy elect, the practical adepts in boxing know. As to ourselves, we are too ignorantly phlegmatic to entertain any idea of the heartfelt ecstacy which accompanies the dislocation of a rib, the breaking of a jaw-bone, or the closing up of both the eyes of one of our fellow creatures.

After three paragraphs about Mendoza, the article further praises Mendoza in its report about the night's second battle, which was "of no note, but its being the object of nature – as the other [Mendoza's] was the effort of art."

Mendoza went on to fight three bouts with the aforementioned Humphries, all of which were won by the new "Star of Israel."

WORCESTER, MASSACHUSETTS – 1790 "ADDRESS...TO THE PRESIDENT"

Massachusetts Spy; or The Worcester Gazette, p. 4 (col 1–2) July 1, 1790

The first Jewish community to address George Washington, the newly elected president, was the Hebrew Congregation of Savannah, Georgia on May 6, 1789. Levi Sheftal (b. 1739, Savannah; d. 1809, Savannah) wrote on behalf of the congregation what was largely a statement addressed to the subject of religious toleration. Sheftal thanked the new President for his support of such tolerance: "Your unexampled liberality and extensive philanthropy have dispelled the cloud of bigotry and superstition."

Miscellanies.

ADDRESS *from the* HEBREW CONGREGATION *of the city of* Savannah, *in Georgia, to the* PRESIDENT *of the United States.*

SIR,

WE have long been anxious of congratulating you on your appointment by unanimous approbation to the Presidential dignity of this country, and of testifying our unbounded confidence in your integrity and unblemished virtue : Yet, however exalted the station you now fill, it is still not equal to the merit of your heroick services through an arduous and dangerous conflict, which has embosomed you in the hearts of her citizens.

Our eccentrick situation, added to a diffidence founded on the most profound respect has thus long prevented our address ; yet the delay has realized anticipation, and given us an opportunity of presenting our grateful acknowledgements for the benedictions of Heaven through the energy of Federal influence and the equity of your administration.

Your unexampled liberality and extensive philanthropy have dispelled that cloud of bigotry and superstition, which has long as a veil shaded religion—unrivetted the fetters of enthusiasm—enfranchised us with all the privileges and immunities of free citizens, and initiated us into the grand mass of legislative mechanism. By example you have taught us to endure the ravages of war with manly fortitude, and to enjoy the blessings of peace, with reverence to the Deity, and benignity and love to our Fellow Creatures.

May the great Author of worlds grant you all happiness—an uninterrupted series of health—addition of years to the number of your days, and a continuance of guardianship to that freedom which under the auspices of Heaven your magnanimity and wisdom have given these States.

LEVI SHEFTAL, *President,* (*in behalf of the Hebrew Congregation.*)

The ANSWER.

To *the* HEBREW CONGREGATION *of the City of* Savannah.

GENTLEMEN,

I THANK you, with great sincerity, for your congratulations on my appointment to the office which I have the honour to hold by the unanimous choice of my fellow citizens ; and especially for the expressions which you are pleased to use in testifying the confidence that is reposed in me by your Congregation.

As the delay which has naturally intervened between my election and your address has afforded an opportunity for appreciating the merits of the federal government, and for communicating your sentiments of its administration—I have rather to express my satisfaction than regret at a circumstance, which demonstrates (upon experiment) your attachment to the former, as well as approbation of the latter.

I rejoice that a spirit of liberality and philanthropy is much more prevalent than it formerly was among the enlightened nations of the earth ; and that your brethren will benefit thereby in proportion as it shall become still more extensive. Happily the people of the United States of America have, in many instances, exhibited examples worthy of imitation.—The salutary influence of which will doubtless extend much farther, if gratefully enjoying those blessings of peace which (under favour of Heaven) have been obtained by fortitude in war, they shall conduct themselves with reverence to the Deity, and charity towards their fellow creatures.

May the same wonder working Deity, who long since delivering the Hebrews from their Egyptian oppressors, planted them in the promised land—whose providential agency has lately been conspicuous in establishing these United States as an Independent Nation—still continue to water them with the dews of Heaven, and to make the inhabitants of every denomination participate in the temporal and spiritual blessings of that people, whose God is Jehovah !

G. WASHINGTON.

Washington replied thanking the congregation for its congratulations and confidence in him. He rejoiced that the spirit of liberality and philanthropy "is much more prevalent than it formally was among the enlightened nations of the earth." He concluded with a prayer containing an Old Testament cadence: "May the same wonder-working Deity who long since delivered the Hebrews from their Egyptian oppressors, planted them in a promised land, whose providential agency has lately been conspicuous in establishing these United States as an independent nation, still continue to water them with the dews of heaven and make the inhabitants of every denomination participate in the temporal and spiritual blessings of that people whose God is Jehovah."

Washington's letter, in addition to demonstrating his affection for this nation's nascent Jewish community, was cited more than three decades later, in 1824, in buttressing support for the Jew Bill in Maryland whose purpose was to provide political freedoms they were previously denied (see pages 14 and 195–198).

PHILADELPHIA – 1790
PRESIDENT WASHINGTON RESPONDS
TO KING DAVID'S LODGE'S ADDRESS
Gazette of The United States, p. 4 (col 2)
September 11, 1790

This issue of the quasi-official publication of the Federalist Party contained the full text of the historic public exchange between Moses Seixas, Master, and Henry Sherburne, Committee-member of King David's Masonic Lodge, and President George Washington during Washington's overnight visit to Newport, Rhode Island, on August 17-18, 1790.

In their addresses, Seixas wished that the "Sovereign Architect of the Universe may always encompass [Washington] with his holy protection," and Washington declared that he would be guided by the Masonic principles of "private virtue and public prosperity.*"*

Washington's 1790 visit to Newport ranks among the seminal episodes in the history of American Jewish religious liberty. Moses Seixas (b. 1744; d. 1809) stands out as the main Jewish personage influencing Washington's averring of religious freedom and social tolerance during this visit. Seixas, a Newport merchant, warden of Kaal Kadosh Yeshuat Israel (Newport Hebrew Congregation), and a prominent Mason, remained in the city after it was occupied by the British during the Revolutionary War. He demonstrated his patriotism by a document he signed during the occupation pledging loyalty to the patriotic cause. Significantly, his brother Rabbi Gershon Mendes Seixas, minister of New York's Shearith Israel Congregation, known as the "patriot rabbi," was reportedly one of fourteen clergymen officiating at Washington's 1789 Presidential inauguration (see also page 28).

Washington's trip to Rhode Island was occasioned by two issues. Firstly, he wanted to show his goodwill to this state which had been the thirteenth and final holdout in ratifying the new Constitution. Secondly, the trip was part of a national campaign by Washington to win support for an Amendment to the new Constitution opposing an established church, a goal eagerly sought by this fledgling 2,000-member national Jewish community. Earlier, at the Philadelphia Constitutional Convention, Washington played a pivotal role in opposing any religious qualification for voting.

Following a thirteen-gun salute welcoming Washington to Newport, Seixas occupied a dual role among the dignitaries welcoming the new President. He was not only Master of King David's Masonic Lodge, he was also the leader of the Newport Hebrew Congregation.

In *The Story of the Jews of Newport* [New York, 1936], Morris A. Gutstein noted the key role of Newport Jews such as Moses Michael Hays, David Lopez, Solomon Myers and Seixas in the early history of the Masonic lodge. Masonry was one of the central commitments of Washington's life and clearly he was aware of the role of Brother Seixas in that regard. Illustrating Washington's devotion to Masonry was his having taken the Presidential oath on a Bible from his lodge, and his Masonic attire at the subsequent groundbreaking for the nation's Capitol building.

According to Gutstein, Washington took a walk through Newport on the afternoon of August 17th. "It may well be," wrote Gutstein [p. 208], "that during these walks, Moses Seixas accompanied him to view the beautiful synagogue, which was the only building that retained its full splendor through the hard times after the evacuation." It does not require much imagination to assume the juxtaposition of both the interests of Jewry and and Masonry in the conversation between these two gentlemen.

"The next morning, the 18th," continued Gutstein [p. 209], "shortly before the President prepared to leave, and immediately after breakfast, deputations from the town and the churches as well as from the Masonic fraternity, appeared at his quarters, to present the visitor with formal addresses, expressions of devotion to their leader. Moses Seixas represented two institutions, King David's Lodge and the Hebrew Congregation. From both he carried to the President warm greetings and messages of love and felicitations, which he presented in the name of the respective institutions."

Washington's overnight visit to Newport, August 17-18, 1790, was, in fact, Washington's third time to that city. In 1756, Washington was welcomed to Newport as a young Virginia Colonel in the service of His Majesty King George III. On March 6, 1781, a little over a year after some 8,000 British-led troops fled the city, he went to Newport to honor General Count de Rochambeau who had led the French troops quartered in Newport. During that visit, Washington was entertained at the home of Moses Seixas, one of the city's main Jewish merchants. A Town Meeting was held at the Newport Hebrew Congregation, among the few beautiful colonial structures not destroyed by the British during the fighting.

But the Newport that Washington visited in 1790 had not recovered from the wartime devastation. Its "golden age" in the decades before the Revolution would never return. Gutstein described the depressed scene in *The Story of the Jews of Newport*:

> *In beauty and in commerce it had few rivals. It had been the center of an advanced cultural life, with a growing library, flourishing schools and bookshops. Now it was a barren city with shattered houses, a pillaged library, and commerce practically at a standstill. The Jewish merchants who had formed the nucleus of an extensive export and import trade were gone and the city declared itself to be in a state of abject poverty.*

N——, [xx. 1.] Auguſt 20, 1790.

ADDRESS
OF THE MASTER, WARDENS, AND BRETHREN OF KING DAVID'S *LODGE.*
TO GEORGE WASHINGTON,
PRESIDENT OF THE UNITED STATES OF AMERICA.

WE the Maſter, Wardens, and Brethren of King David's Lodge, in Newport, Rhode-Iſland, joyfully embrace this opportunity, to *greet* you as a Brother, and to *hail* you welcome to Rhode-Iſland.

We exult in the thought, that as Maſonry has always been patronized by the wiſe, the good, and the great, ſo hath it ſtood, and ever will ſtand, as its fixtures are on the immutable pillars of faith, hope and charity.

With unſpeakable pleaſure, we gratulate you as filling the Preſidential Chair, with the applauſe of a numerous and enlightened people—whilſt at the ſame time, we felicitate ourſelves in the honor done the Brotherhood, by your many exemplary virtues, and emanations of goodneſs proceeding from a heart worthy of poſſeſſing the ancient myſteries of our Craft, being perſuaded that the wiſdom and grace, with which Heaven has endowed you, will ever *ſquare* all your thoughts, words and actions by the eternal laws of honor, equity and truth ; ſo as to promote the advancement of all good works, your own happineſs, and that of mankind. Permit us then, illuſtrious Brother, cordially to ſalute you, with *Three* times *Three*, and to add our fervent ſupplications, that the Sovereign Architect of the Univerſe may always en-*compaſs* you with his holy protection.

MOSES SEIXAS, *Maſter,* }
HENRY SHERBURNE,   } *Committee.*
By Order,   WILLIAM LITTLEFIELD, *Sec'ry.*
Newport, Auguſt 17, 1790.

———

TO THE MASTER, WARDENS *AND* BRETHREN *OF* KING-DAVID'S *LODGE, IN NEWPORT, RHODE-ISLAND.*
GENTLEMEN,

I RECEIVE the welcome which you give me to Rhode-Iſland with pleaſure—and I acknowledge my obligations for the flattering expreſſions of regard contained in your addreſs with grateful ſincerity.—Being perſuaded that a juſt application of the principles on which the Maſonic Fraternity is founded, muſt be promotive of private virtue and public proſperity, I ſhall always be happy to advance the intereſt of the Society, and to be confidered by them as a deſerving Brother.—My beſt wiſhes, Gentlemen, are offered for your individual happineſs.
GEORGE WASHINGTON.

PHILADELPHIA – 1790
PRESIDENT WASHINGTON RESPONDS
TO HEBREW CONGREGATION
Gazette of The United States, p. 596 (col 2–3)
September 15, 1790

ADDRESS
Of the HEBREW CONGREGATION in Newport, Rhode-Island.
To the PRESIDENT of the UNITED STATES of AMERICA,

SIR,

PERMIT the children of the stock of Abraham, to approach you, with the most cordial affection and esteem for your person and merit—and to join with our fellow citizens in welcoming you to Newport.

With pleasure we reflect on those days—those days of difficulty and danger, when the God of Israel, who delivered David from the peril of the sword, shielded your head in the day of battle ; and we rejoice to think, that the same spirit who rested in the bosom of the greatly beloved Daniel, enabling him to preside over the provinces of the Babylonish empire, rests, and ever will rest, upon you, enabling you to discharge the arduous duties of CHIEF MAGISTRATE in these States.

Deprived as we heretofore have been of the invaluable rights of free citizens, we now (with a deep sense of gratitude to the almighty disposer of all events) behold a government erected by the MAJESTY OF THE PEOPLE—a government, which to bigotry gives no sanction—to persecution no assistance ; but generously affording to ALL liberty of conscience, and immunities of citizenship: Deeming every one of whatever nation, tongue or language, equal parts of the great governmental machine. This so ample, and extensive federal union, whose base is philanthropy, mutual confidence, and public virtue, we cannot but acknowledge to be the work of the great God, who ruleth in the armies of heaven, and among the inhabitants of the earth, doing whatsoever seemeth to him good.

For all the blessings of civil and religious liberty, which we enjoy under an equal and benign administration, we desire to send up our thanks to the ancient of days, the great preserver of men, beseeching him that the Angel who conducted our forefathers through the wilderness into the promised land, may graciously conduct you thro all the difficulties and dangers of this mortal life —And when like Joshua, full of days and full of honors, you are gathered to your fathers, may you be admitted into the heavenly paradise, to partake of the water of life, and the tree of immortality.

Done and Signed by order of the Hebrew Congregation, in Newport, (Rhode-Island).
[Signed]   MOSES SEIXAS, Warden.
Newport, August 17, 1790.

This exchange of messages between President George Washington and Moses Seixas (see also pages 188–189), Warden of the Newport Hebrew Congregation, is considered the most treasured newspaper item of Judaica Americana, as well as a bedrock expression of national religious liberty. The phrase describing a government that "gives to bigotry no sanction, and to persecution no assistance," originally coined by Seixas in his moving, Biblically-toned greeting to the president, and repeated by Washington in his reply, is among the most cherished in the American historical vocabulary.

While various organizations and churches presented messages and greetings to the honored president, who would depart from Newport later that day, it was this poignant yet sentimental statement from Moses Seixas that became embedded in both American and Jewish history.

———

**ADDRESS Of the HEBREW CONGREGATION
in Newport, Rhode-Island
to the PRESIDENT of the UNITED STATES of
AMERICA,**

SIR,
Permit the children of the stock of Abraham to approach you with the most cordial affection and esteem for your person and merit – and to join with our fellow-citizens in welcoming you to Newport.

With pleasure we reflect on those days of difficulty and danger when the God of Israel, who delivered David from the peril of the sword, shielded your head in the day of battle and we rejoice to think that the same spirit that rested in the bosom of the greatly beloved Daniel, enabling him to preside over the provinces of the Babylonian Empire, rests and ever will rest upon you, enabling you to discharge the arduous task of the CHIEF MAGISTRATE of these States.

Deprived as we heretofore have been of the invaluable rights of free citizens, we now (with a deep sense of gratitude to the almighty dispenser of all events) behold a government erected by the MAJESTY OF THE PEOPLE a government which to bigotry gives no sanction – to persecution no assistance; but generously affording to ALL liberty of conscience, and immunities of citizenship: Deeming every one of whatever nation, tongue or language, equal parts of the great governmental machine. This so ample, and extensive federal union, whose base is philanthropy, mutual confidence and public virtue, we cannot but acknowledge to be the work of the great God, who ruleth in the armies of heavens, and among the inhabitants of the earth, doing whatsoever seemeth to Him good.

For all the blessings of civil and religious liberty, which we enjoy under an equal and benign administration, we desire to send up our thanks to the ancient of days, the great preserver of men, beseeching Him that the Angel who conducted our forefathers through the wilderness into the promised land, may graciously conduct you thro all the difficulties and dangers of this mortal life – And when like Joshua, full of days and full of honors, you are gathered to your fathers, may you be admitted into the heavenly paradise, to partake of the water of life, and the tree of immortality.

Done and signed by order of the Hebrew Congregation in Newport (Rhode-Island).

[Signed]   MOSES SEIXAS, Warden

Newport, August 17, 1790.

———

To the HEBREW CONGREGATION in Newport, Rhode Island,

GENTLEMEN,

While I received with much satisfaction your Address, replete with expressions of esteem, I rejoice in the opportunity of assuring you, that, I shall always retain grateful remembrance of the cordial welcome I experienced in my visit to Newport, from all classes of citizens. The reflection of the days of difficulty and danger which are past, is rendered the more sweet from a consciousness that they are succeeded by days of uncommon prosperity and security.

If we have the wisdom to make the best use of the advantages with which we are now favored, we cannot fail, under the just administration of a good government, to become a great and happy people.

The citizens of the United States of America, have a right to applaud themselves for having given to mankind examples of an enlarged and liberal policy: A policy worthy of imitation. – All possess a like liberty of conscience, and immunities of citizenship. It is now no more that toleration is spoken of, as if it was the indulgence of one class of people, that another enjoyed the exercise of their inherent natural right. For happily the government of the United States, which gives to bigotry no sanction, to persecution no assistance, requires only that they who live under its protection, should demean themselves as good citizens in giving it on all occasions their effectual support.

It would be inconsistent with the frankness of my character not to avow that I am pleased with your favorable opinion of my administration, and fervent wishes for my felicity. May the children of the stock of Abraham, who dwell in this land, continue to merit and enjoy the good will of the other inhabitants – while every one shall sit in safety under his own vine and fig tree, and there shall be none to make him afraid.

May the Father of all mercies scatter light, and not darkness, in our paths, and make us all in our several vocations useful here, and in His own due time and way everlastingly happy.

(Signed)   G. WASHINGTON

To the HEBREW CONGREGATION, in Newport, Rhode Island,

GENTLEMEN,

WHILE I receive with much satisfaction your Address, replete with expressions of affection and esteem, I rejoice in the opportunity of assuring you, that, I shall always retain a grateful remembrance of the cordial welcome I experienced in my visit to Newport, from all classes of citizens. The reflection on the days of difficulty and danger which are past, is rendered the more sweet from a consciousness that they are succeeded by days of uncommon prosperity and security.

If we have wisdom to make the best use of the advantages with which we are now favored, we cannot fail, under the just administration of a good government, to become a great and a happy people.

The citizens of the United States of America, have a right to applaud themselves for having given to mankind examples of an enlarged and liberal policy : A policy worthy of imitation. All possess a like liberty of conscience, and immunities of citizenship. It is now no more that toleration is spoken of, as if it was by the indulgence of one class of people, that another enjoyed the exercise of their inherent natural rights. For happily the government of the United States, which gives to bigotry no sanction, to persecution no assistance, requires only that they who live under its protection, should demean themselves as good citizens in giving it on all occasions their effectual support.

It would be inconsistent with the frankness of my character not to avow that I am pleased with your favorable opinion of my administration, and fervent wishes for my felicity. May the children of the stock of Abraham, who dwell in this land, continue to merit and enjoy the good will of the other inhabitants—while every one shall sit in safety under his own vine and figtree, and there shall be none to make him afraid.

May the Father of all Mercies scatter light, and not darkness, in our paths, and make us all in our several vocations useful here, and in his own due time and way everlastingly happy.

(Signed)   G. WASHINGTON.

[—673—]

Gazette of the United States.

PUBLISHED WEDNESDAYS AND SATURDAYS BY *JOHN FENNO*, No. 69, *MARKET-STREET*, BETWEEN *SECOND* AND *THIRD STREETS*, PHILADELPHIA.

[No. 67, of Vol. II.] SATURDAY, DECEMBER 18, 1790. [Whole No. 171.]

The Addreſs of the Hebrew Congregations in the cities of Philadelphia New-York, Charleſton, and Richmond.

TO THE PRESIDENT OF THE UNITED STATES.

SIR,

IT is reſerved for you to unite in affection for your character and perſon, every political and religious denomination of men; and in this will the Hebrew Congregations aforeſaid yield to no claſs of their fellow-citizens.

We have been hitherto prevented by various circumſtances peculiar to our ſituation, from adding our congratulation to thoſe which the reſt of America have offered on your elevation to the Chair of the federal government: Deign, then, illuſtrious Sir, to accept this our homage.

The wonders which the Lord of Hoſts hath worked in the days of our forefathers, have taught us to obſerve the greatneſs of his wiſdom and his might, throughout the events of the late glorious revolution; and while we humble ourſelves at his footſtool in thanſgiving and praiſe for the bleſſing of his deliverance, we acknowledge you the Leader of the American Armies, as his choſen and beloved ſervant. But not to your ſword alone is our preſent happineſs to be aſcribed: that, indeed, opened the way to the reign of freedom; but never was it perfectly ſecure, till your hand gave birth to the federal conſtitution;—and you renounced the joys of retirement, to ſeal by your adminiſtration in peace what you had atchieved in war.

To the eternal God who is thy refuge, we commit in our prayer the care of thy precious life; and when full of years thou ſhalt be gathered unto the people, thy righteouſneſs ſhall go before thee, and we ſhall remember, amidſt our regret, "that the Lord hath ſet apart the Godly for himſelf," whilſt thy name and thy virtues will remain an indelible memorial on our minds.

MANUEL JOSEPHSON,

For and in behalf and under the authority of the ſeveral Congregations aforeſaid.

Philadelphia, 13th Dec. 1790.

To which the Preſident was pleaſed to return the following anſwer.

TO THE HEBREW CONGREGATIONS,

In the city of Philadelphia, New-York, Charleſton and Richmond:

GENTLEMEN,

THE liberality of ſentiment towards each other which marks every political and religious denomination of men in this country, ſtands unparalleled in the Hiſtory of Nations.

The affection of ſuch a people, is a treaſure beyond the reach of calculation; and the repeated proofs which my fellow-citizens have given of their attachment to me and approbation of my doings, form the pureſt ſource of my temporal felicity. The affectionate expreſſions of your addreſs, again excite my gratitude, and receive my warmeſt acknowledgment.

The power and goodneſs of the Almighty were ſtrongly manifeſted in the events of our late glorious revolution; and his kind interpoſition in our behalf, has been no leſs viſible in the eſtabliſhment of our preſent equal government. In war he directed the ſword; and in peace he has ruled in our councils. My agency in both has been guided by the beſt intentions, and a ſenſe of the duty which I owe my country.

And as my exertions have hitherto been amply rewarded by the approbation of my fellow-citizens, I ſhall endeavor to deſerve a continuance of it by my future conduct.

May the ſame temporal and eternal bleſſings which you implore for me, reſt upon your congregations.

G. WASHINGTON.

THE Secretary of the Treaſury in his report of ways and means for paying the intereſt which will accrue on the State debts aſſumed, and for a deficiency in a former eſtimate,

		Dollars	
States the amount aſſumed at	- -	21,500,000	
The annual intereſt thereon	- - -	788,333	33
Eſtimated deficiency of the funds already eſtabliſhed for paying the intereſt on the original debt of the United States,	-	38,291	40
Amount wanted,	- Dols.	826,624	73

to raiſe which ſum he propoſes that Congreſs lay additional duties on foreign imported ſpirits, ſo that the amount to be impoſed with what is already impoſed by law (to take place on the 1ſt of January next) may make the amount of the duty propoſed in the draft of a bill accompanying his report to Congreſs on the 9th of January laſt; and to lay the duties propoſed in ſaid bill on ſpirits diſtilled in the United States from foreign materials, and from materials of the United States.

The probable product whereof he eſtimates as follows:

4,000,000 gallons, foreign imported ſpirits at 8 cents,	320,000
3,500,000 gallons diſtilled from foreign materials in the United States at 11 cents, - -	385,000
3,000,000 gallons diſtilled in the United States from their own materials at 9 cents, - -	270,000
	975,000
Deduct drawbacks and expence of collection 10 pr. cent. - - - -	97,500
Net product, - Dols.	877,500
which leaves an overplus of -	50,875 17 cents.

[*The ingenuity and animation of the following paragraphs, from Mr. Bailey's Freeman's Journal, of laſt Wedneſday, muſt inſpire correſponding ideas in every patriotic mind.*]

A PERIOD now commences, ſays a correſpondant, from which future ages ſhall derive new energy given to a republican ſyſtem, whilſt private and public property ſhall be equally ſecured; the power of our rulers, elected by ourſelves, enforced by due laws; morality reſpected, and religion revered. Already that form of government, approved of on mature deliberation, by a vaſt majority of the inhabitants of FREE AMERICA, is in motion. It revolves, through the atmoſphere of reaſon, on the axis of virtue. *Wealth*, whether derived from induſtry or inheritance; *induſtry*, which promiſes to her advocates acceſſion of riches, increaſe of conſequence, and it is hoped, an augmentation of happineſs; the weakneſs of age and the ardor of youth, equally look forward to an æra, merited by patriotiſm, under the guidance of providence.

Whilſt many nations, which lately were deemed highly civilized, becauſe they exhibited the gloſs of faſhion, or boaſted the pomp of luxury, are ſtruggling for a recovery of thoſe rights, which they tamely or ignorantly ſurrendered to one or more tyrants: the United American States have eſtabliſhed a form of rule, which ought rather to be imitated, than envied, by foreign countries.

France has fully caught the ſacred flame: Spain begins to think, that men poſſeſs, or ought to poſſeſs, inherent, unalienable rights; and every other region of the civilized world will follow the example of *Independent America*, (no part of which was known to Europe, or the other two quarters of the globe, 'till about three centuries ago) by liſtening to the dictates of freedom; by recovering, or confirming their rights; by revering their preſent or future WASHINGTONS; and by evincing, that the world will be more worthy of happineſs, when men ſhall truly acknowledge the powers of the OMNIPOTENT, whoſe ſervice is perfect freedom.

But *Waſhington* appears in our great national council—his voice is heard— divoice, which gave vigor to war, gives anim chto peace. He looks—and diſſention is hu thHe ſpeaks— returns on the , a of a cherub. and others th heard, felt, nts, ackn ge, that, al- th idwarded even in odrer homage, than hia, on the eighth day ſeventeen hundred and n

Further Particulars ARMAR's *Expedition ag ans.*

Extract of a letter fro War to the Preſid- ates.

"Lieuten rbally, that after he left F in Kentucky ſeveral men ict, who had been Major Hamtranck a ed a ſeparat

"The fa that Major of the hoſtile riſon and had return ny op cennes, wit out ha et a to poſt e the honor be,

With the higheſt ref SIR,

Your moſt obedi t ſer ant,

H. KNOX, ecretary of War.

The Preſident of the United States

EXTRACT from O

Note. The orders iſſued the march of the troops and militia aſhington, and until they arrived at the Miami Village, relate to the arrangement of the troops, the order of march, of encampment and of battle and the diſcipline neceſſary to be obſerved, all on which are particularly detailed.

GENERAL ORDERS.

Camp of the Miami Village about 170 miles from Fort Waſhington, October 17, 1790.

The General is highly pleaſed with the zeal and alacrity ſhewn by the army (particularly the corps which was detatched under the command of Col Hardin) to come up with the Savages, altho it was impracticable, as they had evacuated their favorite towns, before the light corps could poſſibly reach them.

Leaving behind them ſuch a vaſt quantity of corn and vegetables is a certain ſign that they decamped in the utmoſt conſternation, and dare not face the army.

The army is to remain in its preſent poſition until further orders; in the mean time, Quarter-Maſter Pratt is to have the corn brought in and depoſited in one place, or in as many houſes as he can find, and a guard is to be placed over it for its ſecurity. He will receive directions how it is to be diſtributed.

The ſuperintendant of the horſe department (Mr. Caldwell) is to be reſponſible that his pack-ſaddles are repaired, and put in as good order as poſſible, ready for the next movement of the army.

The General calls upon the commanding officers of battalions not to ſuffer the men to ſtraggle from the encampment, otherwiſe they will certainly ſtand in danger of being ſcalped.

The guards are to be extremely vigilant, to which the field officer of the day is to pay the moſt pointed attention.

A detachment under the command of Lt. Col. Commandant Trotter, conſiſting of

Federal Troops	30
Major Fontaine's light horſe	40
Active riflemen	230
Total	300

are to march to-morrow early.

Lieutenant Colonel Commandant Trotter will receive his orders from the General.

JOS. HARMAR, Brig. Gen.

(To be continued.)

NATIONAL ASSEMBLY.

AUGUST 5th, 1790.

M. Barrere in behalf of the committee of domaines, on the motion of M. Marſanne Fonjulianne.

Your committee of domaines has been inſtructed to preſent to you their opinion on the ſuppreſſion of the *Droit d'Aubaine*. This tax originated at a time when there was no communication among people; it belonged to the King, to the revenue, to the nation, who ſucceeded to the foreigner not naturalized, to the foreigner naturalized when he died inteſtate, and to the native, who in quitting France, had abandoned his country. In conſidering this tax with relation to the conſtitution and to legiſlation, your principles and your decrees have already determined, under the report of fiſcality, that it did not preſent great advantages, as its produce amounted not quite to 40,000 livres. The committee have charged me to preſent to you the following project of a decree.—

The National Aſſembly, after having heard their committee of domaines, conceive that the *Droit d'Aubaine* is contrary to thoſe principles of brotherly love which ſhould connect all men of whatever country or government; that this tax, eſtabliſhed in times of barbarity, ought to be aboliſhed by a people, who have founded their conſtitution agreeable to the rights of man and of the citizen; and that France, being free, ſhould open its boſom to all the people of the earth, by inviting them to enjoy under a free government, the ſacred and unalienable rights of humanity; has decreed, and does hereby decree as follows.—

1ſt. The *Droit d'Aubaine* and that of *Detraction* are aboliſhed forever.

2d. All proceedings, proſecutions and inquiſitions which have theſe taxes for their object, are quaſhed.

This project of a decree was unanimouſly adopted and without diſcuſſion.

Sept. 26. Only 505 Members were preſent, not nearly half of thoſe who compoſe the Aſſembly.

M. Emmery was elected Preſident. He then formed the Aſſembly, that M. Cernon, in the name of the Committee, of Finance wiſhed to make his report on the Exigencies of the ſtate.

He was, conſequently, introduced, and delivered an account of the actual ſtate of the Treaſury.

M. Freteau wiſhed to know what was become of the money which was coined laſt year, and of the patriotic donations? This queſtion induced M. Mirabeau, to make a long harangue on the defects, and abuſes which ſhamefully exiſt in this momentary ſyſtem. He affirmed, that they were ſo dangerous to the public proſperity, that their crowns and louis are ſure to be ſweated on account of the enormous profit which is the conſequence. He put the Aſſembly in mind of an aſſertion which he had made on a former occaſion, that every piece of plate ſent to the Mint, was to be conſidered as an ingot ſent to London.

Ordered, that the Caiſſe d'Eſcompte furniſh the Treaſury with 10 millions of livres.

BOSTON, Dec. 4.

The demand for the produce of our country is rapidly increaſing. To ſhew, in part, the extent of this great ſource of national Wealth, we mention, it as a fact, that one houſe in an adjacent town, has exported and ſold, the late ſeaſon, 2000 barrels Pot and Pearl-Aſhes—2000 barrels Beef—500 barrels Pork—70,000 weight of Butter—1500 buſhels Peas and Beans, beſides other produce. The quantity of beef annually, exported from this State, is upwards of 45,000 barrels—of which JONATHAN WINSHIP, Eſq. of Little-Cambridge, (whoſe beef is ſo highly valued in foreign parts) annually puts up 5000 barrels.

PHILADELPHIA – 1790
"TO THE PRESIDENT…"
Gazette of the United States,
p. 1 (col 1)
December 18, 1790

The first recorded prayer in Hebrew and English for the United States and "His Excellency George Washington, Captain, General and Commander in Chief of the Federal Army of these States" was read by the Reverend Gershom Mendes Seixas at the Consecration Service of the new synagogue of Mikveh Israel in Philadelphia on April 3, 1782. Upon Washington's assuming the post of President of the new republic, he was the recipient of messages of adulation and hope from the various small Hebrew congregations in the nation.

The first Jewish community to address the newly elected George Washington was Savannah, Georgia, followed fifteen months later by Newport, Rhode Island, shortly after the state ratified the constitution. Four months later, on December 13, 1790, Manuel Josephson, president of Philadelphia's Congregation Mikveh Israel, wrote Washington on behalf of his congregation and the Hebrew Congregations of New York, Charleston and Richmond.

Josephson began his letter,

It is reserved for you to unite in affection for your character and person, every political and religious denomination of men...

Washington's response began,

The liberality of sentiment toward each other which marks every political and religious denomination of men in this country, stands unparalleled in the History of Nations....

The Addrefs of the Hebrew Congregations in the cities of Philadelphia New-York, Charlefton, and Richmond.

TO THE PRESIDENT OF THE UNITED STATES.

SIR,

IT is referved for you to unite in affection for your character and perfon, every political and religious denomination of men; and in this will the Hebrew Congregations aforefaid yield to no clafs of their fellow-citizens.

We have been hitherto prevented by various circumftances peculiar to our fituation, from adding our congratulation to thofe which the reft of America have offered on your elevation to the Chair of the federal government: Deign, then, illuftrious Sir, to accept this our homage.

The wonders which the Lord of Hofts hath worked in the days of our forefathers, have taught us to obferve the greatnefs of his wifdom and his might, throughout the events of the late glorious revolution; and while we humble ourfelves at his footftool in thanfgiving and praife for the blefling of his deliverance, we acknowledge you the Leader of the American Armies, as his chofen and beloved fervant. But not to your fword alone is our prefent happinefs to be afcribed: that, indeed, opened the way to the reign of freedom; but never was it perfectly fecure, till your hand gave birth to the federal conftitution;—and you renounced the joys of retirement, to feal by your adminiftration in peace what you had atchieved in war.

To the eternal God who is thy refuge, we commit in our prayer the care of thy precious life; and when full of years thou fhalt be gathered unto the people, thy righteoufnefs fhall go before thee, and we fhall remember, amidft our regret, "that the Lord hath fet apart the Godly for himfelf," whilft thy name and thy virtues will remain an indelible memorial on our minds.

MANUEL JOSEPHSON,

For and in behalf and under the authority of the feveral Congregations aforefaid.

Philadelphia, 13th Dec. 1790.

To which the Prefident was pleafed to return the following anfwer.

TO THE HEBREW CONGREGATIONS,

In the city of Philadelphia, New-York, Charlefton and Richmond:

GENTLEMEN,

THE liberality of fentiment towards each other which marks every political and religious denomination of men in this country, ftands unparalleled in the Hiftory of Nations.

The affection of fuch a people, is a treafure beyond the reach of calculation; and the repeated proofs which my fellow-citizens have given of their attachment to me and approbation of my doings, form the pureft fource of my temporal felicity. The affectionate expreffions of your addrefs, again excite my gratitude, and receive my warmeft acknowledgment.

The power and goodnefs of the Almighty were ftrongly manifefted in the events of our late glorious revolution; and his kind interpofition in our behalf, has been no lefs vifible in the eftablifhment of our prefent equal government. In war he directed the fword; and in peace he has ruled in our councils. My agency in both has been guided by the beft intentions, and a fenfe of the duty which I owe my country.

And as my exertions have hitherto been amply rewarded by the approbation of my fellow-citizens, I fhall endeavor to deferve a continuance of it by my future conduct.

May the fame temporal and eternal bleffings which you implore for me, reft upon your congregations.

G. WASHINGTON.

Supplement to the Columbian, July 3, 1812.

NEW YORK – 1812
"NEW ARMY LIST" FOR WAR OF 1812 INCLUDES JEWISH SURGEON
Supplement to the Columbian
July 3, 1812

Jacob de la Motta (b. Savannah, GA, 1789; d. Charleston, SC, 1845), at age 23, was the highest ranking Jewish medical figure in the military in the early years of the republic. Originally an attending physician at the Charleston Dispensary, he served as an army surgeon during the War of 1812. Later, he returned to Charleston, continued his medical career, and in 1824 was elected as secretary of the Charleston Medical Society. His medical prowess was internationally recognized when he was elected a corresponding member of the Royal Academy of Medicine at Paris in 1836.

Active in Jewish communal affairs, de la Motta helped organize Savannah's Congregation Mikveh Israel and served as its unpaid minister for a number of years. The address he delivered at the synagogue's consecration in 1820 elicited grateful comments from both Jefferson and Madison. Four years earlier he had given a eulogy, later published in pamphlet form, at the funeral service of Rev. Gershom Mendes Seixas of New York City's Congregation Shearith Israel.

In this "New Army List" of the American military in the War of 1812, "Jacob De Lamotte" is listed as the "Artillery, Second Regiment … Surgeon."

NEW ARMY LIST.
[From the National Intelligencer]

The following is an essay towards the formation of a Register of the Additional Army of the United States. The arrangement is only provisional and incomplete. Transfers will reduce the supernumeraries.

Major Generals.
Henry Dearborn — Thos. Pinckney

Brigadier Generals.
Joseph Bloomfield — William Polk
James Winchester — William Hull

Quarter-Master General.
Morgan Lewis.

Deputy Quarter Master.
Bartholomew Shaumburg

Hospital Surgeons
Garret E. Pendergast — David C. Kerr
James Mann

ARTILLERY, SECOND REGIMENT.
Colonel.
George Izard.
Majors.
George C. Mitchell — William Lindsay
Surgeon.   *Surgeon's Mate.*
Jacob De Lamotte — William Southall

Captains
Jesse Robinson — John Goodall
Jacob B. I'On — George W. Russel
Lobert M. Gill — Spottswood Henry
Isaac T. Avery — Joseph Stanford
Philemon Hawkins, jun. — Nathan Towson
Samuel B. Archer — Chs. M. Anderson
John Ritchie — Joseph Phillips

First Lieutenants
Henry Slaughter — Harold Smyth
Lowndes Brown — Thos. M. Randolph, Jr.
Adrian Niel — James G. M'Dowell
Wm. J. Cowan — Jonathan Kearsley
Robert R. Ruffin — Henry K. Craig
Jas. H. Deering — Joseph H. Larwell
John S. Peyton — Peter Parsons
John Fontaine. — John Nevill

Second Lieutenants.
Montgomery Newman — Joseph Hook
Thomas Winn — Robert Stewart
Jacob Warley — Lewis Morgan
Edwin Sharpe — Isaac Davis, Jun.
John Ruffin — James H. Gamble
William Tyler — Alexander A. Meek
John W. Kincaid

BALTIMORE – 1819
JEFFERSON, ADAMS AND MADISON ADDRESS THE "JEW BILL"

Niles' Weekly Register, Supplement to Vol. XV, p. 10
February 20, 1819

In 1776, Maryland's constitution safely protected "all persons professing the Christian religion" yet held no protection for those of other beliefs. In Maryland, unlike any of the other original states, a Jew could not hold any office, civil or military. In 1797, prominent Jews petitioned the Maryland Assembly to rectify this prejudicial issue. Though well received, the petition was rejected. Year after year, as the petition was presented and rejected, new advocates – including several influential and prominent Gentiles – were enlisted. In 1818, Judge H. M. Breckenridge and others introduced legislation, known as the "Jew Bill," to end this discriminatory practice. Despite a vigorous campaign, it would be 1825 before the bill was enfranchised, and another year until it was confirmed.

The full article, on pages 9–13, describes the legislation as "an Act to extend to the sect of people professing the Jewish religion, the same rights and privileges that are enjoyed by Christians." It presents the background and reports on the votes in the legislature as of that time. Of particular significance are letters of support written in 1818 by Thomas Jefferson, John Adams and James Madison.

Jefferson's letter begins, "Your sect, by its sufferings, has furnished a remarkable proof of the universal spirit of religious intolerance ...."

Adams writes, "I wish your nation may be admitted to all the privileges of citizens, in every country of the world...."

Madison opens his letter stating, "Having ever regarded the freedom of religious opinions, and worshippers, equally, belonging to every sect, and the secure enjoyment of it as the best human provision for bringing all into the same way of thinking...." He ends his letter stating, "I observe with pleasure, the view you give of the spirit in which your sect, partake of the common blessings, afforded by our government and laws."

The editor of the National Advocate, at New-York, Mr. Noah, a very intelligent gentleman, and himself a Jew, after making such remarks upon the proceedings of the legislature of Maryland as the case properly warrants, introduces the following letters, on which it is not needful to make a comment:

Extract of a letter from Thomas Jefferson, dated
MONTICELLO, MAY 28, 1818

"Your sect, by its sufferings, has furnished a remarkable proof of the universal spirit of religious intolerance inherent in every sect, disclaimed by all while feeble, and practised by all when in power. Our laws have applied the only antidote to this vice, protecting our religious as they do our civil rights, by putting all on an equal footing.— But more remains to be done—for although we are free by the law, we are not so in practice. Public opinion erects itself into an inquisition, and exercises its office with as much fanaticism as fans the flames of an auto da fe. The prejudice still scowling on your sect of our religion, although the elder one, cannot be unfelt by yourselves. It is to be hoped that individual dispositions will, at length, mould themselves to the model of the law, and consider the moral basis on which our religion rest, as the rallying point which unites them in common interest, while the peculiar dogmas branching from it are the exclusive concern of the respective sects embracing them, and no rightful subject of notice to any other. Public opinion needs reformation on this point, which would have the further effect of doing away the hypocritical maxim of "intus ut lobet, foris ut moris." Nothing, I think, would be so likely to effect this, as to your sect particularly, as the more careful attention to education, which you recommend; and which, placing its members on the equal and commanding benches of science, will exhibit them as equal objects of respect and power."

Extract of a letter from John Adams, dated
QUINCY, JULY 31, 1818.

"You have not extended your ideas of the rights of private judgment and the liberty of conscience both in religion and philosophy, further than I do. Mine are limited only by morals and propriety.

I have had occasion to be acquainted with several gentlemen of your nation, and to transact business with some of them, whom I found to be men of liberal minds, as much honor, probity, generosity, and good breeding, as any I have known in any sect of religion or philosophy.

I wish your nation may be admitted to all the privileges of citizens, in every country of the world. This country has done much, I wish it may do more; and annul every narrow idea in religion, government and commerce.

Let the wits joke; the philosopher sneer! What then! It has pleased the Providence of the "FIRST CAUSE," the Universal Cause, that Abraham should give religion, not only to Hebrews, but to Christians and Mahometans, the greatest part of the modern civilized world!!

Extract of a letter from James Madison, dated
MONTPELIER, MAY 15, 1818.

"Having ever regarded the freedom of religious opinions, and worshippers, equally, belonging to every sect, and the secure enjoyment of it as the best human provision for bringing all into the same way of thinking, or into that mutual charity which is the only proper substitute; I observe with pleasure, the view you give of the spirit in which your sect, partake of the common blessings, afforded by our government and laws."

Religious Liberty.

We are politely favored with the following sketches of Mr. H. M. BRACKENRIDGE's excellent speech in the house of delegates of the state of Maryland...

MR. SPEAKER.—Could I, for a moment, suppose it possible for the bill on your table to lessen, in the slightest degree, the attachment we all profess for our holy religion...

The subject, although of the most fruitful nature, properly resolves itself into three questions. Are the Jews entitled to be placed on a footing with other citizens? Is there any powerful reason, or state policy, compelling us to make an exception unfavorable to them? Is there any thing incompatible with the respect we owe to the Christian religion, in allowing them a participation in civil offices or employments?

But it may be said, that no *force*, or coercion, is resorted to by the state of Maryland, to produce a conformity of belief; that each one is secure in his civil rights, no matter what may be his mode of faith; that no one can be molested on account of his religious opinion; that no one has a right to complain of being excluded from office, if he does not conform to the prevailing religious sentiments of the country. Sir, I contend, that in conformity to the reasons I have advanced, *every* citizen is entitled to *all* the privileges of citizenship; that the religious opinion of no one can be justly visited upon him, either directly or indirectly, as the immediate effect or the consequence of that opinion. If in consequence of my religious belief, I am subjected to disqualifications, while in other respects on a perfect equality with my fellow citizens; while there exists no reasons founded upon the well-being of society, to exclude me from these common benefits, I cannot but consider myself a persecuted man. The persecution is slight I own, but still it is persecution....

the merit of originality in expressing these sentiments. They are those of every American statesman; there is scarcely a distinguished man of our country who has not in some mode or other given them his approbation. They may be regarded as the received and established political doctrines of our country.... Religious institutions, must subscribe to the proposition, that religion is a matter between man and his God, that the temporal arm should be interposed to direct the *actions* of men, and not their *thoughts*. I will take the liberty of reading some passages from different authors of this country who have expressed these ideas in language much stronger than mine: [here Mr. Brackenridge read several passages from Mr. Madison's celebrated memorial on the test laws of Virginia...   boldly declaring the *truth* to his countrymen. That truth has triumphed over bigotry and prejudice; it has planted its victorious standard on that noble monument, the federal constitution—it has prevailed in every state, unless indeed its enemy, driven from every member of the confederacy, *should have found a last intrenchment in the constitution of Maryland;* which God forbid.

I have thus far considered rather what ought to be the right of the citizen, than what it really is, as guaranteed by the charter of his liberties. And here I do not hesitate to assert, that could this question be brought before some tribunal competent to decide, I would undertake to prove, that the right which this bill professes to give is already *secured* by our great national compact, I would boldly contend, that the state of Maryland has deprived, and still continues to deprive, American citizens of their just political rights....

The man who cannot hold the most trifling office in the state of Maryland, may be chosen to preside over its destinies, as a member of the confederacy, he may command your armies and lead you to battle, against the enemy who dares to invade your shores; yet he cannot be an ensign, or lieutenant of a company. He may sit upon the bench, and in the federal courts be called to decide upon the fortune, or the life of the citizen of Maryland; yet he cannot be a justice of the peace, to decide the most trifling controversy. He may be a juror in the circuit court of the United States, and be the arbiter of the fortunes and liberties of the first among you, and yet he cannot sit in the same box, to deal out the measure of justice to the pilfering slave. He may be marshal of the district, and in that capacity entrusted with the most important concerns, at the same time that he is disqualified from performing the duties of a constable! Can it be possible that a discrepancy so monstrous between the general and state governments should not have been perceived, when every part of the system was so admirably attuned to move in unison and harmony? ...

I have had the honor of being acquainted with a number of American Jews, and I have no hesitation in saying, that I have found the same proportion of estimable individuals as in any other class. None, sir, are more zealously attached to the interests and happiness of our common country; the more so, as it is the only one on earth they are permitted to call theirs. None have more gallantly and devotedly espoused its cause, both in the late and revolutionary war; none feel a livelier sense of gratitude and affection for the mild and liberal institutions of this country, which not only allows them publicly and freely the enjoyment and exercise of their religion, but also, with the exception of Maryland, has done away all odious political and civil discriminations. In the city which I have the honor to represent, there are Jewish families who, in point of respectability and worth, are inferior to none; who are known only as differing from the Christian in their religious tenets; who are educated in the same schools with our youth, and like them, *glory in being Americans and freemen.* ...   I content myself with calling your attention to what has been the effects, in this country, of leaving religion to be taught from the pulpit, or instilled by early education. Is there less genuine religion in this country than in any other? For if the interference of government be necessary to support it, such ought to be the natural consequence....

Were we about to attempt the conversion of the Jews to Christianity, the true mode would be to treat them with kindness, and to allow them a full participation in every thing our country affords....

Some reasons have been urged against the passage of this bill, whose force I must own myself unable to comprehend. We are told, that it will hold out inducements to the Jews to migrate to this country from abroad. Without stopping to enquire whether this would be an evil, I shall simply reply that this inducement already exists. If it can seriously be supposed, that *the prospect of obtaining offices* would invite the Jews to this country, has not this invitation been already given by the constitution of the union, as well as of the neighboring states? It has been objected on the other hand, that the number of Jews in this country is but small; that to alter the constitution for these, would be carrying liberality too far. Sir, I think very differently on this subject. If but *one* American citizen be deprived of his just *rights*, and it be in our power to redress them, it is our duty to do so, either by our own act, or by devising other suitable means. It has been repeated that there is no _____ As far as epithets can shew the extent of this bigotry and prejudice, the unfortunate *heretics* are in a situation little better than the unfortunate Jews. This is not the spirit of Christianity. If man errs in his belief is there no judge? There is, and that Judge has emphatically declared to men, "judge not, lest ye be judged."…

… _____ No sir, although the Jews are silent on this occasion, they are far from being insensible. They look to the decision of this house with the deepest interest, as one, that will restore them to their just rank under the constitution, that they are so fully entitled to claim, by every reason of sound policy, as well as by the constitution of the union. It is but a few days since I read an account, in one of the newspapers of Baltimore, of a public examination at the principal seminary of learning in that place. To the son of a Jew, little more than twelve years of age, was awarded the first prize, in every branch of education; and to crown all, he was declared to have surpassed his companions in good conduct and morality, as he had in superior endowments of mind! I own I feel a mortification when I refle… torious deportment of this youth, can lead him to none of the offices and honors of his native state. lieve this fact. The feeling I have for the honor of my country, for the character of this state, is a much more powerful motive for me, in voting for the passage of this bill, than the mere desire of doing justice to the Jews.… _____ I hope for the honor of the United States, and of the state of Maryland, the bill on your table will pass.

I defy any one to produce the dictum, or opinion, of any American statesman, whose opinion is worth citing, in favor of a religious test for political purposes; or the example of any state which has withheld from American citizens of the Jewish religion all eligibility to office.… _____ In every constitution formed since that of the United States, the test has been rejected; and by some it is even provided that none shall ever be required. Jews have been employed both under the state and general governments, in offices of the highest trust and honor.…

But this is a Christian land, and we are Christians! I rejoice that it is so; and I hope we will show ourselves worthy of the name, by acting with Christian spirit. The Great Author of our religion teaches us charity and forbearance to the errors and frailties of our fellow-men. He promised to his followers, not worldly benefits, but crowns of glory in heaven; he emphatically declared, *that his kingdom was not of this world.* Far from inculcating unkindness and resentment to those of the Jews who did not believe in him, he even forgave those among them who were his persecutors and enemies. Do we find any injunction bequeathed to his followers, to pursue his enemies with vengeance? No…

meriting the good will of his fellow-citizens. Until … _____ I dominions, and take their rank among the governments of the earth, THIS IS THEIR CHOSEN COUNTRY; here they can rest with the persecuted from every clime, secure in their persons and property, protected from tyranny and oppression, and participating of equal rights and immunities."

Sir, I have done. I trust I have satisfied every member of this house, of the justice of the positions I have undertaken to maintain. I hope we shall no longer persevere in withholding from the Jews privileges to which they are constitutionally entitled. The attempt to prove that there exists weighty reasons of state why they should not be allowed these privileges, appears to me futile. We run no risk in following the example of the enlightened framers of the federal compact, with the great Washington at their head.

Henry M. Brackenridge

BALTIMORE – 1819 "RELIGIOUS LIBERTY"
Niles' Weekly Register, pp. 226–33
May 29, 1819

Maryland's first Constitution, written in 1776, required all public servants to take a Christian oath. Such an oath not only applied to government officials, but also jurors, lawyers and militia officers. In 1818, Thomas Kennedy (b. Scotland, 1776; d. Maryland, 1832), a member of the Maryland House of Delegates; Col. William G. D. Worthington (b. 1785; d. 1856), who held several positions in city, state and federal government; and Judge Henry M. Brackenridge (b. 1786; d. 1871), a lawyer, journalist and politician, began an eight-year battle to overturn this undemocratic standard. This legislation, known as "The Jew Bill," was originally defeated in 1819, but became law in 1826.

Brackenridge's speech on "The Jew Bill" is considered one of the most powerful statements on Jewish civil liberties in American history. He asked, "Is there anything in the Jewish religious doctrine which disqualify the Jew from discharging the duties and fulfilling all the obligations of a citizen of Maryland?"

Excerpts of his speech – which filled more than 13 columns (almost 8 full pages) of the 9¾" by 6¼" publication – are included here.

NEW-ENGLAND GALAXY.

THE LIBERTY OF THE PRESS AND THE LIBERTIES OF THE PEOPLE MUST STAND OR FALL TOGETHER.—HUME.

No 316.   FRIDAY, OCTOBER 31, 1823.   VOL. VI.

BOSTON – 1823
"THE JEW BILL"
New-England Galaxy, p. 3 (col 3)
October 31, 1823

"The Jew Bill" discusses the fate of legislation in Maryland which would permit Jews to hold public office. Thus far, Jews were not allowed to do so, but the Maryland legislature had approved the "Jew Bill," a measure which would eliminate that restriction.

According to Maryland state law, a second passage of the bill would be necessary in order to make the change final. Ironically, as this article points out, under United States national law, a Jew would be permitted to be elected to the Presidency, while being denied the right to hold public office in Maryland.

The author asks the people of Maryland to follow the spirit of "liberality" rather than "fanatical" zeal and to support the revision. The article criticized the "hypocrisy" of "would-be Christians" who reject the message of "brotherly love" preached by the Savior.

THE JEW BILL.

" In our sister state of Maryland (says the United States Gazette) the bill bearing the above title is very well known—it passed both houses of the Legislature at the last session, but requires the sanction of the next before it can go into operation. It has for its object the abolishing of an odious feature in the statutes of Maryland, in consequence of which a *Jew* is incapable of holding even the office of Constable, although the same voters in whose community he cannot be Constable, have a right, by the Constitution of the United States, to vote for him as President ! For many years the liberal and enlightened citizens of Maryland exerted themselves for a repeal of this unchristian law, and at the last session the " Jew bill" was passed, to the great joy of those who prefer Christian liberality to fanatical folly, but previous to the late election for delegates, which took place a few weeks ago, a number of would-be Christians openly denounced the bill, and in some counties they even expected their candidates to pledge themselves that, in case of their election, they would vote against the confirmation of the law as it passed at the last session, and by that means continue to deny to the inoffensive Jew the same liberties which they themselves enjoy ! In Washington county, the tickets were headed " Jew bill ticket !" and " No Jew bill ticket !" To the astonishment of all enlightened men, the latter succeeded, by a vast majority although the former contained the best talents in the country. We congratulate the unsuccessful candidates on their firmness and independence, and we consider their remaining at home, in consequence of adhering to Christian principles, by far more creditable to their heads and hearts, than to represent a county which, by its vote, has declared its fondness for religious oppression.

We confess that we fear the bill will not be confirmed at the next session ; more time must be allowed for the operation of the spirit of *true* Christianity to enlighten the minds and better the hearts of sundry fanatics in Maryland, and particularly in the county alluded to, for whose vote on this occasion there is so much less apology, as it has every facility for education, and contains within its limits several eminent divines, of various persuasions, all of whom, we trust, inculcate the mild and holy doctrines of our Saviour, particularly those of *brotherly love*, of which he speaks so forcibly and eloquently.

Although this blot on the escutcheon of Maryland may remain for a while, yet we hesitate not to predict, that, ere long, it will be wiped away with scorn, and the maxim to " do unto others as you wish them to do unto you" will take the place of hypocrisy and intolerance.

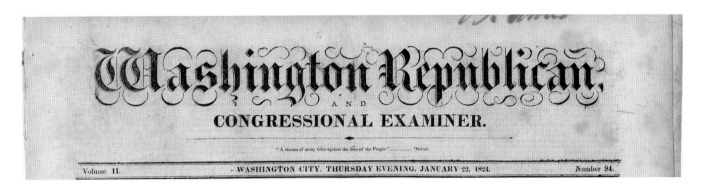

Washington Republican,
AND
CONGRESSIONAL EXAMINER.

"A stream of many tides against the foes of the People." .... *Indian.*

| Volume II. | WASHINGTON CITY, THURSDAY EVENING, JANUARY 22, 1824. | Number 94. |

CITY OF WASHINGTON – 1824
"THIS SPLENDID SCHEME…"
*Washington Republican and
Congressional Examiner, p. 4 (col 5)
January 22, 1824*

This 1824 advertisement for a "magnificent prize" of $100,000 – with only five drawings left "to complete this splendid theme" – invites ticket purchasers to patronize Cohen's Lottery and Exchange Office located on Market Street in Baltimore, Maryland.

The highly reputable lottery company had made history in 1821 when two of proprietor Jacob I. Cohen, Jr.'s brothers, managers of the company's Norfolk, VA office, appealed their conviction for the crime of selling National Lottery tickets in Virginia. Their appeal to the U.S. Supreme Court, Cohens vs Virginia – 19 US 264, led to a major decision regarding the U.S. Court's right to review state courts' decisions in certain criminal cases.

One Hundred Thousand Dollars.
THIS MAGNIFICENT PRIZE

IS still undrawn in the *Grand State Lottery,* besides others of 20,000—2 of 10,000—1 of 5000 DOLLARS, &c. which are *NOW FLOATING.* The drawing will e continued on

Thursday after next,

Only FIVE drawings remain to complete this splendid scheme. Applications for tickets or shares should be made without delay.

| Whole Tickets, | $15 | Quarters, | $3 85 |
| Halves, | 7 50 | Eighths, | 1 87 |

To be had (warranted undrawn) at

C O H E N ' S
LOTTERY AND EXCHANGE OFFICE,
144, *Market Street, Baltimore,*

Where the great capital prize of BOTH the last lotteries were sold, and where MORE CAPITAL PRIZES HAVE BEEN SOLD THAN AT ANY OTHER OFFICE IN AMERICA.

Orders from any part of the United States, either by mail (post paid) or by private conveyance, enclosing the cash, or prizes in any of the Baltimore lotteries, will meet the same prompt and punctual attention as if on personal application, addressed to

Jan 9   J. I. COHEN, Jr. Baltimore.

At the time of the advertisement, Jacob I. Cohen, Jr. (b. 1789; d. 1869), proprietor, was just beginning what would prove to be an illustrious career in both public life and business. In addition to his successful lottery business, Cohen and his brothers established a bank in 1830 that was one of the few to survive the Panic of 1837. Two railroads chartered to link Baltimore with northeastern cities, of which Cohen had been a director for three years, merged into the Philadelphia, Wilmington and Baltimore Railroad just months after he took over as their president. And for twenty years Cohen served as president of the Baltimore Fire Insurance Company.

Cohen's political career is detailed in a "Baltimore – 1826" article on page 114.

214   NILES' REGISTER—NOV. 28, 1829—MISCELLANEOUS.

JERUSALEM. There is a report that the Rothschilds have purchased Jerusalem! We see nothing improbable that, in the pecuniary distress of the sultan, he should sell some part of his dominions to preserve the rest; or that the Rothschilds should purchase the ancient capital of their nation. They are wealthy beyond the desire, perhaps, even of avarice; and so situated, it is quite reasonable to suppose that they may seek something else to gratify their ambition, that shall produce most important effects. If secured in the possession, (and which may be brought about by *money*), they might instantly, as it were, gather a large nation together, soon to become capable of defending itself, and having a wonderful influence over the commerce and condition of the east—rendering Judea again the place of deposite of a large portion of the wealth of the "ancient world." To the sultan, the country is of no great value; but, in the hands of the Jews, directed by such men as the Rothschilds, what might it not become, and in a short period of time?

The sultan is in great difficulty—Baron Rotchschild was proceeding to Constantinople; and a second re-building of the temple is not among the most strange things expected in these strange times, by some of the Jews.

BALTIMORE – 1829
ROTHSCHILDS PURCHASE JERUSALEM
Niles' Weekly Register, p. 214
November 28, 1829

A report that the Rothschilds "have purchased Jerusalem" from the Sultan draws a highly positive reaction from this article's author. Given the great wealth of this banking family, notes the author, it is not surprising that they would engineer such a move.

The author furthers notes that as owners of Jerusalem, the Rothschilds might "gather a large nation together, soon to become capable of defending itself, and having a wonderful influence over the commerce and condition of the east—rendering Judea again the place of deposite of a large portion of the wealth of the 'ancient world.' To the sultan, the country is of no great value; but, in the hands of the Jews, directed by such men as the Rothschilds, what might it not become, and in a short period of time?"

This "report" the *Register* cited was clearly *not* based in fact; according to history, the Rothschilds had never purchased Jerusalem.

PHILADELPHIA/RICHMOND – 1840
"MEETING OF THE ISRAELITES."
United States Commercial & Statistical Register, p. 184
September 16, 1840

The Damascus blood libel of 1840 holds an important role in American Jewish political activism, marking the first time the American Jewish community organized itself politically to aid a threatened Diaspora community. In this accusation of blood libel in which the Damascus Jews were falsely accused of murdering a Christian monk, eight prominent Jews were arrested and tortured, some dying in jail and one forced to convert to Islam.

Western opinion at many levels protested these charges of ritual murder. The *London Times,* in a show of support, published a translation of the entire Passover *Haggadah,* the first time such a work was carried in an English language newspaper. Sir Moses Montefiore, backed by other Western leaders, led a delegation urging the Sultan of Egypt and Syria to call a halt to this blood libel campaign. Eventually, the remaining Jewish prisoners were released, and an edict was issued stopping these attacks.

In a groundbreaking move, the 15,000-member American Jewish community staged protests touching on the politics of foreign policy on behalf of their imprisoned Damascus brethren. Protests were held in six cities, including the one in Richmond cited here. For the first time an American president, Martin Van Buren, was petitioned to act on behalf of Jewry abroad and the American consul in Egypt filed an official protest.

According to Hasia R. Diner, *The Jews of the United States, 1654–2000* (Berkeley, 2004), "For the Jews, the Damascus affair launched modern Jewish politics on an international scale, and for American Jews it represented their first effort at creating a distinctive political agenda. Just as the United States had used this affair to [proclaim its presence on the global scale], so too did American Jews. in their newspapers and at mass meetings, announce to their coreligionists in France and England that they too ought to be thought of as players in global Jewish diplomacy."

Meeting of the Israelites.

Richmond, August 18, 1840.

At a Meeting of the Israelites of the State of Virginia, held in pursuance of public notice, on Sunday, the 16th inst., at the Hebrew Sunday School Room, in the city of Richmond, G. A. Myers was called to the chair, and J. Ezekiel appointed Secretary. The following Preamble and Resolutions were adopted:

Whereas, we have heard with deep felt sorrow of the persecution and sufferings of our oppressed brethren in Damascus and Rhodes, together with the foul charges alleged against the Tenets of our Holy Religion, and being desirous of uniting our efforts, with those of our brethren, and others already engaged in support and defence of the rights of humanity. Be it therefore—

Resolved, That the Israelites of the State of Virginia unite in sentiments of sorrow and sympathy, for the unparalleled cruelties and sufferings inflicted on their innocent and unoffending brethren of Rhodes and Damascus, as also in abhorrence of the foul aspersions and calumnies alleged against their Holy Religion, so utterly opposite to the sacred tenets they profess.

Resolved, That we view with feelings of grateful admiration, the laudable and liberal efforts made by our Christian brethren in union with our own, as evinced by a meeting held in the city of London on the 3d July last, for the purpose of obtaining redress, and preventing future aggressions.

Resolved, That the Israelites of Virginia will cordially unite with their brethren throughout the Union and elsewhere, in adopting such measures as may be thought expedient in effecting to the utmost of their power, a general emancipation, by diffusing the blessings of civil and religious liberty which they enjoy among their fellow-men and brethren throughout the world.

Resolved, That a committee of twelve be appointed to correspond with such other committees as may be selected by their brethren in the United States, and vested with power to elect one or more delegates to meet and confer with others, who may be chosen for the purpose of adopting necessary measures for carrying the above resolutions into effect.

The following gentlemen were nominated a Committee, agreeably to the 4th resolution, viz: Rev. A. H. Cohen, Messrs. Abram Levy, Jacob A. Levy, Isaac Levy, Samuel Marx, L. M. Goldsmith, Henry Hyman, A. Mordecai, Isaac Hyneman, Samuel H. Myers, Myer Angle, Elias Markins, to which was added, Gustavus A. Myers, Esq., Chairman, and Jacob Ezekiel, Secretary of the meeting.

On motion,

Resolved, That the proceedings of this meeting be published in the Whig and Compiler, with a request that they may be also inserted by such Editors as are favorable to the cause.

And then the meeting adjourned.

GUSTAVUS A. MYERS, Chairman.

J. Ezekiel, Secretary.

Among the four resolutions passed at this "Meeting of the Israelites," two show their growing political security in this nation. One expresses "feelings of grateful admiration for the laudable and liberal efforts made by our Christian brethren in union with our own" on behalf of Damascus Jewry. Another resolution praises the freedom that these Jews of Virginia enjoy in the United States, calling for "diffusing the blessings of civil and religious liberty which they enjoy among their fellow-men."

This issue of the *United States Commercial & Statistical Register* also contains an elaborate two column report on page 191 that captured the pageantry and prayers that accompanied the dedication of the new "House of Israel" synagogue on Adelphia Street. Rev. S.M. Isaac from New York served as "the officiating clergyman."

NEW YORK – 1865
"SERMONS BY OUR LEADING CLERGYMEN: THE SYNAGOGUES"
The New York Herald, p. 2 (col 4–6)
April 20, 1865

Most of this black bordered issue deals with the outpouring of grief in response to the assassination of President Abraham Lincoln. Coverage starting on page two discusses the outpouring as expressed in various religious services through-out New York City. "The first religious services to the memory of Mr. Lincoln," the article notes, "were held in the Jewish synagogues on Saturday." The President had died early that Sabbath morning, succumbing to the gunshot wounds he had received the night before.

More than a full column is devoted to "THE SYNAGOGUES," describing first the services at seven New York City synagogues, each with its own subsection noting the names of their rabbis (in keeping with the standard reference to clergymen at the time, the rabbis are called "Rev."). This is followed by a blurb saying that "Similar services, with addresses by the rabbi preachers, were held … in most of the principal Jewish houses of worship."

The next subsection covers "Decorations of the Jewish Synagogues," noting that synagogues met on Sunday (i.e., not on the Jewish Sabbath) to direct the arrangements. Five individual synagogues are discussed, most having black drapery on the exterior of their buildings, with black and white linen and floral combinations atop their Arks. The last sentence of the article lists four more synagogues followed with the conclusion that, "in fact, every synagogue throughout the city presents the same somber aspect."

THE SYNAGOGUES.

Greene Street Synagogue.
REV. ISAAC NOOT.

A special service was held at this synagogue at eleven o'clock A. M. After the chanting of several appropriate hymns by the officiating minister, Rev. Ansel Leo, Mr. Isaac Noot delivered a brief address. He remarked that they assembled this day on an occasion which caused every heart to throb with sorrow and grief and to pay the last tribute of respect to our country's illustrious Chief, whose name is and ever will be united with virtue, patriotism and humanity, and whose memory will be impressed and embalmed upon the young hearts of children. Was it not a dream that a few days ago Abraham Lincoln was still in the land of the living, nobly performing his mission of peace and strenuously laboring in behalf of that loved country for which he lived, and in whose glorious cause he died. Yes, the heart that so unceasingly throbbed for his country, has now ceased to beat—that heart within whose portals sympathy and humanity ever dwelt—that heart within whose recesses the flame of patriotism burned unceasingly—that heart has been stilled by an assassin's foul act. The brain that worked so nobly for our cause is now at rest; the hand that was ever extended in friendship, and which signed the emancipation of millions, is now powerless. Never in our country's history was there a Chief Magistrate who entered on his career with so many difficulties and dangers, and who departed from it so suddenly and so mournfully. Never did a Chief Executive enter upon the duties of his office with so many obstacles to contend against—a civil strife fiercely raging throughout the land, spies lurking in every nook of the Capitol, and everywhere organized bands of conspirators secretly scheming for the destruction of the great ship of state. Our chosen but now martyred chief, nothing daunted, bravely stood at the helm, encountered the terrible breakers of rebellion and the storms of treason with courage and fortitude, never forsaking his post until he had nearly landed his ship safely in the haven of peace. That dauntless helmsman was now no more, the angel of death had claimed him. "The Lord has given, the Lord has taken. Blessed be the name of the Lord."

After a brief allusion to President Johnson, the speaker concluded with a very eloquent prayer.

Broadway Synagogue.
REV. S. M. ISAACS.

This synagogue, which had been neatly and tastefully draped in the habiliments of mourning, was opened for divine service at half-past eleven, the exercises commencing at noon with the hymn, "There is none like our God." Psalms 16, 91 and 109 were then chaunted by the assistant reader, Rev. Mr. Phillips, and the solemn chorals at the opening of the ark were finely rendered by the choir. With a "scroll of the law" in his hand, the officiating reader offered up the "Prayer for the Government," and the minister then delivered special prayers for the repose of the soul of the lamented dead and for the restoration of the Secretary of State and his family. The procession then returned to the ark, the choir chaunting "And as the ark rested."

The minister, Rev. S. M. Isaacs, ascended the pulpit and delivered an impressive discourse, taking his text from Genesis, xv., 1:—"Fear not, Abraham, I am thy shield. Thy reward shall be exceedingly great." Introducing his theme, he remarked that there are times when the spiritual instructor finds himself totally unable to convey the sentiments of his heart through the medium of words. We had assembled to give expression to our sorrow at the calamity which has befallen the nation in the cruel murder of the good, the amiable, the patriotic Abraham Lincoln. It was a question with many philosophers whether intelligent men should mourn, seeing that their knowledge of moral good and evil is so imperfect, and that what efficacy can there be in sorrow? Can it

Back to this mansion call the fleeting breath?

But we are told by the wisest of men "there is a time to mourn;" and what can more impressively evoke such emotion than the assassination of our loved President, to whom the angelic hosts are commissioned to speak, "Thy reward shall be exceedingly great." Selected to be President over a vast country, an intellectual and free people, amid the most gigantic and causeless rebellion that ever afflicted mankind; at the summit of power when it is so difficult to maintain an equilibrium, Abraham Lincoln remained steadfast, unmoved, incorruptible. In all his dignity he never forgot that he was but man. His goodness of heart and honesty of purpose; his extreme disinterestedness; his disposition to "forgive and forget," endeared him to every American. All sectional differences and partisan distinctions merge in the common recognition of the common loss. "May the soul of our late Chief be bound up in everlasting life, and under the shadow of Almighty God may he find a stay and refuge." The reverend gentleman then alluded to the context of the motto he had chosen, words spoken to Abraham after the "Battle of the Kings," when he was offered the booty if he returned to the King of Sodom the captives he freed. In words indignant and emphatic he spurned the offer. His object was freedom for those unjustly held in bondage; he refused to be enriched by the spoils of battle. Then spake the Almighty:—"Fear not, Abraham; I am thy shield; thy reward shall be exceedingly great." How singularly apposite to the being whose cruel murder we deplore! He also battled for a principle—to prevent the extension of slavery; and when, apprehensive of his course, a portion of the people rebelled he buckled on his armor and now saw the four years of war eventuating in welcome peace and reunion. And now he determined to be merciful. Even when his ardent friends counsel'd him "the wicked should be punished with evil," his answer was, as Abraham of

(continued)

old, "Give me but the persons!" "Let slavery be abolished, let our country be truly free, and we will have peace." He sought no personal aggrandizement, no extension of dominion. And for such sterling patriotism, which corrupt politicians do not find in their vocabulary. The Supreme seems to say—"Fear not, Abraham; I am thy shield. Thy reward shall be exceedingly great." He then adverted to the fearful crime that had been committed in this boasted age of enlightenment and civilization, in the cold-blooded assassination of the good President. The assassin's deadly aim had only partially succeeded. The martyred President was unconscious of suffering. Quietly and calmly he sank to rest, while the heart of the nation was cruelly lacerated. He commented on the words of King David, as set forth in the 109th Psalm, and applied them to the circumstances of the death we are lamenting, and concluded an interesting discourse with an earnest and fervent prayer, after which the *Kadish*, or Prayer for the Dead, was said, the choir chaunted the concluding hymn—Universal Lord—and the congregation dispersed.

Congregation Shaary Berachah.
REV. H. WASSERMAN.

The neat little synagogue of this congregation, in East Ninth street, was yesterday noon the scene of very impressive ceremonies. At that hour the building was filled to overflowing with a very respectable audience, mostly dressed in deep mourning, to participate in the services commemorative of the death of Mr. Lincoln.

After reciting Psalms 1, 4, 5, 6, 7 and 19, the *Kadish*, or Prayer for deceased persons was said, and the Minchah Prayer intoned, at the close of which, Rev. H. Wasserman delivered the funeral sermon.

The preacher, after forcibly contrasting the joy of the congregation on the first days of the Passover, with their sorrows on the closing days of the festival, exhorted the people to put their trust in God, who did all for the best. A man had been taken from us who, by his wisdom and his goodness of heart, had elicited the admiration of the entire world. The loss was a serious one, but the Jew, full of faith in the wisdom of God must say, "Praised be the Judge of Truth." This Judge would certainly unravel the mystery which overclouded the commission of this, the greatest of all crimes, and bring to justice the perpetrator. To those who were left behind was bequeathed the duty of praying for their country and their rulers, and the Jews should more especially do so, as in this land they were permitted to say with the prophet, "I am a Hebrew, and I fear the Lord who made the Heaven and the Earth."

After a fervent Prayer for the repose of the soul of the deceased President, and the recovery of the Secretary of State and his son, the services were closed.

Congregation Shaari Zedek, Henry Street.
REV. MR. ROSENFIELD.

The congregation assembled at two o'clock, and the afternoon service was read by the Rev. Max Cohen. The Ark was opened and a prayer for the repose of the soul of Abraham Lincoln, late President of the United States, offered up in a very fervent manner by the Rev. Mr. Cohn, minister of the congregation. The following psalms were then chaunted by the congregation for the recovery of Secretary Seward and son:—47, 5, 12, 14, 27, 28, 38, 57, 69, 119, 91. A lecture was then delivered by the Rev. Mr. Rosenfield in a very impressive manner.

Prayer was then offered up for the President, and for the recovery of Secretary Seward.

Congregation Beth Israel Bikur Cholim.
REV. MR. SCHWALBE.

A large congregation convened in this synagogue, 56 Chrystie street, for solemnizing the obsequies of the late President of the United States. The inside of the synagogue was appropriately and tastefully dressed in black. The services commenced with the singing of Psalms 22, 102, 106, 25, 90, 91, 110. Rev. Mr. C. Schwalbe then delivered a discourse rarely equalled for impressiveness and solemnity, in view of the recent terrible calamity; after which the Kadish prayer was said by the whole congregation. The audience were evidently fully impressed with the solemnity and importance of the occasion.

Congregation of Aderath El.
REV. J. WALZ.

The synagogue of the Congregation Aderath El, East Twenty-ninth street, between Lexington and Third avenues, was heavily draped in black within and without, and quite a large audience had assembled there at twelve o'clock, when the services commenced. First some psalms were recited antiphonally, followed by a Hebrew prayer for the peace of the soul of the departed President. Mr. J. Walz then ascended the pulpit and addressed the congregation. He quoted Isaiah XI., 2, "And on him rested the spirit of the Lord, the spirit of wisdom and understanding, the spirit of counsel and of might, the spirit of knowledge of the fear of God," as peculiarly applicable to our late Chief Magistrate. He then drew a picture of his excellent character, describing him as a good, wise and great man. He was great, not like Cæsar, Alexander and Napoleon, who, with great talents, overleaped the ordinary barriers, and dazzled a world, struck with wonder and awe; but, like Washington, whom the world admires, loves and strives to imitate. The greatest and most enduring work of his life is the proclamation of emancipation, which he has now signed with his life blood. The speaker concluded with an earnest prayer in behalf of the late President, his bereaved family, the mourning nation, his successor, Andrew Johnson. Hebrew prayers were then offered for the recovery of Mr. Seward and the welfare of the new incumbent of the Presidential office. The congregation then sang the hymn, "Yigdal," and dispersed after the ordinary vesper service had been recited.

Thirty-fourth Street Congregation.

There was a very large attendance at this new synagogue. After a very impressive mortuary service by the Rev. Mr. Kramer, a very eloquent address was delivered by the Rev. Dr. Raphall.

Similar services, with addresses by the rabbi preachers, were held in the following synagogues:—Nineteenth street, Rev. J. J. Lyons; Twelfth street, Dr. Adler; Twenty-ninth street, Dr. Bordi; Norfolk street, Rev. Mr. Sternburger, and in most of the principal Jewish houses of worship.

Decorations of the Jewish Synagogues.

As already announced in the HERALD, the first religious services to the memory of Mr. Lincoln were held in the Jewish synagogues on Saturday. On Sunday meetings were held at the respective synagogues and resolutions adopted directing the edifices to be draped with suitable emblems of mourning. Among the first to lead was the

TEMPLE EMANUEL,

located in Twelfth street. A national flag was hung half-mast, and the exterior draped in long garlands of black and white. In the interior the reading desk and ark were covered with crape.

THE THIRTY-FOURTH STREET SYNAGOGUE

was draped on the outside with a twining chain of black, looped up with white rosettes and a large white centre. The basement room, which is used as a synagogue till the main edifice is completed, is hung all around with black. The pillars supporting the roof are covered with entwinings of black and white linen.

THE GREENE STREET SYNAGOGUE

presents a very neat appearance. The echol or ark is so draped as to form a mourning arch. The circle is composed of black linen with white medallions. The sides are formed by the posts of the ark, which are imbedded in black, looped up at intervals with white rosettes.

THE NORFOLK STREET SYNAGOGUE.

The outside of this building and the entrances are covered with black and white drapery arranged in festoons, with medallions in the centre. On the inside all the tiers are covered with the emblem of woe, while over the ark and around the pulpit are crescents of mournful colors.

THE CLINTON STREET SYNAGOGUE

was very tastefully draped on the inside with festoons along the walls of black and white, with large white favors. The ark was covered with crape; and each chandelier was covered with trappings of woe.

The Broadway, Rivington and Stanton, Twenty-ninth, Thirty-fourth, and, in fact, every synagogue throughout the city presents the same sombre aspect.

THE NEW YORK HERALD.

THE NEW YORK HERALD.

WHOLE NO. 10,462. NEW YORK, FRIDAY, APRIL 21, 1865. PRICE FOUR CENTS.

IN STATE.

THE DEAD BODY IN THE CAPITOL.

THE GUARD OF HONOR.

An Immense Number of Citizens View the Remains.

THE METROPOLIS YESTERDAY

Services in Trinity and Other Churches.

BROADWAY ON FAST DAY.

The Preparations for the Funeral.

Arrangements for One of the Longest and Most Imposing Processions the World Ever Saw.

Celebration of the Funeral Rites Throughout the Country.

FEELING OF THE SOLDIERS.

Deep Despondency Prevailing

THE SYNAGOGUES.

Service Held at the Congregation "Bnai Israel."

REV. M. R. DELEEUW.

On Wednesday, April 19, after appropriate psalms sung by the congregation, the minister ascended the pulpit and commenced the following oration:—

O, how doth she sit solitary; the city that was full of people hath become a widow.—Jer. i., 1.

In every corner where I cast mine eyes mourning greets the gaze. The aged and the infant, men and women, palaces and huts, alike draped in the sable hue of desolation; and for whom? In the midst of the greatest rejoicing the administration deprived of its head, and the people of its father; Joachin and Boaz, the pillars of the edifice, felled by the hand of the assassin; Abraham Lincoln, of blessed memory, the victim of their bloodthirsty desperation. William H. Seward, the great statesman of the age, we trust in Thee, oh God, to restore him, that we may reap the benefit of his wisdom, and that he may be enabled to guide us through the death-throes of the rebellion. "In those days I, Daniel, was mourning three full weeks; I ate no pleasant bread, neither came flesh nor wine in my mouth; neither did I anoint myself at all till three full weeks were fulfilled." (Daniel x., 2 and 3.) And who could, my friends, after the dire intelligence conveyed to us on the Sabbath abstain from mourning like unto Daniel. The great grief with which the whole country was stricken so unexpectedly, and which sent forth from the breast of millions a wail of lamentation, and bowed every head with a burden of a great sorrow, finds on this day its culmination when the precious dust of the great and good departed is laid in the grave to rest till the last "trump" sounds and time will roll into eternity. The thought that his remains were yet among us has pent up in our hearts a moiety of our grief, which will burst forth in a more overwhelming stream as the grave closes over the mortal remains of our murdered President. The fear of the land is the beginning of knowledge.—Proverbs i, 7. A pious fervency and just appreciation of the Almighty pervaded the public actions of Abraham Lincoln; trusting in God he met unflinchingly and calmly the storm of rebellion that broke over him upon entering on his first term. For four long years, unmindful of jeers and taunts and derision, he moved calmly, and assured of the justice of

the cause he had to defend, and trusting in God to judge the merits of his actions, the Lord blessed his works; and though his toil was arduous, but, in the words of Solomon, he gave no sleep to his eyes nor slumber to his eyelids.—(Proverbs vi., 4.) Ever watchful and unremitting in his endeavors, under the divine guidance, he triumphed. And when his eyes closed in death, although torn from the earth in a manner worthy the wild beast of the forest, his foes were scattered and silenced; and he had lifted a multitude of his fellow beings from the depth of degradation to manhood's estate. And the Lord said unto Moses, Thou shalt not go over this Jordan.—(Deuteronomy xxxi., 2.) Yet thou shalt see the land before thee, but thou shalt not go thither unto the land which I give the children of Israel.—(Deuteronomy xxxii., 52.) And thus, in the mysterious dispensation of the Lord, Abraham Lincoln was not destined to taste the sweets of the peace he had so zealously labored to establish. Like unto Moses, who had brought the children of Israel from the land of bondage within sight of the promised land, so he had brought this nation within reach of the great boon he sought to attain; and unto his successor, as unto Joshua, remains this task of finally occupying the promised land, as Moses said unto the children of Isreal, "The Lord thy God, he will go over before thee, and he will destroy these nations before thee, and thou shalt possess them."—Deut. xxxi., 3. And so we trust may the Lord do by this nation on this day. The character of our late Chief Magistrate, whose place in our hearts will ever be next to the Father of our Country, his character was marked by generous forbearance and magnanimity, to the grand development of which the glory of our arms had just given force when he was stricken down. Let us hope that his successor will carry out the course he had proposed to himself. The memory of the just is blessed; but the name of the wicked shall rot—Prov. x., 7. Abraham Lincoln! That name, with the many associations that cluster around it, the memory of his kindness and geniality, will ever couple its repetition with a blessing, words of sympathy and sweet remembrance in every household and to every individual of this great nation; to the world it will prove a watchword, a tower of strength for men to rally around, to move them to combat manfully for right.

As for his assasin, who, taking advantage of the confiding nature of his victim—which refused any guard but the honesty of purpose of his fellow citizens—to assassinate him, intending by his foul deed to erase his memory from the world's record, in his purpose he has signally failed, as its baseness merits, and his name shall rot and be forgotten, as his bones, in an unhallowed obscurity. While, in succeeding years, as our grief

(continued)

NEW YORK – 1865
"THE SYNAGOGUES" MOURN PRESIDENT LINCOLN, DAY TWO
The New York Herald, p. 1 (col 5–6)
April 21, 1865

In this second black bordered issue, taken up exclusively with the aftermath of the assassination of President Lincoln, almost another entire column was devoted to the reaction of "The Synagogues." These services and sermons, held Wednesday April 19 at three synagogues, were reported on in detail under four subheads. Two articles spoke about Congregation B'nai Israel, the first quoting the oration given by the Rev. M. R. DeLeeuw, including a moving Biblical analogy noting: "And the Lord said unto Moses … Yet thou shalt see the land before thee, but thou shalt not go thither unto the land … (Deutoronomy xxxii, 52.) And thus, in the mysterious dispensation of the Lord, Abraham Lincoln was not destined to taste the sweets of the peace he had so zealously labored to establish." Shorter coverage was given to Congregation Bikur Cholim U-Kadisha, a "neat little house of worship [which] was, on Wednesday afternoon, the scene of very solemn ceremonies," and to Congregation Shaari Zedek, where the Rev. Max Cohn offered a prayer, "prepared exclusively for this occasion," in which he asked for the highest privileges for Lincoln's soul.

The issue noted that the funeral procession would pass through New York City on its way to Lincoln's burial in Illinois.

subsides and the victim's good work is surveyed, his memory will grow more green in our hearts, and freshen the cherished remembrance of our President martyr.

The ark was then opened by the President of the congregation. (*Al Mola Rachamin.*)

Prayer for the repose of our late President was said. Hymns were sung, and the congregation dispersed.

Services at the Synagogue of Bnai Israel.

This synagogue, situated at the corner of Stanton and Forsyth streets, was thrown open to the congregation on Wednesday for the purpose of holding services appropriate to the occasion. After the usual ceremonies a very eloquent and touching eulogy on the martyred President was pronounced by the Rev. M. R. De Leeuw, having a powerful effect upon all who heard it. The synagogue was very neatly decorated. The arc was covered with mourning. The two fine pillars supporting it were draped in black, while the top held a sable curtain dotted with rosettes and pendants. The reader's desk was covered with a white richly worked cloth, its single pillar being draped in black muslin.

Bikur Cholim U-Kadisha Synagouge, 63 Chrystie Street.

This neat little house of worship was, on Wednesday afternoon, the scene of very solemn ceremonies. The Ark, the galleries and in fact the whole house were most handsomely draped in mourning.

The ceremonies were opened by a choir with the opening prayer (Matowah), after which a vesper service was read by M. Bermas, Esq., and the congregation.

The Rev. Dr. M. Wasserman then offered a very impressive prayer, after which he chose as a text, chapter xl., verse 8, from the Prophet Isaiah, upon which he delivered a most affecting and instructive sermon, at times affecting the audience to tears. After paying a high tribute to the lamented Chief Magistrate, during which he compared him to the best and most righteous man that the world has yet produced, and said that in losing him the nation had lost a tree in full bloom and just as the rich fruit was about to be tasted. The Israelites cannot enough express the sorrow of their hearts were they even, as of old, to clothe themselves in sackcloth and ashes.

After the close of the sermon, Psalms 27, 31, 37 and 91 were said by the congregation; also the prayer for the dead by the reader, Mr. Goldstein. Rev. Dr. Wasserman then breathed a fervent prayer for the prosperity of President Johnson, the health of Secretary Seward and family, and the strengthening of all the officers of the government, State and city; also for the family of the late President.

Rev. Mr. Goldstein closed the solemn ceremonies by chanting Yidgdal, the whole audience joining. The house was well filled, and every face expressed the deep sorrow that had befallen the nation.

Congregation of Shaari Zedek.

During the services at this synagogue the following prayer, prepared expressly for the occasion, was offered up by the Rev. Max Cohn, minister of the congregation:—

Omnipotent God of Life, we pray Thee have mercy over him, thou King of the Universe, for with Thee is the fountain of life! O may he continually be led in the land of the living, and may his soul receive rest in the bundle of life. O may the Gracious, in His many mercies forgive his sins; and may his good works be present in His sight and be placed in His view, together with all His faithful ones, and may he be led in His presence in the land of the living. O may he have a good memorial before his rock, that he may inherit of riches of Him who formed him, that he may approach to His light, remain in His vision and in the vision of His word, since my covenant of life and peace was with Him; therefore let his soul receive rest in the bundle of life. O mayest thou find the gates of heaven open, and mayest thou behold the city of peace and the dwelling place of the just, and may the angels of rejoicing approach thee, and the High Priest stand ready to receive thee, and mayest thou go to thy end and receive thy firm stand and rest. May thy soul go to the cave of Machpelah, and thence to the cherubim where God will guide it, and there thou wilt behold a pillar attracted from above, and not remain without, and mayest thou go to thy end. Michael shall open the gates of the sanctuary, and offer thy soul as an offering before God, and there will be found with thee the redeeming angel to the gates of the pleasant place where Israel is; in this place mayest thou merit to stand. O may thy soul be bound in the bundle of life, together with the heads of the colleges of and captivity with the Israelites, priests and Levites, and with the seven companies of the just and perfect, and in the garden of Eden mayest thou receive thy firm stand and delight, and thou go to thy end and receive thy firm stand and rest.

Chapter #10

Jews and the Civil War

*From the documentary, "Jewish Soldiers in Blue & Gray," produced
by Indigo Films, courtesy of the Shapell Manuscript Foundation.*

By the outbreak of the Civil War, the nation's Jewish population
numbered 150,00 with a majority living in the northern states.
Theologically, there were strong divisions as to Biblical attitudes towards
slavery. Certain rabbis held that there existed Scriptural support for
slavery, while others condemned the institution's inhumanity. During the
war itself, President Lincoln, for the first time in the nation's history,
authorized the establishment of a Jewish chaplaincy. The high point of
anti-Semitism during the war was the issuance by General Ulysses Grant
in 1862 of an Order expelling Jews from the southern military district that
he supervised.

NEW YORK – 1861 "EX-SENATOR BENJAMIN ON HUMAN PROPERTY" & "DR. RAPHALL'S BIBLE"

New-York Daily Tribune,
p. 4 (col 3–5)
January 7, 1861

On January 4, 1861 – designated a national day of fasting and humiliation by President James Buchanan – Rabbi Morris J. Raphall, one of New York City's most prominent rabbis, delivered a sermon in seeming support of slavery based on his Biblical interpretation and set off both a moral and political storm. Three days after the sermon, the editorial page in Horace Greeley's *Tribune* devoted two columns to first attack the ideas of Raphall's "co-religionist" Judah P. Benjamin (see pages 11 and 118) on the subject of "Human Property" and then vent its objections to Raphall's sermon.

Benjamin had recently resigned as a United States Senator from Louisiana and would soon be named Secretary of State of the Confederacy. In taking issue with Benjamin's views, Greeley did not fail to remind his readers of Benjamin's "Israelitish"

(continued)

EX-SENATOR BENJAMIN ON HUMAN PROPERTY.

There are two formulas, both propounded by distinguished and widely different men, which laconically express the fact and the fallacy of slaveholding. "Property in man!" said Dr. Channing, with his usual elegance, and more than his usual vigor, "you might as well talk of "property in angels!" On the other hand, Mr. Clay, with the crisp and axiomatic brevity of a lawyer, said: "That is property which the law "makes property;" which sufficiently would settle the whole question, provided the law *could* make property of whatever law-givers might please to call by that name. If Mr. Clay had considered the matter philosophically and not passionately, he would have seen that, potent as Senators and Representatives usually are, they cannot control the forces and the facts of Nature. A law requiring all apple-trees to blossom in October and to bear in March, though enacted *nemine contradicente*, and approved by a regiment of governors, and declared to be a Christian ordinance by a score of synods, and sanctioned as constitutional by whole benches of judges, would not put a single pippin upon the boughs or into the barrels in the specified month. When Senator Benjamin—we beg his pardon: we must give him a title of which we suppose he is proud —when ex-Senator Benjamin of Louisiana made his recent dramatic display in the Chamber, to the noisy and outrageous glee of the galleries, he talked of four billion dollars worth of men, which gave his peroration rather a pecuniary than a pathetic tint. No Yankee, fresh from swops and dicker, could have taken more kindly than Mr. Benjamin did to the shilling side of the question. Our property, our ravished property, our endangered property—this was the burden of his Senatorial swan-song. He was indignant, just as a farmer is indignant upon discovering his hen-house ravished—to all the statesmanship consistent with a pervading sordidness did Mr Benjamin rise—to nothing higher and manlier.

It is unfortunate for Mr. Benjamin that his idea of property is one which has never been admitted by lexicographers, or logicians, or political economists. Property refers, not to *men*, but to *things*. Property, according to Worcester, is "the *thing* possessed." Property in law, according to Burril, cited by Worcester, is "the un-"restricted and exclusive right to a *thing*." The uality of property is permanence. Acres do ot abscond. Houses never run away. These re *real* property. Then, of property which is alled *personal*, we notice that it does not contain within itself the power of effecting transfer. There must be donor *and* donee, vendor *and* vendee, pledger *and* pledgee. Bullion, which is he symbol of all personal property, is said to take wings; but it does not *take* them before some active intelligence has *made* them. The Treasury securities did not commit larcenies of themselves the other day; they were stolen by their custodian. Horses, to be sure, run away, and so do negroes, and so did our New-York Postmaster; but if this proves negroes to be horses, it also proves Isaac V. Fowler to be a horse. Senator Benjamin, if we may credit his own statement, is about to run away, or has

already run away, from duties which he is sworn to fulfill; but this does not prove him to be a horse, or even an ass, except figuratively; it does not prove him so, if for no other reason, because horses are incapable of committing perjury.

The late Senator from Louisiana and all slaveholding Senators, late or present, grievously blunder when they talk of slaves as property in a plain and unqualified way. They do not see that it is the qualification in the mind of every thinking person that saves them and their inconsistent chattel system from contempt and hatred. The South has lived for more than half a century upon good-natured Northern extenuations—upon the prevalent desire to make out slaveholding something better and different from man-holding, wife-selling, or child-stealing. That is to say: when philanthropists have talked of the auction-block, philanthropists of another sort have talked of the black man's beautiful cottage. When honest men have objected to the wholesale bastardizing and exposure in market-overt of the yellow progeny of the planters, somebody always steps in with an armfull of statistics to prove that the poor blacks are greatly given to church-going. Many of these animals are ill-treated, to be sure, but numbers of them are indulgently treated, which proves—that they are not animals at all! Doctors of Divinity and constitutional lawyers, out of the Bible, out of the Pandects, have labored to convince us that Slavery is a social system pleasing to God, the regenerate heart, and political common sense. We have heard, times without number, from uncounted pulpits, that the slave is a member of society, which, in spite of Mr. Benjamin's Israelitish protest, we declare that "property" never is and never can be. If Slavery is a social relation, then it is not a system of property. Southern philosophers and Northern sycophants may choose between the two theories; but they are not entitled to the benefit of both, because the two are absolutely incompatible.

If, then, Slavery be considered as a mere social relation, the whole plea for equality of privileges in the Territories falls to the ground. Mr. Benjamin has undoubtedly a right to emigrate to Kansas; but it does not follow that he has a right to carry there the social relations of Louisiana. He might as well insist upon taking with him Mr. Livingston's Code or the Municipal Law of New-Orleans. Suppose gambling-hells and bawdy-houses are licensed in the Crescent City; does it follow that faro and prostitution will be legal in Nebraska? These illustrations may be thought impolite, and so let us offer others. Mr. Benjamin may be married (if he is not already married) in a certain way at home; would he have a right to be married in the same way in Oregon? Polygamy is, or was recently, just as firmly established in Utah as Slavery is in South Carolina; may Brigham Young, then, go to housekeeping in this city with his ninety-and-nine wives? Property is everywhere protected by the comity of civilized nations. Can Mr. Benjamin, therefore, flog, paddle and pickle his negro in full conventicle at Exeter Hall? Piracy was for many years a social institution of Algiers; man-eating was the same in New-Zealand; but in no Christian waters did the corsair swim with impunity. [...] spring babies for his table.

origins. What set off this editorial criticism was Benjamin's assertion that Southern slaves represented some $4 billion worth of "property." In the second paragraph the newspaper challenged Benjamin's definition, "…his idea of property is one which has never been admitted by lexicographers…". Toward the end of the next paragraph it continues, "…in spite of Mr. Benjamin's Israelitish protest… property [it] never is and never can be."

- - - - -

In "Dr. Raphall's Bible," the second part of the newspaper's scathing commentary, the rabbi is chided as sharing with Benjamin the characteristic as "an Israelite with Egyptian principles." This article asserts that Rabbi Raphall incorrectly claimed the New Testament was not opposed to slavery. "…Suppose a son or daughter of the Rev. Dr. Raphall were this day a slave in Dahomey, would he doubt its application to the case?"

Furthermore, slavery had "vanished" in Europe "in the light of Christian equity, the force of Christian love." How could Rabbi Raphall have presented a defense of slavery, asked the editorial, inasmuch as "no people on earth have been more oppressed… and persecuted than the Jews?"

Surely, Rabbi Raphall's views are hardly followed by his co-religionists, "We rejoice in the knowledge that only a part of them are thus perverted…."

Slavery being a social relation—and it can be nothing else—the slave cannot be regarded merely as a beast. No man holds social relations—certainly not in this part of the country—with his hog or his donkey. If they prefer such swinish or asinine company in Louisiana, we are quite free to say that it is none of our business, and one of those questions of taste about which there can be no dispute. If Mr. Benjamin likes a theory which may make *things* his cousins, *goods* his uncles, and *chattels* his aunts, we wish him joy of his family, and so leave him; with our hearty protest, notwithstanding, against such Circean transmogrifications in yet untainted Commonwealths.

DR. RAPHALL'S BIBLE.

The Rev. Dr. Raphall is a burning and a shining light in our New-York Israel. As Senator Wade said of his co-religionist, Judah P. Benjamin, he is "an Israelite with Egyptian principles." On the President's Fast-day, he preached a sermon in the Greene-street Synagogue, wherein he demonstrated, to his own satisfaction, that Human Slavery is sanctioned by Divine law. Now, in so far as the Rev. Dr. assumed to quote and to expound the Law of Moses, we let him pass, and proceed to the other branch of the subject. We quote from a report of his discourse as follows:

"But, as that Rev. gentleman [Henry Ward Beecher] takes a lead among those who most loudly and most vehemently denounce slaveholding as a sin, I wished to convince myself whether he had any Scripture warranty for so doing; and whether such denunciation was one of those 'requirements for 'moral instruction' advanced by the New Testament. I have accordingly examined the various books of Christian Scripture and find that they afford the Reverend gentleman and his compeers no authority whatever for his and their declamations. The New Testament nowhere, directly or indirectly, condemns slaveholding—which indeed is proved by the universal practice of all Christian nations during many centuries."

—Dr. Raphall is an educated and reverent expounder of the Law given by Moses, and we have therefore not seen fit to put our authority against his in the interpretation of that Law. But, when he comes to the New Testament, we feel that we have him at a decided disadvantage. We have been studying that book a good many years, receiving it as a message from on high; while he deems it an imposture, of no Divine authority, and appears to have only casually looked it through to see whether it does or does not sustain Slavery. He says "the New Testament nowhere, directly or indirectly, condemns slaveholding;" we say it does, especially in this passage, which is the center and sun of the whole system of Christianity:

"ALL THINGS WHATSOEVER YE WOULD THAT MEN SHOULD DO TO YOU, DO YE EVEN SO TO THEM."   [Matt. vii. 12.

Jesus of Nazareth, who lays down this broad, comprehensive, universal rule of human conduct, adds "for this is the Law and the Prophets," and we believe he had a clearer, deeper, truer comprehension of their spirit than has Mr. Raphall; yet we will not dispute with the Rev. Doctor on that point. But that the Author and Finisher of the Christian faith intended to lay down as absolute and without exception the rule that we must never, under any circumstances, do to another what we would not have that other, if our positions were reversed, do to us, the universal, emphatic accord of Christian commentators for nearly twenty centuries, has affirmed; and the context renders it certain that Christ meant just this, and nothing else. We might quote other passages to the same effect, particularly that concerning "a certain "man" who "went down to Jericho" and "fell "among thieves," and, being by them "stripped, "and wounded, and left for dead," was looked upon and left to get on as he might by "a

"priest," and "a Levite," who, we judge by certain characteristics, to have both been ancestors of the Rev. Dr. Raphall. But Christ explicitly condemned their heartless conduct, commending that of the good Samaritan, who, seeing a fellow creature in distress, stopped not to consider that he was of a detested race and lineage, but flew to his relief, bound up his wounds, and ministered to his every need. He who does not feel that this narrative is aimed directly at such religionists as Dr. Raphall may be a very good Jew (we don't believe he is, but the Dr. is better authority for that than we are); but he is certainly the poorest sort of Christian.

Can any one need to be shown that Christ's Golden Rule is utterly, irreconcilably hostile to Slavery? Suppose a son or daughter of the Rev. Dr. Raphall were this day a slave in Dahomey, would he doubt its application to the case? And if that rule condemn the enslavement of a Jew by a negro, just as clearly does it condemn the enslavement of a negro by a Jew. No Hebraist pretends that the Slavery allowed by Moses ("for the hardness of your "hearts") was the Slavery of negroes exclusively, or was confined to any particular race or color. The "heathen round about" the Israelites, when the Law was given by Moses, were not negroes, nor anything like negroes, but Arabs and Phœnicians, scarcely distinguishable by physical or mental characteristics from the Hebrews themselves.

Christ was born into a world full of Slavery, as Dr. Raphall asserts. Where is that Slavery now? Vanished—melted away in the light of Christian equity, the fire of Christian love. On Sunday next the very last Christian nation in Europe that held slaves will cease to hold them, leaving Mohammedan Turkey the only slaveholding country in the most enlightened and Christian quarter of the globe. The Catholic Church has formally declared that Slavery was overthrown by Christianity, which no one who studies history can doubt. Christianity is gradually rooting out Slavery in Asia and America, and fighting it even in Africa. In the presence of these facts, what weight is due to the circumstance that Christ never specially condemned Slavery? "By their "fruits ye shall know them,"

It is a sad, a deplorable fact, that Slavery unfits men for Freedom. The slave of yesterday is the hardest master to-day, and the Irish kerne, trampled under foot for twenty generations, make just about the meanest Doughfaces in America. No people on earth have been more oppressed, robbed, trodden down, and persecuted, than the Jews; hence we naturally look to them to furnish apologists and pettifoggers for Slavery. We rejoice in the knowledge, however, that only a part of them are thus perverted, but that thousands of the children of Abraham, purified and made wiser by suffering, are among the most faithful and consistent upholders of the inalienable Rights of Man.

NEW YORK
– 1861
"SLAVERY
AND THE
HEBREW
SCRIPTURES"
*New-York
Daily Tribune,
p. 5 (col 4–6)
January 15,
1861*

For the second week, the *Tribune* addressed Rabbi Morris J. Raphall's unconventional sermon which presented slavery as a divinely ordained institution, a discourse that was bound to raise the hackles of a tensely divided nation only three months away from the outbreak of the Civil War. Rabbi Raphall, founding spiritual leader of the upscale B'nai Jeshurun Synagogue, gave his Biblically-based theoretical defense of slavery at the Green Street Synagogue on President Buchanan's national day of fasting and humiliation, January 4, 1861.

The distinction drawn by Rabbi Raphall between the Biblical notion of slavery which recognized the "human dignity" of the slave, and the practice of slavery in the South where the slave was reduced to a "thing," did not please the editorial writers of the *Daily Tribune*. The paper challenged Rabbi Raphall's contentions in an editorial on January 7th and then dismissed them as "vulgar pro-slavery nonsense" in an editorial in this issue.

In addition to the editorial, the issue included a 3-column article by M. (Michael) Heilprin (b. Poland, 1823; d. New York, 1888) – credited as stemming from a learned rabbinic family – in which he sharply attacked both the erudition and philosophy of Rabbi Raphall in a three-column rebuttal, claiming he was "outraged by the sacrilegious words of the rabbi." Heilprin comments that, "Day after day brings hosannas to the Hebrew defamer of the law of the nation….," and later adds that while "all this, I trust, will convert few rational Jews or Christians to the infamous doctrines of Slavery, … it may induce many people to believe that the God of the Jews was or is, after all, a God of Slavery."

Heilprin accused Rabbi Raphall of wrongly holding up the Biblical Noah as a supporter of slavery. He cited German translators of the Old Testament such as Moses Mendelssohn and Leopold Zunz as translating the Hebrew word *Eved* to mean "servant" (a much less degrading term) rather than "slave." If Rabbi Raphall wanted the Bible to be "regarded as divine," challenged Heilprin, he should teach it as "pure, just and humane." Otherwise, Heilprin concludes, regard the Bible as an object of "human frailty."

SLAVERY AND THE HEBREW SCRIPTURES.

REPLY TO THE RABBI RAPHALL.

… Being a Jew myself, I felt exceedingly humbled, I may say outraged, by the sacrilegious words of the Rabbi. Have we not had enough of the "reproach of Egypt?" Must the stigma of Egyptian principles be fastened on the people of Israel by Israelitish lips themselves? Shall the enlightened and humane of this country ask each other, "Are these "the people of God, who have come from his land?" I hoped, however, that, amid the flood of scum that is now turned up by the turbulent waves of this stormy time, the words of the Rabbi would soon disappear, like so many other bubbles, and the blasphemous teachings of a synagogue find no longer echoes than those of Christian Churches. But I am grievously mistaken. Day after day brings hosannahs to the Hebrew defamer of the law of his nation; and his words are trumpeted through the land as if he were the messenger of a new salvation. So depraved is the moral sense of our Pro-Slavery demagogues, so debauched the mind of their mammon-worshiping followers, so dense the Egyptian darkness which covers their horizon, that, all other false lights being exhausted, a spark of Hebrew Pro-Slavery rhetoric is hailed as a new lightning from Sinai, as a new light from Zion, sent to guide the people of the United States safely through the dark tempests that threaten to destroy their ship of State. Down with conscience, humanity, reason, experience! Just listen to the angelic Hebrew sounds of the God-sent Rabbi! He has scrutinized the Hebrew Scriptures and their commentaries, the Mishna, the Gemara, the mediæval Rabbis, perhaps also the Cabalists. If he has not discovered truth, nobody will. And what a stupendous knowledge of profane history, from antediluvian times down to the day when the Rev. H. W. Beecher last preached in Plymouth Church! All this, I trust, will convert few rational Jews or Christians to the infamous doctrines of Slavery, but, on the other hand, it may induce many people to believe that the God of the Jews was or is, after all, a God of Slavery. Allow me, therefore, to show both Christian and Jewish readers of THE TRIBUNE the real value of the Rabbi's biblical scholarship, and, if space permits, also of his logic. "Because of Zion I will not be silent."

Of course, he commences with Noah, and tells us how it came that that man, who first planted a grape-vine, &c., &c., was acquainted with the condition of an *'ebed* (or *ngebed*, as the Rabbi spells it), which he translates by "slave," and not, like the English version, by "servant," and arrives "at the conclusion that, next "……mestic relation of husband and wife, parents "and children, the c……t relation of society with which "we are acquainted is that of master and slave." A fine discovery, which must have been charming to the ears of the Southern part of his hearers! The peculiar domestic institution almost as old as the fratricide of Cain, and certainly as old as the time when the earth was full of violence, and the Lord, repenting that he had made man, determined to destroy him from the face of the earth (Gen. vi.)! Thus biblical criticism, a blessed instrument in the hands of a competent scholar, traces everything to its origin, and naturally links together the brother of Abel with the late Preston S. Brooks, Lamech with Rhett, and perhaps even sister Carolina's going out of the Union, with mother Eve's going out of Paradise! Who the serpent was, has long been discussed. It remains only to be proved that the tree of knowledge was the first full grown palmetto.

Now, being a Hebrew myself, and pretending to an equal knowledge of the beautiful tongue of my ancestors with the Rev. gentleman, I must tell you, statesmen of these United States, that if you undertake to reconstruct the shattered Constitution of your Great Republic on the basis of the learned Rabbi's translation of that word, you will find yourselves woefully mistaken. I doubt if there be one Jewish authority in favor of the Rabbi's preference, but certainly for every one there are ten against him….

NEW-YORK DAILY TRIBUNE, TUESDAY, JANUARY 22, 1861.

4

New-York Daily Tribune.

TUESDAY, JANUARY 22, 1861.

ONE JEW AND A COUPLE OF CHRISTIANS.

When men are out of money they go to the Jews but we never have expected to find Prof. Mors and Hiram Ketchum so short of speech as to be obliged to ask Rabbi Raphall to speak for them. The Rabbi, however, has been induced to repeat his Fast Day discourse, of which we have said all that we think it worth while to say, except that we cannot but express the opinion that twenty-four hours in a good old-fashioned

NEW YORK – 1861
"ONE JEW AND A COUPLE OF CHRISTIANS."
New-York Daily Tribune, p. 4 (col 5)
January 22, 1861

For the third week in a row, Rabbi Morris Raphall was the topic of an angry *New-York Daily Tribune* article. In this article, the author says of the Rabbi's infamous "Fast Day discourse," which the Rabbi has been asked to repeat: "We have said all that we think it worthwhile to say, except that we cannot but express the opinion that twenty-four hours in a good old-fashioned Spanish Inquisition would materially open the Rabbi's eyes."

As spiritual leader of New York City's Congregation B'nai Jeshurun, Rabbi Raphall had antagonized many northerners by his defense of slavery as a "divinely ordained institution" just a few weeks before the outbreak of the Civil War. This article's author expressed no sympathy for the "pretentious Jewish priest" and had many nasty things to say about the two Christians who asked Rabbi Raphall to speak.

Spanish Inquisition would materially open the Rabbi's eyes, and so in some sort benefit him, even if he did come from the rack a perfect india-rubber man. What Dr. Raphall's views are worth, on the subject of Slavery, in this day and generation, i. e., what they are worth to professed Christians, even admitting that he is learned in Old Testaments and Old Talmuds, in which Mr. Heiprin has proved him to be profoundly ignorant, we certainly cannot conceive. If Prof. Morse and Esquire Ketchum are to pin their faith to the Rabbi's phylacteries, then the sooner both of them are circumcised, the better for their souls and their consistency. Will Prof. Morse say that the New Testament teaches no new duties of self-sacrifice, of benevolence, and of broad human charity? If Hiram Ketchum is to swear by the Mosaic Law, why does he accept a part of it and leave the rest? Does he adhere to the "eye for an eye," and the "tooth for a tooth" system? Does he sacrifice goats, kids, and rams? Does he keep the Passover, or the seven days' feast of unleavened bread? Does he keep a Sabbath on the first day of the seventh month? Does he observe the Sabbatical year? Or the jubilee of the fiftieth year? Ah! that he would, and "proclaim liberty throughout all the land unto "all the inhabitants thereof!" Does Prof. Morse suppose that the Lord would be angry, if a "flat-nosed," or "a broken-footed, or a broken-"handed or crooked-back man, or a dwarf," were made a Doctor of Divinity? Does he start with abhorrence when, before a smoking sirloin, cooked to a turn, he notices that the gravy follows the knife, and does he, remembering that the Jews were forbidden to eat blood, discard gravy from the dish? What nonsense it is for him, then, an intelligent man, to rest himself upon the misinterpreted teachings of the Old Testament, and upon the decisions of a pretentious Jewish priest, who cannot by any possibility, according to Prof. Morse's doctrine, get by St. Peter and into Heaven! With all due civility, we must say to the Professor that he knows better. And as for Hiram Ketchum, will he have the New-York statutes abolished and Leviticus or Deuteronomy enacted in their stead? He might as well insist that the tables in our legislative halls shall be made of shittim wood, two cubits being the length thereof, and a cubit the breadth thereof, and a cubit and a half the hight thereof, according to the prescription in he book of Exodus.

NEW ORLEANS – 1861 "TYRANTS OF THE PAST AND TYRANTS OF THE PRESENT"
Sunday Delta, p. 2 (col 3–4) December 8, 1861

In this "sketch of a sermon" in the *Sunday Delta,* a Confederate Rabbi, Bernard Illoway (b. Bohemia, 1814; d. near Cincinnati, 1871), of the Rampart Street Synagogue in New Orleans, draws an analogy between the Confederacy's struggles against President Lincoln's forces and the struggles in the Bible of Judas Maccabee and the wicked Greek Antiochus.

The sermon told how, disgraced from being defeated by the Romans, Antiochus tried to *"blot out the stain… with the glory of … the total and cruel subjugation of the land of*

(continued)

THE SUNDAY DELTA

PUBLISHED BY THE NEW ORLEANS DELTA NEWSPAPER COMPANY.

TERMS—PER ANNUM:

DAILY DELTA, (invariably in advance).....$10
WEEKLY DELTA, do.   do. 2
SUNDAY DELTA, do.   do. 3
For any time less than one year the DAILY DELTA will be delivered to City Subscribers at 20 cents a week.

ADVERTISING RATES

Advertisements $1 a Square for the first insertion. Every subsequent insertion 50 cents.
Advertisements on the Second Page $1 per measured Square each insertion.
Advertisements at intervals $1 a Square each insertion.
Marriage and Funeral Notices $1 each insertion.
A Liberal Discount made to regular Advertisers.
The SEMI-WEEKLY DELTA is issued every Tuesday and Friday morning, at $5 per annum.

SUNDAY MORNING, DECEMBER 8, 1861.

THE TYRANTS OF THE PAST AND THE TYRANTS OF THE PRESENT.

A SKETCH OF A SERMON DELIVERED BY REV. DR. ILLOWAY, IN THE RAMPART STREET SYNAGOGUE.

At the downfall of the Persian monarchy, Alexander the Macedonian became master of the Judea, and after his death, it fell from one to another of his successors, until at last it remained with Antiochus Epiphanes, King of Syria.

Antiochus, commonly called Epimanes, which signifies a mind-man, having been disgracefully defeated in a war with the Romans, tried to blot out the stain of this defeat and crown himself with the glory of a new victory by the total and cruel subjugation of the land of Judea; but, when he found out that this could not be so easily effected as he thought, he declared the country as being in a state of rebellion. He then marched with a powerful army against Jerusalem, and butchered without remorse or pity thousands of helpless citizens, and sold thousands of freeborn men into slavery. But this excess of cruelty did not yet satisfy this bloody heathen king, for superadded to his numerous deeds of barbarity, he now began a war against the religion of the Lord; he pillaged the temple and desecrated the holy Altar by commanding unclean animals to be sacrificed upon it. Though so much blood was already shed, Antiochus's thirst for slaughter was not yet stilled, and, in fact, he determined to exterminate the whole race of Israel. The tyrant found a ready instrument in a man by the name of Apollonius, who, whilst the people were engaged in peaceful worship on a Sabbath day, in the city consecrated to the service of the Lord, ordered his soldiers to fall upon the unresisting and defenseless multitude; and fearfully did the slaughter rage, for all the males were slain until the streets were red with the streaming gore of uncounted victims; and women and children were led away as captives into hopeless slavery. Apollonius next broke down the walls of the city, pillaged it, and set fire to it in many places; and, as

if not enough had yet been done, Antiochus now commanded that all his subjects should conform to one mode of worship, prohibited by the penalty of death the covenant of Abram, interdicted the observance of the Sabbath, compelled many to eat forbidden food, and a statue of an idol was by his order erected on the altar of burnt offerings, where the heathens then worshiped, in the place of God's chosen priests.

There lived at this time, in the town of Modin, an aged man by the name of Mathias, son of Johannen, the high priest, famed for his virtues and ardent zeal for his religion and his country. He was the father of five sons, of whom every one was worthy of such a glorious parent. It happened at this time that an officer of Antiochus, who arrived at Modin with the commission to enforce the king's decrees against the Jewish religion, tried to bring Mathias over to the cause of the king by bribery and the most tempting offers. But the venerable man would not listen to his insidious proposals, and he proclaimed aloud that the faith which his fathers acknowledged was the only one to which he would adhere to the moment of his dissolution: " As long as I live I shall stick to my God and my country as the brick sticks to the wall, and should every man in Israel leave the true God of his fathers, I and my sons we will forever remain faithful to Him; we are ready to live for Him, to fight for the honor of His name, and to die for the righteous cause of our country;" and when the messenger of Antiochus continued in his seductive proposals the old man slew him in his ardent fervor, and he fell by his sword.

The sacred work once begun, he now summoned all the citizens to follow him. In the mountains they organized themselves, and rapidly the number of the defenders increased. With prudence and unflinching courage they conducted their heroic enterprise, and they proceeded to overturn the heathen altars in many places, to enforce the observance of the law, and to establish places for public worship. Mathias had the happiness to behold the prosperous work of regeneration of his people, and, crowned with immortal glory, he resigned his command to his son Judas, after which the aged warrior sunk in the arms of death, and was buried in his native city, Modin.

Judas, surnamed the Maccabee, was a worthy successor of his glorious parent. He initiated his warriors by many a gallant deed of arms—by surprising fortified places, which he secured to himself as places of retreat in case of any misadventure. Having thus trained his small army, he at length took the field against the proud and confiding enemy, where he was met by Apollonius, at the head of a powerful army, whom he conquered and slew. But Antiochus was not willing that the despised Jews should so easily regain their independence. He therefore sent an immense host to exterminate the nation of Israel, which he hated, and whose power he esteemed lightly. Three of his best generals, Nicanor, Gorgias and Ptolomey Necron advanced against the feeble army of Judas with an army of sixty thousand foot and seven thousand horse, and in their train followed a great number of slave-dealers, who were to purchase as many of the Israelites as should be made captives. But, vain imaginations; for no booty, no captives fell into their hands. Overwhelmed with confusion, they were compelled to fly before the handful of those who shed their blood in the cause of their God and their country; and Nicanor, the great general, who had advised that slave-dealers should follow the army, was compelled to fly to Antiochus disguised as a slave. Strange retribution; but how just.

Judea." Illoway's tyrant in 1861 sought his glory by subjugating the people of the South.

"When Antiochus found out that this [subjugation] could not so easily be effected..., he declared the whole country as being in a state of rebellion...," and thousands fell, innocent victims of his ambition.

Illoway points out that was not the more powerful but the one with the righteous cause that won and continues, *"This is a history of by-gone ages, but let me ask you ... whether you did not find in it a faithful mirror in which all our present untoward circumstances are strikingly reflected."*

After a point by point comparison of past and present he urges:

"Israelites, let this… be a useful lesson ... the tyrant is still alive."

After this victory Judas assembled six thousand men in the city of Mizpah, who, according to the ancient and hallowed custom, fasted and prayed fervently for protection from above. Here Judas made a proclamation, in obedience to the mosaic law, that every one that was afraid to meet the foe, or who built in this year a new house or planted a vineyard, should return home; and in consequence of this proclamation but three thousand men remained with him. But every breast of this little band was a fortified tower, and the enemy dared not hope to march to victory but upon the prostrate bodies of every one of these fearless defenders of their righteous cause. After several more important victories, Judas, with his men, who did not fight for fame, for wealth, or for extension of rule, solely for the protection of his religion and his country, succeeded in regaining the desolate ruins of Jerusalem.

But who can paint the anguish of the people when they found shrubs growing in the temple yards, the walls of the sacred edifice defaced, and every thing profaned by the sacreligious and unclean hands of the pagans. Judas commenced immediately the work of purification, reinstalled the expelled priests, and then celebrated the feast of dedication for eight days amidst rejoicing and universal thanksgiving.

I am now done, my brethren, with the principle part of the history of the regeneration of the people of Israel, the recovery of their independence and the dedication of the temple, the memory of which we solemnly celebrate to-day. Thereby I have shown you that great deeds can be accomplished if God superintends our affairs by very small means, and that the victory lies not always in the heavier scale of power, but on the side of those whose cause is a righteous one. It is this a history of by-gone ages, but let me ask you, my brethren, whether you did not find in it a faithful mirror in which all our present untoward circumstances are strikingly reflected. Suppose we would merely change in the pages of history the names of Antiochus and Apollonius into those of our modern tyrants, would we not, by this insignificant alteration, all at once convert the past into the present, and a tale of olden days into a living fact.

The essay is very easy; let us draw a line, and then compare, point by point, the events of the past with those of our own of the present day.

Antiochus sought glory in subjugating the Israelites. Our tyrant was seeking his glory in subjugating the people of the South.

When Antiochus found out that he could not so easily subjugate the Israelites, he declared the whole country as being in a state of rebellion; he treated them as rebels, and thousands and thousands fell as innocent victims of his ambition. Is the same not the case with us? Why are we treated as rebels? Because our noble representatives mightily resisted the wicked designs of the tyrant to subjugate us. Why are our cities pillaged, our villages laid in ashes, our ports blockaded? For no other crime than this—of not suffering a despotic tyrant to subjugate freemen. Why must the precious blood of our valiant and brave sons redden our streams? For no other purpose than to still the thirst for slaughter of an ambitious and perfidious government.

Antiochus soon found a ready instrument in Apollonius, who was soon superseded by others who understood it better to please the tyrant.

How many such slave-hearted subjects did our tyrant had as ready instruments, who were superseded one by another, because they could not bring him blood enough as he wanted and booty enough as he needed.

Antiochus' bitter persecution had its happy effect upon the Israelites, for there was now an opportunity offered to those yet firm and true to their religion and their country to display their constancy, their faithful adherence to the religion of their fathers and their patriotic sentiments and true love to their country.

The persecutions of our tyrants had the same happy effect upon our sons, who availed themselves of the opportunity offered unto them to display their firmness and constancy; for with unflinching courage, resignation and self-denial they left their sweet home, left father and mother and all those dear to their hearts, many their beloved wives and children, and hastened to drive back the bold invader from the soil which he had polluted with the streaming gore of innocent victims, and gladly they expose themselves to the many fatigues of military life, and like our father Jacob when leaving his parental house, they have often no other couch than a moist piece of ground and no other pillow than a cold stone or the hard instrument of defense; and how many of our most prominent citizens embraced a glorious death on the field of honor, to teach the young how to die for to live after death in the heart of those in whose defense they died.

Antiochus ordered that the slave dealers should follow his army to purchase as many of the Israelites as should be made captives.

Our tyrants ordered cotton stealers to follow his army to steal as much as they can of the produce of our blessed soil; but no captives fell into the hands of Antiochus: no cotton shall fall in the hands of our tyrant's cotton heroes.

Antiochus' immense hosts were opposed and defeated by a handfull of brave and lion-hearted Israelites, who fought with an unflinching courage for their God and the righteous cause of their country, and they proceeded from victory to victory; and likewise are the innumerous hosts of our tyrannical oppressor, opposed by a power much inferior to theirs in quantity, but far superior in quality, for we have no mercenaries, only true and faithful sons of the South, who merely fight for their inalienable rights and independence, and who have already proved that they understand to drive the enemy from one defeat to another.

The children of the East at that time were guided by the glorious warrior Judas Maccabee, and we, the children of the South, are guided by a true and faithful son of our country, by the glorious warrior, Jefferson Davis.

Israelites, let this similitude of our present state to this of the past be a useful lesson to you. Remember to-day when we commemorate the happy events of by-gone ages, that Antiochus the tyrant is still alive; he only changed the name; but let us show him that we can oppose him with the same unflinching courage of our ancestors in the East. Israelites, let us prove ourselves as true and faithful sons of our country; let us show ourselves as worthy relations of the glorious family of the heroic Maccabees; let none of us be too old or too young, too feeble or too delicate, too rich or too poor; let us all be inspired by the spirit of freedom and independence; let our watchword be, Glory or Death, and our battle cry, like this of our ancestors, Mikamocha Baalim Adonay, who is powerful like thee, O Lord!

The New-York Times.

VOL. XI—NO. 3191.   NEW-YORK, FRIDAY, DECEMBER 13, 1861.   PRICE TWO CENTS.

JEWISH CHAPLAINS.

Rev. Dr. FISCHEL, of New-York, had yesterday an interview with the President, to urge the appointment of Jewish Chaplains for every military Department, they being excluded by an act of Congress from the volunteer regiments, among whom there are thousands of Israelites. In the meantime the Doctor will take charge of the spiritual welfare of the Jewish soldiers on the Potomac. The President assured him that the subject will receive his earnest attention, and expressed the opinion that this exclusion was altogether unintentional on the part of Congress.

Photo of a religious Jew from the Civil War era, from "Jewish Soldiers in Blue & Gray," produced by Indigo Films, courtesy of the Shapell Manuscript Foundation.

NEW YORK – 1861
RABBIS AS MILITARY CHAPLAINS
The New-York Times, p. 1 (col 3)
December 13, 1861

On July 22, 1861, and again on August 3, 1861, Acts were passed by Congress that restricted the appointment of chaplains in the military to "ordained Christian ministers." The Christian organization that oversaw the chaplaincy program demanded, in September 1861, that a Pennsylvania Calvary regiment remove the Jewish Hebrew teacher they had installed as chaplain. A month later the appointment of the Rabbi chosen by the regiment to replace the teacher was rejected, and a letter from the U.S. Secretary of War advised the rabbi, "Were it not for … the provisions of these two Acts, the Department would have taken your application into its favorable consideration."

In response to these events, the Board of Deputies of American Israelites (see page 77) decided to lobby for the inclusion of Jewish ministers, inviting the Rabbi whose chaplaincy had been rejected – Rev. Dr. Arnold Fischel (b. 1830, Holland; d. 1894, Holland), a former lecturer at Shearith Israel in New York (1856–1861) – to lobby on their behalf.

This *New-York Times* front-page news item reports on the meeting Rev. Dr. Fischel had with President Lincoln as part of the campaign to rescind the limitation. The immediate result of the meeting was that "the Doctor will take charge of the spiritual welfare of the Jewish soldiers on the Potomac." Additionally, "the President assured [Rev. Dr. Fischel] that the subject will receive his earnest attention and expressed his opinion that this exclusion was altogether unintentional on the part of Congress."

The efforts of the Board of Deputies of American Israelites were successful, and on July 12, 1862 Congress voted to reverse itself on the issue.

(After Fischel's successful lobbying, he spent time as a civilian chaplain in the Washington, D.C. area, paid by the Board of Deputies because their application for him to become a military chaplain was rejected due to the small number of Jewish soldiers in that region. When the Board could no longer provide a stipend – and seeing a lack of support for other projects he had hoped to initiate to benefit Jewish soldiers – Fischel returned to Holland.)

VOL. 9.   HARRISBURG, PA., THURSDAY, SEPTEMBER 4, 1862.   NO. 2.

HARRISBURG, PENNSYLVANIA – 1862
"THE ISRAELITES AROUSED."
Patriot Union, p. 1 (col 6)
September 4, 1862

This front-page article, reprinted from the *Chicago Tribune,* reports how Israelites met spontaneously at Chicago's Concordia Hotel to determine how to raise a company of Jewish troops to fight for the Union cause. The meeting voted to raise $10,000 in order to equip this new company, with a bounty of $100 offered to any man who enlists.

[From the Chicago Tribune.]
THE ISRAELITES AROUSED.

Last evening the Israelites held a spontaneous meeting at Concordia Hall, to take into consideration the best means to raise a company of Israelites for the war.

Mr. M. Gerstley was appointed Chairman, and Joseph Frank and T. Florsheim Secretaries. The Chairman called the meeting to order, and stated that this meeting was called to devise means to afford material aid to the Government to crush out this rebellion, and to support the Government and Constitution.

Henry Greenebaum proposed that a committee of five be appointed to draft resolutions. Carried.

The Chairman appointed the following gentleman: H. Greenebaum, B. Scholneman, M. Seitz, G. Shoyer and Samuel Cole.

Stirring war speeches were made by Henry Greenebaum, Maj. E. Solomon, Leopold Mayer, Lyon Silverman of Port Washington, and A. Kohn, all advocating in unmistakeable terms the duty of our Israelite citizens toward their adopted country.

The committee on resolutions reported the following:

WHEREAS, The present crisis in the affairs of our nation directly appeals to every citizen enjoying the inestimable blessings of American freedom, to exert himself to his utmost in assisting the Government in its efforts to maintain the integrity of the Union and the crushing out of the rebellion, which must and shall be done, a number of Israelites of this city, for the first time since their residence here have met together as such, to act upon any public matter whatever, and this time for the purpose of making a united effort in support of a vigorous prosecution of the war. It is hereby

Resolved, That as Israelites we disclaim toward each other any and all relations aside on one common religious belief, except such as should exist among citizens. In all questions of a political nature the Israelite is untrammeled and free to act for himself, and does exercise his individual judgment and discretion.

Resolved, That having contributed individually heretofore, whenever called upon, in support of the war, we are impelled only by the deepest sense of patriotism and a sincere attachment to this land of our choice and love to make an united effort in behalf of our country.

Resolved, That we will raise the sum of $10,000, or more, among the Israelites of this city, for the purpose of immediately recruiting and organizing a company for active service in the war.

Resolved, That an Executive Committee of seven be appointed by the Chairman of the meeting, to carry out the object of these resolutions.

Resolved, That the Jewish company will join the new Hecker Regiment.

These resolutions were carried unanimously.

After the adoption of the resolutions, a subscription list was opened, and in a short time the splendid sum of $6,200 was subscribed.

The above splendid subscription was made in exactly ten minutes.

A recruiting office will be opened to-day, and a bounty of $100 is offered to any man who will enlist. The Israelites have taken hold of this matter with a determination to succeed. All honor to them for their patriotic efforts and munificent liberality. It can not be surpassed.

NEW YORK – 1863
ORDER NO. 11 EXPELS JEWS
The New York Herald, p. 1 (col 3)
January 5, 1863

During the Civil War, Northern textile mills were dependent on Southern cotton, and a limited number of government licenses were given for trade in this commodity. This situation led to a black market with unlicensed traders bribing army officers. General Grant suspected that Jews were mainly behind this illegal operation. On December 17, 1862, he issued the notorious General Order No. 11,

> **General Grant's Order Expelling the Jews from Paducah, Ky.**
> GENERAL ORDER—NO. 11.
> HEADQUARTERS THIRTEENTH ARMY CORPS, DEPARTMENT OF THE TENNESSEE, OXFORD, MISS., Dec. 17, 1862.
> The Jews, as a class, violating every regulation of trade established by the Treasury Department, also department orders, are hereby expelled from the department within twenty-four hours from the receipt of this order by post commanders. They will see that all this class of people are furnished with passes and required to leave, and any one returning after such notification will be arrested and held in confinement until an opportunity occurs of sending them out as prisoners, unless furnished with permits from these headquarters. No passes will be given these people to visit headquarters for the purpose of making personal application for trade permits. By order of
> Major General GRANT.

expelling Jews from the military district he supervised which consisted of Mississippi, Tennessee and Kentucky.

The Herald printed the text of this regulation on its front page in a one paragraph report titled "General Grant's Order Expelling the Jews from Paducah, Ky." *The Herald* simply published this Order and carried no background or explanations.

In response to protests from members of the Jewish community, the press and members of Congress, President Lincoln overruled Grant and withdrew this Order, the announcement being made (in the *Tribune* article that follows) on the same day as this issue of *The Herald* came out.

Grant subsequently claimed this Order was drafted by a subordinate, and he signed it without having first read it.

NEW YORK – 1863
"ORDER AGAINST JEWS REVOKED"
New-York Daily Tribune, p. 5 (col 2)
January 5, 1863

In what is regarded as one of the most blatant anti-Semitic actions of the nineteenth century, General Ulysses S. Grant issued Order No. 11 on December 17, 1862 expelling all Jews from the administrative area of Tennessee which included the states of Tennessee, Kentucky and Mississippi. Prompting Grant's order were allegations that Jews were the principal black-market traders in Southern cotton which was sold to factories in the North. Jews were given 24 hours to leave their homes as a result of this order.

> **GEN. GRANT'S ORDER AGAINST JEWS REVOKED.**
> Deputations of Jews began arriving here yesterday to solicit the President to countermand or modify the order of Gen. Grant excluding Israelites from his lines. The operation of it upon families and merchants long established in regular business proved exceedingly oppressive and produced great excitement in every city in the West. On the application last night of Mr. Kaskel, one of the expelled Jewish citizens of Paducah, sustained by Representative Gurley of Ohio, the President instructed Gen. Halleck to countermand the order imperatively. Such countermand was sent West this morning by telegraph.

Jews and other Americans telegrammed President Lincoln urging that Grant's decree be rescinded. Rallies protesting the expulsion were held in Cincinnati, St. Louis and Louisville. In a telegram to Lincoln, Cesar Kaskel, representing the thirty Jewish families in Paducah, Kentucky, charged that Grant's order violated "all laws and humanity." Two Union Army veterans were among Paducah's small Jewish community.

In its "From Washington" column on January 5, 1863 – ironically the same date as the *New York Herald's* announcement of the Order – the *Tribune* featured a paragraph carrying the subhead, "Gen. Grant's Order Against Jews Revoked." In it the *Tribune* describes the scene leading to Lincoln's countermand of the Order.

NEW-YORK SEMI-WEEKLY TRIBUNE, FRIDAY, NOVEMBER 27, 1863.

FROM CINCINNATI.

The Fright of the Jews—High Prices—
River Navigation—Damage by Frosts—
Are Farmers Subject to Insanity?

From Our Special Correspondent.

BURNET HOUSE, Nov. 23, 1863.

Quite a sensation exists here and in other
river cities about the order of Gen. Hurlburt at Memphis, by which all the able-bodied men are forced to
enter the military service. Many parties with heavy
stocks of goods went thither to go into business, particularly Jews, and by recent arrivals from Memphis we
learn they are devising every means to leave Memphis
and save their goods, but in vain, for the moment they
leave, their goods will be confiscated. I saw several returning who fortunately had not commenced business.
The fact is, the great majority of these traders are Jews,
and they have not hesitated to go into the smuggling
business. Honest traders will suffer with them, but on
the whole, good will result.

Gen. Stephen A. Hurlbut

NEW YORK – 1863
"THE FRIGHT OF THE JEWS"
New-York Semi-Weekly Tribune,
p. 5 (col 4)
November 27, 1863

The *Tribune*'s "Special Correspondent" reported that traders were being forced to flee the area by an "order of Gen. Hurlburt [sic]" requiring all able-bodied men under his jurisdiction to enter the army. Gen. Stephen A. Hurlbut (b. Charleston, SC, 1815; d. Belvidere, IL, 1882) became a Major General of the Union Army in 1862 and commanded the 4th Division in Tennessee from his headquarters in Memphis.

The article asserted that these traders – "particularly Jews" – arrived in Memphis to go into business, but following the General's order they, "are devising every means to leave Memphis and save their goods, but in vain, for the moment they leave, their goods will be confiscated." The article expressed the same spirit of General Ulysses Grant's Order No. 11 issued earlier that year, alleging Jewish disloyalty. The reporter here stated a second time in his short article that "the great majority of the traders" were Jews and then claimed that these Jews "have not hesitated to go into the smuggling business."

Richmond Dispatch.
BY J. A. COWARDIN & CO.

DAILY DISPATCH.

VOL. XXVII.   RICHMOND, VA., SATURDAY, OCTOBER 22, 1864.   NO. 98.

Richmond Dispatch.
JOB PRINTING NEATLY EXECUTED.

CAPTAIN MADISON MARCUS.

This gallant officer, who was killed on Thursday, the 13th instant, was in command of the heroic defenders of Fort Gilmer when it was attacked by a force of negroes and whites.— His defensive force was composed of five companies of the Fifteenth Georgia regiment and a few stragglers from other commands. He instructed his men to reserve their fire until the enemy were almost upon them; at which time he gave the order, and a more terrible fire from cannon and ringing rifles never greeted any foe.

The negroes, leaping down into the ditch immediately beneath the work, endeavored to hoist up one another on their shoulders; but no sooner did the whites of a negro's eyes gleam over the embankment than they were sealed in death.

Captain Marcus ordered his men to use the shells in the fort as hand-grenades. They accordingly cut off the fuses to two seconds, just giving time to allow their being rolled over the parapet. They exploded before reaching the bottom of the ditch, and many of the negroes were so mangled by this proceeding as to render their features undistinguishable. Our defence was heroic, and the result all that could be desired.

Captain Marcus was a young man, between twenty-five and thirty. He was an Israelite; and although a number of his people who were in the army were granted leave of absence to attend upon the ceremonies of the "Feast of Atonement," which is a season of release from all labor, the Feast of Tabernacles closely following, yet he asked no leave, considering that in performing his duty to his country he worshipped his God in an acceptable manner.

The funeral services were performed in the German Jewish Church, Rev. Mr. Michelbacher.

RICHMOND, VIRGINIA – 1864
JEWISH CONFEDERATE SOLDIER'S OBITUARY
Daily Dispatch, p. 1 (col 1–2) – October 22, 1864

The Soldiers' Section of Richmond's Hebrew Cemetery is believed to be the only Jewish military cemetery outside the state of Israel. Among those interred at this Jewish burial ground is Captain Madison Marcus whose heroic death is reported on the front page of this issue.

The obituary notes that Captain Marcus, "an Israelite" who considered defending the Confederacy an acceptable way to observe Yom Kippur, headed the defenders of Fort Gilmer where he died.

"The funeral services," the tribute concludes, "were performed in the German Jewish Church…." Rev. Mr. Max Michelbacher of Richmond's Congregation Beth Ahabah officiated. The Jewish-American History Foundation has numerous references to Rabbi Michelbacher, including copies of his "Prayer for the Confederacy" and General Robert E. Lee's responses to various requests he made on behalf of Jewish soldiers.

An iron fence with rifles as posts and crossed swords and sabers as railings surrounds an area of five rows holding six fallen Jewish Confederate soldiers each. A headstone proclaims, "To the Glory of God and in Memory of the Hebrew Confederate Soldiers Resting in this Hallowed Spot" and lists the soldiers' names. It is a Jewish custom to place a rock, which unlike flowers is everlasting, on top of the monument when one visits, as is seen here.

Some 3,000 Jews served in the Confederate Army during the Civil War. When the war broke out, and Richmond became the capital of the Confederate States of America, 102 Jews from the city joined the ranks of the South, a proportion larger than the Jewish population of the city. Despite their heroic service, several cemeteries including the one in Fredericksburg, VA, refused to permit Jewish soldiers to be buried with their comrades.

BALTIMORE CLIPPER.

"THE UNION, THE CONSTITUTION, AND THE ENFORCEMENT OF THE LAWS."

VOLUME I.—NUMBER 38.   BALTIMORE, TUESDAY MORNING, FEBRUARY 14, 1865.   PRICE TWO C

BALTIMORE – 1865 "SPEECH OF THE REBEL BENJAMIN."

Baltimore Clipper,
p. 1 (col 1)
February 14, 1865

This front-page article "lays before us" the speech given by Judah P. Benjamin, Secretary of State of the Confederate States of America, "at the great war meeting held in Richmond." In the waning months of the Civil War, a desperate South was already suing for peace. Benjamin emphasized the roles of duty and courage and, most importantly, he advocated freeing Negro slaves as a way of enhancing the man-power of the Confederate Army. Such a move, he said, would add 680,000 additional troops.

Benjamin explained that the plan he was hoping to pass through the Legislature would warn the negroes that if they fled north, they would die in the cold climate.

It is noted that Benjamin then complimented the Virginia ladies "for their patriotism and devotion to the cause" and closed with "an eloquent apostrophe to peace."

NEWS FROM THE SOUTH.

The War Meeting in Richmond.

SPEECH OF THE REBEL BENJAMIN.

He Favors the Arming of Negroes

&c.,   &c.,   &c.

As we have already published the speech of Jeff. Davis on the result of the Peace Conference, it is only needful now to lay before our readers the speech of Benjamin at the great war meeting held in Richmond on Thursday night last, to show the desperate straits to which the leaders of the rebellion are at last reduced:

Hon. J. P. Benjamin, Secretary of State, was the third speaker. He congratulated the large assemblage on the change of sentiment among the people, and apparent in the meeting, in the sudden revulsion from the despondency of a few days ago to the high resolve, holy determination and patriotic emulation of this period. Hope and confidence were renewed in the hearts and minds of men; what is the cause of it? Have any great military successes been announced? No. It is the knowledge and consciousness that has come home to all, that is felt in the core of all hearts, that we must conquer in this fight or die. Thank God, we all know it now, that the path of duty is placed before us clear, straight and plain, and all know that we must tread it or perish. Our terms are independence.

With that one word on our treaty scroll, we say to Lincoln, "Put what you please, we will sign the deed." Mr. Benjamin, at this point of his remarks, entered into a recital of the circumstances that led to the sending by President Davis of commissioners with the terms and instructions under which they were sent. The speaker next touched upon the necessity of supporting the government and reinforcing the army. War was a game that could not be played without men, and *men we must have*. He (the speaker) was here to-day to tell some very unwholesome truths. He would be blamed and abused for them probably, but he could not help that.—When our soldiers in the trenches are sending up earnest appeals for help will you withhold that aid, whether that aid be white or black? (Great cheering.) Mr. Benjamin submitted some statistical facts, showing the fighting element available between the two sections.

In 1860 the Confederate States, exclusive of Tennessee and Kentucky, had within her boundaries one million sixty thousand fighting men between the ages of 18 and 45 years. Against this formidable force the enemy have arrayed three millions of men at various periods since

1861. There are in the South six hundred and eighty thousand black men of fighting age, and capable of being made fighting men. *Let us say to every negro who wants to go into the ranks, go and fight, and you are free. Don't press them, for that will make them run away,* and they will be found fighting against us instead of for us. As yet but one side is told them. The Yankees can beat us from the beginning to the end of the year at making bargains.—Let us stop the negro from going over to the enemy by saying:—if you go over to the Yankees you will get your freedom, but you will perish off the earth, for you cannot live in that cold climate. Fight for your masters and you shall have your freedom without incurring the other danger. Let us promise the negro in good faith that if he will fight for us, he shall have his freedom. [Voice—"Let's try it."]

Yes, let's try it. He, the speaker, had never lived in any but a slave country, and like most of his audience, doubtless, had his black mamma nurse, but he would willingly give up all for the attainment of independence. What State will lead off in sending the black man to the aid of General Lee? (Cheers.) Virginia, who gave birth to secession, and led off in the first cannon shot of the revolution. South Carolina, and one after another the Southern States wheeled into line. Virginia held back, for her love for the Union was as strong and warm and affectionate as the love of a mother for her child. People began to ask what of Virginia? Then came a telegram saying that Virginia was going to abandon the South; that she was lukewarm, reluctant and holding back.—(Voice—"Who held her back?") But soon another telegram informed us that Virginia was with us, and, like South Carolina, we are looking to her to lead in the new measure of war policy, which is inevitable, and come it must. When shall it be done? (Voices—"Now, now, now.")

Yes, now. Ask your Legislature to pass a resolution recommending the measure to Congress, and in twenty days Gen. Lee can be reinforced by twenty thousand men. The speaker was no sensationist, no alarmist. He had come to the meeting for the very purpose of giving utterance to some distasteful truths.— *Without the adoption of some decisive, energetic, full-way measure like this, there was danger—very great danger—to avert which,* were he as much a Virginian as he was a Louisianian, he would not hesitate to make this last sacrifice. Louisiana will follow Virginia, and she cannot take one step to which Louisiana will not respond. This only alternative is presented. Either we must fight the Yankees with our negroes, or they will take and hold them as a shield, fighting us with their emancipation proclamations in force.—And if there be such a place as hell upon earth then it would be illustrated in our condition. This struggle over and our subjugation accomplished, our slaves freed, and we slaves. What the Yankees propose to do by the amendment to the Constitution of the United States is to free the negroes if they conquer us, and if they fail to conquer us to let them remain as they are. In conclusion, Mr. Benjamin paid a compliment to the Virginia ladies for their patriotism and devotion to the cause, and closed with an eloquent apostrophe to peace.

The Pittsburgh Commercial.

THE Jews of this country have shown a full share of patriotism since the war begun. From Ohio 12,000 have gone to fight for the Union flag; from New York 10,000; from Illinois 5,000; from Michigan and Wisconsin 3,000; and from other States enough to make a total of 40,000. They have also given their wealth for the soldiers. They have established five asylums for disabled soldiers, their widows and orphans, the benefits of which are limited to no faith or creed—one at New York, one at Philadelphia, one at Cincinnati, one at Chicago, and one at St. Louis.

PITTSBURGH – 1865
THE SERVICE OF THE JEWS IN THE UNION
The Pittsburgh Commercial, p. 2 (col 1)
April 22, 1865

This issue, published one week following the assassination of President Lincoln, paid tribute to the service of Jews in the Union cause. It begins, "*The Jews of this country have shown a full share of patriotism since the war began*" and goes on to enumerate the numbers of Jews fighting from each state.

"*They have also given their wealth for the soldiers,*" the article points out, after which it lists some of the charitable projects Jews were involved in.

Chapter #11

From and About Israel

THE TOMB OF RACHEL.

A few miles further on are the ruins of the village of Rama, fragments of walls, only a few feet high, are now the only vestiges of the place where the Prophet so beautifully predicted the mourning for the innocent. There is a spot on the plain, at no great distance from the ruined village of much higher interest—the tomb of Rachel. It is one of the few places where the observer is persuaded that tradition has not erred; as it fulfils literally the words of Israel in his last hour, when dwelling on the only indelible remembrance that earth seemed to claim from him. The long exile, the converse with the angels of God, the wealth and greatness which had gathered round him, all yield to the image of the loved and faithful wife; 'And as for me, Rachel died by me, in the way from Bethlehem, and I buried her there.'

The spot is as wild and solitary as can well be conceived; no palms or cypresses give their shelter from the blast; not a single tree spreads its shades where the ashes of the beautiful mother of Israel rests. Yet there is something in this sepulchre in the wilderness, that excites a deeper interest than more splendid or revered ones. The tombs of Zacharias and Absalom, in the valley of Jehosaphat, or of the Kings in the plain of Jeremiah, the traveller looks at with careless indifference; beside that of Rachel his fancy wanders 'to the land of the people of the

East,' to the power of beauty that could so long make banishment sweet; to the devoted companion of the wanderer, who deemed all trouble light for her sake.

The Turks have surrounded most of the burial places of the chief characters of the Old Testament, with more pomp and stately observance than this: over that of David and Solomon, on the declivity of Zion, a mosque is erected; the cave, too, of Machpelah, of Hebron, is covered by a large and ancient mosque and all around, the soil is held inviolable.—The cave is in the middle of the interior of the edifice; its dark and deep entrance only is visible, and it is rarely entered, even by the initiated, even by the steps of the faithful. For more than a century, not more than two or three Europeans are known, either by daring or bribery, to have visited it; the last was an Italian Count, who, by paying very high, was allowed by his guardians to tread the floor of the mosque and descend into the obscurity of the hallowed cavern; this was thirty years since. It is a great pity that so memorable a scene should be closed to the curious eye: the bold valley, in which the ancient town of Hebron stands, is often visited by the steps of the pilgrim and the traveller; but the penalty of death to every Christian who enters within the walls of the mosque, is too dear a payment for the gratification. The cave is said by the Turks to be deep and very spacious, cut out of the solid rock; and that the resting places of the celebrated patriarchs still exist, and are plainly to be discerned.

The tribute paid, however, by the followers of the Prophet to the burial place of Rachel, is far more sincere and impressive, than walls of marble or gilded domes; the desire which the Turks feel that their ashes may rest near hers, is singular in the extreme. All around this simple tomb lie thickly strewn the graves of the Mussulmans. A trait such as this, speaks more for the character of this people than many volumes written in their praise—for it cannot be for any greatness, or wisdom, or holiness, in the character of her who sleeps beneath, (for which qualities they show so much respect to the sepulchres of Abraham, of David, and his son)—but simply for the high domestic domestic virtues and qualities which pertain to Rachel—she was a devoted wife and an excellent mother, as well as the parent of a mighty people; and for these things do the Turks venerate her memory.—*Carnes' Recollections of Travels in the East.*

PHILADELPHIA –
1830
"THE TOMB OF RACHEL"
*The Souvenir, p. 382
June 2, 1830*

The tomb of Rachel "is one of the few places where… tradition has not erred…." It is described as being "as wild and solitary as can well be conceived … [yet it] excites a deeper interest than more splendid or revered ones." Rather than the marble and gold adorning those, the graves of Moslems surround this Jewish matriarch's tomb. The author notes that their yearning to be near her reflects most on "the character of this people;" that it is not "for [her] greatness…but simply for [her] high domestic virtues and qualities… [that] they venerate her memory."

PLAN OF JERUSALEM.

**NEW YORK - 1840
MAP OF JERUSALEM**
*New-York Observer, p. 4
December 12, 1840*

A half page topographical map of Jerusalem is featured on this issue's back page. The map shows such sites as ancient tombs, roads, the Jews Quarter, mosques, churches and the "site of Solomon's Temple, now mosque of Omar." Significantly, no traditional Jewihs sites are included in the "References" at bottom.

REFERENCES.

1. Church of the Holy Sepulchre.
2. Palace of the Knights of St. John.
3. Catholic burying-ground.
4. Armenian burying-ground.
5. Protestant burying-ground.

A. Principal Mosque El Sahara.
B. Eight gateways leading to the great platform.
C. Mosque el Aksa, formerly church of the Purification.
D. Mosque of the Mogrebins.

E. Mosque and Minaret.
F. Garden attached to the Mosque El Aksa.
G. Entrance to spacious subterranean vaults.
H. Golden gateway.
I. Entrance gateway.

SOUTHERN JOURNAL.

FREE TRADE; LOW DUTIES; SEPARATION FROM BANKS; RETRENCHMENT; ECONOMY; AND A STRICT CONSTRUCTION OF THE CONSTITUTION.

R. B. SMITH, W. BARTLETT. } EDITORS.   TALLAHASSEE, FLORIDA, MAY 5, 1846.   } VOLUME I. NUMBER 17.

JEWISH COLONIZATION.

The present extraordinary agitation among the Jews with reference to a return to the land of their fathers, cannot but be regarded with interest by the Christian community, especially by those who believe in their literal restoration to the Holy Land.

TALLAHASSEE, FLORIDA – 1846
"JEWISH COLONIZATION."
Southern Journal, p. 2 (col 1)
May 3, 1846

This article seeks to promote the settlement of Jews in the Holy Land. Jews who are persecuted, notes the writer, are "agitating" for a return to Palestine. The article refers to a meeting in London that established a society consisting of both Christians and Jews, Englishmen and foreigners, for enabling the Jews of Poland to be restored to the Holy Land.

The article speaks of the state of the land, quoting a "distinguished writer who said, "A country, once densely populated, lies solitary…."

---

munity, especially by those who believe in their literal restoration to the Holy Land.

"At a meeting of gentlemen feeling deeply interested in the welfare of the Jewish people, recently held in London, (says the London Watchman,) it was resolved that a society be formed under the title of 'The British and Foreign Society for promoting the colonization of the Holy Land.' The Society is to be restricted to the making all necessary preparations to facilitate the realization of the gradual colonization of Palestine, and the present protection and promotion of the civil and religious rights and liberties of the Jewish people in every part of the world. The committee to consist alike of Jews and Christians, Englishmen and foreigners. The co-operation of politicians and good men of every country, sect, and rank, is invited, it being a fundamental rule of the society that it shall be entirely silent and neutral as to every point of religious controversy."

In reference to the present state of Palestine, as being fully open for a return of the Jews, a distinguished writer says :

" A country, once densely inhabited, lies solitary : her pastoral hills unfrequented by the shepherd ; her rich fields untilled, and shaggy with thistles and prickly shrubs ; her villages sunk into heaps of ruins, and her cities without inhabitants. During the identical years in which Ireland quadrupled its population, the population of Palestine had sunk to a *tenth*. This is surely a very extraordinary fact : and when all seem to agree that there remains nothing but emigration for the sorely afflicted race of Israel in Poland, it seems scarce less generally held that the only land which remains for them to occupy is just the land of Palestine. Nor is it mere enthusiasts of the Jewish or Christian faith that unite in indicating this country as a country eminently fitted for colonization—we find it recommended by men of the most practical character."

MOORE'S RURAL NEW-YORKER

TWO DOLLARS A YEAR.]   "PROGRESS AND IMPROVEMENT."   [SINGLE NO. FOUR CENTS.

VOL. X. NO. 2.]   ROCHESTER, N. Y.—FOR THE WEEK ENDING SATURDAY, JANUARY 8, 1859.   {WHOLE NO. 470.

SCENES IN AND AROUND JERUSALEM.

ROCHESTER, NEW YORK – 1859 "SCENES IN AND AROUND JERUSALEM"

Moore's Rural New Yorker, p. 17 (col 3–4) January 8, 1859

This two-column article with three engravings illustrates the growing interest among American Christians in matters relating to the Holy Land mid-century. The article combines material relating to Biblical descriptions of Jerusalem, the architecture of the city, and what could be called recent developments since the Turk rulers of the area realized "they cannot trample with impunity upon the rights of men and treat as dogs the citizens of other and better lands."

As for Jerusalem's Jews, "they are a down-trodden, mourning people.... They are oppressed not only by their Turkish masters and by those styling themselves Christians, but even by their own Rabbis." One engraving shows "disconsolate Jews" at what "is called the Wailing Place."

"SURELY there is no spot on earth like Jerusalem." Here the faithful ABRAHAM, with a confidence that knew no doubt, and a faith that "laughed at impossibilities," raised his hand in obedience to the divine command, to sacrifice his only son — the child of promise and of his old age;—here the son of JESSE tuned his harp—here SOLOMON, "arrayed in all his glory" astonished the world by his magnificence and wisdom. But, a greater than SOLOMON walked its streets, climbed its mountains, and taught His listening disciples under the shade of its ancient olives. The most hallowed memories, the most enchanting recollections spring at the mere mention of JERUSALEM—"name ever dear." "Beautiful for situation, the joy of the whole earth, is Mount Zion—the city of the Great King." Palestine, the land of Prophets, is now attracting universal attention, and its future is the subject of earnest thought and speculation. Many entertain the belief that it will ere long become truly "the joy of the whole earth." Whether their hopes are to be realized or not, we can say

"Glorious things of thee are spoken,
Zion, city of our GOD."

Palestine it is known, is under Turkish rule. A few years ago no Frank, whether Jew or Christian was permitted to make oath in a Mahommedan court of Justice, nor could he own a foot of land. Death was the penalty inflicted on a Mahommedan who should forsake the religion of his fathers.— The late Russian war, and Anglo-French Alliance, have exerted a humanizing effect on the Turkish government. They seem to have discovered the important fact that they are not independent of the European powers; and that they cannot trample with impunity upon the rights of men, nor treat as dogs the citizens of other and better lands. A salutary and wonderful change has been made, and now the Mahommedan may change his religion without danger to life or property, and foreigners are not only permitted to occupy land in Palestine, but by a late *firman* they are invited to come there, or any other portion of the Ottoman empire, and occupy as much land as they may desire, on terms so extremely liberal as to accomodate the poorest, and astonish a Yankee land speculator.

These, and other events which we will not now mention, have directed especial attention to the land of Judea, and its chief city, and to gratify the earnest desire for knowledge on the subject, we design to present our readers with a series of illustrated sketches of scenes in and about Jerusalem. For the engravings we are indebted to JAMES CHALLEN & SON, publishers of the "City of the Great King," a most excellent work, upon which we shall draw largely for the subject matter of these sketches.

CHURCH OF THE HOLY SEPULCHRE.

OVER the spot where it was supposed the Savior was buried, a magnificent pile of buildings, known as the *Church of the Holy Sepulchre* was erected by order of Constantine, and finished and dedicated in 335. This building was destroyed in 614 by the Persian and Jewish army under Chosroes II. Another series of buildings was, however, soon erected on the site of the former, which remained until 969, when they were burned by order of the Arabs. The church was again rebuilt in 1048, but in a much less imposing style than formerly, and in this state it was found by the Crusaders in 1099. It was soon enlarged and beautified. In 1808 the entire pile of building was again doomed to destruction; but phœnix-like rose from its ashes in 1810.

On entering this church the visitor is surprised and mortified to find the whole premises under the charge of a Turkish guard, armed with guns, swords and cowhides, the latter of which they use on the most trivial occasions. Although in this building is represented to be such an aggregation of rites of important events, as to stagger credulity itself, yet no one can enter it without a feeling of reverence. The body of the building is a large rotunda, about ninety-nine feet in diameter, surrounded by an imposing colonnade supporting the

...continued

Scenes in and Around Jerusalem, *continued...*

galleries and a lofty dome. It is on a slightly elevated platform, directly beneath the skylight of this dome, that we find the beautiful little marble church containing the alleged tomb in which the Lord of Life lay. It is only about ten feet in breadth, and twenty in length and height. Its appearance is very finely represented in the engraving; that is as it appears under ordinary circumstances, but during festal occasions it is very highly decorated.

THE WAILING PLACE.

THE Jews in Jerusalem are a down-trodden, mourning people. The words of HAMAN are as true now as they were when uttered at the time NEHEMIAH attempted the restoration of the city— "The remnant that are left of the captivity, there in the province, are in great affliction and reproach." They are oppressed not only by their Turkish masters, and by those styling themselves Christians, but even by their own Rabbis. Even at the present time it would cost any Jew in Jerusalem his life to venture into the Church of the Holy Sepulchre, or even within the outer court of his beloved temple. The portion of the Temple wall approached by a narrow lane through what is called the Mogrebin Quarter, is esteemed the most sacred of all places to which they have access, on account of its vicinity to the Holy of Holies, and there they repair every Friday — indeed, in greater or less numbers every day — and weep and pray for the advent of the Messiah.

The place frequented for this purpose, is called the *Wailing Place*, and the engraving shows the disconsolate Jews engaged in this mournful service, which is described by an eye-witness as being affecting even unto tears.

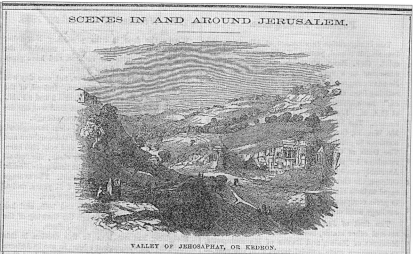

SCENES IN AND AROUND JERUSALEM.

VALLEY OF JEHOSAPHAT, OR KEDRON.

VALLEY OF JEHOSAPHAT, OR KEDRON.

THE valley commencing on the north-west of Jerusalem, in two gentle depressions, and encompassing the city on the north and east, terminating at its junction with another similar valley, is the Kedron of the Bible and Josephus; but is called Jehosaphat by Jews, Christians and Mahommedans. This designation of the valley seems to date far back, but is equally gratuitous and absurd whether due to the mistaken notion that this valley is alluded to by JOEL in his prophecy about the "Valley of the Judgment of God," (*Yehosaphat*,) or to the equally mistaken idea that King Jehosaphat was buried in the tomb that now bears his name, for not only is the term a general, instead of a specific one, and the valley far too limited to contain even a ten-thousandth part of "all nations" of JOEL, but we are expressly informed that JEHOSAPHAT was buried in the city of David. The *Valley of Jehosaphat*, or *Decision*, as described in the Bible, is in all probability the great *Valley of Megiddo* or *Armageddon*, the wide plain of Esdraelon, where so many important battles have been fought by Jews, Assyrians, Turks, Saracens, Franks, &c.

That the *Valley of Kedron*, was known as *Jehosophat*, of which we give an engraving, was used as a place of sepulture, according to the repeated declarations of Scripture, the tombs that abound throughout its length and breadth amply testify. Vineyards, fig-yards, and olive-yards, gardens and patches of green, occupy the entire extent. It may have been called *Kedron*, or *Filthy*, which is the meaning of the word, on account of receiving the blood and other offal from the Temple. RABBI AKABA says there was a certain cave or cess-pool beneath the altar, whereby filth and uncleanness was carried down into the Valley of Kedron; and the gardeners paid so much money as would purchase a trespass offering, for the privilege of fertilizing their gardens with it.

Chapter 12

Conclusion

The Civil War Ends,
A New Year Begins...

Rosh Hashanah
5626 (1865) & 5630 (1869)

In Conclusion

By their mere presence – and the placement they received in their respective publications – the final two items in this *Newfpaper Narrative of Early Jewifh America* attest to the fact that …

Despite their low numbers, by the end of the Civil War,
Jews were no longer *Strangers* in America.
Now a dynamic, significant and recognized force,
they were truly emerging as *Natives*.

JEWISH NEW YEAR.—Yesterday was the beginning of the Jewish New Year, or the anniversary of the creation, and as such celebrated by the Jews all over the world. They account the year now entered upon as the five thousand six hundred and twenty-sixth. All the places of business of the Hebrews are closed. The celebration lasts until sunset to-morrow.

The number of the Hebrew population in this place, and the extent of their business, were plainly perceptible to-day, by the numerous stores, shops and places of business, closed on King street, and in other parts of the city.

ALEXANDRIA – 1865
"JEWISH NEW YEAR"
Alexandria Gazette, p. 3 (col 1)
September 21, 1865

Of the estimated 12,600 population of Alexandria, Virginia recorded in the 1860 census, some 300-400 belonged to the Jewish religion. Yet in this newspaper issue, the Jewish presence seemed to hold more prominence than suggested by the numbers. The Local News column contained two blurbs about that population.

One reported that the previous day was the Jewish New Year, that Jews world-wide were marking the 5,626th year of creation, and that the celebration would last until sunset the next day.

The second reported that "The number of the Hebrew population in this place, and the extent of their business, were plainly perceptible today, by the numerous stores, shops and places of business closed on King street and in other places of the city."

The Charleston Daily Courier.

Vol. LXVII—No. 21,406.   CHARLESTON, S. C., MONDAY MORNING, SEPTEMBER 6, 1869.   ·BY A. S. WILLINGTON & CO.

THE JEWISH NEW YEAR A. M. 5630.—The Israelites will celebrate their "Rosh Hashanah," or New Year A. M. 5630, to-day and to-morrow, the 5th and 6th instant, but the observance of the solemn occasion commences the evening previous, it being their invariable custom to celebrate all their Sabbaths and festivals from sunset to sunset, not alone because in some of their ordinances the words are to be found "from evening to evening shall ye celebrate," &c., but in consequence of the record "the evening and the morning were one day," they compute the day as commencing from evening, or what is generally termed 6 o'clock P. M.

The origin of the New Year observance is to be found in the twenty-third chapter of Leviticus: "And the Lord spake unto Moses, saying, In the seventh month, in the first day of the month, shall ye have a Sabbath, a memorial of blowing of trumpets, a holy convocation." The term *seventh* month is used because from the time of the departure from Egypt the ecclesiastical year was made to begin at *Nissan*, to commemorate the month wherein their glorious deliverance had been wrought. *Tishri*, although thus counted as the seventh month in religious observances, is nevertheless the first month of the year, and the anniversary of the creation of the world.

The cornets or trumpets which were sounded on the New Year were not those of silver which had been made for use in the Tabernacle, but were made of rams' horns, a memorial of the animal which was offered instead of ISAAC when Jehovah tested ABRAHAM's faith, and the anniversary of which event is on the second day of the New Year.

This day is also called a day of *memorial*, because at the close of one year and the commencement of the next all mankind should bring to mind their actions of the past, and after a solemn review of faults and frailties enter, as it were, anew into a covenant with his Maker, the great King of Kings, Creator and Governor of the whole Universe.

The new year also commences the ten days of penitence, the last of which is called "*Yom Kippur*," or day of atonement, of which we will give our readers an account in due time.

The services are of the most solemn and impressive character, and even the lukewarm Israelite always unites with his brethren in the faithful observance of the "Day of Memorial."

CHARLESTON – 1869
"THE JEWISH NEW YEAR A.M. 5630"
The Charleston Daily Courier, p. 1 (col 3)
September 6, 1869

The Jewish New Year of the Hebrew year 5630 is the subject of an informative, six-paragraph, front page article.

Jews will celebrate Rosh Hashanah, notes the article, the next two days, based on the reference in Leviticus 23. The article discusses the fact that *Tishri* (Tishrei), the Hebrew word for the month of the New Year celebration, is considered the seventh month in religious observance which counts from the Jews' departure from Egypt but is actually the first month in that it is the anniversary of the creation of the world.

Rosh Hashanah is also called a day of *memorial* because it begins the ten-day period during which all mankind should review their actions of the past year before standing in judgment on Yom Kippur.

Author Ron Rubin served as professor of political science at the Borough of Manhattan Community College, City University of New York, for more than fifty years before retiring in 2016, setting a record for professorial longevity at the college. Rubin has also served as a Visiting Senior Lecturer at Haifa University, and as a Legislative Assistant in the House of Representatives. A graduate of New York University, where he earned his bachelor's and doctorate degrees in Political Science, and Brown University, where he received his master's degree in Political Science, he is the author of several books, including *The Unredeemed: Anti-Semitism in the Soviet Union* (1968); *Controversies Over the Objectives of the U.S. Information Agency* (1968); *Rudy, Rudy, Rudy: The Real and the Rational* (2000); and *Anything for a T-Shirt: Fred Lebow and the New York City Marathon* (2004). More than 75 of his commentaries were anthologized in 2013 in *A Jewish Professor's Political Punditry – Fifty-plus Years of Published Commentary by Ron Rubin.*

Rubin and wife, Miriam, split their time between homes in Riverdale, NY and Jerusalem, where Rubin continues to be active in Jewish communal activities and to write political commentary.

Developer Peri Devaney is an editorial consultant, copywriter, editor and designer with more than forty years' experience developing and designing magazines, newsletters and marketing materials in the private, corporate and non-profit sectors. A graduate of the State University of New York at Buffalo, this is the fifth full-length book she has played a major role in. It follows the anthology of Ron Rubin's works, of which she was the titled Editor (2013); Rubin's *Anything for a T-Shirt* (2004); *Diary of a Dirty Little War: The Spanish-American War of 1898* by Harvey Rosenfeld (2000); and *Richmond Pearson Hobson: Naval Hero from Magnolia Grove*, also by Harvey Rosenfeld (2001).

Devaney is headquartered in Los Angeles, CA, where she lives with her husband, Michoe-l.